The Rationalists

Critical Essays on the Classics
Series Editor: Steven M. Cahn

The volumes in this new series offer insightful and accessible essays that shed light on the classics of philosophy. Each of the distinguished editors has selected outstanding work in recent scholarship to provide today's readers with a deepened understanding of the most timely issues raised in these important texts.

Descartes's *Meditations:* Critical Essays
  edited by Vere Chappell
Kant's *Groundwork on the Metaphysics of Morals:* Critical Essays
  edited by Paul Guyer
Mill's *On Liberty:* Critical Essays
  edited by Gerald Dworkin
Mill's *Utilitarianism:* Critical Essays
  edited by David Lyons
Plato's *Republic:* Critical Essays
  edited by Richard Kraut
Kant's *Critique of Pure Reason:* Critical Essays
  edited by Patricia Kitcher
The Empiricists: Critical Essays on Locke, Berkeley, and Hume
  edited by Margaret Atherton
Aristotle's *Ethics:* Critical Essays
  edited by Nancy Sherman
The Social Contract Theorists: Critical Essays on Hobbes, Locke, and Rousseau
  edited by Christopher Morris
The Rationalists: Critical Essays on Descartes, Spinoza, and Leibniz
  edited by Derk Pereboom

The Rationalists

Critical Essays on Descartes, Spinoza, and Leibniz

Edited by
Derk Pereboom

ROWMAN & LITTLEFIELD PUBLISHERS, INC.
Lanham • Boulder • New York • Oxford

ROWMAN & LITTLEFIELD PUBLISHERS, INC.

Published in the United States of America
by Rowman & Littlefield Publishers, Inc.
4720 Boston Way, Lanham, Maryland 20706
http://www.rowmanlittlefield.com

12 Hid's Copse Road
Cumnor Hill, Oxford OX2 9JJ, England

Copyright © 1999 by Rowman & Littlefield Publishers, Inc.

All rights reserved. No part of this publication may be reproduced,
stored in a retrieval system, or transmitted in any form or by any
means, electronic, mechanical, photocopying, recording, or otherwise,
without the prior permission of the publisher.

British Library Cataloging in Publication Information Available

Library of Congress Cataloging-in-Publication Data

The rationalists : critical essays on Descartes, Spinoza, and Leibniz
  / edited by Derk Pereboom.
        p.   cm. — (Critical essays on the classics)
     Includes bibliographical references.
     ISBN 0-8476-8910-7 (alk. paper). — ISBN 0-8476-8911-5 (alk.
paper)
        1. Rationalism.   2. Philosophy—History—17th century.
  I. Pereboom, Derk, 1957–   . II. Series.
  B833.R323   1999
  149'.7—dc21   99-16484
                                                          CIP

Printed in the United States of America

∞ ™ The paper used in this publication meets the minimum requirements of
American National Standard for Information Sciences—Permanence of Paper
for Printed Library Materials, ANSI/NISO Z39.48–1992.

Contents

Leibniz

Malebranche

Introduction

For at least a century, it has been customary to divide the European
philosophers from Descartes through Hume into rationalists and empiricists. The philosophers most often cited as rationalists are René
Descartes, Baruch Spinoza, and Gottfried Wilhelm Leibniz, to which
one might add Nicholas Malebranche. In this scheme, the paradigmatic
empiricists are John Locke, George Berkeley, and David Hume. Elements of the old classification include the claim that rationalists, but
not empiricists, tend to doubt the value of sensation for justifying genuine knowledge, and that they instead advocate some type of a priori
methodology, argue that at least some of our ideas and concepts are
innate, express an optimistic view about metaphysics, and perhaps advocate a model for scientific and philosophical method that is indebted
to mathematics. Recently, this categorization has met with important
and powerful challenges (see, for example, Louis Loeb, *From Descartes
to Hume: Continental Metaphysics and the Development of Modern
Philosophy*.[1]) Upon careful examination it is difficult to justify the view
that all of the rationalists and none of the empiricists assent to the
claims classically attributed to rationalism. Perhaps in part because of
this, the influence of the old classification is waning. But it nevertheless
persists as a convenient way of grouping philosophers.

The Philosophers

René Descartes was born in 1596 in La Haye, France, a small town near
Tours later renamed for him. His mother died when he was very young,
and he was raised in his early years by his maternal grandmother. In
1606, when he was ten, he enrolled at the Jesuit College in La Flèche,
where he learned, among other things, Aristotelian philosophy and
theology. After nine years at La Flèche, he earned a doctorate in law at

the University of Poitiers. From 1618 to 1628 he traveled throughout Europe, sometimes joining armies engaged in the Thirty Years' War. During this period he met Isaac Beeckman in Holland, who awakened his interest in science and mathematics. Famously, in 1619, in a heated shed in Bavaria, he experienced a vision of a new mathematical science and philosophy that would replace the Aristotelian consensus. In 1628 he moved to Holland, where he would remain for more than twenty years, frequently changing his residence, and writing all of his important philosophical works.

In 1629, Descartes began working on *The World*, his first general scientific treatise, but in 1633 he abandoned plans to publish it when he heard of the Inquisition's condemnation of Galileo for rejecting the geocentric view of the universe. But then in 1637 he published *The Discourse on Method*, with three other works, *Optics, Meteorology*, and *Geometry*. In 1641 Descartes published his most famous work, the *Meditations on First Philosophy*, together with six sets of objections and replies. His most systematic rendition of his views, the *Principles of Philosophy*, followed in 1644. In 1643 he began a long correspondence with Princess Elizabeth of Bohemia, which ranged over many philosophical issues. Their interaction was dominated by a discussion of ways to achieve emotional well-being, which resulted in Descartes's publication of *The Passions of the Soul* in 1649. In the same year he went to Sweden to become the tutor for Queen Christina, but he died soon thereafter, in 1650.

For Descartes, clear and distinct ideas and not sensations provide the ultimate foundations for knowledge. Propositions become candidates for foundations by virtue of indubitability, which is in turn determined by resistance to skeptical argument. The initial proposition to withstand skeptical argument is *I think*, from which *I exist* follows, hence the renowned *I think, therefore I am*. The veridicality of clear and distinct ideas is guaranteed by the demonstrability of the existence of an essentially perfect being, God. Divine perfection ensures that God is not a deceiver, and God would be a deceiver if clear and distinct ideas were not veridical. Descartes advances a dualistic metaphysics of two types of substance, thinking and extended, according to which the human person consists of a thinking unextended soul and an extended body. Cartesian physics is anti-Aristotelian, denying formal causation in purely physical interactions, and advocating a mechanistic model instead. For Descartes, physics is fundamentally mathematical in nature, and for him mathematical expressibility is a standard for kinds of qualities acceptable in physics.

Baruch Spinoza was born in 1632 in Amsterdam and was raised and educated in that city's Jewish community. The ancestral roots of Spinoza's family, and those of much of this community, were in the Jewish culture of Spain and Portugal. In his early twenties he studied Cartesian philosophy in the school of Francis van den Enden. By this time he had already come to defend unorthodox theological views and had ceased to observe Jewish religious practices. As a result, he was excommunicated from his synagogue in 1656. In 1660 he left Amsterdam to live in various towns in South Holland, first in Rijnsburg (1660–1663), then in Voorburg (1663–1670), and finally in The Hague (1670–1677). During this period he worked as a lens-grinder, aided by his sophisticated understanding of optical theory. Spinoza was acquainted with several other great intellectuals of the time, including Leibniz and Huygens. Partly to safeguard his intellectual freedom, he rejected a position offered to him by the University of Heidelberg. During his lifetime he published only one work under his own name, the *Principles of Descartes' Philosophy* (1663), and one work anonymously, the *Theological-Political Treatise* (1670). Spinoza died of consumption in 1677, and in the same year his friends published his posthumous works as the *Opera Posthuma*, which included his greatest work, the *Ethics, Demonstrated in Geometrical Order*. The *Opera Posthuma* also featured two unfinished works, the *Treatise on the Emendation of the Intellect* and the *Political Treatise*.

Spinoza's *Ethics* contains his original vision of the universe, according to which there exists only one substance, God or Nature. This substance has an infinity of attributes, two of which human beings can comprehend—the mental and the physical—and all of which provide perspectives on the divine nature. Finite things are modes of this single substance. Everything that happens is determined by the divine nature, and consequently we have no free will. Spinoza argues for a parallelism between what happens in the mind and what happens in the body, and further that the mind and body are actually identical. In his conception, there is no psychophysical causation, and, more generally, there is no causation across attributes. Human emotional problems have an intellectual solution, whose highest form involves identification with the divine essence through intellectual activity. In the *Ethics* Spinoza presents these views in accordance with Euclid's geometrical method, proving propositions, corollaries, and scholia on the basis of axioms, definitions, and items previously demonstrated.

Gottfried Wilhelm Leibniz was born in 1646 in Leipzig, in what is now Germany, the son of a professor of moral philosophy. He studied at the University of Leipzig from 1661 until 1666 and then at the University of Altdorf from 1666 to 1667, earning degrees in law and philosophy. After graduating, he declined an academic offer from the University of Leipzig, and instead entered the service of the Elector of Mainz. In 1672 he traveled to Paris as a diplomat, where he stayed until 1676. This period in Paris proved to be of great significance for his intellectual life. There, benefiting from the guidance of Christian Huygens, one of the most important physicists of the time, he became thoroughly acquainted with modern science and philosophy. In Paris he also developed calculus independently of Newton, who formulated it around the same time. After his years in Paris, Leibniz visited England and then the Netherlands, where he met Spinoza. When he returned to Germany he became a counselor at the court in Hanover, which was to be his principal home until his death in 1716.

After setting up residence in Hanover, Leibniz initiated a period of creative and fruitful development of his philosophical views that was to last until the end of his life. He wrote many works during this time, most of which were not published until after his death. In several of these works, the *Discourse on Metaphysics* (1686), the *New System of Nature* (1695), and the *Monadology* (1714), he displays his metaphysical system in outline form. Leibniz's philosophical views on physics are set out in the *Specimen of Dynamics* (1698), *On Nature Itself* (1697), and in his correspondence with De Volder (1699–1706) and with Samuel Clarke, Newton's associate (1715–16). Theology is treated at length in the *Theodicy,* published in 1710, and in his correspondence with Arnauld (1686–1690). In 1704 Leibniz finished a substantial commentary on Locke's *Essay*, entitled *New Essays on Human Understanding.* He had great interest in the works of the important philosophers of his time. Besides the work on Locke, Leibniz wrote about the views of Descartes, Hobbes, Spinoza, Malebranche, Newton, and Berkeley.

At the center of Leibniz's system is the notion of a *monad*, which is an immaterial, simple, mind-like entity modeled on the Cartesian soul. In Leibniz's view, monads are the only substances that exist. Matter, therefore, is not among the fundamental constituents of reality, but is rather an appearance of systems of monads: matter is phenomenal. Hence physics is a study of appearances, and not of ultimately real things. Metaphysics, by contrast, since it has monads in its purview, is about ultimately real things. There is no causation between monads, only within individual monads. The activities of different monads nevertheless cohere because God creates them so that the states of any one harmonize with the states of every other. Leibniz was a determinist in that he held that in virtue of choosing the best of all possible worlds, God determines every event that occurs, including each of our decisions. His greatest philosophical struggles include reconciling divine freedom with God's having to actualize the best of all possible worlds, and human freedom with divine determinism.

Born in Paris in 1638, Nicholas Malebranche received his formal training in philosophy and theology at the Collège de la Marche and later at the Sorbonne. Subsequently, he entered the congregation of the Oratory and was ordained in 1664. In 1674 he published his most important work, *The Search After Truth*. The work is deeply Cartesian, except for two significant doctrines, each based on the Pauline theme "In God we live and move and have our being." The first doctrine is that we see all things in God—that is, the ideas that function in human thought actually exist in the divine mind. According to Malebranche, this fact about human cognition makes possible our clear and distinct apprehension of truth. The second doctrine is occasionalism: that God is the sole cause in the universe. Malebranche held that bodies and minds cannot be genuine causes, and that only the will of an omnipotent being could have this role. For example, the cue's hitting the billiard ball does not itself cause anything to happen. Rather, this event is an occasion for God to cause the ball to move. In 1680 Malebranche published another important work, the *Treatise of Nature and Grace,* and he spent the rest of his life defending and developing his views.

The Articles

This volume contains thirteen essays that represent some of the best contemporary philosophical work on the rationalists. Each of these essays tends towards the sort of history of philosophy that Robert Sleigh has called *exegetical history*, which he distinguishes from *philosophical history*.[2] Exegetical history has two components. The first is fact-finding, and here Sleigh quotes Benson Mates: "the attempt 'to discover and set forth, as accurately, objectively, and as completely as possible, the philosophical views of various historical figures' and to 'set forth the plain facts about what an author thought and said.' "[3] The second is explanatory: "an effort to explain *why* the philosopher under scrutiny thought and said what he did." By contrast, philosophical history attempts "to set out a philosophical theory utilizing *some* doctrines associated with a historical figure, but intentionally introducing revisions where that figure's views are deemed unacceptable," or it "consists in discussing some philosophical topic 'in the company' . . . of some historical figure." Sleigh's examples of philosophical history include Jonathan Bennett's studies of Kant and Spinoza, and J. L. Mackie's work on Locke.

Sleigh points out that until recently exegetical history has been on the defensive. This is surely correct. But over the past two decades history of modern philosophy in the areas of metaphysics and epistemology has been dominated by the exegetical variety. The same cannot be said of the history of modern ethics and political philosophy. Much of the best recent work in that area—Gregory Kavka and Jean Hampton's studies of Hobbes's political philosophy, Annette Baier's work on Humean ethics, Thomas Hill, Christine Korsgaard, Onora O'Neill, and Barbara Herman on Kant's ethics—is reasonably classified as philosophical history. At the same time, this work maintains high standards of textual analysis. Why excellent early modern history of ethics and political philosophy is largely philosophical history while much of the best history of metaphysics and epistemology of this period is now primarily exegetical is worthy of some reflection. Perhaps this is so simply because the ethical and political views of Hobbes, Hume, and Kant, for example, are considered to be as much a part of the contemporary discussion as those of such philosophers as John Rawls and Robert Nozick, while the metaphysical and epistemological views of the early modern period are not widely regarded in this way. But this sort of opinion is subject to change over time. Currently the cutting edge of scholarship in the metaphysics and epistemology of the early modern period strongly inclines to the exegetical, and this is a fact that the essays in this volume reflect.

Janet Broughton's contribution to this volume, "The Method of Doubt," is the result of further reflection on the themes of her influential earlier article, "Skepticism and the Cartesian Circle."[4] A longstanding objection to Descartes's anti-skeptical strategy is that the proof for God's existence requires claims that cannot be established until the existence of God itself is demonstrated. For the proof of God's existence requires that the veridicality of clear and distinct ideas already be established, but this in turn requires that the existence of God already be proven, since it is only by virtue of divine perfection that the veridicality of clear and distinct ideas is guaranteed. This problem is known as the Cartesian circle. Broughton argues that Descartes's strategy against skepticism is to show that the truth of certain claims is a condition of the very possibility of the sort of doubt that he raises in the first Meditation. She then argues that this reading of Descartes provides him with a promising refutation of skepticism, and with a way to avoid the Cartesian circle.

The most important argument for mind-body dualism in Descartes is the argument for the real distinction between mind and body in the Sixth Meditation. In her article, "Descartes's Case for Dualism," Marleen Rozemond develops an original analysis of the argument, drawn from careful textual analysis and a study of related historical material. The result is a reading of the argument which contrasts sharply with the one that is commonly assumed. The received view is that Descartes argues for the real distinction by the claim that I can exist without the body and the body can exist without me. Rozemond argues that the core of the argument is rather that extension and thought are principal attributes, that every substance has only one principal attribute, and that therefore I and my body are distinct substances.

Interpreters often assume that Descartes thoroughly rejects the Aristotelian form-matter metaphysics of the scholastics. In "The Unity of Descartes's Man," Paul Hoffman argues that this is not so, and in particular, that for Descartes the human soul is the form of the human body. In fact, in his view the unity of the person is explained by the soul's being the form of the body, as it is in classical Aristotelianism. Descartes's rejection of hylomorphism is indeed a feature of his physics, but not of his theory of the person.

Many of Descartes's followers embraced an occasionalist position on causation. One argument for occasionalism begins with the Cartesian premise that God conserves the universe by continuously recreating it in its entirety, and concludes that God must be the cause of every change. In "How God Causes Motion: Descartes, Divine Sustenance, and Occasionalism," Daniel Garber argues that Descartes is not committed to occasionalism by his view about divine conservation. Crucially, Descartes distinguishes between a cause of being and a cause of becoming or change. God, in his preservation of the world, is continuously the cause of being of every thing that persists, but it does not follow from this that he is also the cause of changes in the states of these things.

It is uncontroversial that Spinoza advocates determinism, the notion that every event is rendered inevitable by virtue of antecedent conditions. A contested view among interpreters is that he is also committed to necessitarianism, the claim that every actual state of affairs is logically or metaphysically necessary, so that the world simply could not have been any different from how it in fact is. Don Garrett, in "Spinoza's Necessitarianism," argues that Spinoza is indeed a necessitarian, and further, that understanding him as a necessitarian helps us understand two other characteristic doctrines, his view that there is only one substance, and his claim that certain internal features of an idea alone— i.e., clarity and distinctness—are reliable criteria of its correspondence to that which it represents.

In "On the Relationship between Mode and Substance in Spinoza's Metaphysics," John Carriero considers another central but difficult Spinozist doctrine, the claim that all finite things are modes of God. Common assumptions about the relation of modes to substances would suggest that Spinoza holds rocks and trees to be properties that can be predicated of God, a view that seems peculiar. Carriero explores the Aristotelian roots of the notion of what it is for a property to inhere in a substance, and he argues that it is mistaken to explicate this traditional notion of inherence in terms of predication. As a result, the Spinozist doctrine turns out not to be as strange as it might initially seem.

In "Spinoza's Argument for the Identity Theory," Michael Della Rocca examines Spinoza's claim that the mind is identical to the body. Delahunty raises the objection that Spinoza cannot consistently maintain this thesis because it would entail that bodies interact with minds. Spinoza affirms that a body can interact with another body, but if the first body is identical to a mind, then it follows that a mind can interact with a body, which violates Spinoza's ban on causal interactions across distinct attributes. Against this objection Della Rocca develops in detail the claim that causal and related contexts are referentially opaque, and that as a result it does not follow from the fact that a body interacts with another body, and the first body is identical to a mind, that a mind interacts with a body. Della Rocca then provides an account of the reasons why Spinoza held that the mind and the body are identical.

Margaret D. Wilson points out that a notion of causation plays a very important role in the development of many of the key ideas in Spinoza's metaphysics. However, it is notoriously difficult to provide an account of this notion of causation. In "Spinoza's Causal Axiom (*Ethics* I, Axiom 4)" she takes on this task. The axiom is "Knowledge of an effect depends on knowledge of the cause, and involves it." Initially, Spinoza's claim seems counter to common sense. Often we know what has happened without knowing what has caused it—if this weren't so, criminal investigation, for example, wouldn't be needed. Wilson's article provides us with a more plausible reading than these initial reflections suggest. In addition, she discusses the implications of this axiom for understanding Spinoza's mode-attribute relation, for his view that the mind and body do not interact, for his parallelist claim that the order and connection of ideas is the same as the order and connection of things, and for his theory of perception.

In his essay "Phenomenalism and Corporeal Substance in Leibniz," Robert M. Adams sets out Leibniz's account of body. Adams considers two of Leibniz's claims that might seem opposed—that bodies are phenomenal and that they are aggregates of substances—and argues that they can be reconciled on a phenomenalist reading. In the process, he develops an interpretation of Leibniz's notions of corporeal substance and organic body. In addition, Adams argues that Leibniz was perhaps dissatisfied with his main account of the unity of organic bodies in terms of the perceptions of a dominant monad, and this may have led him to consider the notion of a substantial bond as a fundamental feature of reality in addition to monads and their perceptions.

In several of Leibniz's early writings one finds passages that might be interpreted as sympathetic to Spinoza's view that God is the only substance, and that human beings and physical objects are modes of God. In "Leibniz and Spinoza on Substance and Mode," Christia Mercer disputes this interpretation, and in doing so she reveals the rich Neoplatonic background to Leibniz's work. That background, she argues, provides a key to understanding Leibniz's claims about God's relationship to finite substances and about the nature of those finite substances themselves.

In "Natures, Laws, and Miracles: The Roots of Leibniz's Critique of Occasionalism," Donald Rutherford explains Leibniz's views about causation and substance by way of his arguments against occasionalism. He argues that one reason Leibniz opposes occasionalism is that if it were true, there would be no finite substances, where substances are understood to be principles of independent causal power. But if there were no finite substances, then nature, in itself, would be unintelligible—for then the effects of natural things would not be understandable through their own natures, but only through the will of God.

An abstract but nonetheless central feature of Leibniz's system is the notion that relations are ideal, and thus not real. Some commentators have taken this to mean that Leibniz holds that all propositions about relations between substances can be reduced to propositions containing only nonrelational predicates. In "Leibniz's Theory of Relations," David Wong argues against this reductionist interpretation, maintaining instead that for Leibniz propositions about relations are equivalent to propositions that ascribe relational predicates to subjects. In his interpretation, it is only relations considered as abstracted from subjects that are not real, while subjects genuinely have relational properties. Wong also argues that although the reductionist view is false, Leibniz nevertheless holds that the relational properties of a subject are determined by its nonrelational properties. He then explores the significance of these claims for several of Leibniz's characteristic metaphysical doctrines.

In "Occasionalism and General Will in Malebranche," Steven Nadler sets out the fundamental features of Malebranche's occasionalism by way of a response to Antoine Arnauld's interpretation of this position. According to Arnauld, Malebranche's occasionalism consists partly in God's acting only by general volitions, where general volitions are understood as those whose content is general and non-specific, never referring to a particular entity. On this reading, God's causal activity need not be constant and ubiquitous, since he has only to institute general laws at the beginning of creation. Nadler contends that on the better interpretation, Malebranche conceives of God as acting by volitions that are general in the sense that they accord with general laws.

God's volitions indeed have particular content—and they are constant and ubiquitous—but their particular content is always in harmony with the general laws that God set up at the beginning of creation.

I wish to thank Marleen Rozemond, Paul Hoffman, John Carriero, Michael Della Rocca, Robert Adams, Jeremy Hyman, Donald Rutherford, and Steven Nadler for help in planning this anthology.

Notes

1. Ithaca: Cornell University Press, 1981.
2. *Leibniz and Arnauld* (New Haven: Yale University Press, 1990), pp. 2–4.
3. "Individuals and Modality in the Philosophy of Leibniz," *Studia Leibnitiana* (1972), pp. 81–118, at pp. 83–84.
4. *Canadian Journal of Philosophy* 14 (1984), pp. 593–615.

Acknowledgments

The editor and publisher thank the authors and publishers of these essays for permission to print or reprint them in this volume.

Chapter 1, Janet Broughton, "The Method of Doubt," has not been previously published.

Chapter 2, Marleen Rozemond, "Descartes's Case for Dualism," originally appeared in the *Journal of the History of Philosophy* 33 (1995), pp. 29–63.

Chapter 3, Paul Hoffman, "The Unity of Descartes's Man," originally appeared in the *Philosophical Review* 95 (1986), pp. 339–70.

Chapter 4, Dan Garber, "How God Causes Motion: Descartes, Divine Sustenance, and Occasionalism," originally appeared in the *Journal of Philosophy* 84 (1987), pp. 567–80.

Chapter 5, Don Garrett, "Spinoza's Necessitarianism," originally appeared in *God and Nature: Spinoza's Metaphysics*, Y. Yovel, ed. (Leiden: E. J. Brill, 1991), pp. 191–218.

Chapter 6, John Carriero, "On the Relationship Between Mode and Substance in Spinoza's Metaphysics," originally appeared in the *Journal of the History of Philosophy* 33 (1995), pp. 245–73.

Chapter 7, Michael Della Rocca, "Spinoza's Argument for the Identity Theory," originally appeared in the *Philosophical Review* 102 (1993), pp. 183–213.

Chapter 8, Margaret D. Wilson, "Spinoza's Causal Axiom (*Ethics* I, Axiom 4)," originally appeared in *God and Nature: Spinoza's Metaphysics* Y. Yovel, ed. (Leiden: E. J. Brill, 1991), pp. 133–160.

Chapter 9, Robert M. Adams, "Phenomenalism and Corporeal Substance in Leibniz," originally appeared in *Midwest Studies in Philosophy* 8 (1983), pp. 217–57.

Chapter 10, Christia Mercer, "Leibniz and Spinoza on Substance and Mode," has not been previously published.

Chapter 11, Donald Rutherford, "Natures, Laws, and Miracles: The Roots of Leibniz's Critique of Occasionalism," originally appeared in *Causation in Early Modern Philosophy*, Steven Nadler, ed. (University Park: The Pennsylvania University Press, 1993), pp. 135–158.

Chapter 12, David Wong, "Leibniz's Theory of Relations," originally appeared in *The Philosophical Review* 89 (1980), pp. 241–56.

Chapter 13, Steven Nadler, "Occasionalism and General Will in Malebranche," originally appeared in *Journal of the History of Philosophy* 31 (1993), pp. 31–47.

1

The Method of Doubt

Janet Broughton

Between 1635 and 1641 Descartes wrote four works in which he described a special method for guiding inquiry into metaphysics—into the fundamental character of the human mind, of the natural world, and of God, their transcendent ground. This method would enable an inquirer to discover the truth about these matters; to embrace that truth; to forsake many competing beliefs, despite their endorsement by both common sense and the schools; and then to move on to fruitful inquiry in mathematics and the sciences.

The method was the "method of universal doubt."[1] Descartes used it in the *Discourse*, the *Search for Truth*, and the *Principles*, but he worked it out most clearly and powerfully in the *Meditations*, the book that will concern me here. In a prefatory Synopsis to the *Meditations*, Descartes wrote,

> Although the usefulness of . . . extensive doubt is not apparent at first sight, its greatest benefit lies in freeing us from all our preconceived opinions, and providing the easiest route by which the mind may be led away from the senses. The eventual result of this doubt is to make it impossible for us to have any further doubts about what we subsequently discover to be true. (II 9; VII 12)

I will not have much to say here about how methodic doubt is supposed to achieve its "greatest benefit," in loosening the grip of the senses. I want instead to focus on the way in which it is supposed to be a method of successful inquiry, a method that will lead us to the truth.

My aim will be to defend a simple and familiar picture of how the method of doubt yields knowledge of the truth, but my defense will

1

depend upon a new way of understanding the inner epistemic work-ings of the method. I will first sketch out the simple view, along with a basic philosophical problem it seems to entail. Then I will explain a new way of understanding how the method of doubt works. I will con-clude by showing how I think this new appreciation of the method helps to solve the apparent problem attending the simple picture, and by addressing some related interpretative questions.

The Simple Picture

It was Descartes's own mature view that most people, even fairly well-educated ones, have very few beliefs that could pass for knowledge. Many people do have at least a few beliefs in mathematics that consti-tute knowledge of a sort, but the rest of an ordinary person's beliefs are infected with obscurity and confusion, especially through a perva-sive idea that overwhelms us in our infancy.[2] That is the idea that the senses show what we and the world around us are really like. Thus even an ordinary belief like, 'Here's a hand,' is tainted by such implied or presupposed beliefs as these: 'Here's a beige thing,' 'Here's a warm thing,' 'Here's a thing with a power of moving,' 'Here's a part of a rational animal,' and so on. Although there are some clear and distinct ideas mixed in with the rest, the ordinary person gives assent to a mish-mash of ideas, many or even most of which are obscure and confused.

The perspective of the mature Descartes is not, of course, the per-spective of the person beginning the inquiry described in the *Medita-tions*, but that inquirer has just the worry that the mature Descartes thinks he ought to have.[3] He says, "Some years ago I was struck by the large number of falsehoods that I had accepted as true in my child-hood, and by the highly doubtful nature of the whole edifice that I had subsequently based on them" (II 12; VII 17). Of course, here at the outset he is not yet able to trace these falsehoods to their source in the obscure and confused ideas he has concerning the primacy of his senses, nor can he examine his beliefs one by one and distinguish in each between what is obscure and what is clear. He is not in a position (yet) to say to himself, "The idea that this is beige is obscure and con-fused; the idea that it is shaped is not," and so on. Indeed, that is why he *believes* to be *true* the ideas that are, in fact, unrecognized by him, obscure and confused.

Faced with this worry, the meditator proposes for himself the maxim that he will suspend judgment whenever he can discover even a slight reason for doubt. While he may wind up suspending judgment about matters he understands clearly and correctly, by paying this price he can be certain that any judgments the maxim allows him to make will be ones he can make with absolute certainty that they are true.[4]

Of course, there is no reason at the outset to suppose that the maxim *will* allow the meditator to make any judgments, and once the radical grounds for doubt are on the table the prospects for success look bleak. But Descartes thought that using this strategy of methodic doubt would prove to be tremendously fruitful. Let me sketch out the familiar, simple view of how the method's fruits accumulate.

The meditator—let us call him "Descartes"—begins by focusing on those of his beliefs that can survive ordinary skeptical challenges, like 'Were you close enough?' These beliefs concern the things he can see and touch that are not "very small or in the distance" (II 12; VII 18). He then raises the radical skeptical challenges of dreaming and the deceiving God, and carefully considers which of his beliefs can survive them. He does not see how to defend his sense-based beliefs or his clear and distinct ideas in mathematics, and so he suspends judgment about them.

He does, however, see that he *can* defend the beliefs that he exists and that he thinks. But that is not all. Descartes claims that he is somehow also able to add other bits of knowledge to the meager stock of 'I exist' and 'I think.' Understood in a particular way, his beliefs about his own states constitute knowledge: 'I seem to see a light,' for example. Most such beliefs are, at this stage of the inquiry, dead ends; but one—'I have an idea of a benevolent God'—is not.[5] Descartes somehow adds to his stock of knowledge his belief in the general causal principle that something cannot come from nothing, and with it the subsidiary principle that the cause of an idea must have at least as much formal reality as the idea has of objective reality. He puts these causal principles together with his knowledge of his own existence and of his possession of the idea of God, and infers that a benevolent God exists. And then straightaway he can also claim to know that all his clear and distinct ideas are true, since a benevolent God would not have made him so that he clearly understood to be true what actually was false.

From this point on, further inquiry can be safely guided by the rule, 'Accept only what I clearly and distinctly perceive to be true.' At this point in the inquiry, this rule is effective. Descartes has formed various ideas that he can identify as clear and distinct, and his general doubt-induced detachment from his senses allows him to start teasing apart what was obscure and what was clear in his former beliefs. This means that if he heavily qualifies some of his former beliefs, he can stop suspending judgment about them. From here on in, the hard intellectual work comes with the effort to find the right ways to qualify his ideas, that is, to make them clear and distinct.

What I have just sketched out is what I will call the *simple picture* of the way in which the method of doubt leads to knowledge of the first principles of metaphysics. According to this picture, Descartes achieves certainty that all of his clear and distinct ideas are true by achieving certainty that God exists and is not a deceiver, and he achieves certainty about God's existence by achieving certainty about propositions which, taken together, constitute an argument for the conclusion that God exists.

I think most readers find that the simple picture gives a highly natural reading of the first four Meditations, and I think there are many texts that shape such a reading. Two are especially compelling. The first comes at the beginning of the Second Meditation, where Descartes introduces the *cogito* reasoning by saying,

> Anything which admits of the slightest doubt I will set aside just as if I had found it to be wholly false; and I will proceed in this way until I recognize something certain, or if nothing else, until I at least recognize for certain that there is no certainty. Archimedes used to demand just one firm and immovable point in order to shift the entire earth; so I too can hope for great things if I manage to find one thing, however slight, that is certain and unshakeable. (II 16; VII 24)

Clearly 'I exist' is just such an Archimedean point, "firm and immovable," "certain and unshakeable," and Descartes evidently thinks that he can enjoy equal certainty about his attributions of conscious states to himself. The reader naturally expects that Descartes's subsequent achievement of the "great things" he hopes for will rest upon the certainty he first achieves about his existence and states, and perhaps about other matters as well.

The Third and Fourth Meditations strongly suggest that the *first* great thing Descartes produces from knowledge of himself is knowledge that God exists and is not a deceiver, and that *because* he has knowledge of God, he can achieve knowledge of a *second* great thing, namely, the truth of all of his clear and distinct ideas. As Descartes says in the Fourth Meditation,

> from this contemplation of the true God, in whom all the treasures of wisdom and the sciences lie hidden, I think I can see a way forward to the knowledge of other things. To begin with, I recognize that it is impossible that God should ever deceive me. . . . And since God does not wish to deceive me, he surely did not give me the kind of faculty which would ever enable me to go wrong while using it correctly. (II 37–38; VII 53–54)

So the simple picture seems a natural way to depict the way in which Descartes uses the method of doubt in the first four Meditations to achieve certainty that all of his clear and distinct ideas are true.

Complications

But reflective readers are bound to be troubled by a basic philosophical objection to Descartes's procedure as the simple picture depicts it. Early in his inquiry, before he knows that God exists and is not a deceiver, Descartes cannot claim to know something *simply* because he has a clear and distinct idea of it. For all he knows, he has been created by a deceiving God so that he perceives clearly and distinctly to be true propositions that actually are false. The method of doubt thus requires him to suspend judgment about things he perceives clearly and distinctly; he must, for example, suspend judgment about whether 'Two plus three equals five' is true. So consider Descartes's claims to know that he thinks and that he exists, that he has an idea of God, and that the causal principles are true. On the simple picture, Descartes is claiming that somehow he can know each of those things before he knows that God exists and is not a deceiver. But at that same stage of his inquiry, he must suspend judgment about 'Two plus three equals five'! It seems outrageous that he should claim knowledge of his privileged few clear and distinct ideas, when he cannot even claim to know something as simple as the sum of two and three.

Some readers have thought Descartes might have a rationale for giving favored treatment to 'I think' and 'I exist' at this stage of his inquiry. But opinion has varied as to the exact nature of this rationale, and it would still leave unexplained his giving favored treatment to 'I have an idea of God' and to the causal principles. It is very hard to see how Descartes could have a principled reason for saying that the deceiving God argument requires him to suspend judgment about 'Two plus three equals five' but not 'Causes must be adequate to their effects.' Without such a principled account, Descartes seems to be obtuse, or even intellectually dishonest, in his claim for success in using the method of doubt. He seems simply to be ignoring his maxim about suspense of judgment (or ignoring the deceiving God argument) whenever he finds it convenient.

Reflecting on this difficulty, we might try to read Descartes as treating all clear and distinct ideas alike at this stage of his inquiry. Then he wouldn't need a rationale for treating some but not all of them as absolutely certain. There are two general ways to give such a reading. One is to suppose that Descartes assumes that *all* clear and distinct ideas are absolutely certain, even before he has proved that he cannot have been created by a deceiving God. But this is to convict him of circularity: he cannot be in a position to assert absolute certainty about all his clear and distinct ideas until he has shown that God exists and is not a deceiver, but in reaching the judgment that God exists and is not a deceiver he would have to rely upon the assumption that all his clear and distinct ideas are absolutely certain.

The other possibility is to suppose that Descartes thinks *none* of his clear and distinct ideas is absolutely certain before he reaches the conclusion that God exists. This is a possibility that a fair number of readers have pursued. Rather than conclude that Descartes is obtuse or dishonest or arguing in a circle, many readers have rejected the simple picture of how the method of doubt is supposed to lead to knowledge. Taking their cue from some suggestive texts (to which I will turn below), they *complicate* the simple picture. They hold that Descartes intends us not to be absolutely certain about 'I exist,' 'I think,' 'I see a light,' 'I have an idea of God,' and 'Something cannot come from nothing,' until the end of the argument that God exists and is not a deceiver. That is, at an early stage of the inquiry, Descartes is in no better a position to assent to 'I exist' than to 'Two plus three equals five.'

Proponents of this more complicated view face a difficulty of their own, however, for they will need to explain how doubt can yield knowledge of God's existence and the truth of clear and distinct ideas, if not in the simple way I have sketched out. Interpreters of Descartes have been especially clever and imaginative in providing such explanations, and I will briefly return to that enterprise later.

The Method of Doubt

As I have suggested, basic questions about the simple picture turn upon how we understand the method of doubt. I argue that when we understand the method of doubt properly, we will see that Descartes has a rationale, at the early stages of his inquiry, for treating some but not all of his clear and distinct ideas as absolutely certain. In this section of this chapter I will lay out what I believe to be the best way of understanding the method of doubt. In the last section, I will reflect upon what that shows us about the simple picture.

I cannot hope to give a full defense here of the reading I am presenting, but I hope I can say enough about it to make it plausible.[6] The main idea behind this reading is simple to state: in the first three Meditations, Descartes aims to show that the truth of some claims or ideas is a necessary condition of the doubt he raises in the First Meditation. They are thus absolutely indubitable at an early stage of the inquiry. Descartes then shows that some of these claims entail that God exists and is not a deceiver, which in turn entails that our clear and distinct ideas are true. Thus in the first three Meditations he will have argued that the truth of my clear and distinct ideas is a necessary condition of the possibility of raising the doubts of the First Meditation. Only at that point can Descartes claim he is absolutely certain about the truth of *all* his clear and distinct ideas, even those, like 'Two and three equals five,' whose truth is not an immediate condition of methodic doubt. So before this point Descartes can claim to be absolutely certain about the truth of clear and distinct ideas that are conditions of the doubt, but not about any other clear and distinct ideas. The truth of those other clear and distinct ideas is called into doubt by the deceiving God argument. I think it is fair to say that Descartes's arguments are something like transcendental arguments, though that is not a comparison I will elaborate here. What I want to do now is first to explain the notion of indubitability that is connected with the idea of a condition of methodic doubt. Then I will lay out textual evidence in favor of my interpretative claim.

One way in which a claim could be indubitable relative to some set of considerations is if those considerations simply failed to bear upon whatever the claim is about. For example, the dream argument, Descartes says, fails to call his mathematical beliefs into doubt: "For whether I am awake or asleep, two and three added together are five, and a square has no more than four sides" (II 14; VII 20). But the indubitability of some claims does not lie simply in their being beyond the scope of some set of skeptical considerations. Rather, the claims are indubitable because in some way their truth makes doubt based upon some set of considerations possible. Let me describe two ways in which a claim might have this sort of indubitability.

The skeptical considerations Descartes offers in the First Meditation share a general structure: the lunatic argument, the dream argument, and the deceiving God argument[7] all have two main features:

- Each offers an account of how a certain sort of belief arises in me: an account upon which such beliefs are false;[8] and
- I cannot tell whether it is the correct account of my holding that sort of belief or not.

Let me call accounts that meet both these conditions *skeptical scenarios*.

A claim may be indubitable relative to a skeptical scenario by being a claim whose truth is presupposed by the possibility that the scenario is correct. The scenario will be powerless against such a claim, because either it is not possible that the scenario is correct, in which case the scenario cannot generate doubt about anything, or it is possible that the scenario is correct, in which case the claim in question is true.

It might be objected that this would commit Descartes to claiming indubitability for various claims that do not seem as though they ought to be counted as indubitable—for example, the claim that a deceiving God is a possible being.[9] On the view I am attributing to Descartes, that claim indeed cannot be doubted *relative to the deceiving God scenario*. But it *can* be doubted relative to other skeptical scenarios—for example, those involved in the fate-or-chance argument. In what follows it will emerge that for Descartes the claims that have this special indubitability are ones that are implicated in *any* skeptical scenario concerning the relevant belief, or range of beliefs, and so he keeps this complication at arm's length.[10]

There is a second way in which a claim might be indubitable because it is somehow a condition of the possibility of doubt. For someone to engage in the enterprise of methodic doubt described in the First Meditation, it is not enough that there simply *be* a relevant and possibly correct scenario about some set of beliefs. The meditator must also, for example, *consider* the scenario, *recognize* that he cannot tell whether it is correct, and on that basis *entertain doubt* about what he had believed. And arguably he must also be able to *attribute to himself* those states of considering, and so on. This means that there will be some claims that are indubitable in this way: their truth is presupposed by the possibility that someone actually does doubt a class of beliefs by entertaining a skeptical scenario about that class of beliefs.

Now let me turn to textual evidence[11] that Descartes identifies various claims as indubitable in one or another of these two senses. In the Fourth Meditation, Descartes pauses to give us several seldom noticed but very intriguing retrospective accounts of what he has accomplished in his first three Meditations. Concerning the First and Second Meditations, he says,

> during these past few days I have been asking whether anything in the world exists, and I have realized that *from the very fact of my raising this question* it follows quite evidently that I exist. (II 41; VII 58; emphasis added)

Descartes seems to be stressing the fact that my own existence is a necessary condition of my entertaining the doubt of the First Meditation.[12] We are used to reading him as mainly making the point that my existence is a necessary condition of any sort of awareness of anything, and a great deal of the secondary literature on the *cogito* passage focuses on the relation between 'I exist' and 'I think.' But this focus isn't Descartes's own primary focus, as the quotation I've just read makes clear. Rather, 'I exist' must be true if I am to doubt as I in fact *have* doubted in the First Meditation, and so one thing I cannot doubt, as I doubt everything I can, is that 'I exist' is true.

Descartes works through this point twice, with slightly different emphases. Here is the first version:

> I have convinced myself that there is absolutely nothing in the world, no sky, no earth, no minds, no bodies. Does it now follow that I too do not exist? No: if I convinced myself of something then I certainly existed. (II 16–17; VII 25)

The "convincing" is part of the effort of methodic doubt; it is the setting aside of claims by regarding them as no better than false, or by "pretending" (II 15; VII 22) that they are false. Descartes infers that he exists from the fact that he is convincing himself of something, but his *certainty* that he exists is not derived from prior certainty that he is convincing himself of something. Rather *it arises from the fact that his existence makes his doubting possible*, in the second of the senses I have distinguished. Here, Descartes identifies his existence as a condition of his having actually carried out the intellectual activity he described in the First Meditation.[13]

Descartes next works through the same general point with a different aspect of First Meditation doubt in mind:

> But there is a deceiver of supreme power and cunning who is deliberately and constantly deceiving me. In that case I too undoubtedly exist, if he is deceiving me. (II 17; VII 25)

Here again Descartes is identifying his existence as a condition that makes methodic doubt possible, but instead of tying his existence to an aspect of his activity of doubting or suspending judgment, he ties it to an aspect of what I have called a skeptical scenario. A skeptical scenario must describe someone who has been caused to have false beliefs. Thus if there were no one in existence to be deceived (or not, as the case may be) in the beliefs that he holds, the skeptical scenarios could be ruled out as false and would not be *skeptical* scenarios after all, since skeptical scenarios are ones which might, for all I know, be true. So 'I exist' is also indubitable in the first of the two ways I distinguished earlier. (Descartes is here attending only to the deceiving God hypothesis, but the point holds for any of the skeptical scenarios of the First Meditation.)

I think that Descartes exploits both notions of a condition of doubt in the complex passage in which he attributes his states of "thinking" to himself:

> But what then am I? A thing that thinks. What is that? A thing that doubts, understands, affirms denies, is willing, is unwilling, and also imagines and has sensory perceptions. This is a considerable list, if everything on it belongs to me. But does it? Is it not one and the same 'I' who is now doubting almost everything, who nonetheless understands some things, who affirms that this one thing is true, denies everything else, desires to know more, is unwilling to be deceived, imagines many things even involuntarily, and is aware of many things which apparently come from the senses? Are not all these things just as true as the fact that I exist, even if I am asleep all the time, and even if he who created me is doing all he can to deceive me? . . . [I]t is . . . the same 'I' who has sensory perceptions. . . . For example, I am now seeing light, hearing a noise, feeling heat. But I am asleep, so all this is false. Yet I certainly *seem* to see, to hear, and to be warmed. This cannot be false; what is called 'having a sensory perception' is strictly just this, and in this restricted sense of the term it is simply thinking. (II 19; VII 28–29)

Descartes's important claim at the end of this passage—that the claim 'I seem to see' cannot be *false*—can come as something of a surprise. He hasn't done anything to explain how or why such self-reports are incorrigible.[14] In fact, I don't think this is quite the claim he is making. In the earlier parts of the passage he is not arguing, for example, that the self-report, 'I desire to know more,' is incorrigible. Rather, he is arguing that it is *indubitable*, and indubitable in a particular way. He reminds himself that it must be true that he exists if he doubts, but he goes on greatly to enrich his account of the conditions of methodical doubt to include many kinds of states. 'I desire to know more,' 'I am doubting almost everything,' and so on, are claims that must be true if it is to be true that I am engaged in the effort of methodical doubt. That is, these claims are indubitable in the second of the senses I distinguished earlier.

I think Descartes is trying to make a broadly similar point about sense-experiences at the end of the passage, but that he appeals to the first of the ways in which a claim might be indubitable by being a condition of doubt. What are the conditions of my doubting whether I am seeing a light? Well, of course, the doubt Descartes deploys is not the doubt that might arise when there is little or nothing to suggest to me that I *am* seeing a light—when I am wide awake in a very dark room, for example. The doubt that interests him is the doubt that arises when my current experience prompts me to believe that I am seeing a light. If I am to doubt whether I am seeing a light in *those* circumstances, I must be having a particular sort of experience. What sort is that? Descartes cannot answer, 'Seeing a light,' because then doubting whether I see a light would not be possible. His answer instead is, 'Seeming to see a light.' This formula attempts to specify the experience appropriately, without carrying the unwanted implication that I am seeing a light. Again, his point is that the truth of this carefully worded claim is a condition of the possibility of the doubts he has articulated in the First Meditation. This claim must be true if skeptical scenarios about what I see are to be possibly true—or so Descartes is arguing.[15] He means to be bringing out the *indubitability*, not the incorrigibility, of the claim.[16]

There is a closely related movement of thought in the Third Meditation. Again, a retrospective passage from the Fourth Meditation is a good place to start. Descartes recalls his reasons for insisting that he has a clear and distinct idea of God. He says,

> when I consider that fact that I have doubts, or that I am a thing that is incomplete and dependent, then there arises in me a clear and distinct idea of a being who is independent and complete, that is, an idea of God. (II 37; VII 53)

The idea of God does not just happen to arise in him when he considers his limitations; as he had argued in the Third Meditation,

> my perception of the infinite, that is God, is in some way prior to my perception of the finite, that is myself. For how could I understand that I doubted or desired—that is, lacked something— . . . unless there were in me some idea of a more perfect being which enabled me to recognize my own defects by comparison? (II 31; VII 45–46)

Descartes is arguing that having an idea of God is a necessary condition of his awareness of himself as doubting. If we supply the uncontroversial thought that a person could not undertake the First Meditation doubts without being able to be aware that that is what he is doing, we again find that an important step of the overall argument of the first three Meditations turns on identifying a necessary condition of the doubts of the First Meditation. Here, the indubitability of the claim that I have an idea of God arises in the second of the two ways I distinguished earlier.

Let us consider one more retrospective passage from the Fourth Meditation, this one the continuation of the previous one. Descartes has just said, "when I consider the fact that I have doubts . . . then there arises in me . . . an idea of God" (II 37; VII 53). He now continues his review this way:

> And from the mere fact that there is such an idea within me, or that I who possess this idea exist, I clearly infer that God also exists. (II 37; VII 53)

In one way, it is hard to know what to make of this: Descartes is leaving out the causal principles upon which the Third Meditation argument turns.[17] But just because he does, he gives us the impression that a single sweep of argument is taking us from awareness of doubting to the existence not just of the idea of God, but of God himself. Descartes creates a similar impression at the end of the Third Meditation:

> I understand that I am a thing which is incomplete and dependent on another and which aspires without limit to ever greater and better things; but I also understand at the same time that he on whom I depend has within him all those greater things . . . and hence that he is God. The whole force of the argument lies in this: I recognize that it would be impossible for me to exist with the kind of nature I have—that is, having within me the idea of God—were it not the case that God really existed. (II 35; VII 51–52)

Again, the argument, as Descartes swiftly summarizes it, moves us in what seems to be one line of thought from awareness of our limitation to the idea of God and then to the existence of God as the ultimate condition of that awareness.

But what about the causal principles? Descartes hasn't mentioned them in these swift summaries, but of course they are indispensable to the Third Meditation argument for God's existence, and it is hard to see how he could have thought of them as conditions of the possibility of the First Meditation doubt. He didn't ever explicitly tell us how to fit the causal principles into the progressive unfolding of conditions of methodic doubt, but I think we can see a way in which he might have done so, or a reason why he might have assumed that his certainty about the causal principles generated no special problems.

I have argued elsewhere[18] that for Descartes all of the causal principles at bottom express the idea that nothing can happen without a cause, and that indeed it would not make sense to speak of *causes* at all if we allowed that something could happen without a cause, or something could come from nothing. This allows us to see the Third Meditation causal principles as conditions of the possible truth of the skeptical scenarios of the First Meditation. The key idea is that for Descartes, skeptical scenarios are *causal* scenarios, scenarios about how beliefs of a certain sort arise in us.[19] For example, Descartes considers scenarios according to which our beliefs in the existence and nature of physical objects around us arise in us in the way that a lunatic's beliefs, or a dreamer's beliefs, arise. And the more radical scenario is causal, too: it is one according to which even our clear and distinct beliefs occur in us because a deceiving God[20] has caused us to have a nature that finds falsehoods clear and distinct.

On the reading I am proposing, then, each of the premises for the argument that God exists and is not a deceiver is among the clear and distinct ideas that have a special status. All of them can be identified as claims whose truth is a condition of the possibility of First Meditation doubt, even before the skeptical scenarios are ruled out. Once the meditator sees that these absolutely indubitable claims together imply that God exists and is not a deceiver, he is in a position to be absolutely certain that God exists and is not a deceiver, for God's existence is a condition of his doubt, too. And by achieving absolute certainty that God exists, Descartes can also achieve absolute certainty that *all* of his clear and distinct ideas are true.

The Method of Doubt and the Simple Picture

Suppose this account of the method of doubt is correct. Then early in his inquiry Descartes will take himself to have shown that *some* ideas are indubitably true insofar as their truth is a condition of even the most radical of grounds for doubting anything. Among those favored ideas are 'I exist,' 'I am doubting,' 'I desire to know more,' 'I seem to see a light,' 'I have an idea of God,' and 'Something can't come from nothing.' *Not* among these favored ideas are 'Two plus three equals five' or any other mathematical ideas, despite their clarity and distinctness.

Of course, once Descartes sees that some of the favored ideas imply that God is no deceiver and that all his clear and distinct ideas are true, he can be absolutely certain that 'Two plus three equals five' is true, along with any other clear and distinct ideas he finds within him. And Descartes seems confident that using the method of doubt will teach him how to distinguish between what is clear and distinct in his thought, and what is obscure and confused. Using the method of doubt will not only show him that his clear and distinct ideas are true; it will help him to learn how to form and discern ideas that are clear and distinct.[21]

The account I have given of the method of doubt constitutes a defense of the simple picture. The apparent problem with the simple picture was that in the early stages of his inquiry Descartes seemed to have no rationale for claiming to be absolutely certain about *some* of his clear and distinct ideas while nonetheless taking seriously a reason to doubt others. Now what we can see is that there is a rationale behind this discrimination: the truth of some clear and distinct ideas, but not all, is an immediate condition of the possibility of the doubt of the First Meditation.

Does the defense of the simple picture that I have offered constitute a knock-down argument in its favor? If I am right about how the method of doubt is supposed to work in the *Meditations*, then I think this much is safe to say. First, Descartes had in mind a specific *way* in which using the method of doubt can yield absolute certainty even before the skeptical scenarios are vanquished. He uses this device to reach absolute certainty about some, but not all, of his clear and distinct ideas before he reaches the conclusion that God exists and is not a deceiver, and the premises in his argument to that conclusion are among the clear and distinct ideas he is absolutely certain are true. In the first four Meditations, the case for the simple picture seems overwhelmingly strong.

There is one passage in the first four Meditations that might seem to suggest a complicated picture. Near the beginning of the Third Meditation Descartes says that if he does not know that God exists and is not a deceiver, "it seems that I can never be quite certain about *anything else*" (II 25; VII 36; emphasis added). But notice first that Descartes expresses only tentatively the thought that at this stage of his inquiry he cannot be certain of anything: he says this *seems* to him (*videor*) to be true. Second, the sentence appears in a passage of great dialectic complexity. Descartes has reflected on the *cogito* reasoning and noticed its clarity and distinctness. That makes him wonder whether he is yet in a position to say that *all* clear and distinct ideas are true. He certainly cannot see, when he considers a clear and distinct idea, how it could be false, or how he can withhold his assent from it.[22] Then again, as he reminds himself, he has not yet eliminated the deceiving God scenario, and that scenario applies to clear and distinct ideas. It is at *that* point that he says it seems he can't be certain of anything.

Well, it is *hard* for him to see why some clear and distinct ideas cannot be doubted while others—equally clear, distinct and compelling—can be. The sentence in question is an expression of this difficulty, I think. It is not a dismissal of the *cogito* reasoning as merely psychologically compelling. The *cogito* still provides an Archimedean point—an absolutely indubitable idea—from which inquiry can proceed.

So the case for the simple picture that rests simply upon the first four Meditations is compelling, I think. But if we enlarge our view to take in the Fifth Meditation and the Second and Fourth Replies, then I think some readers will want to say that it is not at all clear that the simple picture is the right one. For in one way or another, Descartes seems to be saying that there is certainty and there is certainty, or that there is knowledge and there is knowledge. There is the certainty we may have as we grasp an argument and its conclusion in one sweep of thought, and the certainty we may have when no subsequent considerations can get us to retract our assent to the conclusion, even when we do not recall the argument that leads to it (e.g., II 48; VII 69). There is knowledge that is awareness of primary notions, and knowledge that isn't (II 100; VII 140). Perhaps there is *cognitio* and *scientia.* [23]

The point of these distinctions is very obscure, I think, but because Descartes draws them in the course of replying to the charge of circularity, some readers have taken them to be evidence in favor of a complicated picture of how the method of doubt is supposed to yield its fruits. For example, Alan Gewirth argues[24] that Descartes is illustrating the difference between a kind of certainty we can have whenever we have a clear and distinct idea, and the metaphysical certainty about the truth of clear and distinct ideas that can come only with the defeat of the deceiving God scenario. Before we are metaphysically certain that all our clear and distinct ideas are true, we are metaphysically certain of none of them, though psychologically certain of all of them as we entertain them clearly and distinctly. Bernard Williams takes Descartes to be distinguishing between time-bound certainty, which we may enjoy in having any of our clear and distinct ideas even before we answer the deceiving God doubt, and the acceptance as ongoing beliefs of the matters that we grasp clearly and distinctly, an acceptance that allows us to treat the proof that God exists and is no deceiver as a decisive answer to the deceiving God doubt.[25]

These complicated pictures have two troubling features, however. The first is that they attribute to the meditator the view that he cannot be absolutely certain whether he exists until he knows that God exists and is not a deceiver. This would require the meditator somehow to be taking back what he said in the Second Meditation, when he reasoned,

> but there is a deceiver of supreme power and cunning who is deliberately and constantly deceiving me. In that case I too undoubtedly exist, if he is deceiving me; and let him deceive me as much as he can, he will never bring it about that I am nothing so long as I think that I am something. (II 17; VII 25)

Not only is there no sign that Descartes meant for the meditator to take this reasoning back; he explicitly denied that that was his intention.

Mersenne objected that

> you are not yet certain of the existence of God, and you say that you are
> not certain of anything, and cannot know anything clearly and distinctly
> until you have achieved clear and certain knowledge of the existence of
> God. It follows from this that you do not yet clearly and distinctly know
> that you are a thinking thing. (II 89; VII 124–125)

Descartes replied,

> when I said that we can know nothing for certain until we are aware that
> God exists, I expressly declared that I was speaking only of knowledge of
> those conclusions which can be recalled when we are no longer attending
> to the arguments by means of which we deduced them. (II 100; VII 140)

While there is much in this reply to puzzle us, we must not miss its
main point, which is to *except* the discoveries of the Second Meditation
from the doubts raised by the deceiving God hypothesis.

Second, these complicated pictures of the method of doubt depict
Descartes as achieving metaphysical, or ongoing, certainty that God
exists and is not a deceiver *by first* achieving metaphysical or ongoing
certainty that his clear and distinct ideas are true. For Gewirth, the
order of Descartes's discoveries is this: first he finds that he cannot
clearly and distinctly understand his creator to be a deceiver; second,
that allows him to rule out the deceiving God scenario as a ground for
doubt; third, this leaves him with no reason to doubt the truth of his
clear and distinct ideas; and fourth, that in turn allows him to claim
absolute certainty for his clear and distinct idea that his creator is no
deceiver. For Williams, first Descartes adopts that acceptance rule, "Accept as an on-going belief everything that at any time I understand
clearly and distinctly to be true"; and that leads him to adopt as ongoing the belief that God exists and is not a deceiver.

But both of these versions of a complicated picture reverse the order
of Descartes's discoveries in the Third and Fourth Meditations. As Descartes takes pains to explain, his absolute certainty that all of his clear
and distinct ideas are true *rests upon* his absolute certainty that God
exists and is not a deceiver. I think that an interpretation that reverses
this order must have gone wrong somewhere.

None of this is to say, however, exactly what we are to make of the
passages in the Fifth Meditation and the Second and Fourth Replies
that fuel the complicated picture. So all I want to insist upon here is
this: that our reading of those passages respect the simple picture of
the first four Meditations, whether by rendering them compatible with
the simple picture, or by attributing to Descartes two incompatible ac-

counts of the way in which doubt is supposed to yield knowledge. In other words, I think that there is a compelling case for seeing the simple picture as describing at least one way, and perhaps the only way, in which Descartes thought the method of doubt worked.

Notes

I want to thank audiences at UC San Diego and the University of North Carolina at Chapel Hill for useful questions and comments on an earlier version of this paper. I am grateful to Marleen Rozemond, Nancy Daukas Dowling, and Derk Pereboom for very helpful written comments. Although I have tried to meet their objections, I doubt I have succeeded.

1. *The Philosophical Writings of Descartes*, vol. II, translated by John Cottingham, Robert Stoothoff, and Dugald Murdoch (Cambridge University Press, 1984), p. 270; *Oeuvres de Descartes*, edited by Charles Adam and Paul Tannery (Vrin, 1964–1976), vol. VII, p. 203. Further references to these two volumes will appear in the body of the text; this reference, for example, would appear thus: (II 270; VII 203). See also the Seventh Objections and Replies (II 383; VII 561): "method of doubt."

2. See, for example, the *Principles of Philosophy*, part 1, article 71 (I 218–219; VIIIA 35–36).

3. It is a good question why the inquirer has this worry. The answer will depend in part upon whether we see Descartes as intending for the inquirer to be a philosopher trained in the schools, or an untrained person of common sense, or either indifferently.

4. I do not think that motivating the use of the method of doubt by an ordinary person requires seeing Cartesian doubt as a natural extension of ordinary doubt, or Descartes's setting aside of beliefs as continuous with ordinary doubting. I think the First Meditation doubts should be understood as arising from Descartes's use of a fairly artificial epistemic procedure that is supposed to reach conservative results through unpresuppositious means. In this it is quite unlike Pyrrhonian skepticism. Of course, this leaves unanswered the question whether Cartesian doubt *is* unpresuppositious (or Pyrrhonian skepticism a natural extension of ordinary epistemic practice).

5. Actually, I think Descartes defends this belief a little differently from the way he defends 'I see a light.' I will explain this presently.

6. I am writing a book about the method of doubt that lays out this reading in considerably more detail.

7. Also the argument from fate or chance, which is a deceiving God argument for atheists.

8. See E. M. Curley, *Descartes against the Skeptics* (Harvard University Press, 1978), p. 86.

9. Derk Pereboom has raised this objection in correspondence.

10. Pereboom has also pointed out that considerations can *engender* doubts without constituting reasons or grounds for doubt. So I should say explicitly

that the indubitability at stake here concerns the possibility of treating a skeptical scenario as a *reason* for doubt about some belief or range of beliefs.

11. I will be focusing upon texts in the *Meditations*, but I should add that the *Search for Truth* has a strikingly 'transcendental' cast to it. Descartes's handling there of the idea of a condition of doubt is, however, crude by comparison to the use he makes of it in the *Meditations*. In the *Discourse* the notion of a condition of doubt barely surfaces. I thus speculate that Descartes wrote the *Search for Truth* after the *Discourse* and before the *Meditations*, a chronology that is on historical grounds as possible as any other.

12. The *Search for Truth* puts the point in its own blunt way: "if I did not exist I would not be able to doubt" (II410; X 515). Curley makes much the same point in the fourth chapter of *Descartes against the Skeptics*.

13. Here is one place where my interpretation differs from Curley's. See *Descartes against the Skeptics*, p. 86.

14. See Bernard Williams, *Descartes: The Project of Pure Enquiry* (Humanities Press, 1978), p. 73 ff. and pp. 305–306.

15. I don't think his argument is fully convincing, though the issues involved are very difficult. See John McDowell, "Singular Thought and the Extent of Inner Space," in *Subject, Thought, and Context*, edited by Philip Pettit and John McDowell (Clarendon Press, 1986), pp. 137–168.

16. So why does he say it cannot be false, full stop? I think he is slightly obscuring his point by using the conceit whereby the *dubitable* is treated as *false*.

17. So it is not entirely fair of Descartes to carry on as he does in the letter to Clerselier (II 274; IXA 211).

18. "Skepticism and the Cartesian Circle," *Canadian Journal of Philosophy*, vol. 14, No. 4 (December 1984), pp. 593–615.

19. Barbara Winters argues for the plausibility of such a requirement in "Sceptical Counterpossibilities," *Pacific Philosophical Quarterly*, vol. 62 (Jan. 81), pp. 30–38.

20. Or "fate or chance or a continuous chain of events, or . . . some other means" (II 14; VII 21).

21. I think this pedagogical value is supposed to be connected with the way doubt frees "us from all our preconceived opinions" and provides "the easiest route by which the mind may be led away from the senses" (II 9; VII 12).

22. Though, as Marleen Rozemond has helpfully pointed out to me, even here, where Descartes is dramatizing the assent-compelling character of clear and distinct ideas, he represents 'Two plus three equals five' as being a bit less persuasive than the *cogito*: "*perhaps even (forte etiam)*" 'Two plus three equals five' compels assent (II 25; VII 36). That is, even here, he indicates a distinction between the *cogito* and 'Two plus three equals five' with respect to their indubitability.

23. In "*Cognitio, Scientia* and the Cartesian Circle" (unpublished), John Carriero develops a reading upon which Descartes is making significant use of such a distinction.

24. In "The Cartesian Circle," *Philosophical Review* (1941), pp. 368–395.

25. In *Descartes: The Project of Pure Enquiry*, especially chapters 2 and 7.

2

Descartes's Case for Dualism

Marleen Rozemond

One of Descartes's most lasting contributions to philosophy is his well-known argument for dualism. This argument continues to attract attention not just from historians of philosophy, but from the philosophical community at large. It is generally believed that the modal claim that mind can exist unextended or without body is central to this argument. According to some, Descartes's dualism simply consists in the separability of mind and body. Others hold that it does not consist in this modal claim, but believe that this claim is central to his argument for dualism. I wish to propose a radically different interpretation. It is true that Descartes was concerned with the possibility of mind existing unextended and without body. But I will contend that this idea is not central to the argument. Descartes's dualism does not consist in this modal notion, nor is this notion fundamental to his argument.

The most prominent statement of the argument is to be found in the *Meditations.* In this work the argument has two focal points, one in the Second and the other in the Sixth Meditation. As a result of the skeptical arguments of the First Meditation, Descartes doubts in the Second Meditation that there are any bodies. Nevertheless he is certain that he exists and thinks. Using these observations Descartes argues that he has a clear and distinct perception of the mind as a thinking, unextended thing. In the Sixth Meditation he uses this perception to show that the mind is an incorporeal substance, really distinct from the body. This is the conclusion of what I will call the Real Distinction Argument.[1] What exactly does Descartes think he accomplishes in his discussion of the mind in the Second Meditation, and how does he think he can get from the results of the Second Meditation to the real distinction of mind and body in the Sixth Meditation? The argument is often criticized on the ground that the claims about the mind that Descartes is entitled to in the Second Meditation are insufficient to lead to dualism.

My interpretation of the Real Distinction Argument provides answers to these questions. The argument, I will contend, crucially relies on various aspects of Descartes's conception of substance. Descartes held that each substance has a principal attribute, a property which constitutes its nature or essence.² Other properties of the substance are its modes. The modes of a substance presuppose this attribute: they cannot exist without it, nor be clearly and distinctly understood without it. These aspects of Descartes's conception of substance lead to the real distinction of mind and body in the following way. In the Second Meditation we find we can clearly and distinctly understand a thinking thing while doubting that there are bodies, and while ascribing no corporeal properties to the mind. This leads to the conclusion that thought is not a mode of body, but a principal attribute (sections 2–3). Furthermore, extension is the principal attribute of body (section 4). Finally the argument relies on the idea that a substance has only one principal attribute (section 5). It follows then that mind and body are different substances, and really distinct. After completing my account of the argument I consider its relationship to the idea that mind and body can exist without one another (section 6).

The purpose of this paper is not to claim that Descartes's argument for dualism works. I will, however, conclude that the argument is not vulnerable to various serious objections raised in the literature.

1. The Real Distinction

Before analyzing the Real Distinction Argument we must consider what exactly Descartes means it to show. In the *Meditations* the argument is developed over the course of the whole work. It concludes in the Sixth Meditation as follows:

> Since I know that anything that I clearly and distinctly understand can be brought about by God just as I understand it, it is sufficient that I can clearly and distinctly understand one thing without another in order for me to be certain that one is different from the other, since they can be placed apart [*seorsim poni*] at least by God. And it does not matter by what power that happens, in order for them to be regarded as different. Consequently, from the very fact that I know that I exist, and that at the same time I notice nothing else at all to pertain to my nature or essence, except that I am a thinking thing, I conclude correctly that my essence consists in this one thing, that I am a thinking thing. And although perhaps (or rather, as I will soon say, certainly) I have a body, which is very

closely joined to me, because, however, I have on the one hand a clear
and distinct idea of myself, insofar as I am only a thinking, not an extended, thing, and on the other hand a distinct idea of body insofar as it
is only an extended thing, not thinking, it is certain that I am really distinct
from my body, and can exist without it. (AT VII 78)

Descartes is clearly interested in establishing the modal claim that mind
and body are separable, that is, that each can exist without the other.
He is particularly interested in the idea that he, or his mind, can exist
without his body. This claim is important because it provides hope for
an afterlife, as Descartes explains in the Synopsis to the *Meditations*.[3]
In the Sixth Meditation, however, a different concern is more prominent. Descartes does conclude there that mind can exist without body,
but he does not discuss the issue of the afterlife. His primary concern
there is rather to establish the claim that mind and body are different
substances. Descartes is interested in this claim because he aims to
develop a view according to which mind and body are different kinds
of substances each with different kinds of modes. Descartes pursues
this goal in the Sixth Meditation as follows: immediately after the statement of the final stage of the Real Distinction Argument just quoted,
he discusses the question of which modes belong to which substance. He
argues that sensation and imagination belong to him, that is, his mind;
the 'faculties' for changing location, taking on various shapes and the
like belong to a corporeal substance.[4] The idea that mind and body are
different kinds of substances with different kinds of modes is important
because it allows Descartes to assign to body only those modes that can
be dealt with by mechanistic explanations. The mind is the incorporeal
subject of states that cannot be so understood. In this way he aims to
provide metaphysical support for his view that mechanistic explanations can account for all phenomena in the physical world.[5]

Although Descartes is interested in establishing the separability of
mind and body, the conclusion of the argument is most properly understood to consist in the claim that mind and body are different substances—*diversae substantiae*.[6] It will be important for understanding
the argument to distinguish these two points. I will use Descartes's
characterizations of real distinction and substance found in the *Principles of Philosophy*, which contains the most extensive and most formal
exposition of his metaphysics. Descartes writes there: "a real distinction obtains properly only between two or more substances."[7] The notion of real distinction was not, of course, new with Descartes and had
its roots in the scholastic theory of distinctions. The characterization
from the *Principles* is very close to the one used by scholastics such as
Suárez and Eustacius. They defined real distinction as distinction of

one thing from another: *una ab alia re*. It is crucial in this context that the term thing—*res*—is for them a technical term: modes are not *res* in this sense.[8] In this sense of the term only substances are *res* for Descartes, modes are not. Descartes himself sometimes uses the term *res* in a sense that excludes modes.[9] A difference between Descartes and the scholastics is that for the latter *res* includes real qualities—a category that Descartes famously rejected.

It is often thought that, contrary to the view I am propounding, for Descartes the real distinction of mind and body simply consists in their separability.[10] This interpretation derives support from Descartes's definition of real distinction in the appendix to the Second Replies entitled "Reasons that Prove the Existence of God and the Distinction of the Soul from the Body Expounded in Geometrical Fashion" (hence-forward Geometrical Exposition). He writes there that "two substances are said to be really distinct when each of them can exist without the other."[11] But we must be careful, for elsewhere in the Second Replies Descartes considers separability as a *sign* of real distinction. In re-sponse to the objection that he has failed to show that body cannot think he writes: "I don't really see what you can deny here. That it is sufficient that we clearly understand one thing without another in order to recognize that they are really distinct? Provide then some more certain sign of real distinction; for I am confident that none can be given. For what will you say? That those things are really distinct of which each can exist without the other?" (AT VII 132). Descartes then argues that in order for separability to be sign of real distinction, it must be known. Consequently, he contends, this sign is not an alternative to his way of proving the real distinction; but it leads to his own require-ment that we clearly and distinctly understand one thing without an-other. This discussion suggests that separability does not constitute real distinction.[12]

One might think that Descartes rejects here the idea that separability is a sign of real distinction. But in fact his point is that by itself separabil-ity is not enough: one also needs to know, with certainty, that separa-bility obtains. Even if Descartes does not claim in this passage that sepa-rability is a sign of real distinction, however, the passage strongly suggests that separability is not constitutive of real distinction. For the way in which Descartes considers separability as a candidate for being a sign of real distinction is hard to reconcile with the idea that instead it is constitutive of real distinction. That idea is conspicuously absent. If Descartes thought that real distinction simply consists in separability one would expect him to say so in this context.

It is worth noting that Descartes's position so understood is also the one taken by Suárez. He characterizes real distinction as the distinction of one thing *(res)* from another, and devotes considerable attention to the question how one can detect a real distinction. He discusses various signs of real distinction and separability is one of them.[13]

What is Descartes's notion of substance? In the *Principles* Descartes defines substance as something "that *so exists* that it needs nothing else in order to exist" (emphasis added).[14] There is a temptation to read this definition as saying that being a substance simply consists in having the ability to exist apart from anything else. Descartes's notion of substance is often understood this way. On this interpretation the real distinction of mind and body, the idea that they are different substances would, after all, reduce to their separability.[15] But the definition in the *Principles* makes clear that there is more to Descartes's notion of substance. For it presents the idea that a substance needs nothing else in order to exist not as fundamental, but *as a result* of its actual mode of existence. What could Descartes have in mind?

Descartes's ontology contains substances and modes. A mode exists in or through something else, a substance, whereas a substance exists through itself. Descartes quite frequently characterizes substances as things existing through themselves—*res per se subsistentes.*[16] In Descartes's definition of substance in the Geometrical Exposition this way of distinguishing modes and substances is present in a different way. Descartes does not on this occasion describe substance as a *res per se subsistens,* but he describes it as that through which properties exist. He writes: "Each thing in which inheres [*inest*] immediately, as in a subject, or through which exists something that we perceive, that is, some property, or quality, or attribute, of which a real idea is in us, is called substance."[17] The Aristotelian scholastics commonly distinguished substances and qualities in this way. For instance, Eustacius of St. Paul wrote that a substance is a "being that subsists or exists *per se.*" And he explains: "to subsist or exist *per se* is nothing other than not to exist in something else as in a subject of inherence, in which a substance differs from an accident, which cannot exist *per se* but only in something else in which it inheres."[18]

The idea, I take it, is that a substance, unlike a mode, is a thing in its own right. A substance has its own existence, unlike a mode.[19] Descartes expresses this idea in one of his discussions of the scholastic notion of a real quality—a quality that is supposed to be a *res.* He often criticizes this notion, arguing that it is the result of regarding a quality as a substance—which he thinks is incoherent. Sometimes, when he makes this point, he says that we think of such a quality as a substance because we ascribe to it the capacity to exist separately.[20] But in a letter to Elizabeth he writes about real qualities as qualities "that we have imagined to be real, that is, to have an existence distinct from that of body, and consequently to be substances, although we have called them qualities."[21]

The connection with separability is now as follows: a substance can exist without anything else, because it has existence in its own right, *per se*. Modes are different because they exist by virtue of inherence in something else. Consequently, a mode cannot exist without such a subject of inherence. In non-Cartesian terms the idea is a very simple one. The world contains things and properties. The primary entities are things, which exist in their own right. Properties don't exist in their own right; they exist by virtue of being the properties of things. The basic idea of the distinction between these two categories is not modal, but it does have modal consequences. To take an arbitrary example, a piece of wax is a thing, which exists in its own right. Its shape and size are properties of it, which exist by belonging to the piece of wax. As a result, if one were to destroy the piece of wax, the shape and size would disappear. The piece of wax itself is not a property of something else such that its existence depends on that entity in this way.[22] What Descartes wants to establish then regarding mind and body, is that each is a thing in its own right, and that they are different from each other.

2. Modes and Attributes

The Real Distinction Argument should be understood in terms of Descartes's theory of substance. The crux of this theory can be found at *Principles* I, 53:

> there is one principal property for each substance, which constitutes its nature and essence and to which all the other ones are referred. Namely, extension in length, width and depth constitutes the nature of corporeal substance; thought constitutes the nature of thinking substance. For everything else that can be attributed to body presupposes extension, and is only a mode of some extended thing; and similarly all those we find in the mind, are only different modes of thinking. So for instance, figure can only be understood in an extended thing, motion in extended space; and imagination, sensation or the will only in a thinking thing. But on the other hand, extension can be understood without shape or motion, and thought without imagination or sensation and so on: as is clear to anyone who attends to the matter.

So Descartes thinks that each substance has a principal attribute that constitutes the nature or essence of that substance. All the other (intrinsic) properties of a substance are 'referred to' this attribute; they are modes, ways of being of the principal attribute, and, as Descartes often says, *presuppose* it.²³ A principal attribute constitutes a substance in that it makes it a complete thing, a substance, and makes it the kind of substance that it is. Modes cannot do that.

Descartes wants to argue that mind or thinking substance and body are different substances. In other words, he wants to show that they are not one and the same substance. The Real Distinction Argument can be understood as ruling out various specific ways in which mind and body could be the same substance. First, the discussion of the mind in the Second Meditation leads to the conclusion that thought is not a mode of body but a principal attribute. As a result it is not the case that the mind is a body by virtue of thought being a mode of body. Second, the argument relies on the claim that extension, which constitutes the nature of body, is the principal attribute of body. Consequently mind and body are not identical by virtue of extension being a mode of thought. These results are not yet sufficient to establish the real distinction because they are compatible with the idea that mind and body constitute one substance with two principal attributes. But this possibility is ruled out for Descartes, since he held that a substance has only one principal attribute. I will discuss these three stages of the argument in this order.

The present section will be concerned with what Descartes means to accomplish in the Second Meditation. Interpreters have answered this question in different ways. Descartes might think that he clearly and distinctly perceives that the mind is not extended. In that case dualism would follow quite simply by way of the validation of clear and distinct perceptions. But I will argue that he does not proceed in this way. Sometimes Descartes presents the result of the Second Meditation as a claim about his nature or essence. He says in the Sixth Meditation: "I noticed nothing else to pertain to my nature or essence except that I am a thinking thing." This phrase is ambiguous.²⁴ It could mean either that he did not notice that anything else belongs to his nature or essence, or that he noticed that nothing else belongs to his nature or essence. This ambiguity could be a very serious one. Descartes's argument might rely on ambiguities of this kind in a way that is fatal to it.²⁵ The first of these claims is weaker and easier to establish than the second one. But the question is often raised whether it would be sufficient for establishing dualism. The second claim is obviously harder to defend. Thus a common objection to the argument is that the Second Meditation fails to show that the mind is not essentially extended. Philosophers have questioned the idea that this claim, and dualism, can be established *a priori* by means of a thought experiment of the kind found in the Second Meditation.²⁶

These problems are very pressing if one assumes that the question whether the mind is essentially extended comes down to the question whether it is necessarily extended. But Descartes's use of the thought experiment must be understood in light of his notion of a principal attribute and his view that the essence of a substance consists in such an attribute. The contribution of the Second Meditation is a clear and distinct perception of the mind that shows that thought is such an attribute. From this perspective it will be clear that the argument does not fall victim to ambiguities of the sort noted above, and it will account for Descartes's confidence that the argument succeeded in establishing dualism.

Descartes does not think he has established in the Second Meditation that he clearly and distinctly perceives that the mind is not extended. He addresses this issue in a letter to Clerselier, in which he responds to an objection from Gassendi concerning that Meditation: "I said in one place that, while the soul doubts the existence of all material things, it only knows itself precisely taken, *praecise tantum,* as an immaterial substance; and seven or eight lines below, in order to show that by these words *praecise tantum,* I do not understand an entire exclusion or negation, but only an abstraction from material things, I said that nevertheless one was not assured that there is nothing in the soul that is corporeal, although one does not know anything corporeal in it" (AT IX 215). The Second Meditation itself is quite clear about this point. Descartes argues there that in spite of the skeptical arguments of the First Meditation he is certain that he exists and that he is a thinking thing. Throughout this discussion the crucial doubts are about bodies. After he has established that he is a thinking thing, he considers the question whether he might be a body, but he concludes that he cannot settle that issue yet. He writes: "What else am I? I will use my imagination. I am not that complex of limbs, which is called the human body; I am also not some thin air infused in these limbs, nor a wind, fire, vapor, breath, nor anything that I imagine. For I have supposed those things to be nothing. The position remains: I am nevertheless something. Perhaps it happens to be the case, however, that these very things which I suppose to be nothing, because they are unknown to me, do not in reality differ from that I that I know? I don't know, I don't dispute about this yet: I can only judge about those things that are known to me" (AT VII 27). So here Descartes clearly thinks that he has not established that he (clearly and distinctly) perceives that the mind is not corporeal. Whereas he does not mention extension explicitly in this passage, it is covered by what he says. For earlier he announced: "By body I understand all that which is apt to be limited by some shape, confined in a place, and which can fill a space in such a way that it excludes any other body from it" (AT VII 26). This last characteristic, filling space in a way that excludes other bodies or other things, Descartes identifies with extension, and he sometimes specifies the essence of body in terms of it. For instance, in writing to Hyperaspistes he denies of the mind "real extension, that is, that by which it occupies a place and excludes something else from it."[27]

Let us now turn to what Descartes does think he establishes by means of the Second Meditation. In response to questions from Caterus and Arnauld Descartes defends the argument in the First and Fourth Replies by claiming that he has a clear and distinct conception of the mind *as a complete thing.*[28] As has been pointed out by Margaret Wilson and others this notion is very important for the Real Distinction Argument.[29] A complete thing, for Descartes, is "a substance endowed with those forms or attributes which are sufficient for recognizing it as a substance."[30] In the Fourth Replies he writes: "The mind can be perceived distinctly and completely, or sufficiently for it to be regarded as a complete thing, without any of those forms or attributes from which we recognize that body is a substance, as I think I have sufficiently shown in the Second Meditation" (AT VII 223). Now in the Second Meditation Descartes considers the mind only as a *thinking* thing. The import of the idea that mind can be conceived as complete without any corporeal attributes is thus that thought is perceived to be sufficient for the mind to be a substance.[31] This is what the Second Meditation is supposed to establish.

In terms of Descartes's theory of substance this leads to the result that thought is a *principal attribute* and not a mode.[32] The thought experiment contributes to this result by showing that thought is not a mode of body. In other places the point is that thought does not presuppose *extension.* Thought not being a mode that presupposes extension is precisely what Descartes regarded as sufficient to argue that thought is a principal attribute. The reason is, briefly, that extension is the principal attribute of body, and Descartes is concerned with the question whether mind and body are the same substance. I will return to this question later.[33]

How does the thought experiment of the Second Meditation show that thought is not a mode of body or extension? In the *Comments on a Certain Broadsheet* Descartes provides an explanation: "it belongs to the nature of a mode that although we can easily understand any substance without it, we cannot, however, *vice versa* clearly understand a mode unless we conceive at the same time a substance of which it is a mode; as I explained at *Principles* I, 61, and as all philosophers agree. It is clear from his fifth rule, however, that our author had not attended to this rule: for there he admits that we can doubt about the existence of body, when we do not at the same time doubt the existence of the mind. Hence it follows that the mind can be understood by us without the body, and that therefore it is not a mode of it"(AT VIII–2 350). Descartes makes clear here that the mind is not a mode of body because we can doubt the existence of body while not doubting the existence of mind, and because a mode cannot be clearly understood without conceiving of the kind of substance to which it belongs.[34] In this text Descartes identifies the claim that the mind is not a mode of body with the idea that thought is a principal attribute. A little later he makes basically the same point in terms of attributes: "From this fact that one [attribute] can be understood in this way [that is, distinctly] without the other [attribute], it is known that it is not a mode of the latter, but a thing or an attribute of a thing which can subsist without it" (ibid.). The point is really that the Second Meditation is supposed to show that *thought* is not a mode of body.

We can see now why the thought experiment of the Second Meditation shows that thought is not a mode of body. The reason is that Descartes thought that a mode depends not only ontologically, but also epistemically on its attribute. He believed that a mode cannot be conceived clearly and distinctly without the substance of which it is the mode, or without the attribute of that substance. Thus he claimed in the Sixth Meditation (in language that is very close to that of the *Comments*) that we can see that sensation and imagination are modes of him, that is the mind, because he can clearly and distinctly conceive of himself without them, but they cannot be so conceived without an intelligent substance in which they inhere.[35] Motion, shape and size are modes of the body, and they cannot be clearly and distinctly conceived without extension.

This view of the mode-attribute relation explains why the connection between a mode and its attribute can be detected by the kind of thought experiment executed in the Second Meditation. Descartes makes this point very clear in the letter to Gibieuf of January 19, 1642:

> when I consider a shape without thinking of the substance or the extension of which it is a shape, I make an abstraction of the mind which I can easily recognize afterwards, by examining whether I did not draw that idea that I have of figure alone from some richer idea that I also have in me, to which it is so joined that, although one can think of one without paying attention to the other, one cannot deny it of the other when one thinks of both. For I see clearly that the idea of figure is so joined to the idea of extension and of substance, given that it is not possible for me to conceive a shape while denying that it has extension, nor to conceive of extension while denying that it is the extension of a substance. But the idea of an extended and shaped substance is complete because I can

conceive it all by itself, and deny of it everything else of which I have ideas. Now it is, it seems to me, quite clear that the idea I have of a substance that thinks is complete in this way, and that I have no other idea that precedes it in my mind, and that is so joined to it that I cannot conceive them well while denying one of the other; for if there were such an idea in me I would necessarily know it. (AT III 475–76, K 123–24)

In this letter Descartes allows that we can think of a mode without thinking of its attribute by an abstraction of the mind—that is to say, by not thinking of the attribute at all.[36] But when we consider both the mode and its attribute together we will see that the mode depends on that attribute.

So in order to establish whether some property F is a mode of another property G, one would have to consider them both together, and then see whether one can deny G of F. Or, more properly, the question is whether one could (clearly and distinctly) conceive of something as a thing that has F while denying G of it. Consequently, in order to establish that thought is not a mode of extension, or rather, that it is not a mode of an extended substance, we have to consider whether we can conceive of a thinking thing while denying extension of it. For the purpose of the Real Distinction Argument, then, this is Descartes's task in the Second Meditation. And, of course, what is at issue is the question whether we can have *clear and distinct* conceptions of the right kind. Descartes does not always specify the requirement of clarity and distinctness. In the *Meditations* the notion of a clear and distinct idea or conception does not emerge until after the discussion of the mind in the Second Meditation. Like Descartes, I will sometimes omit it.[37]

In the Second Meditation this strategy is carried out as follows. Descartes doubts that there are bodies, yet he is certain that he exists. He establishes that he is a thinking thing. We saw that then he turns to the question whether he might be a body, and he concludes that he cannot settle that issue yet. But after he has made that point he makes clear that there is something that is certain already: "It is very certain that the notion of this [I] so precisely taken does not depend on those things which I do not yet know to exist; it does not depend therefore on any of those things that I feign in imagination" (AT VII 27–28). In light of his theory of substance and, in particular, the letter to Gibieuf, this passage has the following significance. Before the above quote Descartes establishes that he is a thinking thing: he focuses his attention just on thought while not considering corporeal characteristics—that is, in abstraction from such characteristics. Then he in effect considers thought and extension (as well as other corporeal characteristics) together: he wonders whether he is a body in addition to being a thinking thing. At first he claims he is not a body, since he assumes there are none. But then he considers the possibility that he is, after all, a body, and he says he does not know, that he cannot settle the question now. But what he does think he can claim is that his *notion* of himself does not depend on the objects of the imagination, that is, bodies or extended things.[38]

According to the letter to Gibieuf, if thought were in fact a mode of extension, Descartes would recognize at this point that his idea of a thinking thing depends on the idea of extension, or of extended substance. Given that he knows he is a thinking thing, he would now see that he also is a body. But he doesn't. Then he draws the conclusion that one expects in light of the letter to Gibieuf: the notion that he has of himself at that point, the notion of a thinking thing, does not depend on the objects of the imagination, that is, bodies.[39]

Let us now return to the question whether the Real Distinction Argument relies on a problematic equivocation. We noticed the ambiguity in Descartes's phrase, "I know nothing else to belong my nature or essence except that I am a thinking thing." In the Synopsis to the *Meditations* Descartes explicitly makes the weaker claim and says: "I clearly had no cognition of [*cognoscere*] anything that I knew [*scirem*] to pertain to my essence, except that I was a thinking thing" (AT VII 8). In a moment we will see why Descartes thinks this claim is sufficient.[40]

Descartes uses a variety of other descriptions of the epistemic result of the Second Meditation. These descriptions can often be interpreted in different ways. Some of them suggest that we can form a conception of the mind that excludes extension. Descartes says so in a letter to Mesland: "There is a great difference between abstraction and exclusion. If I said only that the idea that I have of my soul does not represent it to me as dependent on body, and identified with it, that would only be an abstraction, from which I could only form a negative argument, that would be unsound. But I say that this idea represents it to me as a substance that can exist even if everything that belongs to body is excluded from it, from which I form a positive argument, and conclude that it can exist without the body" (AT IV 120). In the letter to Gibieuf Descartes claims that extension can be denied of the mind.[41] But sometimes Descartes's point seems to be that one can form a conception of the mind that merely omits extension. In the Fifth Replies he says that we don't have to regard the mind as an extended thing, and that the concept of it developed in the Second Meditation does not contain corporeal characteristics: "I discover that I am a thinking substance, and form a clear and distinct concept of that thinking substance in which [concept] none of those things that belong to the concept of corporeal substance is contained. This clearly suffices for me to affirm that insofar as I know myself, I am nothing other than a thinking thing, which I affirmed in the Second Meditation. And I did not have to admit that thinking substance is some mobile, pure, subtle body, since I had no reason that persuaded me to do so"(AT VII 355). In the *Comments on a Certain Broadsheet* he describes the point as being that we can doubt the existence of body, while not doubting (and being certain of) the existence of the mind (AT VII–2,350). This analysis also suggests that Descartes is concerned with omission of extension from the conception of the mind.

Thus there is variation in Descartes's formulations of the conception of the mind needed for the Real Distinction Argument. In addition, several of these formulations are susceptible to different interpretations. We have seen, however, that Descartes wants to establish that thought is not a mode of extension. In light of Descartes's views of the relationship between modes and attributes it is now clear what he has in mind. For Descartes believes that a mode depends epistemically on its attribute in such a way that one would see the connection between a mode and its attribute, were one to consider them together—as opposed to not paying attention to corporeal characteristics, as happens in abstraction. Thus if thought were a mode of extension, considering them together would force us to say that a thinking thing must be extended. The crucial result for the Real Distinction Argument is that we are not forced to do so. Given this result one can make various claims that provide what is needed for the argument. One could say that extension can be omitted from the concept of a thinking thing. This claim is insufficient if it is made while abstracting from extension. But it is sufficient if the omission of extension is found possible *while considering the question whether extension should be included.* Descartes's weaker statements must be understood with this qualification in mind. Alternatively, we could say that we can deny extension of the mind, or that we can form a conception of the mind that excludes extension from it in the sense that we can do so coherently.[42] Finally, it should be clear now that the claim that we do not clearly and distinctly perceive extension to belong to the essence of the mind is sufficient if this claim is established while considering whether it does so belong.[43]

So in the Second Meditation we learn that we can consider thought and body together without seeing that a thinking thing must be extended and a body. In terms of Descartes's theory of substance it follows that thought is not a mode of extension and of body. Finally, since thought is not a mode of body, Descartes thinks, it is a principal attribute, and makes something a complete thing. I will now turn to questions one might raise about this last inference.

3. Thought a Principal Attribute

The idea that thought is not a mode of extension is not by itself enough to establish that thought is a principal attribute. Thought could be a mode of some other attribute. It could also be identical with extension, but Descartes does not actively consider this possibility. In the sequel I will assume that the idea that thought is a principal attribute includes the idea that thought is not identical with extension and will usually omit this specification.[44]

The point that thought might presuppose some other property is sometimes raised as an objection to Descartes's argument. The question is whether this possibility threatens the attempt to show that the mind is an incorporeal substance. For if thought were a mode of some other property which is, however, a principal attribute distinct from extension, then the conclusion could still be established. So thought being a mode of some other property would be a problem for the argument if either (a) thought were a mode of some other *corporeal* property, or (b) thought were a mode of some property that is presupposed by both thought and extension. These are the possibilities Descartes needs to rule out.

What does Descartes have to say to this objection? The following considerations address (a). In the Second Meditation Descartes does not merely try to establish that *extension* can be denied of the mind. He uses the assumption that bodies don't exist, and lists various corporeal characteristics. So any corporeal properties thus included in the Second Meditation are supposed to be ruled out on the basis of the thought experiment. Consequently in the *Meditations* Descartes does not assume that thought's not being a mode of extension is sufficient for its being a principal attribute.

Often he does make this assumption, however, and the reason is that extension is the crucial property, because it is the principal attribute of body for Descartes. If one grants Descartes that extension is the principal attribute of body, he has an additional reply to (a). For then all the other properties of body presuppose extension. Consequently if thought presupposed some corporeal property other than extension, it would turn out that in the end thought presupposes extension.[45] Thus if one grants Descartes that extension is the principal attribute of body, showing that thought does not presuppose extension is enough to show that thought is either (i) a principal attribute or (ii) a mode of a principal attribute F which is different from extension, and which—since extension and F are principal attributes—is neither presupposed by extension, nor presupposes it. I have pointed out that (ii) is not a worrisome possibility. So I will disregard it.

What does Descartes have to say about (b), the possibility that there is some other property that is presupposed by both thought and extension? In the first place, Descartes generally neglects this possibility. He seems to assume that he just needs to show that thought is not a mode of body. Accordingly, I will schematize the argument as relying on this assumption. Nevertheless Descartes would have something to say to (b). For a passage in the Third Replies makes it clear that he thinks (b) can be ruled out by considering thought and extension together. There Descartes claims that if one considers modes that presuppose the same attribute together, one will see that they have this attribute in common. Thus he thinks that when we consider the various modes of mind together we see they have thought in common, and similarly for the modes of body. He also claims that we see no connection between thought and extension.[46]

This reply may well leave Descartes's critic unsatisfied. Descartes's approach can only establish that thought does not presuppose extension by virtue of some *a priori* dependence. On Descartes's view, establishing that there is no *a priori* truth by virtue of which thought entails extension is enough to show that thought is not a mode of extension. But one might question Descartes's view that the mode-attribute relation is always detectable *a priori*. Alternatively, one might grant that it is, but doubt that a strategy like the one pursued in the Second Meditation and described in the letter to Gibieuf is enough to see whether some property is a mode of another one. This strategy might not be enough to determine whether there is an *a priori* connection.

This is a very serious problem for the argument. Descartes needs to rule out the possibility that thought might be a way of being extended despite there being no *a priori* connection between thought and extension, or none that is so easily detected. It is important to see, however, that this line of objection could have rather strong implications. For Descartes might be able to develop a response that derives from the particular sense in which a mode is supposed to be a way of being of a principal attribute. This sense is such that a mode cannot be understood without its principal attribute. This view is plausible for examples of modes found in Descartes's writings, such as motion, shape, sensation, imagination. According to this response, the objection about the epistemic relation of modes to principal attributes results in questions about the ontological picture. It would turn the present worries into a questioning not just of the view that modes epistemically depend on their attributes, but of the view that a substance has a principal attribute of which the other properties are modes in Descartes's sense.

4. The Nature of Body

The claim that thought is a principal attribute is not enough to establish that my mind is not actually extended. If my mind is a thinking, complete thing by virtue of the attribute of thought, it follows that my mind could exist as just a thinking thing that is not extended. But that conclusion is compatible with the idea that it is actually extended. Descartes relies on two other premises to conclude that his mind is not extended: the claim that extension is the principal attribute of body, and the claim that a substance has exactly one principal attribute. I will now discuss the claim that extension is the principal attribute of body. This claim rules out the possibility that mind and body are identical by virtue of extension, which constitutes the nature or essence of body for Descartes, being a mode of thought. I wish to emphasize the importance of this premise to the argument. Generally discussions of the argument focus on the mind and pay little attention to Descartes's claims about body. But Descartes's conception of body is absolutely crucial.

Two aspects of the claim that extension is the principal attribute of body are important. (1) The first is the idea that *extension* rather than some other property is the principal attribute of body. Descartes himself regarded this point as important for the Real Distinction Argument, as is clear from the following passage:

> The earliest judgments which we have made since our childhood, and the common philosophy also later, have accustomed us to attribute to the body many things which belong only to the soul, and to attribute to the soul many things which belong only to body. People commonly mingle the two ideas of body and soul in the composition of the ideas that they form of real qualities and substantial forms, which I think should be completely rejected. By examining physics carefully, one can reduce all those things in it which fall under the knowledge of the intellect to very few kinds, of which we have very clear and distinct notions. After considering them I do not think one can fail to recognize whether, when we conceive one thing without another, this happens only by an abstraction of our mind or because the things are truly different. When things are separated only by a mental abstraction, one necessarily notices their conjunction and union when one considers them together. But one could not notice any between the body and soul, provided that one conceives them as one should, the one as that which fills space, the other as that which thinks. (Letter of July 1641, possibly to de Launay, AT III, 420–21, K 109)

Descartes claims here that when we clean up our notions of body and soul, and think of body as what is extended, and of the soul as what thinks, it is easier to see that the body is really distinct from the soul.

Descartes saw his conception of body as an advance over the Aristotelian Scholastic conception which mixed ideas of body and soul.[47]

(2) It is crucial to the argument that body has a *principal attribute* different from thought. That is to say, it is important that body is a substance by virtue of some property different from thought, and does not have to think in order to be a substance.[48] This point is important, because, as we shall see, the argument relies on the idea that extension is a *principal attribute* to show that the mind is not extended. Descartes takes the point that body has a principal attribute different from thought to be pretty obvious, and it will strike most people as not in need of much defense. One can easily conceive of a corporeal, non-thinking complete thing such as a stone, and we easily grant that there are such things. But it is worth pointing out that this claim was denied, for instance, by Leibniz, who thought that all substances are perceiving substances. In Cartesian terms, for Leibniz extension is not a principal attribute, and perception is the only principal attribute.

Although Descartes thought it was an advantage of his conception of body that he regarded its essence as consisting in extension, the argument could have gone through, in principle, on a conception of body as having a different principal attribute. The present point is just that in order to get the conclusion that the mind is not a body, Descartes needs the claim that some property different from thought is the principal attribute of body.

The fact that denial of the possibility of corporeal, nonthinking substances is unusual explains why generally little attention is paid to the role of claims about body in the Real Distinction Argument. But it is important to see that claims about the nature of body are indispensable to Descartes's argument. Central statements of the argument should make this clear. For instance, in the Sixth Meditation Descartes relies on clear and distinct conception of both mind and body—and not just of the mind.

5. Attributes and Substances

How close are we to the conclusion that mind and body are different substances? At this point in the argument it is established that both thought and extension are principal attributes. Consequently two ways in which the mind might be a body are ruled out: thought cannot be a mode of extension, and extension cannot be a mode of thought. What is left, however, is the possibility that the mind has two principal attributes, thought and extension. But Descartes holds that a substance cannot have more than one principal attribute. I will call this premise the Attribute Premise. Given that the mind is a thinking thing and that thought and extension are both principal attributes, it follows that the mind is not extended.

We have, in fact, already encountered the Attribute Premise in Descartes's account of substance. For we saw that at *Principles* I, 53 he writes that each substance has one principal attribute that constitutes its nature or essence. The premise is generally not at all explicit when Descartes argues for the real distinction of mind and body. But Descartes appeals to it in the *Comments on a Certain Broadsheet.*[49] Regius had written: "since those attributes [extension and thought] are not opposites but diverse, there is no obstacle to the mind being some attribute belonging to the same subject as extension, although one is not comprehended in the concept of the other."[50] Descartes writes in reply that this is possible for modes, but: "About other attributes that constitute the natures of things it cannot be said that those that are different and of which neither is contained in the concept of the other, belong to the same subject. For it is the same as saying that one and the same subject has two different natures, which implies a contradiction, at least when the question concerns a simple and noncomposite subject, as is the case here" (AT VII-B 349–50).

Less obviously, the premise is just below the surface in Descartes's discussion of the argument in the Fourth Replies. He writes: "No one who perceived two substances through two different concepts has ever failed to judge that they are really distinct" (AT VII 226). On a simple-minded reading of this sentence Descartes would be suggesting something like this: whenever we have two concepts, and we wonder whether they correspond to one or two substances, we must think there are two. But he cannot mean to say that. The concepts in question are, of course, those of the mind as a thinking complete thing, and the body as an extended complete thing, where neither concept contains what belongs to the other substance. Thus the idea is that mind and body are perceived through thought and extension respectively. I think that what is behind this comment is the fact that for Descartes two principal attributes yield two substances. The comment suggests that Descartes thought this pretty obvious—which view might contribute to an explanation of the fact that the idea is not made more explicit by Descartes.

Descartes's use of the premise in the passage from the *Comments on a Certain Broadsheet* suggests that we need to make a modification in the statement of the premise. For Descartes draws a distinction between simple and composite subjects, and what he says seems to suggest that he allows for complex *substances* which have more than one principal attribute. An example of a complex subject for Descartes is the human being who is a composite of mind and body, and in which more than one attribute can be found. We must be cautious, however, for Descartes does not use the term 'substance' here. But as I understand it the role of the Attribute Premise is compatible with Descartes's accepting complex substances. The role of the premise in the argument is to establish that when there are two principal attributes, there are two substances, but it is compatible with the idea that two substances could in turn compose a third substance. So it leads to the conclusion that mind and body are both substances, while allowing for the possibility that together they compose a third substance, a human being.[51] To put the point slightly differently: according to the Attribute Premise, if there are substances that think and are extended they are always composites of two different substances, a thinking one and an extended one. In the sequel I will leave this complication out of consideration. Supposing that Descartes does allow for complex substances, in effect my discussion will concern simple ones.[52]

The Attribute Premise is generally not explicit in Descartes's discussions of the Real Distinction Argument. But there are good reasons for thinking that the argument relies on it. First, Descartes adhered to the Premise, as is quite clear at *Principles* I, 53, and in the *Comments*. Second, in the *Comments* he does ascribe a role to the Premise in the case for dualism. Finally, there is the philosophical consideration that the argument requires *something* to do the work the Premise does. Without the Attribute Premise the argument establishes the possibility of a thinking, nonextended substance. But it simply does not rule out the possibility that there are thinking substances that are also extended and corporeal (without being composites of a thinking and an extended substance). Thus it does not rule out the possibility that my mind is in fact extended and corporeal. The Attribute Premise solves the problem by appeal to a view Descartes clearly committed himself to, and which he did cite in support of dualism. Of course the role of the Premise is generally implicit. Thus it is quite likely that Descartes himself did not fully appreciate its importance.[53]

Why does Descartes hold the Attribute Premise?[54] The premise makes a strong claim, and the question whether one should accept or reject it is not easy to answer. Descartes never really defends it. The closest he comes is in the passage from the *Comments* where Descartes simply says that a substance cannot have two natures, because this would imply a contradiction. That remark does not teach us much. The question why he might have held this premise is an interesting one, however, and I wish to pursue it to some extent, although doing so is necessarily speculative.

One consideration worth mentioning is the fact that the resulting picture is quite appealing: it is very clean and neat. According to this picture a substance has a very orderly set of properties; a particular kind of substance cannot have just any kind of property. Its properties are unified by means of its principal attribute, which accords with the idea, common in the history of philosophy, that a substance is a unity in some strong sense. In addition, part of the attraction of the resulting view for Descartes is, of course, that corporeal substances can be accounted for entirely mechanistically.

Further examination of the role of the principal attribute in Descartes's conception of substance helps make sense of his adherence to the Attribute Premise from a different angle. It is useful to compare his conception of substance to two others, namely, what I will call the Bare Subject View, and the Aristotelian scholastic conception of corporeal substance. For this purpose we must distinguish between the notion of a substance and that of a subject of inherence. On the Bare Subject View a substance just is a subject of inherence of properties. Properties inhere in the subject, but are not constituents of a substance. The subject constitutes the entire substance.[55] According to the Aristotelian scholastics, on the other hand, a corporeal substance is a composite of prime matter and substantial form. Each of these is a constituent of the substance. Prime matter is a bare subject in the sense that it, too, is in itself featureless and understood as the bare subject for substantial form. But an important difference with the Bare Subject View is that prime matter is merely a constituent of the substance, which in addition includes one or more substantial forms.[56]

Descartes clearly rejects the Bare Subject view, and agrees with the Aristotelians in thinking that the substance itself is more than just a bare subject. He thinks it contains the principal attribute. In fact, often he seems to hold a view that is exactly the opposite of the Bare Subject View. For much of what Descartes says suggests that the principal attribute constitutes the entire substance, and that there is no bare subject of inherence at all. On this view there is nothing to the substance over and above the principal attribute, and the substance is entirely constituted by it.

It is clear that for Descartes the substance includes the principal attribute. Thus in the Fourth Replies he writes that surfaces and lines can be understood as complete things (that is, substances) only if one adds besides length and width also depth.[57] Descartes's point is here that one needs to include the principal attribute of extension in order to get completeness. In the letter to Gibieuf he says that in order to have a complete idea of shape (which is the same as understanding shape as a complete thing)[58] one needs to include extension and substance— not just substance. This point again shows that completeness requires a principal attribute. Otherwise it should be enough for completeness to think of shape as inhering in a substance without including extension. Furthermore Descartes's view that thought is *sufficient* for completeness would be puzzling if the subject by itself constitutes the complete thing or substance.[59]

Various comments Descartes makes suggest that for him there is no bare subject as a constituent of substance at all. He rejects the scholastic notion of prime matter in *The World* as unintelligible, saying "it has been so deprived of all its forms and qualities that nothing remains that can be clearly understood."[60] Matter must be conceived as extended, he contends. In the *Principles* he allows only a distinction of reason between the subject and its principal attribute: "Thought and extension can be regarded as constituting the natures of intelligent and corporeal substance; and then they must be conceived not otherwise than as thinking substance itself and extended substance itself, that is, as mind and body. In this way they are understood most clearly and distinctly. For this reason we understand extended or thinking substance more easily than substance alone when the fact that it thinks or is extended is omitted. For there is some difficulty in abstracting the notion of substance from the notions of thought and extension, because these are different from it only by reason" (*Principles,* I 63). Descartes seems here to *identify* the principal attributes with the substances. If there is only a distinction of reason between principal attribute and substance, then it is impossible to see how there could be anything to a substance over and above the principal attribute. For a distinction of reason is just a conceptual distinction.[61] In the *Comments* Descartes writes: "I have not said that those attributes [thought and extension] are in [incorporeal substance and corporeal substance] as in subjects different from them" (AT VIII-B 348).[62] It is worth pointing out also that in the *Comments* Descartes uses 'thought' and 'mind' interchangeably.

A comparison between Descartes's view and the hylomorphic conception of corporeal substance is interesting at this point. For the Aristotelians a corporeal substance consists of prime matter and substantial form. Descartes eliminates prime matter. In Aristotelian terms the result is that a substance just consists in a substantial form. In Descartes's terms it is that the substance just consists in a principal attribute. Now these notions are different, but it is worth pointing out that the notion of a principal attribute inherited certain features of the notion of substantial form, in particular of a version of this notion found, for instance, in Aquinas and Suárez. On this view substantial forms constitute the natures of substances. For Descartes the principal attribute plays this role. The substantial form of a hylomorphic substance is the principle or source of the properties, faculties, and activities of a substance, and determines what kinds a substance can have; for Descartes its principal attribute determines what kinds of modes belong to a substance.[63] For Aquinas and others the substantial form is what gives the substance its being, its actuality. It makes something a substance.[64] For Descartes the principal attribute makes something a substance, a being in its own right as opposed to a mode, which has being through something else. In the light of these similarities it is significant for our present purposes that Descartes eliminated prime matter. For, in a sense, as a result of eliminating prime matter the substance just consists in the principal attribute.

Descartes's commitment to the identification of principal attribute and substance is not unproblematic. He makes various claims that raise questions about this commitment. It would lead us too far afield to consider these problems.[65] But at least there is a clear tendency in Descartes to make this identification. This tendency provides a very simple hypothesis about why Descartes adheres to the Attribute Premise. For given this identification a substance contains nothing over and above the principal attribute: there are no additional constituents. Consequently where there are two such attributes there must be two substances.

6. Separability

The previous section concludes my account of the structure of the Real Distinction Argument. I now want to return to the issue of the separability of mind and body. I have argued that the real distinction of mind and body does not consist in their separability. But as we saw earlier, Descartes was not just interested in the claim that mind and body are really distinct, that is, actually different substances. He was also concerned with the idea that mind and body are separable, in particular that the mind can exist without the body. What is the relationship between the separability of mind and body and their being different substances, and what is the role of separability in the argument?

One connection between real distinction and separability, as we have seen, is that the first entails the second. For Descartes a substance is a thing in its own right. Furthermore, because a substance exists in its own right, it can exist without anything else. Clearly, then, it follows from the idea that mind and body are really distinct, that is, different substances, that they can exist without one another. But it does not follow from these considerations that this must be the order of inference in the Real Distinction Argument. According to many interpreters the inference goes in the opposite direction: the separability of mind and body is an essential step for deriving their real distinction. Prominent statements of the argument, such as in the *Meditations,* the Geometrical Exposition, and the *Principles* seem to support such an interpretation. I believe, however, that this approach misrepresents the precise significance of separability in the Real Distinction Argument, and overestimates its importance. I now wish to address this issue.

In the Geometrical Exposition Descartes clearly does infer the real distinction of mind and body from their separability. He argues there that mind can be without body and *vice versa* at least by God's power. Then he concludes: "Substances that can be without one another are really distinct (by definition 10). But mind and body are substances (by definitions 5, 6, and 7), that can be without one another (as has already been proved). Therefore mind and body are really distinct" (AT VII 170).[66] But the Geometrical Exposition is unusual in presenting the real distinction so clearly as derived from separability. Whereas the idea of the separability of mind and body is in evidence in the Sixth Meditation and in the *Principles,* in neither of these texts does Descartes clearly infer real distinction from separability. In the Meditations he first makes general claims about how to establish a real distinction. He seems to be saying that it is established via separability, when he says: "Since I know that anything that I clearly and distinctly understand can be brought about by God just as I understand it, it is sufficient that I can clearly and distinctly understand one thing without another in order for me to be certain that one is different from the other, since they can be placed apart [*seorsim poni*] at least by God." But when he moves to the discussion of mind and body in particular, their separability does not figure as a premise. Their separability does show up: Descartes concludes the argument by saying, "it is certain that I am really distinct from my body, and can exist without it." But this sentence is more easily read as presenting the direction of inference to be from real distinction to separability! Finally, in the *Principles* also Descartes seems to conclude that mind and body are really distinct before he addresses their separability.

It is important that on various occasions Descartes presents the real distinction as derived simply from the claim that he has clear and distinct conceptions of mind and body as different substances. The Sixth Meditation can be read that way. Most strikingly in the Synopsis Descartes presents the final stage of the argument as follows: "I concluded that all those things which are clearly and distinctly conceived as different substances, as are mind and body, are substances really distinct from one another" (AT VII 13). Now statements of the argument where he infers that mind and body are different substances simply from the fact that he had different conceptions of them, or, as here, from the observation that he clearly and distinctly conceives them to be different, might be elliptical. There might be an implicit step to the effect that mind and body are separable. But there are two philosophical points to be made here. First, in fact that step is not needed: on my reconstruction the argument arrives at the real distinction without any appeal to separability. Second, interpretations that do see the argument as deriving the real distinction from the separability of mind and body tend to run into problems with respect to this inference. The literature in English has often taken this approach. I will consider two examples.

According to one common analysis the argument works as follows. In the Second Meditation Descartes argues that it is conceivable that he (his mind) exists, and thinks without being extended. Furthermore, he believes that whatever is conceivable is possible. Let us call this the Conceivability Premise. It follows that it is possible for him to exist, and think, without being extended. The argument then needs a further premise to show that he *actually* is not extended, and thus not a body. This job can be done by the premise that what is extended is necessarily extended, where this claim is to be understood *de re*. I will call this premise the Essentialist Premise. The conceivability and possibility of him existing without being extended should also be understood as *de re* claims about a particular. Let us call this the Essentialist Argument.[67]

There are two problems with this interpretation. The first one is that the Essentialist Premise is introduced just on the basis of the philosophical need for it, and not at all on the basis of textual evidence.[68] The second one is that the Essentialist Argument has the following serious philosophical flaw. Descartes might find it conceivable that he exists without being extended, and from this infer, by way of the Conceivability Premise, that it is possible for him not to be extended. But on the other hand, it might be that, unbeknownst to him, he is actually extended. But then by the Essentialist Premise he would be necessarily extended. So given the Essentialist Premise, the conceivability of existing unextended is insufficient to establish its possibility.[69]

Margaret Wilson reconstructs the argument as follows. If A can exist apart from B, and vice versa, A is really distinct from B, and B from A. Furthermore, the argument relies on premises that establish the following: if I clearly and distinctly perceive that A can exist apart from B and *vice versa,* then they can so exist, because God can bring it about, and thus they are really distinct. The question is now: what does it take to perceive that A can exist without B? Wilson says: "I can clearly and distinctly perceive the possibility that A and B exist apart, if: there are attributes ϕ and φ such that I clearly and distinctly understand that ϕ

belongs to the nature of A, and the φ belongs to the nature of B (and φ ≠ φ), and I clearly and distinctly understand that something can be a complete thing if it has φ even if it lacks φ (or has φ and lacks φ)." Thought and extension then fulfill the conditions of φ and φ for mind and body, and it follows that mind and body are really distinct.[70]

On this interpretation the argument relies on the perception that thought belongs to me, and that thought is sufficient to constitute a complete thing. Consequently it establishes that my completeness, my existence as a substance, does not require extension, and that I *can* exist without being extended. But on this interpretation nothing in the argument rules out that *actually* I am extended and a body. This would not be a problem if Descartes was merely concerned to establish that I can exist without body, or, to put it differently, that I can exist in an entirely incorporeal form. Now Wilson thinks that this is all Descartes wants to establish, because she thinks that real distinction is nothing over and above separability. Mind and body are different things, on her view, just in the sense that they can exist apart.[71] But I have argued that there is more to Descartes's notion of real distinction. Mind and body are different substances for him in the sense that each is a thing in its own right different from the other. This idea is important since he thinks each is a subject of inherence for different types of properties. Addition of the Attribute Premise would result in the conclusion that mind and body are different substances in this stronger sense.[72]

Furthermore, once this point is recognized, it should be clear that separability can be dropped from Wilson's reconstruction. On her interpretation, Descartes bases the claim that we clearly and distinctly perceive the separability of mind and body on the claim that we perceive that thought belongs to mind, and extension to body, and that each of these is complete with just the attribute in question.[73] Wilson is right on this point. On the other hand, if one takes the clear and distinct perceptions of mind and body as complete with just thought and extension respectively, the real distinction can be established without an appeal to separability by adding the Attribute Premise (and the validation of clear and distinct perceptions via God).[74] In other words, for Descartes these clear and distinct perceptions allow us to conclude both that thought and extension are principal attributes, and that mind and body are separable. But the first of these two claims is more fundamental philosophically: mind and body can exist without one another because thought and extension are different principal attributes. Moreover, this claim is more important for the argument, since it allows the inference to dualism when combined with the Attribute Premise.

So both these interpretations try to establish the real distinction via separability, and run into obstacles trying to do so. Arguing that mind and body are actually different substances in the sense that Descartes wants by way of their separability is not a trivial matter. The inference from the conceivability of mind existing (as a complete thing) without being extended and without body to its possibility is problematic. Nor is there an automatic step from this possibility to the mind actually not being extended and a body. Furthermore, as we have seen, if the argument is understood in light of Descartes's theory of substance, the separability of mind and body is not needed to establish their real distinction.

Descartes himself did, however, seem to think that one can infer from the separability of mind and body to their being different substances. He did not seem to see the problems with this inference. But these problems are not serious for Descartes since his conception of substance allows the argument for the real distinction to go through without running afoul of them. The reconstruction of the argument I propose avoids philosophical problems that arise from focus on separability and reveals, I believe, the fundamental ideas underlying the argument.[75]

7. Conclusion

The argument can now be schematized as follows:

1. I can doubt that I am extended but I cannot doubt (that is, I am certain) that I think.[76]
2. For any (intrinsic) properties ϕ and φ, if it is possible to doubt that something is ϕ while not doubting (that is, while being certain) that it is φ, then φ is not a mode of ϕ.
3. Thought is not a mode of extension. (1, 2)
4. Extension is the principal attribute of body, that is, corporeal substance.
5. If thought is not a mode of extension, it is a principal attribute distinct from extension.
6. Thought is a principal attribute distinct from extension. (3, 5)
7. Every substance has exactly one principal attribute.
8. The substance that is the subject of my thoughts (= my mind) is not extended. (4, 6, 7)
9. My mind is a different substance from body. (4, 8, LL)
10. If A and B are different substances, they are really distinct.
11. My mind is really distinct from body. (9, 10)

So interpreted, Descartes's argument escapes various philosophical problems, and it explains his confidence in the argument in terms of views he clearly held. It does not suffer from the problems that arise for the Essentialist Argument and Wilson's interpretation that result from focusing on the possibility of mind existing unextended or without body. In addition, my understanding of the argument should do away with ascriptions to Descartes of the so-called 'Argument from Doubt' which runs as follows: "I can doubt that body exists, I cannot doubt that I exist, therefore I am not identical with body," where the conclusion follows simply by an application of Leibniz's Law. Sometimes this argument is attributed to Descartes, but its shortcomings are clear.[77] My interpretation explains the role of the doubt without committing Descartes to the Argument from Doubt. The importance of the doubt is this: because we can doubt that bodies exist while being certain that mind exists, we discover that mind, or thought, is not a mode of body.[78]

We can see now why Descartes thought he could establish dualism by means of the kind of *a priori* reasoning displayed in the thought experiment of the Second Meditation. It is supposed to show that we can form a clear and distinct conception of the mind as a thinking, unextended substance. This result is significant since it supports the claim that thought is a principal attribute. We have seen how that claim is used in the argument.

This virtue of my interpretation of the argument helps meet the following objection. Descartes's theory of substance is not in evidence in the Second Meditation. Consequently one might be puzzled by the idea of understanding the Meditation in terms of this theory. But I have argued that an important part of the point of what he says there *can* be understood in the context of this theory, and that doing so explains Descartes's confidence in the Real Distinction Argument. In addition, it is worth pointing out that his conception of the relationship between modes and principal attributes, which I have claimed is at issue in the Second Meditation, is expressed in the Sixth Meditation. Descartes relies on it in his discussion of the question of what modes belong to what substance, immediately after the conclusion of the Real Distinction Argument. Finally, I do not wish to claim that in writing the *Meditations* Descartes had his conception of substance in mind in precisely the terms in which he expounded it in the *Principles*. I don't know whether he did. The fact is that this conception allows one to understand Descartes's faith in the argument in the *Meditations*. This fact is sufficiently explained if the ideas fundamental to this conception of substance were operative in Descartes's mind—whether or not he had formulated them to himself as he did in the *Principles*.

How defensible is the Real Distinction Argument? Crucial to the argument are the Attribute Premise and Descartes's view that the modes of a substance depend epistemically on its principal attribute. A full critical assessment of the argument would devote much attention to these claims, as they are both strong claims and far from uncontroversial. But such an assessment falls far beyond the scope of this paper.

Notes

I am very grateful to Robert M. Adams, Tyler Burge, Philip Clark, and John Etchemendy for comments on drafts of this paper. It has also benefitted from reactions from Kit Fine, Eckart Förster, Dan Garber, Hannah Ginsborgh, and Jeremy Hyman. But it owes most to Rogers Albritton, who inspired me to formulate my interpretation of the Real Distinction Argument.

1. What I call the Real Distinction Argument is not, however, Descartes's only argument for dualism. Also in the *Meditations* Descartes argues that mind and body are distinct on the ground that the mind is indivisible, while body is divisible (AT VII 85–86). In the *Discourse* and other places Descartes lists various human capacities in favor of the idea that the human being is not just a body (AT VI 55–60). References to Descartes are specified as follows. I always provide the reference to Charles Adam and Paul Tannery, *Oeuvres de Descartes* (Paris: Vrin, 1964–1978), using the abbreviation AT and specifying volume and page numbers. Translations can be found in John Cottingham, Robert Stotthoff, and Dugald Murdoch, trans., *The Philosophical Writings of Descartes* (New York: Cambridge University Press, 1985, 2 volumes), which provides the AT page numbers in the margins. Translations of the correspondence can be found in Anthony Kenny, trans., *Descartes: Philosophical Letters* (Minneapolis: University of Minnesota Press, 1981), abbreviated as K. Translations in the paper are my own.

2. As will become clear later, there are complications regarding this claim (see pp. 51–52).

3. AT VII 13.

4. AT VII 78–79. Whereas Descartes says here that sensation and imagination are modes of his mind, it has been argued that he held (at least at some point) that they really belong to the union of mind and body, rather than just the mind. See Paul Hoffman, "Cartesian Passions and Cartesian Dualism," *Pacific Philosophical Quarterly* 71 (1990): 310–32. See also John Cottingham, *Descartes* (Oxford: Basil Blackwell, 1986).

5. Clear appreciation for both these points can be found in Julius Weinberg, *Ockham, Descartes, and Hume: Self-Knowledge, Substance, and Causality* (Madison: University of Wisconsin Press, 1977), 72. Daniel Garber points out an interesting problem for the argument's success in defending Descartes's view of the scope of mechanistic explanation. See Garber, *Descartes's Metaphysical Physics* (Chicago: University of Chicago Press, 1992), 92–93, 111. An important question about the Real Distinction Argument is this: what exactly was Descartes's view of the nature of mind and body in terms of the kinds of properties that he ascribed to them, and why he held this view. I say little

about this issue in the present paper, which is more concerned with the role of general aspects of his conception of substance in the argument. I address it at greater length in "The Incorporeity of the Mind," in *Essays on Descartes's Philosophy and Science,* ed. Stephen Voss (Oxford: Oxford University Press, 1992).

6. AT VII 13, 78, 226, 423.

7. *Principles* I, 60.

8. See Eustacius, *Summa Philosophiae Quadripartita* (Paris: Carolus Chastellain, 1609), part 4, p. 80. Extensive discussion of these issues can be found in Suárez's *Disputationes metaphysicae* (in *Opera Omnia,* vols. 25–26 [Paris: Vivès, 1856]), Disp. VII. Characterization of real distinction as the distinction of one thing from another is provided at Disp. VII.I.I, and used throughout the disputation. For more discussion of my understanding of the conclusion of the argument, see my dissertation, *Descartes's Conception of the Mind* (University Microfilms International, 1989).

9. In the Fourth Replies Descartes comments on the employment of the term in the *Meditations,* and says that he had used it to stand for complete things, which are substances. He points out that he did not call the faculties of imagination and sensation *res,* but distinguished them accurately from *res sive substantias*—things or substances (AT VII 224). On the other hand, at *Principles* II, 55 Descartes calls both substances and their modes *res.*

10. See Garber, *Descartes's Metaphysical Physics,* 85, 89. Paul Hoffman and Margaret Wilson hold that it is sufficient for real distinction of mind and body that they can exist apart. In principle one might think separability is sufficient for establishing real distinction without being constitutive of real distinction. But Hoffman and Wilson think that real distinction consists in separability. See Hoffman, "The Unity of Descartes's Man," *Philosophical Review* 85 (1986) 339–70, p. 343n., Wilson, *Descartes* (Boston: Routledge and Kegan Paul, 1978), 190, 207. Descartes does think that separability is a sufficient indication, a sign, of real distinction, because he thinks that only two (or more) substances, entities existing in their own right, can be separated from one another.

11. AT VII 162.

12. If Descartes does not think that real distinction consists in separability, the question arises why he provides the definition in the Geometrical Exposition in terms of separability. Descartes must have been moved to do so in view of its use in the argument for the real distinction of mind and body a little later in the text.

13. Disp. VII. II. 9–27.

14. *Principles* I, 51. Strictly speaking, of course, this definition only applies to God, since all created substances depend on Him, as Descartes immediately makes clear in this section of the *Principles.* Something is a created substance, then, when it so exists that it can exist without anything else except God. I will generally omit this qualification.

15. Cf. Garber, *Descartes's Metaphysical Physics,* 65, 85, 89. Wilson also interprets the real distinction as consisting in the ability to exist apart (*Descartes,* 207).

16. AT III 456–57, AT III 502, K 128, VII 222, 226, VIII 348. See E. M. Curley, *Spinoza's Metaphysics: An Essay in Interpretation* (Cambridge: Harvard University Press, 1969), 4–11, for the view that this way of distinguishing substances and modes was common at the time.

In the Fourth Replies Descartes gives a weaker characterization of substance in terms of the *ability* to exist *per se:* ". . . this is the very notion of substance, that it can exist *per se,* that is, without the help of any other substance." On the same page, however, he gives a stronger description of substances as *res per se subsistentes*—not merely as things that *can* exist *per se* (AT VII 226). Existence *per se* is compatible with being joined to another substance in some way other than by inhering in it, and it should be distinguished from existing without or apart from other substances. Thus the mind exists *per se,* without the *help* of any other substance, in particular without inhering in another substance. But it does not, of course, exist without the body existing, or in separation from it, because it is in this life united to the body.

Paul Hoffman has argued that for Descartes the soul is the form of the body. In his defense of this position he relies on the view that for Descartes a substance is something that *can* exist apart, but that also can exist in, inhere in, something else ("The Unity of Descartes's Man," 352–55). The mind does so when it is joined to the body. So Hoffman disagrees with my interpretation of Descartes's notion of substance according to which it does not (and could not) exist in or through something else. But Hoffman's position in fact does not require that a substance can inhere in something else. I regard my interpretation of Descartes's notion of substance as compatible with Hoffman's view that for Descartes the human soul is the substantial form of the body in the sense found in Scotus and Ockham. My reasons are as follows. For the Aristotelian scholastics substantial forms are very different from accidents. Substantial forms fall under the category of substance (although they are incomplete ones); they are not accidents. For present purposes it is important that they thought the relationship that an accident bears to the substance it belongs to is different from that of a substantial form to what it is united with. This difference is manifested by the fact that one can find them saying that accidents inhere in, exist through, or are in substances: substantial forms, such as the human soul, *inform* the body. (Cf. Suárez, *Disputationes metaphysicae,* VII.I.18, p. 256; Eustacius, *Summa,* I, p. 97, IV pp. 45, 46; and a quote in Gilson, *Index scolasticocartésien* [Paris: Vrin, 1979], 275–77.) I am not sure that the precise terminology is essential here, but what is important is that the relationships differ. Thus the view that the soul is the substantial form of the body does not require that it can inhere in the body. This view also does not require that the soul can be a quality of the body. On the contrary. For the Aristotelian scholastics composites of matter and substantial form constitute a genuine, hylomorphic individual, but not composites of substance and accident (cf. Marilyn Adams, *Ockham* [Notre Dame: University of Notre Dame Press, 1987], 633). See also fn. 22 below.

17. AT VII 161. See also AT VII 222.

18. *Summa Philosophiae* I, pp. 96–97. For several more references see Gilson, *Index,* 275–77.

19. Strictly speaking this is not quite accurate, given that Descartes believes God continuously creates the world. Thus really the existence of a substance continuously comes from God. One might say then that God gives a substance its existence directly—its own existence. A mode does not receive existence directly from God, but exists by virtue of inhering in a substance: it participates in the existence of the substance.

20. AT VII 434, and letter for Arnauld, July 29, 1648, AT V 223, K 236.

21. May 21, 1643, AT III 667, K 139. On my interpretation, something that is a substance cannot be a quality for Descartes. There is a passage in the Sixth Replies, however, where he does seem to allow for this possibility. He says that "clothing, considered in itself, is a substance, but when it is referred to a clothed man, it is a quality; and also the mind, although it really is a substance, can nevertheless be called a quality of the body to which it is joined" (AT VII 441–42). Thus the suspicion arises that Descartes did think the mind, a substance, can also be a quality. This fact would be quite problematic given Descartes's contention earlier in the Sixth Replies that "it is contradictory that there should be real accidents"—accidents, that is, that are also substances by virtue of their ability to exist apart from any other subject (AT VII 434). For Descartes all accidents are modes, which cannot exist apart from a subject. Fortunately, he clears himself of this suspicion in the Sixth Replies. After his criticism of real accidents Descartes says that he admits that a substance can be an accident of, or belong to another substance *(unam substantiam alteri substantiae posse accidere)*. But he clarifies this point by saying "it is not the substance itself that has the form of an accident, but only the mode in which it belongs to [*accidit*] the other substance does. Just as when clothing belongs to [*accidit*] a man, it is not the clothing itself, but the being clothed that is an accident [*est accidens*]" (AT VII 435).

Descartes's comparisons of the soul with the scholastic notion of gravity as a real quality might lead one to think that Descartes did think the soul could be a quality. It would lead too far afield to deal with this issue adequately. But on my view Descartes does not use these comparisons to argue that the soul can be a quality. Rather his point is that the soul is whole in the whole body and whole in its parts, and united to the body in such a way that they can interact. See also fn. 17 above.

22. Although it has dependence relations other than this ontological one, such as causal ones. Descartes ignores other kinds of dependence relation, and so will I.

23. This is a bit of a simplification, for Descartes allows for a third category of properties, such as duration, existence, number, that belong to any substance (*Principles* I, 48). For discussion of this issue see Garber, *Descartes's Metaphysical Physics,* 66–67.

Descartes often describes the relationship between modes and their principal attribute using the term 'presupposition'. Descartes says that the modes of body presuppose extension (*Principles* I, 53), and in the Sixth Meditation he argues that the active faculty of producing ideas is not in me because it does not presuppose intellection (AT VII 79). These remarks would seem to imply that the modes of the mind *presuppose* thought. But it is striking that he never explicitly says so. I wonder whether he thought that the term 'presuppose' captures the relationship between thought and its modes less well than the relationship between extension and its modes. Nevertheless I will generally use this term to refer to the relationship between an attribute and its modes. There are two aspects to this relationship, an epistemic and a metaphysical one. It is not clear to which of these the term 'presuppose' is meant to refer. I will use it to refer to the metaphysical aspect.

24. *"nihil plane aliud ad naturam sive essentiam meam pertinere animadvertam, praeter hoc solum quod sim res cogitans"* (AT VII 78, see also AT VII 8, 219). For discussion of this ambiguity see Curley, *Descartes against the Skeptics* (Cambridge: Harvard University Press, 1978), 196, and Anthony Kenny, *Descartes: A Study of His Philosophy* (New York: Random House, 1968), 83ff.

25. Steven J. Wagner has argued for this view in "Descartes's Arguments for Mind-Body Distinctness," *Philosophy and Phenomenological Research* (1983): 499–517.

26. See Sydney Shoemaker, "On an Argument for Dualism," in Carl Ginet and Sydney Shoemaker, eds., *Knowledge and Mind* (Oxford: Oxford University Press, 1983), 233–58.

27. August 1641, AT III 434, K 119–120. He speaks of *real* extension to distinguish the feature that characterizes body from the sense in which he is willing to say that mind is extended. See also the letters of July 22, 1641, possibly to de Launay (AT III 420–21, K 109), to Elizabeth of June 28, 1643 (AT III 694–95, K 143), to More of February 5, 1649 (AT V 269–70, K 238–39),and April 15, 1649 (AT V 341–42, K 248–49), and the Sixth Replies(AT VII 442).

28. AT VII 120–21, 221–27.

29. *Descartes,* 191–97.

30. AT VII 222.

31. The idea that thought is sufficient to constitute a complete thing should not be understood merely modally. One might think the idea is that thought and extension *can* each constitute a complete thing, but that they do not necessarily do so. Instead, however, the idea is that they have what it takes to constitute complete things and thus *do* always constitute complete things. In other words, Descartes thinks that thought and extension are always principal attributes.

32. Taken in one sense, the mere idea that the mind is conceived of as a substance or complete thing is trivial. For on Descartes's view the mind is the substance that thinks, whether this is in fact also a corporeal substance or not. Thus in the Geometrical Exposition Descartes defines mind as the substance that thinks, body as the substance that is the subject of extension, and then says that it remains to be determined whether mind and body are the same substance (AT VII 161–62). The substantive contribution that the Second Meditation makes is then not just the (clear and distinct) idea that mind is a thinking substance, but the idea that it is sufficient for it being a substance that it thinks.

There is a complication in that Descartes also used the term 'thought' to refer to the modes of the mind. He distinguishes carefully between these two uses of the term, however. (Cf. *Principles,* I, 63 and 64, and the letter to Arnauld of July 29, 1648, AT V 221, K 234–35.)

33. There are two aspects to the notion of a principal attribute: (a) it does not presuppose another property; (b) it is presupposed by other properties. The argument as I present it relies on (a), and Descartes's discussions of the argument tend to emphasize this aspect of the notion. But in the Third Replies Descartes presents the case for dualism by emphasizing (b) (AT III 176).

34. In one sense of 'understanding without' or 'conceiving without' this cannot be enough. For when I am certain that my mind exists while doubting the existence of body, I conceive of body. As will become clear in a moment what is important is that one can conceive of the mind without thinking of it as corporeal or as mode of body while conceiving of body.

35. AT VII 78. See also *Principles* I, 53 and 61.

36. See also a letter of 22 July 1641, probably to de Launay (AT III 419, K 109).

37. One might think that in light of the letter to Gibieuf Descartes should be saying that he knows he is not a body. But that is not so. The letter to Gibieuf explains how one can find out whether the *idea* of a thinking substance depends on the idea of extension, and thus whether the idea of a thinking thing is an idea of a complete thing. It does not say that one can find out whether any thinking thing has the property of extension by means of the procedure described. This is an important point, for it is consistent to hold that the completeness of some entity, that is, its status as a substance, might be guaranteed by thought and not require extension, while the entity is extended. Failing to see this distinction would amount to confusing having a complete idea of something (which is the same as having an idea of it as complete) with having an adequate idea of it, which requires knowing everything about it. Descartes is careful about this distinction in the Fourth Replies (AT VII 220–21).

38. We saw above (p. 39) that although Descartes does not mention extension explicitly here, it is covered in this passage.

39. Really what Descartes should be saying here is that his notion of himself does not depend on his *notion* (or idea) of body, rather than body. But this must be what he means. It is what he needs, and in addition, it is more plausibly what he is entitled to rather than the claim that the notion of himself does not depend on body. What he has said in this paragraph provides support for the idea that his notion of a thinking thing does not entail corporeity, but it does not directly address the question whether this notion could exist without body existing (although Descartes thinks that this also is true).

40. Descartes was asked this question by his contemporaries, and was clearly confident that it posed no problems for him (AT VII 8, 219, 355).

41. See also AT VII 121, 227.

42. Descartes would say also that sensation can be denied of the mind: it is merely a mode of it. But it does not follow that the mind does not have the faculty of sensing or does not actually sense.

There is an ambiguity in the claim of exclusion. Descartes might mean that we can exclude extension from our conception of the mind, or that we can form a conception of the mind as something from which extension is excluded. This ambiguity, however, makes no difference to Descartes's purposes. They are hardly different, and Descartes would wish to make both claims given that the point is that one is not forced to think of a mind as extended.

43. Sometimes Descartes seems to commit himself to the idea that the argument relies on the stronger claim that he clearly and distinctly perceives that extension does not belong to the essence of the mind. Passages that suggest this commitment can be found at AT VII 13, 169–70, 219, 226. He is entitled to such a perception when the implications of the weaker claim (that he does not perceive that extension belongs to the mind) are combined with further views he held and that the Real Distinction Argument relies on. The weaker claim supports the idea that he perceives that thought is not a mode of body, but a principal attribute. Given Descartes's view that the essence of a substance consists in its principal attribute, and that a substance has only one such attribute, he can derive the clear and distinct perception that extension does not belong to the essence of mind. These aspects of Descartes's views can explain the occurrence of that stronger claim. But the contribution of the thought experiment by itself is just the weaker one.

44. In the Sixth Replies he does seem to say that he used to identify thought and extension. He writes: "although the mind had the idea of thought no less than of extension, since it did not understand anything unless it also imagined something, it identified them [*utrumque pro uno et eodem sumebat*], and referred all the notions which it had of intellectual things to the body" (AT VII 441). In other places he addresses the question of whether thought might be identical with motion. At one point he allows that one might think so, though only if one made the mistake of relying on one's imagination(AT VII 425). But elsewhere he seems to think this mistake is out of the question, and that the only error one might make is ascribing both thought and motion to the same thing (AT VII 422–23). The passage quoted above combines both ideas applied to extension instead of motion. The cure for identifying thought with motion or extension seems to consist in using one's pure intellect. This cure is provided by the withdrawal from the senses, including the imagination (cf. *Meditations,* AT VII 28) that the first two Meditations are supposed to produce. But I don't think Descartes really meant to be *arguing* that thought is not extension.

45. I know of only two places where Descartes seems to allow for the possibility of a mode presupposing another mode which then in turn presupposes a principal attribute. In Meditation III Descartes seems to describe the modes of body as ordered in a hierarchy of presupposition (AT VII 43). In a letter (probably to Mersenne for Hobbes) he says "there is no problem or absurdity in saying that an accident is the subject of another accident, as one says that quantity is the subject of other accidents" (AT III 355). The example Descartes is interested in there is the relationship between movement and its determination.

46. AT VII 176. In the letter to Gibieuf Descartes makes a comment that suggests that if there were such a connection, and we did not know of it,

God would be a deceiver. He writes: "I do not deny that there may be several properties in the soul or body of which I have no ideas. I only deny that there are any that are inconsistent with the ideas of mind and body that I have, including my idea of their distinctness. For otherwise God would be a deceiver, and we would have no rule for assuring ourselves of the truth" (AT III 478, K 152).

47. In the *Meditations* this point is not made explicit. A well-known comment in a letter to Mersenne of March 4, 1641, suggests that this is intentional. Descartes says to Mersenne: "I will say to you, between us, that these six Meditations contain all the foundations of my Physics. But please do not say so, for those who favor Aristotle might cause more problems for their approval. And I hope that those who will read it, will get used to my principles without noticing, and that they will recognize the truth before realizing that they destroy those of Aristotle" (AT III 298, K 94).

48. Strictly speaking, neither of these two points about body relies on peculiarities of the notion of a principal attribute. The first one could be stated by saying that the essence or nature of body is extension. The importance of the second point lies in the idea that something can be a corporeal, nonthinking substance. I have stated both in terms of the notion of a principal attribute, because that notion does play a role in the way in which the premise currently under discussion ("extension is the principal attribute of body") gets used. For it is combined with the premise that a substance has just one principal attribute to reach the conclusion that mind and body are really distinct.

49. This passage was pointed out to me by Jeremy Hyman.

50. AT VIII 342–43.

51. The view that Descartes held this position is defended by Paul Hoffman in "The Unity of Descartes's Man." Insofar as I know, Descartes never calls the human being a substance, although he does call it here a (complex) subject (see also AT VII 425) and elsewhere an *ens per se* (in letters to Regius, December 1641, AT III 460; K 121–22, January 1642, AT III 493, 508–509; K 127, 130) and *unum per se* (AT VII 222). I owe this observation to Jeremy Hyman. Though I find this fact intriguing I am not sure what its significance is. Descartes does claim that there is a substantial union between mind and body (letter to Regius, January 1642, AT III 493, 508, K 127, 130, letter to Mesland, February 9 1645, IV 166, K 157, and VII 219, 228, 585). Geneviève Rodis-Lewis defends the idea that Descartes thinks the human being is a genuine individual without claiming he regards it as a substance (*L'individualité selon Descartes* [Paris, Vrin, 1950], 74–81).

52. The quote from the *Comments* suggests that Descartes might have yet another qualification in mind, namely, that the Attribute Premise applies only to attributes that constitute the natures of things and *neither of which is contained in the concept of the other*. Clearly that condition applies to thought and extension. I don't know of an example in Descartes of attributes that constitute the natures of things without satisfying this condition. Moreover, perhaps Descartes did not really mean to suggest that there are such attributes. The clause might be there just because he wanted to mention this characteris-

tic of attributes that constitute the natures of substances. I will leave this condition out of consideration.

53. It is worth noting that Descartes's statements of the argument in major texts such as in the *Discourse, Meditations,* and *Principles* tend to be quite elliptical and omit not just the role of the notion of a principal attribute. When responding to questions and objections he came up with various elaborations that have contributed significantly to our understanding of the argument and Descartes's confidence in it. For instance, whereas in the Replies and in correspondence Descartes is quite explicit about the importance for the argument of the notion of a complete thing, his statements in these major texts do not appeal to this notion. Whereas for the *Discourse* and the *Meditations* the explanation could be that the role of the notion of a complete thing was really an elaboration Descartes developed later, that explanation does not apply to the *Principles.*

54. Stephen Schiffer defends something like this premise in "Descartes on His Essence," *Philosophical Review* 85 (1976): 21–43. See especially 36–37.

55. This view can be found in Locke, for instance, in Bk. II, ch. 23 of *An Essay concerning Human Understanding,* ed. P. H. Nidditch (Oxford: Clarendon Press, 1975). For a discussion and more references see Edwin McCann, "Cartesian Selves and Lockean Substances," *The Monist* 69 (1986): 458–82. Locke's conception of substance is controversial, however. For a different interpretation see M. R. Ayers, "The Idea of Power and Substance in Locke's Philosophy," in *Locke on Human Understanding,* ed. I. C. Tipton (Oxford, 1977).

56. There was debate among the scholastics about the question whether a substance can have more than one substantial form. For this debate see Marilyn McCord Adams, *Ockham,* part IV, ch. 15; and Robert Zavalloni, *Richard de Mediavilla et la controverse sur la pluralité des formes* (Louvain: Éditions de l'Institut Supérieur de Philosophie, 1951).

57. AT VII 228.

58. See AT VII 221.

59. AT VII 219.

60. *The World,* AT XI 33, 35.

61. In a letter to an unknown correspondent of 1645 or 1646 Descartes claims that a distinction of reason is always founded in a distinction in reality (AT IV 349–50, K 187–88). So there is a distinction in reality, though not a *real* distinction, between the principal attribute and the substance, and it results from the fact that there is a subject of inherence. A real distinction, *distinctio realis,* is a distinction between *res,* things, but for Descartes a principal attribute and its subject of inherence are not two different *res.*

This letter does not show, however that there is a distinction in reality *in a substance* between its principal attribute and the subject of inherence. The question at issue in this letter is the nature of the distinction between essence and existence. The distinction in reality results there, Descartes seems to claim, from the fact that there is a distinction in reality between the *thought* of the essence of the thing and the *thought* of its existence. In addition, there is a distinction in reality between something as it exists in the intellect and as it exists outside the intellect. In the thing as it exists outside thought there is no distinction between its essence and its existence. Thus, similarly, for the subject and the attribute there would not be a distinction in the thing as it exists outside thought.

62. This passage is less clear than the one from the *Principles,* for Descartes's primary concern here is to draw the distinction between modes and attributes. Descartes's point could just be that an attribute is not different from its substance in the way in which a mode is.

63. Cf. Suárez, *Disputationes metaphysicae* XV.1.7, X.64, *De Anima* I.I.9, 11 (in volume 3 of his *Opera Omnia*). Descartes, *Principles* I 53, *Comments on a Certain Broadsheet* AT VIII–2 349. See also Garber, "How God Causes Motion: Descartes, Divine Sustenance, and Occasionalism," *Journal of Philosophy* (1987): 574.

64. Aquinas, *Summa contra Gentiles* II, ed. Leonine (Turin: Marietti, 1946). For a translation see James F. Anderson, trans. (Notre Dame: University of Notre Dame Press,1975), c. 68, p. 204.

65. For a discussion of the question of whether the substance is identical with its principal attribute see Jean Laporte, *Le rationalisme de Descartes* (Paris: Presses Universitaires de France, 1945), 185–90, and "Expérience ontologique et déduction systématique dans la constitution de la métaphysique de Descartes," *Cahiers de Royaumont, philosophie no II, Descartes* (New York: Garland, 1987), 10–71. The latter is a presentation by Fernand Alquié followed by discussion that includes as its main other protagonist Martial Gueroult.

66. See also AT VII 227.

67. Versions of this interpretation can be found in Wagner, "Descartes's Arguments for Mind-Body Distinctness"; Michael Hooker, "Descartes's Denial of Mind-Body Identity," in Hooker, ed., *Descartes: Critical and Interpretative Essays* (Baltimore: Johns Hopkins University Press, 1978), 171–85. Bernard Williams's interpretation is different in important respects, but he also claims the argument relies on *de re* modal claims (*Descartes: The Project of Pure Inquiry* [Penguin, 1978], 115–16). Hooker's interpretation is adopted by James Van Cleve in "Conceivability and the Cartesian Argument for Dualism," *Pacific Philosophical Quarterly* 64 (1983): 35–45. Sydney Shoemaker discusses the argument in "On an Argument for Dualism." He uses Norman Malcolm's interpretation from "Descartes' Proof That He Is Essentially a Non-Material Thing," in *Thought and Knowledge: Essays by Norman Malcolm* (Ithaca: Cornell University Press, 1977), 58–84. The term "Essentialist Premise"is taken from Shoemaker's article. The papers by Van Cleve and Shoemaker are concerned with philosophical rather than scholarly issues. Interpretations that do not ascribe *de re* modal claims to Descartes are Margaret Wilson's (*Descartes,* 185–200), and E. M. Curley's (*Descartes against the Skeptics,* 193–206).

This argument is stated in terms of the ability of the mind to exist without being extended rather than in terms of separability. But separability is at issue in the following sense. The question at issue is, of course, whether a person's mind is identical with her body or a thing distinct from it. If the mind can exist without being extended, it can exist without this body with which it might be identical.

68. Stephen Wagner pays more attention than others to the question of textual evidence for the Essentialist Premise. He claims that there is no question that Descartes held it. But he thinks that Descartes failed to supply it explicitly, or argue for it, and suspects confusion on Descartes's part on the distinction between the Essentialist Premise, which is a *de re* claim, and the *de dicto* claim that necessarily bodies are extended. Insofar as I know there is no textual evidence for Descartes's adhering to this premise, let alone for the idea that he regarded the argument as relying on it.

69. Thus a conflict arises between the Essentialist Premise and the Conceivability Premise. One might drop the premise that what is conceivable is possible. The question then arises how else one could establish that it is possible that one exists and thinks without being extended. Sidney Shoemaker has argued that there is no way of doing so without begging the question ("On an Argument for Dualism," 247–48). For a different version of the same criticism see Van Cleve ("Conceivability and the Cartesian Argument," 41).

On my interpretation Descartes's argument is not vulnerable to these problems. It does not rely on the Essentialist Premise nor on the Conceivability Premise. This latter premise is supposed to capture how one can use the result of the thought experiment of the Second Meditation. It is a very strong claim about *a priori* access to what is possible, as it contends that *anything* that is conceivable is possible.(Other notions of conceivability are possible, but would not be appropriate in an interpretation of the Real Distinction Argument, which is meant to be *a priori.*) Descartes's argument does require, however, the narrower claim that the connection between modes and attributes is an *a priori* matter. This claim allows one to conclude that thought is a mode of extension on the basis of the thought experiment. It is compatible with the Essentialist Premise, which, however, is not used in Descartes's argument.

An important feature of Descartes's argument is brought out by the following difference between it and the Essentialist Argument. Sidney Shoemaker has claimed about the Essentialist Argument that it may be thought to work because it is assumed that if dualism is true for some thinking subject, then it is true for every thinking subject. His point, I take it, is this. One might find the notion of a thinking substance that is not extended coherent, and infer that it is possible for there to be such an entity. But supposing these claims are correct, it still does not follow about any particular thinking thing (such as Descartes or his mind) that it is unextended ("On an Argument for Dualism," 248–49). Descartes's argument, however, tries to *establish* that dualism is true for any thinking subject. For it purports to establish that it is impossible for any thinking thing to be an extended thing.

70. *Descartes,* 185–200.

71. *Descartes,* 190, 207.

72. Curley tries to accomplish this by appealing to the notion of a rigid designator developed by Kripke (*Descartes against the Skeptics,* 201–206).

73. Cf. *Descartes,* 193–98, esp. 193–94.

74. Two other items that tend to figure in Descartes's statement of the argument do not appear in my reconstruction of it, namely, Descartes's references

to clear and distinct perceptions and to God. The reason is as follows. I think that the role of God in the argument is just to validate clear and distinct perceptions. It is needed given the skeptical arguments of the First Meditation. The notion of clear and distinct perception enters into the argument only to make the point that a reliable cognition is at issue, a perception of the kind we know to be true. If skeptical worries are ignored the philosophical structure of the argument does not include explicit reference to God or the notion of clear and distinct perception. Descartes himself seemed to see the argument this way (cf. Synopsis to the *Meditations* AT VII 13, Fourth Replies AT VII 226), but this interpretation is not uncontroversial. It is often thought that God plays a bigger role. (See Curley, *Descartes against the Skeptics,* 198–200; Wagner, "Descartes's Arguments for Mind-Body Distinctness.")

It is worth pointing out that the fact that Descartes invokes God's power (rather than his veracity) in the argument is not sufficient to show that his role goes beyond the validation of clear and distinct perceptions. For Descartes clearly thought that limits on God's power would create problems for the reliability of our perceptions (cf. *Meditations,* AT VII 21). For this issue see also Geneviève Rodis-Lewis, *L'oeuvre de Descartes* (Paris: Vrin, 1971), 338–39, and Martial Gueroult, *Descartes' Philosophy Interpreted According to the Order of Reasons,* Roger Ariew, ed. and trans. (Minneapolis: University of Minnesota Press, 1985), II, 48–49. Both Rodis-Lewis and Gueroult point out the relevance of the fact that Descartes tries to establish the real distinction in the face of the union of mind and body. In a different context Gueroult argues that God's veracity follows entirely from his omnipotence, as deception is an imperfection for Descartes (21–26).

76. One reason, of course, why separability is found to emerge in Descartes's statements of the argument is because he is interested in separability in view of the issue of the afterlife. Another relevant point is the fact that, as the French commentators like to point out, Descartes clearly thought that the close union of mind and body constituted an obstacle to recognition of the real distinction. For this issue see the references to Gueroult and Rodis-Lewis in the previous footnote.

76. One might think that by virtue of (1) the argument relies on *de re* modal claims about particulars. But it should be clear from (3) that the argument relies on what (1) shows about thought, not on what it shows about a particular, namely, me.

77. Cf. Wilson, *Descartes,* 190.

78. There are places where it does look as if Descartes uses the Argument from Doubt for real distinction, in particular in the *Search for Truth* (AT X 518), *Discourse* (AT VI 32–33) and at *Principles* I, 8. Wilson thinks that it is not necessary to attribute the argument to Descartes in the latter two places. Furthermore, since the *Search* is a questionable source it does not force one to attribute the argument to Descartes (*Descartes,* 242–43). I think that the passage in the *Discourse* is the most troubling, and that it is very hard not to see Descartes as using the argument in that passage—if read in isolation. But

elsewhere Descartes claims that in the *Discourse* he is summarizing arguments which really require more extensive treatment (letter of May 1637 to an unknown correspondent, AT I 352, K 34). The Real Distinction Argument receives such treatment in the *Meditations* and other places, where the role of the skeptical doubts is more complicated.

3

The Unity of Descartes's Man

Paul Hoffman

Introduction

One of the leading problems for Cartesian dualism is to provide an account of the union of mind and body. This problem is often construed to be one of explaining how thinking things and extended things can causally interact. That is, it needs to be explained how thoughts in the mind can produce motions in the body and how motions in the body can produce sensations, appetites, and emotions in the mind. The conclusion often drawn, as it was by three of Descartes's illustrious successors, Malebranche, Spinoza, and Leibniz, is that mind and body cannot causally interact.[1]

I mention this problem of the interaction between thinking things and extended things only to distinguish it from the problem concerning the union of mind and body which I wish to discuss. Some commentators, such as Daisie Radner, maintain that the union of mind and body is metaphysically more fundamental than their interaction and is meant to account for the possibility of such interaction.[2] But not everyone agrees that Descartes should or even can draw a distinction between the union of mind and body and their causal interaction. Margaret Wilson attributes to Descartes a theory of mind-body union which she refers to as the "Natural Institution" theory.[3] According to this theory, "to conceive mind and body as united is just to conceive of mind as subject, at a given time, to experiencing certain sorts of sensations in response to certain movements in the brain; and the brain as subject to certain movements as a result of certain thoughts or volitions in the mind."[4] As she explains, "on the Natural Institution theory, then, it would seemingly be wrong to say that we experience sensations in different parts of our bodies *because of* a state of affairs designated as the

59

close or intimate union or intermingling of mind with body. Rather, what we call the close union or intermingling of this mind with this body is nothing but the arbitrarily established disposition of this mind to experience certain types of sensations on the occasion of certain changes in this body, and to refer these sensations to (parts of) this body."[5] Despite the occasionalistic ring to this latter quotation, her point is that on what she refers to as "Descartes's best account of embodiment," the union of mind and body is nothing other than their interaction.[6]

Wilson does acknowledge that it is an important feature of Descartes's theory of embodiment that he does not rest content with the Natural Institution theory and instead tries to account for the interaction of mind and body on the basis of another theory of their union which she refers to as the "Co-extension" theory.[7] However, she dismisses this Co-extension theory as "seemingly almost ineffable."[8] Thus she seems to think both that it would have been better if Descartes had stuck solely to the view that the union of mind and body just is their interaction and that his attempt to draw a distinction between their union and their interaction rests on a hardly intelligible theory of the nature of their union.

It is this problem of the nature of the union between mind and body, as opposed to the problem of their interaction, which is the subject of this paper. Moreover, I do not wish to discuss the nature of the union of mind and body with respect to its success in solving the problem of mind-body interaction. I disagree with Radner's seeming belief that the sole problem that the notion of the union between mind and body is meant to solve is the problem of their interaction.[9] Instead, I think that it also has a more important task, which is to explain how two really distinct things, mind and body, can somehow generate another thing, the man or human being, which is itself a unity, that is, a genuine individual or an *ens per se.* Thus, what I want to ask is whether there is in Descartes's philosophy a notion of the union of mind and body which gives a satisfactory account of the unity of the man or human being, that is, an account according to which a human being has an intuitive claim of being one thing, and not merely two things conjoined.

That Descartes considers a human being to be a genuine individual is an underappreciated fact among English-speaking commentators. To take an extreme case, in a recent article, Fred Sommers alleges that "a Cartesian person is a non-individual, since it is composed of a mind and a body," and he leaves the impression that it is Descartes's intention to characterize human beings as non-individuals.[10] And even Wilson, who does acknowledge that one of the defects of the Natural Institution theory is that it "can be construed as having unorthodox implications with respect to the unity of man," fails to give due weight to the seriousness of this defect.[11] However, as I shall argue below, whether or not Descartes succeeds, it is surely his intention to leave the man intact as an individual.

The French commentators, much more than their English-speaking counterparts, do put appropriate emphasis on the unity of Descartes's man. But while they grant Descartes the intention to preserve the unity of a human being, they deny that he is successful. Étienne Gilson, for example, asserts that "medieval philosophy distinguished the body and soul less really than Descartes, in that they did not make two complete substances, and this is why they had less difficulty than Descartes in uniting them."[12]

In what follows I want to defend Descartes's account of the unity of a human being. In Part I, textual evidence will be cited in support of the view that Descartes does think that his man is a unity. In Part II, it will be argued that Descartes believes mind inheres in body as form inheres in matter, and that this hylomorphic conception of the union of mind and body does real philosophical work for him, and is not, as several commentators state, a conception to which he gives, to quote Bernard Williams, "little metaphysical weight."[13] In discussing the most important objection against taking his hylomorphism seriously, I will argue contrary to Gilson that Descartes's account of the per se unity of his man compares favorably with medieval accounts of per se unity, and, indeed, is remarkably close to the views of Scotus and Ockham.

I. Descartes's Belief that a Human Being is a Unity

It is certainly true that Descartes emphasizes the real distinction between mind and body much more than the unity of a human being. He admits as much in a letter to Princess Elizabeth and gives a hint as to why:

> There are two facts about the human soul on which depend all the things we can know of its nature. The first is that it thinks, the second is that it is united to the body and can act and be acted upon along with it. About the second I have said hardly anything; I have tried only to make the first well understood. For my principal aim was to prove the distinction between soul and body, and to this end only the first was useful, and the second might have been harmful. (AT III, 664; K 137)[14]

In another letter, this time to Regius, he makes a very similar remark:

> many more people make the mistake of thinking that the soul is not really distinct from the body than make the mistake of admitting their distinction and denying their substantial union, and in order to refute those who believe souls to be mortal it is more important to teach the distinction of parts in man than to teach their union. (AT III, 508; K 130)

But to teach the distinction between mind and body is not to deny their union.[15] Earlier in the same letter to Regius, Descartes advises him to say that he believes a human being is a true *ens per se:*

> And whenever the occasion arises, in public and in private, you should give out that you believe that a human being is a true *ens per se,* and not an *ens per accidens,* and that the mind and the body are united in a real and substantial manner. You must say that they are united not by position or disposition, as you say in your last paper—for this too is open to objection and, in my opinion, quite untrue—but by a true mode of union, as everyone agrees, though nobody explains what this means and so you need not do so either. (AT III, 493; K 127)

These three passages from the letters to Princess Elizabeth and Regius give clear indication that, contrary to the claim of Sommers, Descartes does not call into question the Aristotelian and common sense view that a human being is a genuine unity, that is, an individual. However, the evidence from the letter to Regius might be challenged on the grounds that Descartes's advice to him does not reflect his real views, but is merely a strategic response to avoid further controversy. Regius, an exponent of Descartes's views at the University of Utrecht, had offended his Aristotelian colleagues, who, led by Voetius, attempted to get the magistrates to forbid him to teach. In this letter Descartes is coaching Regius how to respond to a public disputation in which the followers of Voetius had challenged Regius's claims that a human being is an *ens per accidens,* that the earth moves around the sun, and that substantial forms should be rejected (K 126).

Although I acknowledge that accusations of disingenuousness are difficult to defeat, my own belief is that this letter does reflect Descartes's real views.[16] Even though he admonishes Regius for his lack of tactfulness in openly denying substantial forms instead of merely showing their uselessness, his own reply scarcely conceals his contempt for substantial forms, not to mention his contempt for Aristotelians in general and Voetius in particular. Moreover, one wonders what motivation he would have had for concealing his real views from Princess Elizabeth.

There is other important evidence that Descartes believes a human being is an individual. In the *Sixth Meditation* he asserts that he is not united to his body as a pilot to a ship, but is "closely joined and, as it were, mixed together with it, so that I make up one thing with it" (AT VII, 81; HR I, 192). Moreover, there are several passages in which he refers to the substantial union of mind and body.[17] By using the expression 'substantial union' I take him to be pointing out not merely that the union is a union of two substances, which he does think is the case, but that the product of the union is itself a substance.[18] The fact that Descartes considers a human being to be a substance provides further evidence that he thinks that a human being is a genuine individual, since a substance just is an individual. Descartes uses the terms 'substance', *'ens per se',* and 'complete thing' interchangeably, and all of them I take to be equivalent to my terms 'individual' and 'genuine unity'.[19]

There is a standard picture of the Cartesian created universe which perhaps contributes to the tendency to deny that Descartes conceives of a human being as a genuine individual. According to this picture, the Cartesian created universe is populated by a lot of minds, but by only one extended substance, the entire extended world, of which individual bodies are merely modes. Such a picture makes it difficult to see how a human being could be a genuine individual. How could a substance, in this case a mind, be combined with a mode of another substance, in this case a human body, to form a genuine unity?

Martial Gueroult, the most persuasive defender of the view that Cartesian bodies are not substances but modes, ascribes to Descartes a very strong notion of what it is to be a created substance in the strict sense, according to which only God can cause substances to come into or to go out of existence, and according to which substances can go out of existence only by annihilation.[20] If this strong conception of created substance were the proper conception, it would exclude human beings from the class of substances not only indirectly, by entailing, as Gueroult at least thinks it does, that there is only one extended substance of which individual bodies are modes, but also directly: first, human beings go out of existence when other bodies cause the death of the human body, and second, on Descartes's view a human being need not be annihilated to go out of existence, since he thinks the soul survives. The key evidence in favor of Gueroult's interpretation is a famous passage from the Synopsis of the *Meditations:*

first, it must be known that absolutely all substances or things which must be created by God in order to exist, are by their nature incorruptible, nor can they ever cease to be unless they are reduced to nothing by God denying them His concurrence, and second, it must be noted that body, at least taken generally, is a substance and for that reason never perishes. But the human body differs from other bodies only insofar as it is composed of a certain configuration of members and other such accidents; while the human mind is not similarly composed out of any accidents, but is a pure substance; for although all its accidents are changed, so that it understands other things, wills others, senses others, etc., the mind does not for that reason become something else; however, the human body becomes something else from the sole fact that the shape of some one of its parts is changed; from which it follows that body very easily ceases to exist, whereas the mind by its nature is immortal. (AT VII, 13–14; HR I, 141)

Even this passage, however, does not provide unambiguous evidence for the standard picture of the Cartesian extended universe. First, it is not at all clear that Descartes is referring to the extended universe taken as a whole when he says that body, at least taken generally, is a substance ("corpus quidem in genere sumptum esse substantiam").[21] Second, he falls short of saying that individual bodies are modes.

Nor do I think Gueroult has made a convincing case that the strong conception of created substance is the proper conception. Noting that elsewhere Descartes does explicitly refer to bodies as substances, Gueroult also ascribes to him a loose conception of created substance in addition to the strong conception of the Synopsis.[22] Any subject is a substance in this loose sense. I agree that Descartes does have both a strong and a weak conception of created substance. But I disagree that entities which are substances in the weak sense, such as bodies, are, strictly speaking, modes and not full-fledged substances. To respond briefly, Gueroult does not cite a single passage where Descartes says that bodies are modes to offset the passages where Descartes says they are substances. Moreover, Descartes seems committed to denying that bodies are modes, since he says that bodies are parts of matter and denies that modes are parts.[23]

In the Synopsis passage quoted above, Descartes suggests that entities which satisfy the conditions of the strong conception of created substance are not composed of parts or other similar accidents. Following his language in that passage, we can refer to such substances as pure substances. But even though bodies are composed of parts and so fall short of being pure substances—we might call them impure substances—they nevertheless should still be considered as full-fledged substances. Therefore, contrary to the standard picture of the Cartesian created universe, Descartes, in constructing a human being, does not face the impossible task of generating a unity out of a substance and a mode of another substance. His task, which may seem equally impossible, is that of generating a unity out of two substances.[24]

II. Descartes's Hylomorphism

It is well known that Descartes rejects substantial forms and real qualities. This creates a certain skepticism toward the claim that he conceives of the mind as the substantial form of the man. But what is less well known, indeed the main passages have never been translated into English, is that in the same letter to Regius cited above, which is where he makes his most concerted attack on substantial forms, he also asserts both that the human soul is the substantial form of the man and that it is the only substantial form, whereas the rest of the so-called substantial forms are composed of the configuration and motion of the parts of matter (AT III, 503 & 505).

As I have already mentioned, there is some controversy whether this letter should be taken at face value. But it should not be so surprising that Descartes would consider the human soul or mind to be the only substantial form. Neither of his two major reasons for rejecting substantial forms applies to the human soul. First, one of his major reasons for rejecting substantial forms and real qualities is that explanations which appeal to them are anthropomorphic, that is, they attribute to bodies properties which properly belong only to the human soul:

> But it is clear that the idea of gravity was taken partly from that which I had of the mind primarily from the fact that I thought that gravity carried bodies toward the center of the earth as if it contained in itself some knowledge of this center within it. For this could not be done without knowledge, and there cannot be any knowledge, except in the mind. (AT VII, 442; HR II, 255)

> The first is that I do not grant there are in nature any *real qualities,* which are attached to substances, as little souls to their bodies, and which can be separated from them by divine power. (AT III, 648; K 135)

> The earliest judgments which we made in our childhood, and the common philosophy later, have accustomed us to attribute to the body many things which belong only to the soul, and to attribute to the soul many things which belong only to the body. So people commonly mingle the two ideas of body and soul when they construct the ideas of real qualities and substantial forms, which I think should be altogether rejected. (AT III, 420; K 109)

Obviously, this objection that explanations appealing to substantial forms are anthropomorphic does not apply to an explanation which takes the human soul to be a substantial form.

Second, Descartes's other major reason for rejecting substantial forms is that they are merely theoretical entities which he thinks are dispensable because they have no explanatory value, whereas explanations in terms of the motions and configuration of the parts of bodies are successful (AT II, 200; K 59: AT XI, 25–6; M 39). The human soul, in contrast, is not a mere theoretical entity. That he exists and that he is a thinking thing are the first two propositions Descartes claims to know with certainty in the *Second Meditation* (AT VII, 25 & 27; HR I, 150 & 152). Thus, on my view, he should not be construed as first rejecting substantial forms generally, and subsequently making an exception of the human soul in order to do some required philosophical work. On the contrary, he is to be construed as beginning with the view that the human soul is a substantial form and as rejecting the attempt to use the human soul as a model for explanations of the non-human physical world.

In addition to these passages in the letter composed for Regius in which he asserts that the soul is the substantial form of the man, there are several other texts which support the view that he thinks the mind inheres in the body as form inheres in matter. In the *Rules* he says that the mind informs the body, and in the *Principles* he says that the human soul informs the whole body (AT X, 411; HR I, 36: AT VII, 315; HR I, 289). In the *Third Meditation* he says that he judges that he exists in the body (AT VII, 50; HR I, 170). In the *Replies to the Sixth Objections* he says that the mind, even though a substance, can be said to be a quality of the body to which it is connected (AT VII, 441–2; HR II, 254–5).[25]

Despite the fact that there are numerous passages in which Descartes seems to commit himself to the view that the soul informs the body as form inheres in matter, many commentators are inclined to dismiss them. The one notable exception among contemporary commentators is Geneviève Rodis-Lewis, who does take these remarks seriously as expressing Descartes's own views.[26] But, as already mentioned, Bernard Williams alleges that Descartes gives them little metaphysical weight. Gilson argues that "even though we do not forget the art that Descartes always had to put new wine in old bottles," in this instance it is a case of not preserving anything of the idea with the expression.[27] Henri Gouhier, perhaps even less charitably, claims that "what Descartes retains from scholastic philosophy is precisely what is not philosophical."[28]

In what follows I shall defend Descartes's account of the unity of a human being by responding to various reasons for thinking that the old scholastic notions of form inhering in matter cannot do for him the philosophical work of uniting mind and body into a single entity. I shall consider four different sorts of such objections to Descartes's hylomorphism.

The first objection is that Descartes believes thought and extension are incompatible because any extended thing is divisible whereas no thinking thing is divisible (At VII, 85–6; HR I, 196). Therefore, a human being could not be an individual, because, having both attributes, thought and extension, it would be both divisible and indivisible. My reply is that it is only the mind considered alone which he thinks is indivisible. He does not say of the composite human being that it is indivisible.[29]

The second objection, that the Cartesian mind is not the right sort of entity to inhere in a substance, can be generated from remarks made by Gouhier. Gouhier asserts that according to Descartes's two definitions of substance, a substance is a subject which, metaphysically as well as grammatically, can never be an attribute, where the term 'attribute' is being used in its more general sense to mean quality.[30] Thus, if, by definition, no substance can ever be a quality, then since the mind is a substance, it would be contradictory for Descartes to maintain that the mind can be a quality of body, that is, could inhere in a body.

This argument can be readily dismissed. Gouhier is simply mistaken in ascribing to Descartes the view that no substance can be a quality. It is not, as Gouhier claims, a consequence of either of Descartes's two definitions of substance. The definition from the *Replies to the Second Objections,* that a substance is a thing in which or through which qualities exist as in a subject, does not entail that a substance itself could not exist in a thing as in a subject (AT VII, 161; HR II, 53). The *Principles* definition, that a (created) substance is a thing which needs only the concurrence of God in order to exist, also does not entail that no substance can be a quality (AT VIII, 24–5; HR I, 239–40). What it does entail is that a created substance, unlike a mode or attribute, can exist without existing in a subject, that is, it can exist without being a quality (of a created substance). But it does not follow from the fact that in order to be a substance a thing must be able to exist without existing in a subject that it cannot exist in a subject.[31]

Moreover, there is decisive textual evidence that Descartes's conception of what it is for a thing to be a (created) substance is, unlike Aristotle's, sufficiently weak to require only that the thing be able to exist without existing in a subject and not that it never exist in a subject. One important piece of evidence is the terminology itself. That a substance or *ens per se* is a thing which can exist with only itself as a subject, or alternatively, without any subject, follows directly from the supposition that Descartes uses the word *'per'* to mean the same thing in the term *'ens per se'* and in the definition of substance in the *Replies to the Second Objections,* where it is used to characterize the relation between a quality and its subject (AT VII, 161). Another piece of evidence is that the entities he cites as examples of incomplete things are modes, for example, motion, shape, and the faculties of mind (AT VII, 120 & 224; HR II, 22 & 100), and modes are dependent because they must exist in something in order to exist (AT VII, 222; HR II, 98). Third, and most important, in arguing against real accidents, he makes it clear that he thinks the kind of separate existence which is sufficient for a thing to be considered a substance is its capability of existing apart from a subject.

> Secondly it is contradictory that real accidents should exist, because whatever is real can exist separately apart from any other subject; but whatever can exist separately is substance not accident. And it makes no difference whether it be said that real accidents can be disjoined from their subject, not naturally, but merely by the divine power; for coming to pass naturally is nowise different from coming to pass by the ordinary power of God, which does not differ at all from his extraordinary power, and does not make any further contribution to things, so that if everything which can exist naturally apart from a subject is substance, so whatever by the power of God, however extraordinary it may be, is capable of existing without a subject, must likewise be termed substance. (AT VII, 434; HR II, 250)

More specifically, it is useful for our purposes to mention his analogy of mind-body union with what he considers to be the ordinary, but mistaken, view of the relation between gravity and body. He argues that just as gravity is considered to be a real quality, that is, a quality which exists in body but can exist apart from it, so the mind can be said to be a quality of body, even though it can exist apart from body (AT VII,441–2; HR II, 254–5). Although this account of gravity is incorrect, because if it were something which could exist apart from a subject, it would be a substance, which it is not, Descartes believes that anyone who had accepted this account of gravity should be willing to accept the notion of mind–body union.[32] As he says in a letter to Arnauld,

> So it is no harder for us to understand how the mind moves the body, than it is for them to understand how such gravity moves the stone downwards. Of course they deny that gravity is a substance, but that makes no difference, because they conceive it in fact as a substance since they think

that it is real and that it is possible, even if only by Divine power, for it to exist without the stone. (AT V, 222–3; K 236)

The third sort of objection includes those which attack his use of the hylomorphic model of mind-body union by challenging this analogy with gravity. One such objection is made by Wilson. She notes that on what she refers to as the Co-extension theory of mind-body union, the mind, like gravity, is said to be "co-extensive with the body, 'whole in the whole and whole in any of its parts.' "[33] Her objection is that this talk of gravity and co-extensiveness is merely obfuscating.[34] To evaluate this charge, it will be useful to have Descartes's statement of the gravity analogy before us. What he says is the following:

> although I imagined that gravity was diffused throughout the whole of the body possessing weight, . . . I also saw that while it remained coextensive with the heavy body, it could exercise its force at any point of the body, because whatever the part might be to which a rope was attached, it pulled the rope with all its weight, exactly as if the gravity resided in the part alone which the rope touched and was not diffused through the others. Indeed it is in no other way that I now understand mind to be coextensive with the body, the whole in the whole, and the whole in any of its parts. (AT VII, 442; HR II, 255)

He seems to be suggesting here that since the entire gravity of a body can act at any part to which a rope is attached, it must exist in the body whole in any of its parts. What I like about this example is that it provides a picture of how something which exists in a whole body can nevertheless be conceived to exist whole in one of its parts. It exists whole in one of its parts if the whole of it can act in that part. But if I understand Wilson, she seems to find the analogy obfuscating because she is still left wondering how he can reconcile his assertion that the soul "exercises its functions more particularly" in the pineal gland with, first, the assertion that the soul exists whole in the whole body, and, second, that it exists whole in every distinguishable part of the body.[35]

I agree that the gravity analogy does not help us understand how the soul exists whole in the whole body, nor does it explain how the soul exists whole in every distinguishable part of the body, although the last sentence of the quotation—"indeed it is in no other way that I now understand mind to be coextensive with the body, the whole in the whole, and the whole in any of its parts"—suggests that Descartes thinks it does. What the analogy does illuminate is how something which we already take to exist whole in the whole, such as gravity, can still exist whole in a part. But I disagree that he should find it especially difficult to find "some sort of accommodation" between his claim that the soul acts on the pineal gland and his claims that it exists whole in the whole body and whole in any part of the body.[36]

In defense of Descartes, let me begin by pointing out that Aquinas had similar worries about reconciling his own view with that of Aristotle. In the *Summa Theologica* one of the objections he considers to his own view that the soul exists whole in each part of the body is Aristotle's assertion in *On the Movement of Animals* that "there is, then, no need of soul in each part: it is in some governing origin of the body, and other parts live because they are naturally attached, and do their tasks because of nature."[37] Aquinas's solution to this objection is to say that Aristotle is speaking of the motive power of the soul.[38] According to Aquinas, since the soul is the substantial form of the body, it must exist whole in each part of the body, but its powers need not exist in every part of the body.

Not only could Descartes make this same distinction between the soul and its power to move the body, but he actually does make it in the *Passions of the Soul*.[39] In Part I, Article 30, he says:

> the soul is truly joined to the whole body, and one cannot properly say that it is in some one of its parts to the exclusion of others. (AT XI, 351; HR I, 345)

And in Article 31, he says:

> although the soul is joined to the whole body, there is nevertheless in the body a certain part in which the soul exercises its functions more particularly than in all the others. And it is usually believed that this part is the brain, or perhaps the heart.(AT XI, 351–2; HR I, 345)

When he speaks of the soul exercising its functions, I take him to be referring to what Aquinas refers to as the motive power of the soul. Thus the major difference between Descartes and the Aristotelians on this score, as Descartes sees it, is that he associates the motive power of the soul with a part of the brain, whereas they have associated it with the whole brain or with the heart. But there is no reason why he should be any less justified than Aquinas in asserting both that the soul exists whole in the whole body and whole in each of its parts, even if its motive power does not exist whole in each of its parts. According to Aquinas, if a form is not divided when its subject is divided, then it follows that the whole of it is in each part of the body.[40] This is precisely what Descartes claims about the human mind in Article 30, as well as in the *Sixth Meditation*—it is not divided when the body is divided (AT VII, 85–6; HR I, 196). Still, one might object that all this consideration shows is that if the human body were the subject of the mind, the mind would exist whole in every part of the body. But it does not settle the issue of whether the human body, as opposed to the pineal gland, is the mind's subject. So on what grounds can Descartes claim that the whole body is the mind's subject? Aquinas seems to think that the subject of the soul is that which is actualized by the soul.[41] Is there any suitably powerful sense in which the Cartesian mind can be said to actualize the human body? I think that there is. In a letter to Mesland, February 9, 1645, Descartes says:

First I consider what is the body of a man, and I find that this word 'body' is very ambiguous, because when we speak of a body in general, we mean a determinate part of matter, and the whole of the quantity of which the universe is composed, so that if the least bit of that matter were removed we would judge at once that the body was smaller and no longer complete; and if any particle of that matter were changed we would at once think that the body was no longer totally the same, or *numerically the same*. But, when we speak of the body of a man, we do not mean a determinate part of matter which has a determinate size, but we mean only all of the matter which is together united with the soul of this man, so that, even though this matter changes and its quantity increases or decreases, we still believe that it is the same body, *numerically the same,* while it remains joined and substantially united to the same soul; and we believe that this body is entirely whole while it has in itself all the dispositions required to conserve that union. There is no one who does not believe that we have the same bodies which we have had since our infancy, although their quantity has much increased, and even though according to the common opinion of doctors, and without doubt according to the truth, there is no longer in them any part of the matter which was in them before, and even though they no longer have the same shape; so that they are only *numerically the same* because they are informed by the same soul. Personally, having examined the circulation of the blood and believing that nutrition takes place by a continual expulsion of the parts of our bodies, which are driven from their place by others which enter it, I do not think that there is any particle of our members which remains *numerically* the same for a single moment, although our body, insofar as it is a human body, always remains *numerically* the same while it is united to the same soul. Moreover, in that sense, it is indivisible, because if an arm or a leg of a man is cut off, we think correctly that his body is divided, taking the word 'body' in the first sense, but not taking it in the second sense; and we do not think that someone who has an arm or leg cut off is less a man than any other. Finally, whatever matter it is and whatever size or shape it can be, so long as it is united to the same rational soul, we still take it as the body of the same man, and we take it as the entire body, if it does not need to be augmented by other matter in order to remain joined to this soul. (AT IV, 166; K 156)

Similarly, in another letter to Mesland, dated 1645 or 1646, he says:

> it does not cease to be true to say that I have now the same body that I
> had ten years ago, even though the matter of which it is composed has
> been replaced, because the numerical unity of the body of a man does
> not depend on its matter, but on its form which is the soul. (AT IV, 346)

What these passages suggest is that if the determinate part of matter
which is united to my mind ceases to be united to my mind, it will
cease to constitute the body I now have. It may perhaps continue to
exist as a body, in this case a corpse, depending upon the circumstances of my death, but it will no longer constitute my body. My body
will have ceased to exist. There is, therefore, a suitably powerful sense
in which the mind actualizes the human body—a human body exists
only so long as it is united to the mind.[42] Moreover, the entire human
body cannot be constituted by the pineal gland alone, because the pineal gland needs "to be augmented by other matter in order to remain
joined to the soul." It does not have "in itself all the dispositions required to conserve that union."

It is true that for Aquinas, as well as for Aristotle, closely associated
with the notion of a part of the body being actualized by the soul is the
notion of that part of the body retaining its proper action or function.
It is a necessary condition of a body and its parts retaining their proper
functioning that it be ensouled.[43] In contrast, Descartes, as an element
of his mechanism, banishes the notion of bodies or their parts having
a proper action or function to the realm of God's inscrutable will. But
I do not think that this difference, as important as it is, somehow makes
it implausible for him to say that the subject of the mind is what we
normally take to be a human body and instead commits him to the
view that the pineal gland is the subject of the mind. And even for
Descartes, the notion of the soul's actualizing the body is not entirely
divorced from the notion of teleological explanation.[44] To the extent
that teleological explanation of the behavior of bodies retains a place
in Descartes's philosophy, it is the purposeful behavior of human bodies which is accounted for, as it was for the Aristotelians, by their being
ensouled.[45]

A second objection to the gravity analogy is raised by Gilson. He
accuses Descartes of offering a closed and exceedingly short circle of
explanation which is consequently empty. He points out that on the
one hand Descartes uses the gravity analogy to make sense of the relation between mind and body, and that on the other hand, as we have
seen, Descartes asserts that our understanding of gravity rests on a
confusion of our ideas of mind with those of body.[46]

Gilson is correct that we gain no understanding from the gravity analogy of how mind can exist apart from body, because it is only by confusing gravity with mental substance that we think gravity can exist apart
from body. But the understanding of what it is to exist whole in any of
the parts, which we do gain from the gravity analogy, is not under-
mined when we see that there are certain flaws in our conception of
gravity which arise from importing notions which properly belong only
to mind, namely, that it can exist apart from body and that it must have
knowledge. However, it might be claimed in defense of Gilson, even
though he himself does not make this argument explicitly, that it is not
just the conception of gravity as capable of existing apart from body
and its having knowledge which illegitimately import notions which
properly belong only to mind, but that our conception of gravity as
existing whole in any of the parts does as well.[47] One such argument
points out that to exist whole in any of the parts is for the whole to be
capable of acting in any of the parts, but only minds can act. Another
argument points out that even if things other than minds can act, for
Descartes there is no such thing as gravity which acts. If the term 'gravity' is used properly, it refers to a certain effect which is explained by
his vortex theory of motion.

The second argument does tell against the gravity analogy. But there
is another analogy available. Descartes could have instead compared
the mind with what he called the quantity of motion of a body which
collides with another body. He would have been willing to say, I think,
that the entire quantity of motion of the body acts in the point which
touches the other body. And I do not think that this analogy is circular,
since I do not see how this conception of the quantity of motion acting
at a point imports notions belonging to mind.

The fourth and most important sort of objection to the view that
Descartes can use the form-matter model to explain the unity of the
man derives from medieval accounts of per se unity, and ultimately
from Aristotle. The objection is that even if the mind does inhere in
the body as form inheres in matter, nevertheless, no substance, and
hence nothing which is an *ens per se,* can be constituted from another
substance or substances. While Aristotelian substances are themselves
composites of form and matter, the composite of a substance and an
accident, for example, Socrates and whiteness, is not an *ens per se,* but
an *ens per accidens.* Thus the charge against Descartes is that he cannot consistently maintain that the body, the mind, and the man are all
substances.[48]

In defense of Descartes, I shall argue, relying heavily on a late draft
of a chapter from Marilyn Adams's forthcoming book on Ockham, that
his account of composite unity compares favorably with those of Aqui-

nas, Scotus, and Ockham.[49] Indeed, I will argue that despite termino-
logical differences, his account is really the same as that of Ockham
and Scotus.

Aquinas's position is that an *ens per se* cannot have a plurality of
actual constituents. Thus he concludes that a substance can have only
one substantial form, and he relegates prime matter from the realm of
actuality to the realm of pure potentiality. But Aquinas was in the mi-
nority. To quote Marilyn Adams, "most others were convinced by a
variety of arguments that prime matter must have an actuality of its
own and living substances a plurality of substantial forms, and inferred
that a plurality of actual constituents does not interfere with a thing's
being one per se."

These arguments, at least as presented by Adams, I find completely
devastating of Aquinas's position, although she herself is more sympathetic to him. Let me mention one argument by Scotus which I think
is especially powerful. He alleges that prime matter, conceived as pure
potentiality, cannot fulfill its role of being the ultimate subject of inherence, on the ground that pure potentiality is simply non-being, and
non-being cannot be an ultimate subject of inherence.

Ockham and Scotus, in contrast with Aquinas, hold that an *ens per
se* can be composed of a plurality of actual things. For example, on
Ockham's view, prime matter, the form of corporeity, the sensory soul,
and the intellectual soul are all actual constituents of a human being,
which he thinks is an *ens per se*. Their view is that what permits the
essential unity of the composite is not the non-actuality of all but one
of the components, but rather that none of the components is itself a
complete thing, that is, a substance. Consequently, on the surface at
least, they disagree with Descartes about what kinds of entities can
combine to form an *ens per se,* because Descartes wants to assert that
really distinct substances can unite to form an *ens per se.*

However, the Cartesian conception of what it is to be a (created)
substance or complete thing, namely, that a substance is a thing which
can exist without existing in anything as in a subject, is sufficiently weak
that entities which Scotus and Ockham consider to be mere actual
things, such as prime matter, the form of corporeity, and the intellectual soul, would, if they had the property Scotus and Ockham ascribe
to them of being able, at least by divine power, to exist apart from other
things, count as Cartesian substances. Therefore, Scotus, Ockham, and
Descartes are in fundamental metaphysical agreement that things
which can exist apart from each other can form an *ens per se,* provided
that they stand in the appropriate relation to one another. And all agree
that the relation in question is the inherence relation. Where they disagree is first, with respect to their judgments as to which entities in

fact have the capability of existing apart from one another, and second, with respect to the meaning of the term 'substance' or 'complete thing'. For example, Scotus and Ockham would agree, but Descartes would disagree, that whiteness can exist apart from a substance.[50] Moreover, Scotus and Ockham would agree that it does not follow from the fact that whiteness can exist apart from a subject that it is a substance, whereas Descartes would assert that if whiteness could exist apart from a subject, then it would be a substance. Nevertheless, since Descartes is in fundamental agreement with Scotus and Ockham on the formal conditions for the per se unity of composites, he is equally entitled to claim that his man is an *ens per se.*

However, to defend Descartes's account of the unity of a human being by arguing that it is no worse than that of his predecessors is not necessarily to mount a very strong defense. There remains a serious question whether any hylomorphic ontology can generate a human being which is a genuine unity. Since the hylomorphic complexes of Scotus, Ockham, and Descartes contain components which can exist apart from the others, it would seem to follow that it is only a contingent fact about the components that they are united at all, so the unity would be a mere accidental unity and not a per se unity.

One strategy that Descartes could use to reply to this objection is suggested by his account of the identity of the human body mentioned above, according to which the numerical identity of the human body is determined by its union with the soul. He could propose that a union of things generates a per se unity when that union is not accidental to at least one of the components. This would entail that a human being is an *ens per se,* provided that a human being is understood to be a composite of a mind and a human body, as opposed to being a composite of a mind and a determinate part of matter.

This strategy might seem unsatisfactory because it might seem that by generating a sufficient dependency between mind and body to claim that their union is not accidental, he undermines his claim that they are really distinct. If the human body cannot exist without being united to the mind, it would seem to follow by his own criteria that mind and body are only modally distinct. I have argued elsewhere, however, that his account of real distinction does not require that mind and body can each exist out of real union with the other. Instead, what he does require for real distinction, namely, that each can exist without having the essential attribute of the other existing in it, is consistent with the claim that the body must be united to the mind in order to exist.[51]

But this strategy is still objectionable because it appeals to a very weak notion of per se unity. Instead of a composite being an *ens per se* just so long as the union *is not* accidental to at least one of the components, it would seem that, on the contrary, a composite is an *ens per accidens* just so long as the union *is* accidental to at least one of the components. Thus instead of inferring that a human being is an *ens per se* because the union is not accidental to the human body, we should infer that a human being is an *ens per accidens* because the union is accidental to the mind.

Let me mention two possible replies to this objection. The first reply provides what I consider to be a more philosophically satisfying solution to the objection, but Descartes himself seems to have endorsed the second. According to the first reply, he should have conceded that in the ordinary case a composite is an *ens per accidens,* if the union is accidental to one of the components, but then added the proviso that the composite is an *ens per se* if it is only in virtue of divine power that the union is accidental to one of the components. There is some textual evidence in support of this reply. In a letter of December 1641, in which he is again coaching Regius, under fire for asserting that a human being is an *ens per accidens,* he advises him to say that it is not absolutely accidental to the mind that it be united to the body or to the body that it be united to the mind, and tells him not to deny that it is only due to a miracle that they can exist apart.

> It may be objected that it is not accidental to the human body that it should be conjoined to the soul, but its very nature, since, when a body has all the dispositions required to receive the soul, without which it is not a human body, it cannot, without a miracle, be that the soul is not united to it. Moreover, it may be objected that it is not accidental to the soul that it should be joined to the body, but it is only accidental to it that it should be separated from the body after death. All of this should not be denied, lest the theologians be offended again, but nevertheless, it ought to be responded that these things can on this account be said to be accidental, that considering the body alone, we clearly perceive nothing in it on account of which it demands to be united to the soul, as we perceive nothing in the soul on account of which it must be united to the body, which is why I said above that it is in a certain manner accidental, not that it is absolutely accidental. (AT III, 460; K 122)

It is important to note that when he says in this passage that in considering the body alone, we perceive nothing in it demanding union with the soul, he suggests, contrary to what I have said so far, that the mind's subject is a body whose identity conditions do not depend on its being united to the mind. Hence the body which is the mind's subject would be not the human body, but the determinate part of matter. In that case, there would no longer be any clear sense in which the mind actualizes its subject. But, as we have seen, part of Scotus's attack on Aquinas's account of composite unity is to deny that a substantial form needs to actualize its subject, because a subject must already be actual. This might seem to reintroduce the problem of fixing which determinate part of matter is the mind's subject—why isn't it just the pineal gland? But the same answer is still available. Descartes can respond that the pineal gland by itself cannot be the mind's subject because it needs to be augmented by other matter in order to remain joined to the mind. Moreover, according to the proposal under consideration of distinguishing between *entia per accidens* and *entia per se* on the basis of the distinction between ordinary accidental unions and those unions which are accidental only because God has the power to create one of the component parts out of real union with the others, Descartes could still maintain that a human being is an *ens per se* even if the mind's subject were not the human body but the determinate part of matter. It would still be the case that it would require a miracle for the determinate part of matter with all the dispositions required to receive the soul to exist apart from it.

One problem with this strategy of distinguishing between an *ens per accidens* and an *ens per se* on the basis of the distinction between an ordinary accidental union and a union which is accidental only because God has the power to create one of the component parts out of real union with the others is that Descartes only attributes the latter distinction to his opponents; he does not endorse it. And indeed, in the *Replies to the Sixth Objections,* he denies that such a distinction can be made:[52]

coming to pass naturally is nowise different from coming to pass by the ordinary power of God, which does not differ at all from his extraordinary power. (AT VII, 435; HR II, 250)

But I do not myself see why Descartes could not have allowed such a distinction. There is no incoherence in maintaining both that it is a sufficient condition for a thing's being a substance that it can exist apart from a subject, even if only by divine power and not naturally, and that it is a necessary condition for things to constitute an *ens per se* that they can exist out of real union only by divine power and not naturally. Nor does such a distinction appear to conflict with any other Cartesian doctrine.

Such a defense of the per se unity of a human being does, however, create a difficulty for my account of the status of bodies. I have alleged that Descartes believes bodies are substances and that he uses the terms 'substance' and '*ens per se*' interchangeably. Yet since a union of parts of bodies can be disrupted naturally, by the actions of other bodies, and moreover, since those parts can continue to exist without any special action by God, it would follow that bodies are not *entia per se,* and hence, not substances. Now what I think is the best response to make on Descartes's behalf here is to concede that in the end there is a distinction to be drawn between an *ens per se* and a substance. To be a substance it is sufficient to be able to exist apart from a subject, whereas for a substance to be an *ens per se* it is necessary that whatever parts it has can exist out of real union with one another only by divine power.

The other response to the objection that Descartes's human being is not an *ens per se* is found in the same letter to Regius. He advises Regius to say that something can be both an *ens per se* and an *ens per accidens:*

> That which is an *ens per se* can be made *per accidens,* for mice are generated or made by accident from dirt, and yet are *entia per se.* (AT III, 460; K 122)

A human being is an *ens per se* because

> body and soul, in relation to the whole human, are incomplete substances, and it follows from their being incomplete that what they constitute is an *ens per se.* (AT III, 460; K 122)

A human being is an *ens per accidens* because

> considering the body alone, we clearly perceive nothing in it on account of which it demands to be united to the soul, as we perceive nothing in the soul on account of which it must be united to the body, which is why I said above that it is in a certain manner accidental, not that it is absolutely accidental. (AT III, 460; K 122)

Even I have been tempted to say that in advising Regius to assert that a human being is in one sense an *ens per se* and in another sense an *ens per accidens,* he is simply trying to avoid controversy. But this letter is not the only passage where he suggests such a response. In the *Replies to the Fourth Objections* he asserts that a hand is both complete, when considered by itself, and incomplete, when referred to the whole body of which it is a part, and he uses this example as an analogy to illustrate how mind and body are at once complete and incomplete (AT VII, 222; HR II, 99). So his endorsement of this solution does now strike me as sincere. But I have been unable to discover a way to defend its philosophical merits. Allowing one and the same thing to be both an *ens per se* and an *ens per accidens* seems to stretch those concepts beyond the breaking point.

May others speak on his behalf.

Conclusion

I have argued that Descartes does take seriously the hylomorphic model of mind-body union. Moreover, I have argued that his account of the unity of a human being compares well with those of his medieval predecessors. The key move in making this comparison has been to point out that his conception of (created) substance is much weaker than the Aristotelian conception—he requires of a substance only that it be able to exist apart from a subject. Thus if his Aristotelian predecessors are permitted to allow as constituents of an *ens per se* actual things which can exist apart from each other, at least by divine power, then so should he.

Abbreviations to editions of Descartes's works:

AT   *Oeuvres de Descartes,* Vols. I–XII and Supplement, edited by Charles Adam and Paul Tannery (Paris: Leopold Cerf, 1897–1913).

HR   *The Philosophical Works of Descartes,* Vols. I and II, translated by Elizabeth S. Haldane and G. R. T. Ross (Cambridge: Cambridge University Press, 1911–1912 and 1931).

K   *Descartes: Philosophical Letters,* translated and edited by Anthony Kenny (Oxford: Clarendon Press, 1970).

M   *Le Monde, ou Traité de la lumière,* translation and introduction by Michael Sean Mahoney (New York: Abaris, 1979).

Notes

This paper was inspired by a remark made in conversation by Joshua Cohen. I am especially grateful to Marilyn Adams, to my dissertation committee chair Robert Adams, and to Rogers Albritton. I would also like to thank John Carriero, James Conant, Dan Garber, Hannah Ginsborg, Marjorie Grene, Jeremy Hyman, Edwin McCann, Michele Moody, Margaret Wilson, Kenneth Winkler, and the editors at *The Philosophical Review.* Jennifer Whiting deserves special mention for several helpful suggestions as I was preparing the draft first submitted for publication.

Earlier versions were read at UCLA and at the University of Wisconsin, Madison and discussed at the College of William and Mary.

1. See Nicholas Malebranche, *The Search after Truth,* translated and edited by Thomas Lennon and Paul Olscamp (Columbus: Ohio State University Press, 1980), pp. 446–452; Baruch Spinoza, *Ethics,* Part III, Prop. 2; Gottfried Leibniz, *The Monadology,* Paragraph 17.

2. Daisie Radner, "Descartes' Notion of the Union of Mind and Body," *Journal of the History of Philosophy* 9 (1971), pp.159–170.

3. Margaret Wilson, *Descartes* (Boston: Routledge and Kegan Paul, 1978), p. 205.

4. Ibid., p. 219.

5. Ibid., p. 211.

6. Ibid., p. 218.

7. Ibid., p. 211. Wilson, however, does not mention that in a letter to Regius, January, 1642 (which will figure prominently in my interpretation of Descartes's view) Descartes tells Regius that he thinks it is untrue that mind and body are united by position or disposition (AT III, 493; K 127). See page 62 below.

8. Ibid., p. 207.

9. Radner, *op. cit.,* p. 162.

10. Fred Sommers, "Dualism in Descartes: The Logical Ground," *Descartes: Critical and Interpretive Essays,* ed. Michael Hooker (Baltimore: Johns Hopkins University Press, 1978), p. 224.

11. Wilson, *op. cit.,* p. 214.

12. Étienne Gilson, *Études sur la rôle de la pensée médiévale dans la formation du système cartésien* (Paris: J. Vrin, 1930), p. 250.

13. Bernard Williams, *Descartes: The Project of Pure Enquiry* (New York: Penguin Books, 1978), p. 280.

14. A translation is my own if it differs from the English source cited.

15. There is one important passage in another letter to Princess Elizabeth, which has generated some discussion lately, in which he does seem to assert that to teach their distinction is to deny their union:

> It does not seem to me that the human mind is capable of conceiving at the same time the distinction and the union between body and soul, because for this it is necessary to conceive them as a single thing and at the same time to conceive them as two things; and this is absurd. (AT III, 693; K 142)

In commenting on this assertion Wilson says that it is hard to avoid interpreting it "as an overt admission on Descartes's part that his position on the mind-body relation is self-contradictory" (Wilson, *op. cit.,* p. 207). Thus on her reading, Descartes thinks it would be harmful to discuss the union, given his aim of trying to prove the real distinction, because he thinks the two views are incompatible. But since she thinks that the two views are not incompatible, she is puzzled as to what could have motivated him to make such a statement. On her view, all that is required for a real distinction between mind and body is that they are capable of existing apart. Therefore, he could have consistently conceived of them as really distinct yet as "temporarily constituting one thing as a result of their present conjunction." In other words, she is relying on the quite plausible intuition that there is no difficulty in conceiving a proposition of the form "not p and possibly p," where "not p" is the proposition that mind and body do not exist apart and "possibly p" is the proposition that mind and body can exist apart.

I agree with Wilson that it is sufficient on Descartes's view for mind and body to be two things that they be capable of existing apart and that it is sufficient for them to constitute a single thing that they not exist apart. Thus it is not contradictory that mind and body should at the same time be two things and constitute a single thing. [My view, however, differs from hers as to what existing apart amounts to. In my dissertation, *Metaphysical Foundations of Descartes' Concept of Matter* (UCLA, 1982), I argue that what he means by the elliptical expression 'exist without the other' is that each can exist without the essential attribute of the other, and not, as Wilson and others seem to think, that each can exist without the other existing (Wilson, p. 190).] But let me offer the following conjecture, which I think is interesting but problematic, as to why Descartes might have thought it is impossible for us simultaneously to *conceive* of mind and body being two things and constituting a single thing. I think that Descartes might not distinguish between conceiving of p and conceiving of possibly p. In making this conjecture I do not see myself as attributing a mistake to Descartes, because I myself have doubts as to whether such a distinction can be drawn. I can see no difference in what I do when I conceive of it snowing in July and when I conceive of it possibly snowing in July. This is not to say there is no difference between the proposition that it will snow in July and the proposition that possibly it will snow in July, for surely these propositions have different truth values and we can believe one without believing the other. But that sort of distinction in modality does not enter into our conception. Thus I think it would be entirely plausible for Descartes to maintain that we conceive the very same thing when we conceive of mind and body existing apart and when we conceive of them possibly existing apart. So if there is no distinction between conceiving of p and conceiving of possibly p, and if we cannot conceive of the state of affairs not p and p, then it would follow that we cannot conceive of the state of affairs not p and possibly p.

One merit of this conjecture is that it helps clear up some of the confusion surrounding Descartes's remarks about the relation of clear and distinct conception to reality. He is widely held to maintain, and in fact he does state in the *Third Meditation,* that whatever we clearly and distinctly conceive is true (AT VII, 35; HR I, 158). But in the *Sixth Meditation,* from the premise that we can clearly and distinctly conceive mind apart from body and body apart from mind, he draws only the weak conclusion that mind can exist apart from body, when one would have expected him to conclude that they do exist apart (AT VII, 78; HR I, 190). This has led to a misreading of the conclusion, which Wilson points out, as stating that they do exist apart (Wilson, p. 197). Her reading is wrong because he consistently describes what is or can be conceived as their separate existence, not their possible separate existence (AT VII, 78; HR I, 190: AT VII, 121, 223, 355, 444; HR II 22, 99, 209, 256: AT VIII, 25; HR I, 241). Of course, it is not significant on my reading whether we describe what is conceived as their separate existence or their possible separate existence, but it is on hers. Now the language of the *Meditations* might support an interpretation according to which whatever we *do* clearly and distinctly conceive is true, and that whatever we *can* clearly and distinctly conceive is possible. But this reading is philosophically idiotic. Surely Descartes does not believe this: we do not conceive of the separate existence of mind and body, but we can conceive of it.

Instead, I think Descartes is best interpreted as believing that whatever we can or do clearly and distinctly conceive is possible, and that we can infer that something is true only if we can or do clearly and distinctly conceive that it cannot not be true. This interpretation finds support in a letter to Mersenne, March 1642:

> you quote as an axiom of mine: whatever we clearly conceive is or exists. That is not at all what I think, but only that whatever we perceive clearly is true, so it exists, if we perceive that it cannot not exist; or that it can exist, if we perceive that its existence is possible. (AT III, 544–5; K 132)

This passage supports my reading insofar as it denies that whatever we clearly and distinctly conceive is true. But it does not offer unequivocal support for my reading. Instead of saying that whatever we clearly and distinctly conceive is possible, he says that if we conceive that something is possible we can infer that it is possible. This might seem to suggest what I want to deny, that he does see a distinction between conceiving of p and conceiving of possibly p. But in that case one would have expected him to tell us in this passage what we can infer from conceiving p, in addition to telling us what we can infer from conceiving that p is impossible and that p is possible. However, since no such account is provided, let me conjecture that it is not provided precisely because he sees no distinction in conceiving p and in conceiving possibly p. It should be noted that Wilson thinks this strong condition on what sort of conception is required to guarantee truth is too strong for Descartes's purposes (Wilson, p. 142).

16. It was gratifying to discover that I am in agreement with Leibniz on this reading of Descartes. See his *New Essays on Human Understanding*, translated and edited by Peter Remnant and Jonathan Bennett (Cambridge: Cambridge University Press, 1981), p. 317. I would ask of those who think Descartes is being disingenuous to play along with my attempt to take his remarks at face value.

17. See AT III, 493; K 127: AT III, 508; K 130: AT IV, 166; K 157: AT VII, 219; HR II, 97: AT VII, 228; HR II, 102–3.

18. Janet Broughton and Ruth Mattern understand his use of the expression 'substantial union' in the same way. See their article "Reinterpreting Descartes on the Notion of the Union of Mind and Body," in the *Journal of the History of Philosophy* 16 (1978), p. 27.

19. The key passage is AT VII, 222; HR II, 98–9. Descartes's use of the term 'per se' is obscured by the French translation, which translates 'a se' as 'par soi', and 'per se' as either 'par soi' or 'de soi' (AT IX, 35 & 173). Haldane and Ross make use of the terms 'per se' or 'self-derived' where 'a se' is found in the Latin, although in a footnote to one passage they do point out that the

Latin is 'a se' (HR II, 4 & 14). The crucial evidence that 'a se' and 'per se' have different meanings is found in the *Replies to the Fourth Objections*. Unlike his translators, Descartes is careful to restrict the use of the term 'a se' to the "Reply to the Second Part, concerning God," where it is used to characterize God's power of causing his own existence (see also AT VII, 110; HR II, 15), and the use of the term 'per se' to the "Reply to the First Part, concerning the Nature of the Human Mind," where he makes it explicit that the distinction between things which can exist per se and things which cannot exist per se is the very same distinction as that between complete and incomplete things:

> But if they are said to be incomplete, because they cannot exist per se alone, I confess it seems to me contradictory that they are substances, that is, things subsisting per se, and at the same time incomplete, that is, not able to subsist per se. (AT VII, 222; HR II, 99)

20. Martial Gueroult, *Spinoza* (Hildesheim: G. Olms, 1968), Vol. I, App. 10, pp. 540–555, and *Descartes selon l'ordre des raisons* (Paris: Aubier, 1953), Vol. I, pp. 107–118.

21. As Jean Laporte argues in *Le rationalisme de Descartes* (Paris: Presses Universitaries de France, 1950), pp. 187–188, *in genere* is not *in globo*.

22. See AT III, 477; K 124: AT VII, 222; HR II, 99: AT VIII, 71 for passages in which Descartes asserts that bodies or parts of extended substance are themselves substances. See AT IV, 349; K 186: AT VII, 255; HR II, 121: AT VIII, 28; HR I, 243 where he makes assertions which entail that they are substances.

23. See AT VII,433; HR II, 249 where Descartes asserts that modes cannot be parts and AT VIII, 53; HR I, 266 where he identifies bodies and parts of matter.

24. It is clear that the issue as to whether Descartes's human being can claim to be a unity is not whether it satisfies the conditions of the strong conception of created substance. Accordingly, I am not referring to the strong conception when I say that he uses the term 'substance' to mean a unity. In discussing his strict conception of created substance, Gueroult curiously fails even to mention Descartes's claim that a human being is an *ens per se*. Perhaps this omission can be explained by his view expressed in *Descartes selon l'ordre des raisons,* Vol. II, pp. 65–66 and Chapter XV, that Descartes thinks the substantial union of mind and body is incomprehensible from the point of view of our finite intellects, even though it is an indubitable fact made known by sensation and made possible by God's omnipotence.

25. Radner, *op. cit.,* p. 165, contrasts the hylomorphic model of mind-body union with a model according to which mind is said to be a quality of body:

> Descartes himself seems to be dissatisfied with the whole idea of one substance being styled a quality of another. For elsewhere, when he uses the analogy of gravity, as well as when he uses the other two analogies mentioned above, what he seems to have in mind is not one substance considered as a quality of another, but a special kind of relationship between two kinds of substances considered as such.

But I think there is an important sense in which Descartes sees no distinction between the two models. To consider a substance as a quality of another just is to conceive a special kind of relationship, namely inherence, between two substances considered as such. However, I think that Radner is probably correct in suggesting that to consider one substance as a quality of a second substance is to deny that the first is the substantial form of the second, even if the first does inhere in the second. Thus this passage from the *Replies to the Sixth Objections* only supports the view that the mind is a form of the body, not that it is the substantial form of the body.

26. Geneviève [Rodis-]Lewis, *L'individualité selon Descartes* (Paris: J. Vrin, 1950), pp. 76ff.

27. Gilson, *op. cit.*, p. 247.

28. Henri Gouhier, *La pensée métaphysique de Descartes* (Paris: J. Vrin, 1962), p. 351.

29. See the *Notes against a Programme* for the clearest exposition of Descartes's view that attributes which constitute the essence of a thing are incompatible in a simple substance, but not in a composite substance (AT VIII–II, 349–350; HR I, 436–7).

30. Gouhier, *op. cit.*, p. 353.

31. Nor does it follow from the strong conception of substance discussed above in the Introduction that a substance cannot exist in a subject.

32. These remarks about gravity indicate that closely linked to Descartes's modification of the concept of substance is a modification in his concept of what it is to be in a subject. For Aristotle, part of what it is to be in a subject is to be unable to exist apart from it (*Categories*, 1a 23–25). But Descartes, following his medieval Aristotelian predecessors, thinks that some things, such as gravity, which exist in a subject can nevertheless exist apart from it. He differs from the Aristotelians by insisting that such things are substances.

33. Wilson, *op. cit.*, p.213.

34. Ibid., p. 214.

35. Ibid., p. 213.

36. Ibid.

37. Thomas Aquinas, *Summa Theologica*, Pt. I, Q. 76, Art. 8; Aristotle, *De Motu Animalium*, text with translation, commentary and interpretive essays by Martha Craven Nussbaum (Princeton: Princeton University Press, 1978), 703a 37, p. 52.

38. See also *Summa Contra Gentiles*, Bk. 2, Ch. LXXII.

39. After having come to the conclusion that such a distinction is available to Descartes, it was only upon rereading Wilson and noticing her juxtaposition of these two articles from the *Passions* that it occurred to me that he actually makes the distinction. My translations of the articles closely follow hers.

40. Aquinas, *Summa Contra Gentiles*, Bk. 2, Ch. LXXII.

41. Aquinas, *Summa Theologica*, Pt. I, Q. 76, Art. 4.

42. Ferdinand Alquié, in his edition of Descartes's works, alleges in a footnote [*Descartes: Oeuvres philosophiques* (Paris: Garnier Freres, 1967), Vol. III, p. 976] that the *Passions,* Part I, Art. 30, conflicts with this claim that the iden-

tity of the body derives from the soul. There Descartes asserts that "the body is one and in a certain manner indivisible because of the disposition of its organs, which are so related to one another that when any one is removed, that renders the whole body defective." However, I am not so sure there is a conflict. There would be a conflict if Descartes asserted that the identity of the human body derives solely from its union with the soul. But in the letter to Mesland he seems to think that the identity of the human body depends on both its union with the soul and the dispositions of its organs. Geneviève Rodis-Lewis makes what I take to be a similar response to Alquié in "Limitations of the Mechanical Model in the Cartesian Conception of the Organism," fn. 37, in Hooker, *op.cit.*, p. 169.

43. Aquinas, *Summa Theologica*, Pt. I, Q. 76, Art. 8; Aristotle, *De Anima*, Book II, Ch. 1, 412b 10–24. But I do not think that even for the Aristotelians it is a necessary condition of a part being a part of my body that it retain its proper functioning—my eye will continue to be part of my body, should I go blind, even though it will cease to be an eye.

44. I am indebted to Jennifer Whiting here.

45. It might well be argued in further defense of Descartes that there is no need for me to concede any significant difference between his views and the Aristotelians' on the relation of ensoulment and teleological explanation. Gueroult, most prominently, thinks that the substantial union of mind and body "is the basis of the teleology of human nature and the finality of the human body" (*Descartes selon l'ordre des raisons,* Vol. II, p. 187). He even goes so far as to claim that finality is spread through the whole human body, down to its smallest parts to infinity (p. 186), where the end in question is the conservation of the union of mind and body (p. 180). Gueroult's attribution of finality to the human body derives from Descartes's suggestion in the *Sixth Meditation* that God gave us the particular sensations we have because they indicate what is beneficial or detrimental to the composite human being. Indeed, this is why Gueroult says that it is sensation that transforms the human machine into an end (p. 180).

But in providing such an explanation of our sensations, Descartes is violating his own strictures against appeals to God's will (my thinking on this issue has been influenced by an unpublished paper by Janet Broughton). Thus it strikes me that the issue as to whether teleological explanation plays only a very limited role in Descartes's account of human beings, as I was suggesting, namely, in the explanation of behavior that derives from the will of human beings, or whether it plays a more comprehensive, Aristotelian role of the sort Gueroult suggests, hinges on resolving Descartes's conflicting remarks about our access to God's will. I hope to say more on this problem in the future. Other references include Laporte, *op.cit.*, pp. 343–361, and Rodis-Lewis, in Hooker, *op.cit.*, pp. 152–170.

46. Gilson, *op. cit.*, p. 247–248.

47. John Carriero pointed out to me that Gilson might be defended along these lines.

48. Radner makes what might be construed to be a similar objection

(Radner, *op. cit.*, pp. 162–164, 168). She points out that in a letter to Elizabeth, Descartes asserts that there are three primary notions in his philosophy, that of mind, that of body, and that of the union between them (AT III, 665; K 138). She equates these primary notions with his simple natures, and concludes that since simple natures cannot be analyzed by the mind into others more distinctly known, the union of mind and body cannot be a unity of composition, because a unity of composition can be analyzed into its components. Therefore, the objection is that Descartes's account of the union between mind and body is inconsistent because he wants to maintain both that it is a unity of composition and that it is a simple nature.

This objection has force only if one understands Descartes's assertion that the union of mind and body is a primary notion to be a claim about the man, that is, if one understands the term 'union' to refer to that entity which results from uniting mind and body. But it might instead refer to the relation which unites mind and body. In that case, what he would be saying is that the relation of informing or inhering in is unanalyzable. This fits well with his advice to Regius that he need not give an account of this relation, since no one else has either (AT III 493; K 127). (See Broughton and Mattern, *op.cit.*, for another defense of Descartes against Radner's criticisms.)

But more important, even if Descartes did slip in the way Radner suggests by demanding of the composite that it be unanalyzable, that is an entirely different sort of objection from the fourth objection. No Aristotelian would demand of an essential unity that it be unanalyzable. Even someone who thinks that in the most proper sense of the term 'substance', composites of form and matter are not substances, but that rather only the form is substance, is not going to deny that substance is capable of definition. But see Donald Morrison, *Three Criteria of Substance in Aristotle's Metaphysics: Unity, Definability, Separation* (unpublished Ph.D. dissertation, Princeton, 1983) Chapter 3, for an interesting discussion of the paradox in Aristotle's demand that a definition be a unity.

49. Marilyn Adams, *Ockham* (Notre Dame: University of Notre Dame Press, forthcoming Part IV, Chapter 15, "The Metaphysical Structure of Composite Substances."

50. At least where divine power is limited by what we can clearly and distinctly conceive. But without such an assumption, Descartes's theory of distinction—real, modal, and of reason—disintegrates.

51. In my dissertation, *Metaphysical Foundations of Descartes' Concept of Matter* (UCLA, 1982), I argue that the notion of separate existence required for a real distinction between mind and body is not that each can exist without the other existing, nor that each can exist out of real union with the other, but that each can exist as a complete thing without having the essential attribute of the other. Thus mind can exist as a complete thing without being extended and body can exist as a complete thing without thinking. And since, as discussed above on pages 67–68, it is sufficient for being a complete thing or substance that a thing be able to exist apart from a subject, the human body can still be considered a substance even though it cannot exist without being the subject

of the mind, because it does not need the mind as its subject. That is, on my interpretation of the sort of separability that is required for real distinction, body not only can be separated from mind, it is separate from mind (because it does not exist in the mind), even though it is and must be united to the mind (because its existence requires the mind to exist in it). But only God, on my reading, has the power to separate mind from body, that is, to keep the mind in existence when it is not in the body (which is a different power from that which bodies have of causing the composite human being to go out of existence by interfering with the human body). On this understanding, the relation of being separate is not symmetrical.

52. Michele Moody raised this objection.

4

How God Causes Motion: Descartes, Divine Sustenance, and Occasionalism

Daniel Garber

In his *Traité de l'esprit de l'homme* (1664),[1] Louis de la Forge, one of Descartes's early followers, wrote:

> I hold that there is no creature, spiritual or corporeal, that can change [the position of a body] or that of any of its parts in the second instant of its creation if the creator does not do it himself, since it is he who had produced this part of matter in place A. For example, not only is it necessary that he continue to produce it if he wants it to continue to exist, but also, since he cannot create it everywhere, nor can he create it outside of every place, he must himself put it in place B, if he wants it there, for if he were to have put it somewhere else, there is no force capable of removing it from there. (*Ibid.*, p. 240)

De la Forge's argument is an interesting one. He begins with two premises. The first is the doctrine of divine sustenance, that God must sustain the existence of every body, indeed, of every thing, mind or body, at every moment of its existence. Secondly, de la Forge assumes as a result, it would seem, that God causes motion in the material world by recreating bodies in different places at different times. From this de la Forge draws the conclusion that *only* God can move a body. When God sustains bodies, he must sustain them in *some* place or other; he cannot sustain them everywhere, nowhere, or in any way independently of some place or other. And so causes of motion beside God, causes of motion like our own minds are supposed to be, are neither possible nor needed; if motion and rest are direct results of God's sustenance of the material world, it would seem that there can be no room for other causes.

The position de la Forge is trying to establish here is a variety of occasionalism, and the argument I have sketched is one among many which Descartes's followers used to establish the claim that God is the only genuine cause in the material world, at least.[2] On this view, causal relations between two bodies, or between a mind and body, are not true causal links, but only occasional links which depend for their efficacy on God actually to impart the appropriate motion to the appropriate body. What is especially interesting is that de la Forge starts from what many commentators assume to be genuinely Cartesian doctrines to establish his conclusion. Descartes emphasizes in a number of places that "we have no force through which we conserve ourselves," and so for this we must turn to God, who "continually reproduces us, as it were, that is, conserves us" [Pr I 21].[3] Descartes appeals to this doctrine of divine conservation in proving his laws of nature, both in *Le Monde* and in the *Principia Philosophiae,* arguing that God is the first and continuing cause of motion in the world, and that acting with constancy in preserving his material creation, he must necessarily sustain the world in such a way that certain general constraints on motion are satisfied; quantity of motion is thus conserved, as is motion along a straight path [Pr II 36–42]. The close connection between God's sustenance of the world and his role as cause of motion in the inanimate world has led a number of commentators to see something like de la Forge's view in Descartes, the view that God's role as a cause of motion in the world is inseparable from his role as a sustainer of the world, that God causes motion by creating bodies in different places at different times.[4]

De la Forge's premises seem to belong to Descartes as well. But, if so, then it would appear that, like it or not, Descartes too must be committed to de la Forge's conclusion that God can be the *only* cause of motion in his material world, that, contrary to our "most certain and most evident experience," mind cannot really cause motion in the world [AT V 222 (K 235)]. This is the question I would like to examine in this essay. In the end, I shall argue that, when we understand Descartes's doctrine of divine sustenance and of the way God enters the world as a cause of motion, we shall see that, wherever de la Forge's views lead him, Descartes need not be committed to occasionalism, at least not in this way. When we understand just how God causes motion, we shall see that Descartes's God can leave plenty of elbow room for other causes to produce their effects, indeed, produce them as directly as God himself does.

I.

It will be helpful to begin the story with a brief discussion of Descartes's doctrine of divine sustenance. Descartes writes in Meditation III:

> All of the time of my life can be divided into parts, each of which is entirely independent of the others, so that from the fact that I existed a short time ago, it does not follow that I ought to exist now, unless some cause as it were creates me again in this moment, that is, conserves me. [AT VII 49 (CSM II 33)]

Now, Descartes argues, "plainly the same force and action is needed to conserve any thing for the individual moments in which it endures as was needed for creating it anew, had it not existed" [AT VII 49 (CSM II 33)]. Clearly such a power is not in us; if it were, Descartes reasons, I would also have been able to give myself all of the perfections I clearly lack [AT VII 168 (CSM II 118)]. And so he concludes that it must be God that creates and sustains us [AT VII 111, 165, 168, 369–370 (CSM II 80, 116, 118, 254/5); Pr I 21]. This conclusion, of course, holds for bodies as well as for us. It is not just *souls,* but *all* finite things that require some cause for their continued existence. And, as with the idea of ourselves, "when I examine the idea of body, I perceive that it has no power [*vis*] in itself through which it can produce or conserve itself" [AT VII 118 (CSM II 84); cf. AT VII 110 (CSM II 79)]. And so we must conclude that the duration of bodies, too, must be caused by God, who sustains the material world he created in the beginning.

Descartes conceives of God's continual sustenance of his creatures as their *efficient* cause: "I should not hesitate to call the cause that sustains me an efficient cause" [AT VII 109 (CSM II 79)]. But God's causality here is in one respect importantly different from other efficient causes that we are familiar with from our experience. In reply to Gassendi's *Fifth Objections,* Descartes distinguishes between two sorts of efficient causes, a *causa secundum fieri,* a cause of becoming, and a *causa secundum esse,* a cause of being. Roughly speaking, as Descartes understands the notions, a *causa secundum esse* is a cause which must continue to act for its effect to continue, unlike a *causa secundum fieri,* which produces an effect that endures, even after the cause is no longer in operation or even in existence. An architect, thus, is the cause of becoming with respect to a house, as is a father with respect to his son. But Descartes claims

> the sun is the cause of the light proceeding from it, and God is the cause of created things, not only as a cause of becoming, but as a cause of being,

and therefore must always flow into the effect in the same way, in order
to conserve it. [AT VII 369 (CSM II 254/5)]

And so, just as we ordinarily think that the sun must continue its illumi-
nation for daylight to persist, so must God continue his activity in order
for the world and its motion to be sustained.[5] This continual sustenance is also unlike the more ordinary efficient causes insofar as it
requires a kind of power beyond the capacities of created things.
Whereas finite things may be able to stand as the efficient causes *secundum fieri* of things in the world, only God, strictly speaking, can
stand as their cause *secundum esse*. As we noted earlier, in *Meditation
III* Descartes declares that: "plainly the same force and action is needed
to conserve any thing for the individual moments in which it endures
as was needed for creating it anew, had it not existed" [AT VII 49 (CSM
II 33)]. From this Descartes infers that, "it is also one of those things
obvious by the light of nature that conservation differs from creation
only in reason" [AT VII 49 (CSM II 33)]. That is, the activity and power
needed to sustain a thing in its existence is identical to the activity and
power necessary to create anything from nothing [cf. also AT VII 165,
166 (CSM II 116, 117)]. Elsewhere he puts the point a bit differently,
suggesting that conservation is to be understood as the "continual production of a thing" [AT VII 243 (CSM II 169); cf. Pr II 42], or, more
guardedly, suggesting that God *as it were (veluti)* continually reproduces his creatures [Pr I 21; cf. AT VII 110 (CSM II 79)].

In the following section, we shall investigate how Descartes's God
causes motion while sustaining the world. But, before turning to that
question, I would like briefly to discuss an issue closely related to the
questions under discussion here, that of temporal atomism. A number
of commentators take Descartes's language quite literally when he says
that God must continually recreate his creatures. On their view, Cartesian time must, as a result, be a series of discrete timeless instants,
created one after another like the frames of a motion picture.[6] Such a
view seems inevitably to lead to a position like de la Forge's. The cartoonist creating an animated cartoon can cause his creatures to move
only by drawing them in different positions in successive frames; so
too for God, it would seem, were we to conceive of him as the grand
cartoonist with respect to his creation. In this way, God's sustenance
would seem to be inseparable from his role as cause of motion, and all
genuine causes of motion other than God would seem to be frozen
out.

But it is not at all clear that Descartes held such a position. In a
recent study, Jean-Marie Beyssade[7] has argued that Descartes's God
sustains the continuously flowing time of our experience. On Beys-

sade's view, time for Descartes is much like body, infinitely divisible and not composed of any ultimate elements, elements like the durationless temporal atoms are supposed to be. Beyssade does not deny, of course, that Descartes is concerned with timeless instants in a number of important contexts, and, indeed, that he even talks about God conserving bodies as they exist at a given instant [AT XI 44 (CSM I 96); Pr II 39]. But, Beyssade argues, such instants are not, strictly speaking, *parts* of duration. A hunk of extended substance can be divided into innumerable parts. But, for these divisions to be genuine *parts* of a body, they must be extended as well. Points, lines, surfaces, and geometrical objects that lack extension in length, width, and breadth are not *parts* of a body, but *limits* or *boundaries*. So, Beyssade suggests:

> In the same way, every duration or part of duration contains a before and after . . . ; the instant is its limit or boundary. If we are not mistaken, Descartes always takes this word ['instant'] and its Latin original '*instans*' in the strict sense of a limit. (*ibid.*, p. 348; cf. p. 353)

Durations, no matter how small, can be parts of an enduring world, and thus can be candidates for God's sustaining activity. But, although there may be instants *in* duration as boundaries of finite durations, instants, Beyssade suggests, cannot be *parts* of an enduring world; they cannot compose durations, nor can we intelligibly talk about God creating a single instant by itself without creating the duration it serves to bound, any more than we can talk about God creating a two-dimensional surface, a mode of body, without the body that it bounds [AT VII 250/1, 433 (CSM II 174, 292)].

With this in mind, it is easy to see that there is really nothing in Descartes's texts that unambiguously implies temporal atomism. The idea that all the parts of time are independent, the view we saw earlier in Meditation III, certainly does not; the parts of time in question there might plausibly be read as genuine parts of time, parts with duration, parts which are independent in the sense that God could create any stretch of time without creating preceding or succeeding portions of time. One can give similar readings to other passages in which Descartes talks about the independence of the present time from other moments or moments from one another. Even where Descartes talks of creating the things anew at every moment, even where Descartes makes it clear that God sustains things as they are in a timeless instant, there is no need to attribute temporal atomism to him.[8] To say that God recreates the world at every instant is to say that every instant can be regarded as the beginning, as the boundary of a newly created world. But, although every instant can be regarded as a moment of creation, it does not follow that what is being created is a bare instant or a sequence of bare instants, or that God could create an atemporal instant without creating a duration for that instant to bound.

But, just as Descartes was not committed to temporal atomism, neither was he committed to its denial; I know of few passages that cannot be plausibly interpreted either way. Indeed, I know of no passage to suggest that Descartes was particularly *interested* in the question of temporal atomism, one way or the other. And so it seems improper to argue from Descartes's supposed temporal atomism to the claim that God causes motion through recreating bodies in different positions at different times. If we want to know how God causes motion for Descartes, we should face the question directly.

II.

In presenting his account of God as continual sustainer of the world, Descartes did not think he was telling his readers anything they had not already heard. As far as he was concerned, he was appealing to an old and widely accepted doctrine with which his audience could be expected to be both familiar and generally sympathetic. When in the *Fifth Objections* Gassendi challenged his appeal to a conserving God [AT VII 300 (CSM II 209)], Descartes responded: "When you deny that to be conserved we require the continual influx of a first cause, you deny something that all metaphysicians affirm as obvious" [AT VII 369 (CSM II 254); cf. AT VI 45 (CSM I 133)]. And, in defending himself against Gassendi's criticisms, he seems to have turned directly to his copy of St. Thomas Aquinas.[9] God's sustenance of this world of created things is explicitly discussed in the *Summa Theologiae* I, q 104, a 1, and this passage may be the source of Descartes's answer to Gassendi. Like Descartes, Aquinas distinguishes between causes *secundum fieri* and *secundum esse,* and appeals to the same examples Descartes does—the builder of a house, the parent of a child, and the sun as illuminator—to clarify the sense in which God is the cause of the world as enduring [ST I, q 104, a 1 c]. And, although Aquinas does not say exactly that God's activity in sustaining the world is identical with his activity in creating it, many of Descartes's contemporaries would have been happy to agree with Descartes that "this conservation is the very same thing as creation, differing only in reason."[10]

In his monumental commentary on the *Discours,* Étienne Gilson[11] noticed this similarity between Descartes and Aquinas. But Gilson also noted an apparent (and important) difference as well:

> The being of the things Descartes's God conserves is so different from
> that which St. Thomas's God conserves, that there is a profound differ-
> ence between their two notions of continual creation. The Thomist God
> conserves the being of a world of substantial forms and essences. . . . But,
> on the contrary, in Cartesianism, there are no substantial forms any more.
> (*Ibid.*, p. 341)

Gilson goes on to argue that, lacking substantial forms, Descartes, unlike the scholastic, is doomed to a movie-show world of still frames,
mocking the continuity of time and motion that the scholastic is genuinely entitled to. Gilson's full argument is too complex to enter into
here. But I would like to explore his initial observation a bit.

Descartes does, for the most part, reject substantial forms and this
does indeed make a difference, as Gilson emphasizes. But what difference it makes depends upon how the notion is understood, and what
it is that takes the place of the absent forms. Now, the notion of a
substantial form is a basic notion in Aristotelian thought, and there
are important differences of conception among scholastic thinkers with
regard to that notion. But, to understand the importance of the rejection of substantial forms to Descartes's thought, we must begin with
an account of what the notion meant to him.

In very general terms, a substantial form is that which, joined to matter (the *materia prima* of the scholastics, ultimately) results in a complete substance. But, more substantively, substantial form is that from
which the characteristic behavior of the various sorts of substances derives. And so, Descartes notes, writing to his then disciple Henricus
Regius in January 1642, "they [i.e., forms] were introduced by philosophers to explain the proper action of natural things, of which action
this form is the principle and the source" [AT III 506 (K 129)]. Or, as
the Conimbrian Fathers wrote in a book Descartes likely learned from
as a schoolboy,

> There are individual and particular behaviors [*functiones*] appropriate to
> each individual natural thing, as reasoning is to human beings, neighing
> is to horses, heating to fire, and so on. But these behaviors do not arise
> from matter. . . . Thus they must arise from substantial form. (Gilson,
> *Index*, §209)

More concretely, Descartes views substantial forms as substances of
a sort: "by the name 'substantial form' I have understood a certain
substance joined to matter, and with it composing something whole
that is merely material" [AT III 502 (K 128)]. And the sort of substances
they are is mental substance, Descartes thinks, "like little souls joined
to their bodies" [AT III 648 (K 135)].[12] And so Descartes characterizes

the scholastic account of heaviness which he himself once held as follows:

> But what especially showed that the idea I had of heaviness was derived
> from that of mind was the fact that I thought that heaviness bore bodies
> toward the center of the earth as if it contained in itself some knowledge
> of it [i.e., the center of the earth]. For this could not happen without
> knowledge, and there cannot be any knowledge except in a mind. [AT VII
> 442 (CSM II 298)]

If substantial forms are supposed to explain the characteristic behavior
of bodies of various sorts, then we must be thinking of them as intentional entities, agents of a rudimentary sort, things capable of forming
intentions and exercising volition, little souls joined to matter. And so
the scholastic doctrine of form and matter is, in a sense, just the image
of the Cartesian human being, an unextended soul united to extended
body and projected out onto the material world. Indeed, Descartes
often uses the supposed familiarity of the scholastic model of heaviness
(which everyone would have learned at school) to persuade those who
have trouble with mind-body interaction on his view that they already
understand how interaction is possible; if one can understand the scholastic account of heaviness, then one can understand how the soul can
move the body, Descartes reasons, since the two cases are just the
same.[13]

It should be evident from Descartes's account of substantial form
that he does not reject forms altogether. Given that the human mind
is the very model of a form, it is not surprising to find Descartes saying
from time to time that the human soul is "the true substantial form of
man" [AT III 505]; indeed, it is "the only substantial form" he recognizes [AT III 503; cf. AT IV 346, AT VII 356 (CSM II 246)]. Descartes
from time to time also uses scholastic terminology and talks of the soul
"informing" the body [AT IV 168 (K 158); AT X 411 (CSM I 40)]. In this
sense, Gilson perhaps overestimates the difference between the world
Descartes's God sustains and that which Aquinas's sustains, insofar as
both contain at least some substantial forms.[14]

But it is significant that Descartes's world has many fewer forms than
Aquinas's does, that Descartes rejects all forms but those which pertain
to human beings.[15] This raises something of a problem for Descartes,
however. The substantial form was that in terms of which the characteristic behavior of a body of a certain sort was to be explained. But, without form, what is to explain why horses neigh and fire heats, why cannon balls fall and smoke rises? In one sense, the replacement for
explanation in terms of form is explanation in terms of size, shape, and

motion—mechanical explanation. Indeed so, but the story does not end there. In order to explain the behavior of a body (say a cannon ball) mechanistically, we must know more than just the size, shape, and motions of its parts and the surrounding medium; we must also know the relevant laws of motion, how a body as such can be expected to behave, what results when two bodies of given sizes, shapes, and motions encounter one another in collision, etc. Descartes replaces the multiplicity of Aristotelian substances, each with its own form and distinct characteristic behavior, with one kind of body which fills the entire universe and behaves everywhere in accordance with the same laws [cf. Pr II 23]. But, in the absence of scholastic substantial forms, Descartes must find some way of explaining the characteristic behavior of material substance, the laws of motion. And it is here that God enters as the "universal and primary [cause of motion], which is the general cause of all motions there are in the [physical] world" [Pr II 36]. God is the cause of motion, what takes the place of the scholastic forms Descartes banished from the inanimate world of nonhuman beings.

But this, of course, leads us back to the question I posed earlier in this paper: How does God cause motion in the world? And how is God's role as cause of motion related to his role as sustainer of body?

To answer this first question, we must, I think, reflect on how souls and the other forms Descartes attributed to the scholastics were thought to cause motion. We must keep in mind here that the issue is under a cloud, so to speak, and it may turn out that, because of an argument like the one de la Forge gave, Descartes is not entitled to hold that the human soul causes motion. But, *prima facie* and despite the doubts of a number of his readers, Descartes certainly thought the question relatively unproblematic. Writing to Arnauld on 29 July 1648, Descartes noted:

> That the mind, which is incorporeal, can impel a body, is not shown to us by any reasoning or comparison with other things, but is shown daily by the most certain and most evident experience. For this one thing is among the things known *per se,* which we obscure when we try to explain through other things. [AT V 222 (K 235)]

The mind can cause motion in a body, Descartes holds; it is something we know through experience directly, something we cannot explain in other terms. Insofar as we comprehend it, it is because "we have within us certain primitive notions, on the model of which we form all our other knowledge," Descartes explains to Elisabeth [AT III 665 (K 138)]. And, Descartes goes on to explain, we understand the schoolman's substantial forms to work in exactly the same way; indeed, as I noted earlier, the understanding we have of forms derives from the notions we were given to understand how human mind works on body.

Descartes is not very informative about just how mind (or form) moves body; on his view, there is not much that *can* be said, other than to direct our attention to the experience we all have that is supposed to make it all clear.[16] But, although there is not much we can say, there is no confusing the sense in which mind causes motion in a body with the way God sustains the body that mind supposedly moves. One of the axioms Descartes uses in the geometrical presentation of his arguments appended to the *Second Replies* reads as follows: "It is greater to create or conserve a substance, than it is to create or conserve the attributes or properties of a substance" [AT VII 166 (CSM II 117)]. The passage is not without its difficulties.[17] But the clear sense is that Descartes wants to distinguish causes that change the modes or properties of a thing (modal causes, as I shall call them) from causes that create or sustain the very being of a substance (substantial causes, perhaps). God, sustaining the world, is clearly a substantial cause. But minds are clearly not; insofar as they cause changes in the motion of bodies, they at best can count as modal causes. And, insofar as substantial forms are understood on the model of souls acting on bodies, Descartes would have had little trouble classifying them, with minds, as modal causes; they are causes of motion, a mode in bodies assumed to be sustained by the divine sustainer who is the unique substantial cause.

God enters Descartes's physics to do the business substantial forms did in the Aristotelian system, as he understood it, to cause bodies to behave in their characteristic ways. And, I claim, when doing the business of forms, Descartes's God is understood to cause motion in just the way forms were taken to do it, that is, on Descartes's account, in just the way that we do it: by way of an impulse that moves matter in a way that we can comprehend only through immediate experience. This is not at all clear as late as 1644 when, in proving his laws of nature in the *Principia*, Descartes's account of God as cause of motion is deeply (and obscurely) intertwined with his account of God as sustainer of the world [Pr II 36–42]. But, by April 1649, Descartes wrote to Henry More:

> Although I believe that no mode of acting belongs univocally to God and to his creatures, I confess nevertheless, that I can find no idea in my mind which represents the way in which God or an angel can move matter, which is different from the idea that shows me the way in which I am conscious that I can move my own body through my thought. [AT V 347 (K 252)]

And, so Descartes suggests to More, God is conceived to move bodies in just the way we do, using the same primitive notion we use to understand how we move our own bodies.

If this is how we conceive of God as a cause of motion, then, it would seem, we are conceiving of him as a *modal cause* when it comes to motion. Conceived as such, there would appear to be a distinction between God as sustainer of the world, a substantial cause keeping things in existence, and God as cause of motion, a modal cause causing bodies to have the particular motion they have, determining, at least in part, their modes. The difference between these two roles God plays for Descartes comes out again in the correspondence with More. In his letter of 5 March 1649, More asked Descartes if "matter, whether we imagine it to be eternal or created yesterday, left to itself, and receiving no impulse from anything else, would move or be at rest?" [AT V 316]. Descartes answers in his letter of August 1649: "I consider 'matter, left to itself, and receiving no impulse from anything else' as plainly being at rest. But it is impelled by God, conserving the same amount of transference in it as he put there from the first" [AT V 404 (K 258)]. The picture that comes through here is a simple one. Bodies can be conserved with or without the divine impulse. Without the impulse, they are at rest; with it, in motion. God's conservation of body seems separable from his role as cause of motion, and as cause of motion, he seems to act as we would in the circumstances; God's motion seems to result from a divine act of will, a divine shove.

III.

Now that we understand something of how God causes motion, we can return to the question originally posed and offer an answer.

As de la Forge construed Descartes's views on God, continual recreation, and God's role as cause of motion, Descartes seems pushed inevitably toward occasionalism and the view that God is the only genuine cause of motion in the world; if God causes motion by recreating bodies in different places at different times, then there seems to be no room for finite causes to act. But by now it should be clear why Descartes need not be committed to such a view.

I have argued that, for Descartes, God enters as a cause of motion in order to replace the scholastic's substantial forms, and, in that role, he can (and, in the More letters, at least, *is*) construed as acting in just the way forms were thought to cause motion, that is, in just the way *we* cause motion. As such, God both sustains bodies in their being and sustains bodies in their motion. But, it is important to note, *these two activities seem to be quite distinct;* in the one case, God is acting as a modal cause, in the other, as a substantial cause. This is an extremely important observation. There is no substantial cause but God, nor can there be, since no other being has the ability to create and sustain the universe. But, although God is a modal cause with respect to motion, there is no reason to hold that God is the *only* such cause. God is conceived to act as we do in causing motion; just as the finite cause of motion does not exclude others, so the fact that God causes motion does not seem to exclude other causes. This seems true even when we are talking about causing motion *in the same body.* Just as two human beings can exert their contrary impulses on the same bit of matter, so can we impose an impulse contrary to the one God imposes. Indeed, we do so every time we lift a stone, on which God is imposing an impulse to move toward the center of the earth.

And so Descartes would have to agree with de la Forge that God cannot sustain bodies that are in no place at all or in indeterminate places; the very possibility is absurd. But, I think Descartes might insist, although God sustains bodies that *have* place, it is not the act of sustaining them that *gives* them place. What gives them place and the motion that puts them in different places at different times is impulse or the lack thereof, a cause quite distinct from that by which bodies are sustained. These impulses may come from God himself, but they might come from other causes, like our own minds [cf. AT V 403/4 (K 257)]. And, when they come from God, they are not to be identified with the cause by which he sustains the bodies he moves.

There are a number of important questions relevant to the topic at hand which space will not permit us to discuss. Most importantly, it would be valuable to discuss the relations between the conception of motion and its divine cause which I have been developing with the discussion of motion and rest and their laws in part II of the *Principles* and in ch. 7 of *The World*—the sense in which motion and rest are distinct and the sense in which they are not, the sense in which motion and rest are states, and the way in which motion and rest give rise to forces that come into play at the time of collision. My story will not be complete until we see how the way in which Descartes's immutable God causes motion leads him to the conception of motion (and its associated forces and laws) which underlies his program in natural philosophy.

But, incomplete as my preliminary sketch of Descartes's position may be, it allows us to see one important feature that differentiates Descartes's metaphysic of motion and his use of God as cause of motion from that of his avowedly occasionalist followers. What lies behind occasionalism as advanced by de la Forge and by many Cartesians of his generation is a deep worry about causality in the world of finite things; what comes up again and again is the view that finite things are incapable of any genuine causal efficacy, that producing an effect is beyond the power of any finite thing. God enters as the *only* being capable of producing any change in the world.[18] Descartes's view is quite different. Descartes *never* rejects finite causes as such; indeed, it is on the model of one particular finite cause, us, that *all* causes are understood, conservation excepted.[19] When God enters as a cause of motion, it is simply on account of the fact that some finite causes needed to do the job are not available. But, even when God undertakes this task, it seems to me that Descartes can quite well hold that finite causes of motion are in no way squeezed out. Mind, indeed, can remain as direct a cause of motion for Descartes as God himself.

Notes

Many thanks to Roger Ariew for a prompt, careful reading of an earlier draft.

1. Pierre Clair, ed, *Louis de la Forge: Oeuvres Philosophiques* (Paris: Presses Universitaires de France, 1974). A similar argument is also found in dialogue seven of Nicolas Malebranche, *Dialogues on Metaphysics,* Willis Doney, trans. (New York: Abaris Books, 1980).

2. For a brief account of occasionalism among 17th Century Cartesians, see ch. 5 of Jean-François Battail, *L'Advocat philosophe Géraud de Cordemoy (1626–1684)* (The Hague: Martinus Nijhoff, 1973). There are a number of varieties of occasionalism. Here I am only concerned with the claim that God is the only genuine cause of motion in the material world.

3. The numerous references to Descartes's texts will be given in the body, for the most part, using the following abbreviations. AT: Charles Adam and Paul Tannery, eds., *Oeuvres de Descartes* (Paris: J. Vrin, 1964–1978); CSM: John Cottingham, Robert Stothoff, and Dugald Murdoch, trans., *The Philosophical Writings of Descartes* (New York: Cambridge, 1985); K: Anthony Kenny, trans., *Descartes: Philosophical Letters* (Minneapolis, Minn: University Press, 1981). The original language text in AT will be cited first, followed by a translation in CSM or K (if available). The one exception to this is the *Principia Philosophiae,* abbreviated 'Pr', and cited by part and section number. The original Latin can be found in AT VIII A, and translations in CSM I.

4. See e.g., Jean Wahl, *Du rôle de l'idée de l'instant dans la philosophie de Descartes* (Paris: Felix Alcan, 1920); Martial Gueroult, "The Metaphysics and Physics of Force in Descartes," in Stephen Gaukroger, ed., *Descartes: Philosophy, Mathematics and Physics* (Sussex: Harvester Press, 1980), pp. 196–229, esp. 218–220; G. Hatfield, "Force (God) in Descartes' Physics," *Studies in History and Philosophy of Science,* X (1979): 113–140, esp. 127.

5. Descartes does concede, under challenge, that the sun may not be

an especially good example of a *causa secundum esse*. See AT III 405, 429 (K 115/6).

6. See, e.g., the references cited in note 4.

7. *La philosophie première de Descartes* (Paris: Flammarion, 1979), pp. 129–143.

8. For the former formulations see AT VII 49, 109 (CSM II 33, 78/9); for the latter see AT XI 44, 45 (CSM I 96/7), Pr II 39.

9. In December 1639, Descartes tells Mersenne that he owns *"une Somme de S. Thomas,"* though it is not altogether clear to me whether this means a copy of Aquinas's *Summa Theologiae* or a *summary of* Aquinas. See AT II 630 (K 69).

10. Guilelmus Amesius, *Medulla theologica* (1628), quoted in Heinrich Heppe and Ernst Bizer, ed., *Die Dogmatik der evangelisch-reformierden Kirche* (Neukirchen, kreis Moers: Buchhandlung des Erziehungsvereins, 1935), p. 208. For other of Descartes's contemporaries on the question, see Heppe, *Dogmatik,* Locus XII; G. T. Thomson, *Reformed Dogmatics,* Heinrich Heppe, trans. (London: Allen and Unwin, Ltd., 1950), ch. XII; Étienne Gilson, *Index Scholastico-Cartesien* (Paris: J. Vrin, 1979), §§64, 112.

11. *Discours de la méthode: texte et commentaire* (Paris: J. Vrin, 1967).

12. The remark in question relates to real qualities, strictly speaking, qualities that follow directly from forms. But, in his polemics against the scholastics, Descartes drew no distinction between substantial forms and real qualities.

13. For a fuller account of this, see §II of Daniel Garber, "Understanding Interaction: What Descartes Should Have Told Elisabeth," *Southern Journal of Philosophy,* XXI supp. (1983): 15–32.

14. For a recent discussion of the human soul as substantial form in Descartes, see Marjorie Grene, "Die Einheit des menschen: Descartes unter den Scholastikern," *Dialectica,* XL (1986): 309–322.

15. For the still standard account of Descartes's rejection of forms, see Gilson, *Études sur le rôle de la pensée médiévale dans la formation du système cartésien* (Paris: J. Vrin, 1975), pp. 141–190.

16. This, in any case, is what he insisted on in writing to Elisabeth. See AT III 663–668, 690–695 (K 137–143). What exactly he meant here is not entirely clear.

17. The passage raises an obvious question about the relation between an attribute and a substance, a question the young Burman raised to Descartes in coversation. See AT V 154, and John Cottingham, trans. and ed., *Descartes' Conversation with Burman* (New York: Oxford, 1976), pp. 15, 77–80.

18. See especially Nicolas Malebranche, *De la récherche de la vérité,* bk. VI pt. II, ch. III, and the XVe *Éclaircissement.*

19. See Garber, "Understanding Interaction," *op. cit.*

5

Spinoza's Necessitarianism

Don Garrett

In a letter dated July 22, 1675, Henry Oldenburg advises Spinoza not to include in his "five-part Treatise [the *Ethics*] anything which may appear to undermine the practice of Religious virtue" (Letter 62). In response to Spinoza's subsequent request to know the specific doctrines that he intends (Letter 73), Oldenburg reports on the reactions of readers of the earlier *Theologico-Political Treatise:*

> I will tell you what it is that causes them most distress. You seem to assert the fatalistic necessity of all things and actions: and they say that if this is admitted and affirmed, then the nerves of all laws, of all virtue and religion, are cut through, and all rewards and punishments are empty. (Letter 74)

To this, Spinoza replies immediately and firmly:

> At last I see what it was that you asked me not to publish. Since, however, *this very thing is the principal basis of all those which are contained in the Treatise* [the *Ethics*] *I had intended to publish,* I want to explain in what sense I maintain the fatalistic necessity of all things and of all actions.
>
> For in no way do I subject God to fate, but I conceive that everything follows with inevitable necessity from the nature of God, just as all conceive that it follows from the nature of God Himself that He should understand Himself. (Letter 75; my emphasis)

Spinoza develops this "principal basis" throughout Part I of the *Ethics,* concluding that "In nature there is nothing contingent, but all things have been determined from the necessity of the divine nature to exist and produce an effect in a certain way" (EIp29), and that "Things could

103

have been produced by God in no other way, and in no other than they have been produced" (EIp33).

How are these conclusions to be understood? It is widely agreed that Spinoza's position entails determinism: the doctrine that every event is causally determined from antecedent conditions by the laws of nature. But there has been little consensus concerning the further question of whether his position also entails what we may call "necessitarianism": the doctrine that every actual state of affairs is logically or metaphysically necessary, so that the world could not have been in any way different than it is—or, to adopt the Leibnizian mode of expression, that the actual world is the only possible world. Stuart Hampshire has asserted that Spinoza is indeed committed to necessitarianism; Curley has argued that he is best interpreted as committed to its denial; Matson, Jarrett, and Bennett have maintained that he inconsistently commits himself to both necessitarianism and its denial; while Delahunty appears to hold that Spinoza's formulations are sufficiently ambiguous that he commits himself neither to the doctrine *nor* to its denial.[1]

With respect to the actual substance, its attributes and its infinite modes, Spinoza's position seems straightforward: they exist of necessity, and are the only ones there could have been.[2] If there is any contingency to be found in his universe, therefore, it evidently rests with the finite modes. But the possibility of different modes is a more difficult question. EIp28 asserts that every finite thing is caused to exist and to produce an effect by another finite cause that is caused to exist and to produce an effect by yet another finite cause, "and so on, to infinity." Since causes produce their effects necessarily for Spinoza (EIax3), it follows that the existence and action of each finite mode is, given the antecedent existence of its cause, inevitable at the time it is produced. Moreover, because the chain of prior finite causes for each finite mode reaches to infinity, it also follows that there has been no point in the entire duration of the universe at which two different prospective sets of finite modes constituted genuinely alternative possible futures. Nevertheless, even this latter conclusion does not entail that the actual total series of finite modes as a *whole* is a necessary one; for it leaves open the question of whether there could not instead have been, from eternity, some other equally possible total series of finite modes, one equally compatible with all of the necessary constraints on such a series. If Spinoza allows that there could have been a different total series of finite modes, then for all its invocation of necessity and inevitability his metaphysics will not be necessitarian. For, to each such total series there will correspond a different "possible world"—that is, a different way the universe genuinely could have been. Thus, the question of

Spinoza's necessitarianism is largely centered on the necessity or contingency of the total series of finite modes.

In this paper I will argue for three theses: (1) Spinoza is *not* positively committed by anything he says to the denial of necessitarianism; (2) Spinoza *is* positively committed by what he says to the truth of necessitarianism; and (3) if we do understand Spinoza as a necessitarian, then we can make better sense of two fundamental Spinozistic doctrines—his monism and his doctrine that every internally adequate idea corresponds to its object—as doctrines that are indeed founded on the "principal basis" of the "necessity of all things and actions." Although each of the three theses for which I will argue is deductively independent of the others, in the sense that they could be true or false in any combination without contradiction, they are nonetheless mutually supporting. Taken together, these theses constitute a strong case for regarding Spinoza as a necessitarian. I will defend the theses in order.

I

There are three textual grounds on which Spinoza has been thought to be committed to a plurality of possible worlds and hence to the denial of necessitarianism: (1) the relation he describes between the finite modes and the "absolute nature" of the attributes; (2) his distinction between essences that involve necessary existence and those that do not; and (3) his distinction between essential and inessential characteristics of things.

1. *Finite modes and the "absolute nature" of attributes.* EIp28d states that

> what is finite and has a determinate existence could not have been produced by the absolute nature of an attribute of God; for whatever follows from [*sequitur*] the absolute nature of an attribute of God is eternal and infinite. (by P21)

There are two different ways in which this claim might be thought to commit Spinoza to a plurality of possible worlds.[3]

a. *"Following from."* The first and more general of these ways does not demand that we assign any specific interpretation to the "absolute nature of an attribute" at all, so long as that "nature" is taken to be expressible in some propositional content. The argument, proposed by

Bennett, is as follows: EIp21 and EIp28d both entail that finite modes do not "follow from" the absolute nature of any attribute; but it is a theorem in most systems of entailment logic that a necessary truth is entailed by—i.e., "follows from"—any proposition whatever; hence, we must conclude that the existence of any particular finite mode cannot be a necessary truth.[4]

Bennett himself sets this argument aside on the grounds that the relevant theorem of entailment logic has not always been well-known and remains controversial, so that there is no reason to think Spinoza was aware of it or held it. In fact, however, we can go further: Spinoza can and must reject the theorem, at least as a claim about the relation that *he* intends by "following from."

He *must* reject it in view of its unacceptable consequences. To take one example, the existence of every infinite mode is necessary; but if every infinite mode therefore "followed from" every other infinite mode, Spinoza's distinction between immediate and mediate infinite modes, which is drawn in terms of that relation (EIp23d; see also Letters 63–64), would collapse. Moreover, he clearly intends "*y* follows from *x*" to entail "*x* causes *y,*" as the cited passage from EIp28d indicates.[5] Yet, surely he could not accept the consequence that every necessary state of affairs is a *cause* of every other. If it were, then every infinite mode of a given attribute would be both cause and effect of every infinite mode of every *other* attribute, contrary to EIIp6; and, even worse, every infinite mode would also be the cause of God's existence, contrary to EIIp6c.

He *can* reject the theorem because, in saying that "*y* follows from *x,*" he means considerably *more* than simply that "*x* entails *y,*" as the latter proposition is understood in most contemporary modal and entailment logics. In these logics, the meaning of "*x* entails *y*" is exhausted by the claim that there is no possible world in which *x* is true and *y* is false. For Spinoza, in contrast, to speak of *x* as following from *y* is to locate *x* specifically as a necessitating *cause and ground* of *y* within a causal order of the universe that is at once dynamic and logical. Thus, if the Spinozist "following-from" relation is to be identified with a kind of entailment at all, it must be identified with the entailment relation of a "relevance logic," one whose relevance condition is satisfied only by priority in the causal order of nature.[6] Relevance logics, because of the additional requirements they impose on the entailment relation, generally do not satisfy the theorem Bennett cites.

b. *"Absolute nature."* However, that theorem is by no means the only basis on which EIp21 and EIp28d may be thought to be incompatible with necessitarianism. For it may be argued that once we understand more specifically what is *meant* by "the absolute nature" of an attribute (alternatively: an "attribute . . . insofar as it is considered absolutely" [EIp23d]), we will see that the failure of finite modes to follow from *this* nature will require them to be contingent. If, for example, we interpret the "absolute nature of an attribute" to be its true or complete nature, then it will be difficult to see how finite modes could be rendered fully necessary *without* following from an attribute's "absolute" nature—for the attributes constitute the essence of God, who is the only independently necessary being.

There is reason to doubt, however, that "absolute nature" should be interpreted as "true or complete nature" in this context. For Spinoza also asserts repeatedly that *all things*—clearly including finite modes—must "follow from the necessity of God's [or "the divine"] nature" (EIp16, EIp17s, EIp26d, EIp33d, EIp33s1). At EIp29s, moreover, he equates "following from the necessity of God's nature" with following "from any of God's attributes." Hence, the finite modes *do* evidently follow from the attributes, but *not* from the "absolute nature" of the attributes—which would be a contradiction if "absolute nature" meant simply "real or complete nature."[7]

Can the notion of "absolute nature" be given a different interpretation, not subject to this difficulty? Its use in the *Ethics* gives us two clues. The first clue is in EIp21d, where Spinoza offers two parallel *reductio ad absurdum* arguments. The first argument concludes that whatever follows from the absolute nature of an attribute of God must be infinite, while the second concludes that whatever follows from the absolute nature of an attribute must have always had to exist or be eternal. The first argument, which for the sake of definiteness uses "thought" as a representative attribute, may be outlined as follows:

1. "in some attribute of God [for example, "thought"] there follows from its absolute nature something that is finite" (Spinoza's assumption).
2. Every attribute of God, including thought, is "necessarily . . . infinite by its nature" (by EIp11).
3. A thing can be finite only if it is limited or "determined through" something of the same nature (by EIdef2).
4. There is thought that does not constitute the finite thing in question (from 1–3).
5. "*on that account* [the finite thing] does not follow necessarily from the nature [of this thought] insofar as it is absolute thought." (from 4; my emphasis)
6. whatever "follows from the necessity of the absolute nature of the attribute itself . . . must necessarily be infinite" (from the con-

tradiction between 1 and 5, thus discharging Spinoza's original assumption).

As the direct inference from (4) to (5) shows, Spinoza regards it as self-evident that whatever follows from the "absolute nature" of a thing must necessarily be manifested *pervasively* throughout that attribute. The second, parallel argument of the demonstration—concerning eternity and "determinate existence or duration"—similarly takes it as self-evident that whatever follows from the absolute nature of an attribute necessarily exists *permanently,* or without durational limits, throughout that attribute.

The second clue is in EIp28d. There Spinoza argues that, since finite modes must be determined to exist and to produce their effects by God, yet cannot follow from the "absolute nature" of any attribute, they must follow instead from the attribute "insofar as it is considered to be affected by some mode." "Following from the absolute nature of an attribute" is thus contrasted *not* with failing to follow from the attribute at all, but rather with following from the attribute as that attribute is considered in a different *way.*[8]

From these two uses of the notion of "absolute nature of an attribute," we can form a reasonable hypothesis about its purpose. An attribute, if it is to have any internal diversity or change, must be qualified in different ways at different places and times. Now, some things about an attribute will follow from the very nature of the attribute regardless of *how* it is qualified or "affected," and thus will follow equally from it under all circumstances; accordingly, things of this kind must be infinite and eternal, in the sense of being necessarily pervasive and permanent throughout the whole range of the attribute. This is the argument of EIp21d concerning infinite modes. Other things, however—those local and temporary features that actually constitute the attribute's diversification and change—cannot similarly follow from the nature of the attribute *without regard* to how it is qualified or "affected"; otherwise, they would be necessarily pervasive and permanent as well. Hence, these finite things must follow only from some non-pervasive or non-permanent qualifications or "affections" of the attribute. In order to be non-pervasive or non-permanent, these affections must themselves follow from non-pervasive or non-permanent affections, and so on to infinity. This is the argument of EIp28d concerning finite modes. The distinction at issue—between that which follows from the attribute "absolutely" or without regard to how it is affected, and that which follows from the attribute only where and when the attribute is qualified or affected in some particular way—is, thus, one that Spinoza would be committed to drawing simply by a commitment to the attributes' manifesting internal diversity and change through their modes, regardless of his attitude toward the contingency or necessity of the series of those modes.

Still, it is one thing to say that Spinoza's use of the distinction need not be *motivated* by a belief in the plurality of possible series of finite modes, and another to say that his use of the distinction does not *require* such a plurality. Could Spinoza allow the actual series of finite modes to be necessary while denying that those finite modes follow from the "absolute" nature of the attributes? In order to answer this, we must first ask how, if at all, he could suppose the actual series of finite modes to be necessary.

How could the series of finite modes be the only possible one? To put the question more precisely, how could there be only *one* possible solution to the problem of how an attribute is to be diversely modified by an infinite series of finite modes? Of course, such necessarily pervasive and permanent features of the attribute as its laws of nature—contained or "inscribed" in the attribute or its infinite modes (*Treatise on the Emendation of the Intellect* 101)—will provide one kind of necessary constraint. Even so, however, the hypothesis that the actual total series of finite modes is the *only* one that is completely consistent with the laws of nature may seem too wildly optimistic for Spinoza to have accepted it.

To this it might be replied simply that: (i) these laws of nature may be highly complicated, and (ii) it also seems wildly optimistic to suppose that the actual set of laws of nature is the only completely consistent set, yet Spinoza evidently does accept *that* hypothesis. However, there is another, fuller response available; for, in addition to the general laws of nature, Spinoza can allow a further, crucial, necessary constraint on the series of finite modes. He holds that everything whatever exists unless prevented from doing so (EIp11d), that a substance's power to exist varies with its reality and perfection (EIp11s) and that everything expresses some degree or other of reality and perfection (EIp16d; reality and perfection are identified in EIIdef6). Furthermore, he evidently holds that "substance with less than the greatest possible number of attributes" is a contradiction, on the grounds that greater number of attributes is correlated with greater reality (by EIp9), so that the existence of God is necessary, while the existence of substances of fewer attributes is impossible.[9] It is therefore plausible that he would also regard "substance whose attributes express less than the greatest possible reality and perfection through their series of finite modes" as a contradiction, thus making the series of finite modes that expresses the highest degree of reality and perfection necessary, and all lesser series impossible. As Donagan has noted, this constraint is suggested by EIp33s1: "From the preceding it clearly follows that things have been produced by God with the highest perfection, since they have followed necessarily from a given most perfect nature."[10] (See also EIp16d itself.)

It now remains for us to consider whether a series of finite modes that is necessary in such a way would be compatible with Spinoza's claim that finite modes do not follow from the absolute nature of the attributes. For, after all, it might be objected, if there is only *one* possible solution to the problem of how to realize a series of finite modes for an attribute, then that series *must,* after all, follow (either immediately or mediately) from the absolute or unqualified nature of the attribute itself.

To this objection there are two alternative replies. First, if Spinoza accepts the requirement that the series of finite modes must express the highest degree of reality and perfection, then he could well maintain that the series of finite modes does *not* follow from the absolute nature of the attribute, but only from that nature *together with* this additional necessary constraint. This constraint, it might be argued, pertains to the nature of the attributes, but not to their *absolute nature,* as evidenced by the fact that the constraint requires *different* modifications at different places and times.

Second, however (and this reply is available whether he accepts the additional constraint or not), Spinoza nowhere denies that the whole *series* of finite modes follows from the absolute nature of the attributes. His claim is only that no *individual* finite mode follows from it. Indeed, if the total series of finite modes as a whole were *itself* an infinite mode—not an implausible suggestion, given its pervasive and permanent extent—then it would *necessarily* "follow from" the absolute nature of the attributes, by EIp23. In that case, the total infinite series of finite modes would be an infinite mode having finite modes as parts; but that is not unprecedented, since the human mind is a finite mode that is nevertheless a part of the infinite intellect of God, by EIIp11c. In fact, the total infinite series of finite modes might well turn out to be identical with the "whole of nature [as] one Individual, whose parts . . . vary in infinite ways, without any change [in] the whole Individual" that Spinoza describes in lemma 7s preceding EIIp14, and which he seems, in Letter 64, to identify as a mediate infinite mode. The crucial point, however, is that no finite mode would follow, *considered independent of its membership in this series,* from the nature of an attribute. For, if the mode followed *independently,* it would have to be necessarily pervasive and permanent throughout the attribute, i.e., it would have to be an infinite mode. Instead, each finite mode would follow from the nature of an attribute, but *only in virtue of its member-*

ship as part of the one consistently constructible or maximally perfect series of finite modes. As a result, it would follow from an attribute *only insofar as the attribute is considered to be affected by particular modes*—just as EIp28d asserts.[11] Hence, the failure of individual finite modes to follow from the nature of an attribute "considered absolutely," is, on the proposed interpretation, compatible with there being only one possible total series of such modes.

2. *Essence and necessary existence.* EIIax1 reads: "The essence of man does not involve necessary existence."[12] At first glance, this axiom may suggest that the existence of particular men is not necessary, and hence must be contingent. Yet EIp29 asserts that "In nature there is nothing contingent," and EIp33s1 asserts that "A thing is called contingent only because of a defect of our knowledge." Is this not a contradiction?

We may begin by noting that the axiom does not claim that the *existence* of particular men is not necessary; it claims, rather, that necessary existence is not "involved" *in the essence* of men. It is thus simply a particular instance of the distinction drawn at EIp33s1:

> A thing is called necessary either by reason of its essence or by reason of its cause. For a thing's existence follows necessarily either from its essence and definition or from a given efficient cause. And a thing is also called impossible from these same causes—viz. either because its essence, *or* definition, involves a contradiction, or because there is no external cause which has been determined to produce such a thing.
>
> But a thing is called contingent only because of a defect of our knowledge. For if we do not know that the thing's essence involves a contradiction, or if we do know very well that its essence does not involve a contradiction, and nevertheless can affirm nothing certainly about its existence, because the order of causes is hidden from us, it can never seem to us either necessary or impossible. So we call it contingent or possible.[13]

This distinction is often interpreted as one between two degrees of necessity: real logical or metaphysical necessity, on the one hand, and mere causal inevitability in virtue of antecedent conditions, on the other. The "contingency" that Spinoza contrasts with both would amount, on this interpretation, simply to chance, or an absence of inevitability; and his denials of such contingency would therefore be simply assertions of determinism rather than of necessitarianism.

It must be emphasized, however, that Spinoza does not present the distinction as one between two *degrees* of necessity, but rather as one between two *sources* of necessity: a thing's own essence, and a cause other than the thing itself. And, once again, this is a distinction that Spinoza would have to draw, given his commitment to the internal diversification of the attributes through a series of finite modes, whether he were a necessitarian or not. For the essence of an actually existing finite mode cannot contain a contradiction; if it did, it would be like a square circle, incapable of existing at all. On the other hand, the finite mode's own essence cannot "involve," or be the sufficient source of, its existence; for then it would require no external cause for its existence and could not be prevented, through the absence of such a cause, from existing pervasively and permanently (see EIIp11d). Hence, the individual members of a series of finite modes must have essences that, taken by themselves, do not necessitate the thing's existence *without regard* to external circumstances; rather, their essences must be capable of being instantiated under appropriate conditions (i.e., affections of the attribute), as part of a series of finite modes. (One might say that it pertains to their essence not to exist *simpliciter,* but rather to exist given the presence of a particular efficient cause.)

If the cause of such a finite mode is itself inevitable but only contingent, then the resulting finite mode will be inevitable but contingent. If, on the other hand, the series of causes that determines the finite thing to exist and to act at a particular time and place is itself the only possible series, then the existence of the finite mode at that time and place will itself be completely necessary, even though the necessity of its limited durational existence is derived from its place in the only possible series, rather than from its own essence considered in isolation. It might of course be argued that if the series of finite modes is completely necessary, then the limited durational existence of a finite mode must after all "follow from," and hence be "involved in" the thing's own essence; but this conclusion is warranted only if we accept the theorem that whatever is necessary "follows from" everything whatever; and this is a theorem that, as we have already seen, Spinoza can and must reject.

3. *Essential properties.* Throughout the *Ethics,* Spinoza appears to employ a distinction between the characteristics of a thing that are essential and those that are not essential. It may be argued, however, that if every actual state of affairs is necessary, then every characteristic of a thing must be essential to it, so that Spinoza's use of the distinction is incompatible with necessitarianism. As Bennett expresses it:

> The strongest pressure on Spinoza to allow that at least some propositions are contingent comes simply from its being hard to do good philosophy while staying faithful to the thesis that this is the only possible world. . . . For example, his uses of the concept of a thing's *essence,* meaning those of its properties which it could not possibly lack, are flattened into

either falsehood or vacuous truth if there are no contingent truths; because then every property of every thing is essential to it.[14]

Bennett offers EIp5d and EIIIp6d as examples of arguments that are said to rely crucially on an essential/inessential distinction, and hence on the existence of contingent truths.

a. *Essence, property and accident.* In assessing this line of argument, we must distinguish between two senses of "essence." In the first sense—due ultimately to Aristotle's *Posterior Analytics,* and common particularly in scholastic philosophy—the essence of a thing consists of the characteristics in virtue of which it is the thing that it is, and which, therefore, the thing must always have. This essence is distinguished both from the thing's properties and from its accidents. The properties are characteristics that do not belong to the essence but follow from and are deducible from it; for this reason, a thing must always have all of its properties. The converse, however, does not hold: the essence is not properly deducible from the properties.[15] Accidents, in contrast, are characteristics that do not follow from the essence of the thing at all, and which the thing may therefore either acquire or lose without affecting its identity; their source is thus at least partly outside the essence of the thing. In the *second* sense of "essence"—historically derivative from the first, and common particularly in contemporary modal logic—a characteristic is said to be essential, or to be part of a thing's essence, if it is a characteristic that the thing has in every possible world in which the thing exists at all. For lack of better terms, I will speak of essences of the first kind as "scholastic" essences, and essences of the second kind as "logical" essences.

It is clear that Spinoza uses "essence" and related locutions to denote scholastic essences. At TIE 95, for example, he insists that a perfect definition "will have to explain the inmost essence of the thing, and to take care not to use certain properties [*propria*] in its place"; and at TIE 96, in discussing the conditions for a good definition of a created thing, he stipulates that we require "a concept, *or* definition, of the thing such that when it is considered alone, without any others conjoined, all the thing's properties can be deduced from it." The same distinction between essence and properties is clearly evident in the *Ethics* at EIIp40s2, where Spinoza contrasts knowledge of the second kind, which depends on "adequate ideas of the properties of things," with knowledge of the third kind, which "proceeds from an adequate idea of the formal essence of certain attributes of God to the adequate knowledge of the . . . essence of things." Other particularly explicit invocations of the essence/property distinction occur at EIp16d, and at EIIIdef.aff.VIexp and XXIIexp.[16]

The essence/property distinction, as Spinoza draws it, does not require that a property belong to its bearer only contingently; on the contrary, it *must* belong to it necessarily, since all properties are deducible from the essence alone. Consider Spinoza's own example:

> If a circle, for example, is defined as a figure in which the lines drawn from the center to the circumference are equal, no one fails to see that such a definition does not at all explain the essence of the circle, but only a property of it. (TIE 95)

Spinoza is certainly well aware that this property, though not the essence of the circle, is a necessary rather than a contingent feature of it.

Spinoza also clearly allows that things have characteristics that are neither part of the thing's essence nor properties of it, characteristics that do not follow from the essence of the thing alone, and in that sense correspond to the "accidents" of the traditional distinction. Among the most important examples of such characteristics, for Spinoza's purposes, are human passions. But the fact that such characteristics do not follow solely from the essence of their bearer requires only that their source be at least partly outside the bearer; it does *not* require that there be a possible world in which the bearer would *not* have been caused to have them. Hence, neither Spinoza's own distinction between essence and properties, nor the distinction between these and characteristics that are imposed from outside, commits him to a denial of necessitarianism.

b. *Essence in EIp5d.* Spinoza's own uses of the term "essence" are most naturally understood in the scholastic sense, a sense in which the existence of "inessential" characteristics is compatible with necessitarianism. Still, it may be objected, Spinoza might nonetheless *rely* on the supposition that some things have some of their characteristics only contingently, without using the *term* "essence" in connection with it. And, in fact, in neither of the two arguments Bennett cites as examples—EIp5d and EIIIp6d—does the term "essence" occur. Thus, we must still investigate whether these arguments commit Spinoza to the existence of *logically* inessential properties, under whatever name, and hence to a denial of necessitarianism.

EIp5 and its demonstration read as follows:

P5: In nature there cannot be two or more substances of the same nature *or* attribute.

Dem.: If there were two or more distinct substances, they would have to be distinguished from one another either by a difference in their attributes, or by a difference in their affections (by P4). If only by a difference in their attributes, then it will be conceded that there is only one of the same attribute. But if by a difference of their affections, then since a substance is prior in nature to its affections (by P1), if the affections are put to one side and [the substance] is considered by itself, i.e. (by D3 and A6), considered truly, one cannot be conceived to be distinguished from another, i.e. (by P4), there cannot be many, but only one [of the same nature *or* attribute], q.e.d.

One of the main problems in understanding this demonstration is to understand why EIp1 ("A substance is prior in nature to its affections") entitles us to put "the affections . . . to one side." Bennett's suggestion is that:

If we take this [IP1] to entail that any state of a substance is accidental to it, i.e., that a substance could have lacked any of its actual [affections], then we get the following argument. Distinct substances must be unalike in respect of some properties which they cannot lose; for if they were unalike only in respect of their accidental properties they could become perfectly alike, and so, by the identity of indiscernibles, become identical. It is obviously intolerable to suppose that two substances could have been—or could become—one. So between any two substances there must be an unlikeness in respect of nonaccidental features, i.e., of attributes.[17]

Ingenious as this proposed interpretation is, it is nevertheless subject to a number of serious objections. First, as Bennett emphasizes, it would be a logical fallacy for Spinoza to argue from "*x* and *y* are unalike only in respect of their accidental properties" to "*x* and *y* could become exactly alike." Second, it would be a further logical fallacy for Spinoza to move from "*x* and *y could have been* exactly alike" to "*x* and *y could become* exactly alike." Third, although Spinoza would indeed reject the claim that two substances could have been or could become one, he is not yet in a position to reject such a claim at EIp5. Indeed, the clearest grounds on which Spinoza could reject it would be EIp14 and EIp14c1, which assert that God is necessarily the only substance; but EIp14 is derived in part from EIp5, and so could hardly serve as a justification for it. Fourth, the kind of priority at issue in EIp1 must be a kind of priority derivable from the premises of EIp1. These premises are simply EIdef3 and EIde5, the definitions of "substance" and "mode," which mention only the priority of "being in" and "being conceived through." These kinds of priorities may well be related to the *scholastic* inessentiality to substance of its modes, but the definitions do not imply that modes must be *logically* inessential, as the proposed interpretation requires. Finally, and perhaps most decisively, the proposed interpretation requires that Spinoza identify the distinction between a substance's attributes and its affections or modes—as employed at EIdef1—with the distinction between its logically essential and logically inessential characteristics; but this Spinoza could not and would not do, regardless of his attitude toward necessitarianism, since the infinite modes are, by EIp21, logically (although not scholastically) essential to God.[18]

For these reasons, it is unlikely that the proposed interpretation of EIp5d is correct. The interpretation could be rejected with greater certainty, of course, if we had a more satisfactory interpretation to offer in its place. I will outline such an interpretation—one that depends on a necessitarian reading of Spinoza—in the final section of this paper. But the objections just considered are sufficient for us to conclude that he need not be construed as a necessitarian on the basis of EIp5d.

c. *Essence in EIIIp6d.* EIIIp6 states that, "Each thing, as far as it can by its own power, strives to persevere in its being." The demonstration appeals, in part, to the claim that "no thing has anything in itself by which it can be destroyed, *or* which takes its existence away (by P4)"; or, as Bennett expresses it, that "nothing can, unaided, cause its own destruction." Bennett then asserts that "if all a thing's properties are essential to it, then this argument ought to conclude that nothing can, unaided, cause any change in itself." His line of thought, presumably, is this: a logically essential characteristic of a thing is one that it has in all possible worlds in which the thing exists at all; necessitarianism requires that all characteristics of things be logically essential to them; hence, necessitarianism requires that if a thing lost one of its characteristics, it would cease to be that thing, so that all change would be destruction.

We must distinguish, however, characteristics whose permanent possession is logically essential from characteristics whose temporary possession is logically essential. Spinoza certainly recognizes some characteristics of the first kind, such as each individual's "fixed proportion of motion and rest." Necessitarianism, however, by no means requires that every characteristic be of this first kind; it requires only that, whenever a thing has some characteristic for a temporary part of its duration in one possible world, it must have that characteristic for that *same* temporary part of its duration in every possible world. To put the point in another way, necessitarianism does not require that nothing undergo change, but only that the series of a thing's actual changes constitute its only possible biography. For Spinoza, this would indeed be the case if the actual infinite series of finite modes was the only possible series. Necessitarianism is therefore compatible with EIIIp6d.

Thus far, I have argued that Spinoza is not committed to the denial of necessitarianism by (1) his claim that finite modes do not follow from the absolute nature of the attributes, by (2) his distinction between things whose essences include necessary existence and those whose essences do not, or by (3) his explicit or implicit use of an essential/inessential distinction. I have not yet argued that he is committed to necessitarianism. It is to this thesis that I now turn.

II

There are three chief textual grounds for the conclusion that Spinoza is committed to necessitarianism in *Ethics* I: EIp16, which claims that "infinitely many things in infinitely many modes" follow from the necessity of the divine nature; EIp29, which denies any contingency in nature; and EIp33, which claims that "Things could have been produced by God in no other way, and in no other order" than that in which they have been produced. I will consider these three grounds in order. In the course of considering EIp16, I will argue that, independently of these three propositions, Spinoza is also committed to the denial of other possible series of finite modes by the doctrines of *Ethics* II.

1. *EIp16: The divine nature and the infinite intellect.* EIp16 and its demonstration read as follows:

> P16: From the necessity of the divine nature there must follow infinitely many things in infinitely many modes (i.e., everything which can fall under an infinite intellect).
>
> Dem.: This Proposition must be plain to anyone, provided he attends to the fact that the intellect infers from the given definition of any thing a number of properties that really do follow necessarily from it (i.e., from the very essence of the thing); and that it infers more properties the more the definition of the thing expresses reality, i.e., the more reality the essence of the defined thing involves. But since the divine nature has absolutely infinite attributes (by D6), each of which also expresses an essence infinite in its own kind, from its necessity there must follow infinitely many things in infinite modes (i.e., everything which can fall under an infinite intellect), q.e.d.

Bennett outlines two different ways in which this proposition appears to commit Spinoza to necessitarianism: the first concerns the relation between the actual and the necessary, while the second concerns the relation between the possible and actual. I will argue that Spinoza is committed to necessitarianism in both ways.[19]

a. *Necessity and actuality.* Spinoza is committed to each of the following claims:

1. Everything that falls under an infinite intellect follows from the necessity of the divine nature.
2. "The necessity of the divine nature" is something necessary.
3. Whatever follows from something that is necessary, is itself necessary.
4. Everything that is actual falls under an infinite intellect.

(1) is simply a paraphrase of EIp16 itself. Spinoza's commitment to (2) is evidenced not only in his reference to the "necessity" of the divine nature, but in the demonstration of EIp16 itself. For the demonstration argues as follows: (i) from the definition or essence of a thing, properties necessarily follow; (ii) the greater the reality contained in the essence, the more properties will follow in this way; (iii) God's essence is utterly infinite (by EIdef6); and, hence, (iv) from God's essence, infinitely many things must follow. The demonstration thus takes the "divine nature" to be equivalent to God's essence, which, by EIp20c1, is an eternal and, hence, necessary, truth.

(3) is an evident consequence of the character of the "following from" relation as a necessitating logical and causal relation, as is apparent from its use in EIp21–28. It might be suggested, however, that we could reject the application of (3) in this context on the following basis: Even if the series of finite modes were contingent, each finite mode could still be said to follow at least *partially* from the nature of the attribute. For finite modes follow from other finite modes *by means of* the laws of nature governing them. And these laws, at least—laws contained in the attribute or its infinite modes—do follow from the absolute nature of the attribute, whether there could have been a different total series of finite modes or not. Hence (1)—the claim that everything falling under an infinite intellect follows from the divine nature—can be construed as claiming only that such things follow *at least partially* from the divine nature. But it is not true that whatever follows *partially* from something necessary must be itself necessary; hence (3) ought not be interpreted as applicable to (1). (A similar line of argument has been suggested to reconcile EIp16 with EIp21 and EIp28d; see note 7.)

This argument, however, is subject to two serious objections. First, it requires Spinoza to trade tacitly (and equivocally, given EIp21 and EIp28d) on the very distinction between an adequate cause and a partial cause that he draws quite clearly at the outset of *Ethics* III, one that he could easily have drawn in *Ethics* I had he thought it would be useful. Second, the demonstration of EIp16 makes it clear that the relation between the divine nature and the infinitely many things said to follow from it is to be understood as the relation between a scholastic essence and its properties (in effect, the demonstration claims that infinitely many things are "properties" of God); yet, as we have already seen from TIE 96, the properties of a thing are all deducible from the essence of the thing *alone*.

Finally, Spinoza's commitment to (4) is evident from the definition of "infinite" at EIdef2. For EIp16 equates "what falls under an infinite intellect" with "infinitely many things"; and, by definition, a collection of things cannot be infinite if it leaves any thing of the same kind outside itself. Moreover, numerous later passages (EIp17s, EIp26d, EIp33d, EIp33s) confirm that the "infinitely many things" that follow from the divine nature comprise "all" things, or everything. (4) is also independently required by Spinoza's commitment to the parallelism of the attributes—i.e., that "the order and connection of ideas is the same as the order and connection of things" (EIIp7; EIIp7c in effect draws (4) as a consequence). But from (1–4) we can infer:

5. Everything that is actual is necessary.

(5) is equivalent to necessitarianism.

b. *Actuality and Possibility.* As Bennett observes,[20] Spinoza also appears to be committed to the following two claims:

6. Everything that falls under the infinite intellect is actual.
7. Everything that is possible falls under the infinite intellect.

(6) is directly entailed by EIp16 itself, since EIp16 states that whatever falls under an infinite intellect actually follows from the divine nature. It is also confirmed in EIp30, which states that, "an actual intellect, whether finite or infinite, must comprehend God's attributes and God's affections, and nothing else"; and it is confirmed again in EIp33s. Moreover, it is required by the parallelism of the attributes (EIIp7): for if the infinite intellect contained an idea of a non-actual thing, it would be an idea without a corresponding object.[21]

Regarding (7), Bennett says only that "Spinoza sometimes uses the notion of an 'infinite' or unlimited intellect to express the notion of what is possible."[22] I have been unable to confirm this by a definitive passage, but it might be regarded as evident simply from the definition of "infinite" (EIdef2), on the grounds that the failure to conceive something that is genuinely possible constitutes a limitation. This interpretation of the definition would be strengthened by Spinoza's apparent willingness to construe "infinite attributes" in the definition of "God" (EIdef6) as meaning "all possible attributes." But, from (6) and (7) we can infer:

8. Everything that is possible is actual.

(8) is also equivalent to necessitarianism.

c. *Parallelism and causal independence.* Even if we set aside EIp16 and EIdef2, however, Spinoza is still ultimately committed to (6) and (7) by doctrines he advances in *Ethics* II. We have already noted that he is committed to (6) by the parallelism of the attributes (EIIp7); I will now argue that *Ethics* II commits him to (7) as well.

Since there is in God an idea of every actual thing (EIIp7c), and since there could have been no substances, attributes, or infinite modes other than the actual ones, the question of how the infinite intellect could lack the idea of something genuinely possible may be reduced to that of how God could fail to have an idea of a possible but non-existent finite mode—i.e., of a finite mode that exists in some possible world, but not in the actual one. As we have already seen from EIp28, if there are to be genuinely possible but non-existent modes, they must belong to a total causal series of finite modes that is itself possible but not actual. But if there are such possible series of modes, what could prevent the occurrence of a corresponding series of *ideas* of those modes in the infinite intellect? There are only three alternatives: (i) the cause is to be found in the attribute of Thought itself; (ii) the cause is to be found in the non-existence of the objects of the ideas; or (iii) there is no cause, but the non-existence of the series of ideas is a brute contingent fact.

None of these alternatives, however, can be acceptable to Spinoza. If the non-existent series of finite modes is indeed a genuinely possible series, then the series of ideas of those finite modes must be a genuinely possible series of finite modes of thought; and hence we cannot say that the idea is prevented from existing by the attribute of Thought itself. Yet, to say that the series of ideas is prevented from existing by the non-existence of their objects would be to contradict EIIp5:

> The formal being of ideas admits God as a cause only insofar as he is considered as a thinking thing, and not insofar as he is explained by any

other attribute; i.e., ideas, both of God's attributes and of singular things, admit not the objects themselves, *or* the things perceived, as their efficient cause, but God himself, insofar as he is a thinking thing.

The remaining alternative is to say that, just as the series of finite modes itself could have existed but as a brute contingent fact did not, so the series of finite ideas of those objects could have existed but as a matter of brute contingent fact did not. But this too is unacceptable. For, if the existence or non-existence of a particular series of finite modes is an independent matter of chance within each attribute, then it will be only a matter of chance whether the series of finite modes from different attributes happen to correspond with one another. Moreover, we will never be in a position to know whether or not they *do* correspond. For example, from the existence of one's own mind, which is part of a series of finite modes in the attribute of Thought, one would not be able to determine whether the series of finite modes that includes one's own body has or has not been realized in Extension. EIIp7 (which asserts the parallelism of the attributes) and EIax4 (from which EIIp7 is derived) would then be, if not false, at least contingent, uncertain and unknowable. Hence, the infinite intellect must contain an idea of every possible thing, since the idea of any possible thing could be excluded from it only by violating either the causal independence or the necessary parallelism of the attributes. But the claim that the infinite intellect contains an idea of every possible thing is (7); and together with (6)'s requirement that every idea in the infinite intellect have an actual object, it entails (8), the doctrine that everything possible is actual—i.e., necessitarianism.

We may also put this same line of argument in somewhat more popular theological terms. If God is to know everything that is the case without error, his set of ideas about what series of finite modes is actual in each attribute must correspond precisely to the actual series of finite modes in that attribute, without positing any *other,* non-existent, finite modes as actual. But this perfect correspondence between things and ideas can be assured—and hence a source of knowledge—in only two ways: either (i) God's ideas are *caused or explained* by the actuality of the series of things itself, or (ii) there is for each attribute only one *possible* total series of finite modes, and one corresponding *possible* series of ideas of finite modes. Since Spinoza rejects the former alternative, he must accept the latter.

2. *EIp29: Necessity and contingency.* EIp29 states:

> In nature there is nothing contingent, but all things have been determined from the necessity of the divine nature to exist and . . . produce an effect in a certain way.

EIp29 differs from EIp16 in only three respects: (1) its explicit use of the term "contingency," (2) its reference to "all things" as opposed to "infinitely many things," and (3) its explicit application both to the existence of things and to their actions. The demonstration justifies this greater explicitness on the basis of the more specific developments of EIp21–28. The heart of the demonstration, however, is the claim (EIp16) that infinitely many things follow in infinitely many ways "from the necessity of the divine nature." If, as I have argued, the necessity of EIp16 must be construed as logical or metaphysical necessity, and not as mere "inevitability in light of antecedent conditions," then the denial of contingency in EIp29, which is derived from and paraphrased in terms of that proposition, must be understood in the same sense.

3. *EIp33: The order of nature.* EIp33 and its demonstration read as follows:

> P33: Things could have been produced by God in no other way, and in no other order than they have been produced.
>   Dem.: For all things have necessarily followed from God's given nature (by P16), and have been determined from the necessity of God's nature to exist and produce an effect in a certain way (by P29). Therefore, if things could have been of another nature, or could have been determined to produce an effect in another way, so that the order of Nature was different, then God's nature could also have been other than it is now, and therefore (by P11) that [other nature] would also have had to exist, and consequently, there could have been two or more Gods, which is absurd (by P14C1). So things could have been produced in no other way and no other order, etc., q.e.d.

The crucial question in the interpretation of this proposition is this: how are we to understand "in no other way, and in no other order?" If this expression refers only to the attributes, the infinite modes, and their laws—which in a sense determine the "way" and "order" in which finite modes follow from one another—then the proposition is compatible with a plurality of different possible series of finite modes. If, on the other hand, this "way" or this "order" includes the finite modes as well, then the proposition will deny the possibility of even finite modes other than the actual ones.

As the demonstration makes clear, the "order" in question is the "order of Nature" *(naturae ordo)*. Of Spinoza's many uses of this term, in the *Ethics* and elsewhere, nearly all at least suggest that the order of nature includes particular finite modes as parts, and several imply it more directly. For example, in the *Treatise on the Emendation of the Intellect,* he proposes that we should "attend to the order of Nature"

(TIE 65), as the chief remedy against the formation of imaginative "fictions" concerning the existence of particular durational things—advice that would presumably be useless if such particular things were not to be found as parts of that order. EIp11d asserts that

> the reason why a circle or triangle exists, or why it does not exist, does not follow from the nature of these things, but from the order of the whole of corporeal Nature. For from this [order] it must follow either that the triangle necessarily exists now or that it is impossible for it to exist now.

Perhaps most directly of all, EIIp24d speaks of the relation between a part of the human body and "a singular thing [i.e., a finite mode or a concerted association of them, by EIIdef7] which is prior, in the order of nature, to the part itself." Spinoza also consistently uses such related terms as "common order of nature" *(communis ordo naturae)* and "order of causes" *(ordo causarum)* to include the finite modes.[23] Moreover, as Bennett points out,[24] Spinoza characterizes his position in EIp33d and EIp33s2 as a denial that "things could have been of another nature," that God could "decree anything different," that God could have "willed and decreed something different concerning nature," and that "things could have been produced otherwise than they are now." Taken together with the demonstration's reliance on EIp16 and EIp29, these facts strongly suggest that EIp33 is intended to rule out not merely any alternative possible attributes and infinite modes, but any alternative possible series of finite modes as well.

In this section, I have argued that Spinoza is committed to necessitarianism by three propositions in *Ethics* I: EIp16, 29, 33. I have also argued that he is independently committed to that claim by the conjunction of two doctrines expressed in *Ethics* II: the causal and explanatory independence of the attributes (EIIp5), and the necessary parallelism of the attributes (EIIp7).

III

Thus far, I have argued that Spinoza is not committed to the denial of necessitarianism, and that he is committed to its truth. But, does the question of necessitarianism have any bearing on our interpretation of the rest of his philosophy? I believe that it does, with respect to at least two topics: his monism, and his view of the relation between the internal adequacy of an idea and its external correspondence to its object.

We are now in a position to explore briefly the bearing of necessitarianism on these topics.

1. *Monism and the sharing of attributes.* Spinoza's monism is stated in EIp14: "Except God, no substance can be or be conceived." The formal demonstration is straightforward: (i) God is by definition a being "of whom no attribute which expresses an essence of substance can be denied" (by EIdef6), and (ii) "he [God] necessarily exists" (by EIp11); but (iii) two substances cannot share an attribute (by EIp5); hence (iv) God is the only substance.

The demonstration of EIp14 relies, however, on EIp5; and the demonstration of the latter proposition has puzzled commentators. As we have seen, EIp5d begins by asserting (i) that two or more distinct substances would have to be distinguished either by a difference of *attributes* or a difference of *modes* ("affections"). Spinoza then argues (ii) that a difference of attributes would entail that there was only one substance *of the same* attribute; and he infers from EIp1—that is, "A substance is prior in nature to its affections"—(iii) that we may set the modes "to one side." He then concludes (iv) that there cannot be two substances with the same attribute. Perhaps the most puzzling feature of the argument is its claim that we are entitled by EIp1 to put the affections or modes of substance "to one side" in the attempt to distinguish two substances of the same attribute. Few commentators have agreed that Spinoza is entitled to do so. The fullest attempt to explain his grounds for so doing is that of Bennett, discussed above, according to which Spinoza's argument commits him to a plurality of possible worlds. Bennett himself rightly characterizes as "fallacious" the argument he is forced to ascribe to Spinoza; and I have argued that it is subject to a number of additional difficulties as well.

If, however, we interpret Spinoza as a necessitarian, then we find that he does have grounds for putting the modes "to one side" that are both comprehensible and sound. If all modes follow from attributes in such a way that no attribute could possibly have given rise to a *different* set of modes, then we will indeed be *entitled* to set the modes to one side in our attempt to distinguish two different substances with the same attribute; for any difference in modes will necessarily be *due* to some difference of attributes, and hence the second alternative for distinguishing two substances (difference of modes) will reduce to the first (difference of attributes).

Spinoza's necessitarianism is of course not yet articulated at this point in the *Ethics.* But it does not need to be for the purposes of EIp5. He needs only the claim of EIdef 3 and EIdef5, that modes must be conceived through substance, together with the equation of "substance" with "attributes" that EIp4d makes for this context. From a strong reading of this claim of priority, expressed in EIp1, he can infer that any *difference* of modes must be conceived through a *difference* of attributes. He need not appeal to the more explicit claim that modes are conceived through their attributes *because* they are causally necessitated by them—although this more explicit claim is arguably already available from the claim (in EIax4) that effects should be conceived through their causes, together with the description (in EIax3) of the causal relation as necessitating.

The question of how Spinoza reduces differences of mode to difference of attribute is by no means the only question that can be raised about the argument for EIp5.[25] But, if we construe the dependence of modes on attributes in the strict way dictated by a necessitarian interpretation of Spinoza, then we have a much more natural and persuasive basis for one crucial step of the demonstration of EIp5, and hence for one crucial step in his argument for monism.

2. Internal adequacy and correspondence. EIIdef4 states that:

> By adequate idea I understand an idea which, insofar as it is considered in itself, without relation to an object, has all the properties, *or* intrinsic denominations of a true idea.

In the *Meditations,* Descartes devotes a great deal of effort to arguing that a certain internal characteristic of an idea—namely, its clarity and distinctness—is and should be treated as a reliable criterion of the idea's agreement with or correspondence to that which it represents. In striking contrast, Spinoza seems at EIIdef4 simply to take it for granted that there is a certain internal characteristic belonging to all and only ideas that are true—i.e., ideas that, by EIax6, agree with their objects. Similarly, in the TIE he asserts without argument that truth involves both an "internal" and an "external" denomination (TIE 69). How could Spinoza simply *presuppose* a correlation between an internal characteristic of ideas and their external correspondence to their objects, particularly when Descartes had tried so carefully and elaborately to establish such a correlation?

If there are genuinely possible but non-actual series of finite modes, then it is difficult to see how any *intrinsic* characteristic could reliably distinguish a "true" idea affirming the existence of a really existing finite mode from a "false" idea affirming te existence of a non-existent but equally possible mode. Furthermore, as we saw in our earlier discussion of the infinite intellect, there could be no guarantee that such false ideas would not exist, given the requirement of the explanatory independence of the attributes in EIIp5. Hence, if Spinoza regards the series of finite modes as contingent, his assumption that there is an internal characteristic of ideas possessed only by those that correspond truly to their objects would be unwarranted.

If, however, we interpret Spinoza as holding that the attributes necessitate a unique series of modes, so that no other series is possible, then he will have a comprehensible and sound justification for his assumption. Necessitarianism entails that nothing is logically or metaphysically possible except what is actual. Hence, if an idea possesses enough internal consistency or "adequacy" to show that what it represents is a genuine *possibility,* it will thereby also show it to be *actual.* Of course, in Spinoza's view no idea affirming the existence of a finite mode actually possesses this degree of adequacy, *as the idea exists in any human mind,* since this adequacy requires a knowledge of all of the finite mode's causes (EIIp24–27). However, he also requires that ideas affirming the existence of particular finite modes *must* be "adequate" *in God* (EIIp9, EIIp32); and this internal adequacy could not guarantee the idea's correspondence with actually existing modes unless those modes were the only ones genuinely possible.

Conclusion

I have argued that Spinoza is not committed to the denial of necessitarianism by any of the three textual grounds on which he has been taken to be so committed. I have argued that he is committed to necessitarianism by three propositions of *Ethics* I, and, on independent grounds, by the doctrine of attributes contained in *Ethics* II. Finally, I have argued that if he is interpreted as a necessitarian, then both his monism and his view that internal "adequacy" is correlated with external correspondence can be given a sounder basis in his philosophy than they can be given otherwise. Taken together, these results make a strong case for the claim that Spinoza is a necessitarian. They also suggest that his doctrine of necessity is, indeed, a "principal basis" of at least some of the central doctrines of the *Ethics.*

Notes

1. Stuart Hampshire, *Spinoza* (New York: Penguin, 1951), p. 54; Edwin Curley, *Spinoza's Metaphysics* (Cambridge, Mass.: Harvard University Press, 1969), especially pp. 106–109; Wallace Matson, "Steps Towards Spinozism," *Revue Internationale de Philosophie* 31 (1979): 76–83; Charles Jarrett, "The

Logical Structure of Spinoza's *Ethics,* Part I," *Synthese* 37 (1978): 55–56; Jonathan Bennett, *A Study of Spinoza's* Ethics (Indianapolis: Hackett, 1984), 111–124; R. J. Delahunty, *Spinoza* (London: Routledge and Kegan Paul, 1985), pp. 155–165. Although I am in general agreement with Hampshire's characterization of Spinoza's position, I find his one-line justification of it, in terms of the co-extensivity of *Natura naturans* and *Natura naturata,* to be too brief and general to be helpful. I am inclined to classify J. I. Friedman with Curley, as one who interprets Spinoza as a non-necessitarian, on the basis of his "Spinoza's Denial of Free Will in Man and God," in *Spinoza's Philosophy of Man,* ed. Jon Wetlesen (Oslo: Universitetsforlaget, 1978), pp. 58–63; I do not do so because I am sufficiently confident that I know what he means by the locution "causally but not logically necessary" in the context of the paper. It should be noted that only Delahunty actually uses the term "necessitarianism," and that he uses it in a somewhat broader sense than I have given it here.

2. In the course of *Ethics* I, he asserts that God necessarily exists (EIp11), and that there could exist no other substance but God (EIp14). He defines God as the substance of infinite (unlimited or all possible) attributes (EIdef6), which, given God's existence, entails that there could have been no attributes other than those actually possessed by God; and he asserts that all of God's attributes are eternal (EIp19), which, by the definition of "eternity" (EIdef8), entails their necessary existence. He affirms that whatever things follow from the absolute nature of any of God's attributes have always had to exist and be infinite, and are eternal through that attribute (EIp21), and that every infinite mode must so follow, either immediately or mediately, from the absolute nature of some attribute of God (EIp23d). Assuming that no attribute could have had a different "absolute nature" from the one it actually has, and that nothing could have followed from such an absolute nature except what actually does follow from it, we may conclude not only that every infinite mode exists necessarily, but also that there could not have been any infinite modes other than the actual ones. Furthermore, Spinoza holds that nothing exists except substance and modes (EIp6c, EIp15d and EIp28d), and does so on cited grounds (EId3, EId5, and EIax1) that presumably render this restriction a necessary truth for him as well.

3. Of these two ways, only Bennett describes the first. The second is to be found in Curley, Matson, Jarrett, and Bennett (cited in n. 1).

4. Entailment is, of course, primarily a relation between states of affairs or propositions, whereas for Spinoza the "following from" relation is primarily between things. I shall not insist on the distinction here, however, and will instead speak indifferently of a mode, its existence, and the proposition that it exists. For present purposes, nothing turns on the distinction.

5. This is clear from the fact that a claim about "production" is inferred directly from a claim about "following from." It is also especially evident in the derivations of EIp16c1–3, each of which infers a claim about the character of God's causality directly from EIp16's claim that infinitely many things "follow from" the necessity of the divine nature.

6. This is presumably a condition that could not be formalized. For a dis-

cussion of formalizable relevance logics, see Alan Ross Anderson and Nuel Belnap, *Entailment: The Logic of Relevance and Necessity* (Princeton: Princeton University Press, 1975). As we shall soon see, Spinoza also holds that, in some cases, a y can "follow from" some x "insofar as" x is "considered in" one way, but not "insofar as" x is "considered in" another way. This is a related respect in which his "follows from" relation differs from, and is less formalizable than, other entailment relations.

7. One might seek, as Jarrett suggests, to reconcile this contradiction by interpreting Spinoza as employing his own later distinction between adequate and partial causation at this point, so that EIp21 and EIp28d refer to following *adequately*, while the other passages refer to following *partially* (p. 55). I discuss this interpretation and my reasons for rejecting it below, in section II.

8. Note that these two ways of following from the attribute need not be mutually exclusive; the demonstration implies that mediate infinite modes follow in *both* ways, although immediate infinite modes follow only in the former, and finite modes follow in only the latter.

9. For an examination of the role of this principle in explaining why God is the only possible substance, see my "Spinoza's 'Ontological' Argument," *The Philosophical Review* 88 (1979): 198–223.

10. Alan Donagan, "Spinoza's Proof of Immortality," in *Spinoza: A Collection of Critical Essays,* ed. Marjorie Grene (New York: Doubleday, 1973), p. 249. This constraint would also explain why the attributes must express themselves through finite modes at all. To the question of why there are any finite modes, Spinoza could reply as he does to the question of why God has created men who are not governed by reason: "because the laws of his nature have been so ample that they sufficed for producing all things which can be conceived by an infinite intellect" (EIapp; Curley, p. 446).

11. Of course, the absolute nature of the attribute would "entail" the existence of each individual finite mode, in the sense that there would be no possible world in which the attribute had that absolute nature and yet the finite mode did not exist; but, as we have already seen, Spinoza requires more than this of the "following from" relation. In his view, a finite mode can be said to "follow from" an attribute "considered" in one way, but fail to "follow from" it when it is considered in another, more restricted, way—a distinction that makes good sense when taken as expressing a finite mode's dependence for existence on its membership in the only constructible or maximally perfect infinite series of such modes, but a distinction for which the modern entailment relation simply makes no allowance.

12. Spinoza's own gloss of this axiom continues: "i.e., from the order of nature it can happen equally that this or that man does exist, or that he does not exist." I discuss the interpretation of this gloss below, in n. 21. If what I argue in this section is correct, then it will be evident that both of the plausible interpretations of the gloss are compatible with necessitarianism.

13. For similar distinctions, see also TIE 53 and *Metaphysical Thoughts* I:3. Reference to EIax2, EIp33s1, or both figure in Curley, Bennett, and Friedman.

14. Only Bennett offers this argument (p. 114). As the quoted passage sug-

gests, however, it constitutes his chief grounds for regarding Spinoza as committed to a denial of necessitarianism.

15. If a thing's having its essence is a necessary truth, of course, then its doing so is *entailed* by anything whatever, in one sense of "entailment" discussed above. This only shows, however, that the sense of "deducible from" in question here is not identical with that sense of "entailed by."

16. The scholastic essence/property distinction is also in accordance with the definition of the "essential" offered at EIIdef2:

> D2: I say that to the essence of any thing belongs that which, being given, the thing is necessarily posited and which, being taken away, the thing is necessarily taken away; or that without the thing can neither be nor be conceived, and which can neither be nor be conceived without the thing.

For a thing can be conceived (simply by conceiving its essence) *without* conceiving its properties. This does not mean that we can conceive that the essence might fail to give rise to the properties, but only that conceiving the essence does not require us to conceive the properties. (This situation is somewhat analogous to that of the attributes: we conceive each attribute without the aid of any other (EIp10s), but we cannot conceive that one should exist and that another should not, since that would involve conceiving that an attribute failed to exist.) Similarly, the thing does not causally *depend* on the properties, and in that sense "can be" without (reliance on) them, even though it cannot fail to give rise to them through its essence. Indeed, EIIIdef.aff.XXIIexp speaks of "an effect or [*sive*] property."

17. Bennett, pp. 67–68.

18. The infinite modes do not, of course, constitute respects in which substances of the same attribute might *differ*. The objection is rather to the reading of EIp1 that Bennett's interpretation requires.

19. These two ways, which I outline below, are based specifically on Bennett, p. 122; the argumentation that Spinoza is committed to their individual elements is my own.

20. Bennett, p. 122.

21. It is worth taking note of a weaker sense in which there *are* ideas of non-existent finite modes—for example, of unicorns, conceived as a species of one-horned equine animals. This is the sense of EIIp8; and if having an idea of a non-existent thing in *this* sense were sufficient to make something "fall under the infinite intellect," 7 would follow immediately. But as EIIp8 explains, such an idea is *not* an idea having no object, which would violate EIIp7; rather it is an idea having a truly existent thing as its object. This truly existent thing is not an existent unicorn, however, but rather the formal *essence* of a unicorn. This essence is "comprehended" in the attribute of Extension. As I understand it, this means that the essence is itself a real, existent, feature of Extension: specifically, the pervasive and permanent feature that Extension's *general* laws are such as to permit the unicorn-mechanism to exist whenever and wherever the series of finite modes and causes should dictate. The idea of a "non-existent thing" in EIIp8 is simply the idea of this essence (which I

construe to be an infinite mode); indeed, the idea is the very *same* mode as this essence, but manifested under the attribute of Thought (EIIp7s).

In the case of actually existing finite modes, however, there is in God not only an idea of their permanent *essence,* but also an idea of their *actual existence* (EIIp8c). This idea of the actual existence of a finite mode is itself a finite mode, and is indeed the very same finite mode manifested under the attribute of Thought, as part of a causal order paralleling the causal order containing its object (EIIp7s; EIIp9,d). The human mind is an example of such an idea of an actually existing finite mode (EIIp11), and all such ideas of the actual existence of finite modes are in the infinite intellect of God (by EIIp11c, whose demonstration is completely general). (To put the matter in more popular terms, God not only knows what essences there are; he knows which particular finite modes actually exist.) It is such finite ideas of the actual existence of finite modes that I am discussing in the text.

22. Bennett, p. 122.

23. In fact, there is only one passage that even appears to contradict this interpretation. Spinoza continues in EIIax1 ("The essence of man does not involve necessary existence") as follows: "i.e., from the order of nature it can happen equally that this or that man does exist, or that he does not exist [hoc est, ex naturae ordine, tam fieri potest, ut hic, & ille homo existat, quàm ut non existat]." There are two possible interpretations of this gloss that are compatible with Spinoza's determinism: (a) that the existence of a particular man in itself neither contradicts nor is required by the general and pervasive *laws* ("order") of nature, or (b) that the man's *essence* does not determine whether he exists or not, but that his existence is instead determined as part of the actual *series* ("order") of natural causes and effects. The first interpretation requires that the "order of nature" not include finite modes, but the second interpretation requires that it *should* include finite modes. The first interpretation is particularly suggested by the Curley and Shirley translations; the second is particularly suggested by the Elwes and White-Sterling translations.

24. Bennett, pp. 119–120.

25. For an excellent presentation of some of these issues, see Bennett, pp. 66–70. I have discussed these issues in "Ethics IP5: Shared Attributes and the Basis of Spinoza's Monism," contained in a collection of essays written in honor of Jonathan Bennett, ed. Mark Kulstad and Jan Cover (Indianapolis: Hackett, 1990).

6

On the Relationship between Mode and Substance in Spinoza's Metaphysics

John Carriero

A central if difficult position taken in Spinoza's *Ethics* is that things in the universe other than God—including rocks, trees, ideas, and minds—are modes of God; according to Spinoza, produced things are modally dependent on God. How are we to understand this relation of modal dependence? Spinoza inherits the term *mode* from Descartes, who was using the term as a replacement of sorts for the Aristotelian *accident*. In the Aristotelian tradition, accidents are supposed to inhere in their subjects. Is modal dependence for Spinoza basically the same thing as the traditional relation of inherence?[1]

Some commentators have argued not. Explicating the traditional idea of inherence in terms of predication (so that the relation of inherence is supposed to amount to the relation between a property or quality and the subject of which the property or quality is predicated),[2] these commentators suggest that to interpret Spinoza's modal dependence in traditional terms would be to commit him to the view that a produced thing, e.g., Mt. Rushmore, is a quality or property predicable of God. In the view of these commentators, this position is so odd as to suggest that Spinoza's understanding of modal dependence cannot be the traditional idea of inherence but must be fundamentally novel.

This line of reasoning is flawed in that it relies on a misleading caricature of the traditional relation of inherence. In particular, it is a mistake to explicate the traditional relation of inherence in terms of predication. In Section 1, I sketch a traditional medieval Aristotelian conception of the dichotomy between substance and accident which distinguishes inherence from predication. I also show how Spinoza's thinking about the substance/mode dichotomy draws, often in surprising and subtle ways, on that tradition. In the remaining two sections I respond to arguments that have been offered against relating Spinoza's conception of modal dependence to a traditional conception of inherence. In Section 2, I take up Edwin Curley's claim that things like tables and chairs are of the "wrong logical type" to count as modes, which leads him to suggest that all that modal dependence comes to in Spinoza is causal dependence. In Section 3, I consider three of Bayle's objections to Spinoza's claim that produced things are modes of God, objections which Curley has suggested are so compelling as to give us further reason for doubting whether Spinoza understood modal dependence as inherence.

1. Spinoza and a Traditional Aristotelian Conception of Accident

Let's begin by recalling a standard Aristotelian treatment of the distinction between substance and accident.[3] In the *Categories* (1a16ff.), Aristotle develops the notion of substance by presenting a pair of orthogonal distinctions. First, he distinguishes between things that can be said of a subject and things that cannot be said of a subject. *Horse,* for example, can be said of a subject, but *Bucephalus* cannot. Roughly, this first distinction is between universal and particular.[4] Aristotle goes on to draw a second distinction, between things that exist in a subject and things that do not exist in a subject. According to Aristotle, *white* and *being eight feet tall* exist in subjects, say Socrates or Bucephalus, but *humanity* or *horsehood* does not exist in a subject. If whiteness exists in Socrates, why isn't it equally true that humanity exists in him? Aristotle's point here is that Socrates is too closely bound up with his humanity for his humanity to be thought of as existing in him: without his humanity, there would be no "him" for anything to exist in. (By way of contrast, there would still be a subject if Socrates were to lose his whiteness.)

It is the second of this pair of distinctions—the distinction between what exists in a subject and what does not—that is central to Aristotle's notion of substance; substances as opposed to accidents are things which do not exist in subjects. Those things that do not exist in subjects and cannot be said of another (e.g., *Socrates, Bucephalus*) Aristotle terms "primary substances" (πρῶται οὐσίαι); those things that do not exist in subjects and can be said of others (e.g., *human being, horse*) are termed "secondary substances" (δεύτεραι οὐσίαι). While it is undeniable that Aristotle accords a privileged status to individual substances, writing that they are what is called "substance most strictly, primarily, and most of all" (Ackrill translation, 2a11), it is also undeniable that, for Aristotle's notion of substance, the key distinction is the one between what exists in a subject and what does not, and not the orthogonal distinction between what can be said of another and what cannot be.

So accidents are beings which exist in subjects; substances are beings which can serve as the subject of accidents but which do not themselves exist in other subjects. The subject of an accident is either itself an accident, as surface is the subject of color, or a substance, as animal is the subject of mortal. Since there is no infinite regress of accidents and subjects, all accidents ultimately inhere in substances, as color, for example, ultimately inheres in body. Moreover, since accidents depend for their existence on the substances in which they ultimately inhere, whereas substances do not depend on their accidents, substances are prior "in being," or ontologically prior, to accidents.

Since a substance is ontologically prior to its accidents, Aristotelians took it as obvious that a substance could not depend on its accidents for its individuation. (An argument from ontological priority to the individuation thesis might be filled out as follows: It is incompatible with the nature of substance, as an independent being, that it should depend on any of its accidents in order to exist. But a thing depends on its individuating principles for its existence. So a substance cannot depend on its accidents for its individuation.) Rather, accidents are individuated through the subjects in which they exist: Socrates' whiteness is distinct from Plato's (let's say qualitatively identical) whiteness, precisely because Socrates' whiteness exists in Socrates and Plato's whiteness exists in Plato.[5] Indeed, one of the primary ways to attack a theory of individuation in high scholasticism was to argue that the theory had the consequence that substances are individuated by their accidents.[6]

In addition to being ontologically prior to accidents, substances are also definitionally prior to them. In Aristotelianism, a definition, in the philosophically most significant sense of the word, is not an explication of the meaning of a term, but rather an account of a thing's being or essence, that is, an account of what it is to be that thing. For example, if we were to define a human being as a *risible teachable animal,* although we would have provided the means to tell those things which are human beings apart from those things which are not, and so would have provided a working knowledge of how to apply the term "human being," we would not have provided a definition of a human being. This is because *risible teachable animal* does not reveal what it is to be a human being, does not reveal the essence of a human being. *Rational animal,* by way of contrast, which exhibits the ground of risibility (having a sense of humor depends on the ability to understand) and of teachability, does reveal a human being's essence. Now, if a definition of an accident is to reveal its being or essence, and if an accident depends for its existence on inherence in a substance, then the definition must make mention of this inherence. For example, white might be defined as such-and-such a color *of a surface;* snub as such-and-such a curvature *of a nose.* The definition of a substance, by way of contrast, does not need to make mention of anything outside of the being of that substance; human being, for example, is defined simply as *rational animal,* not as *rational animal of such-and-such a subject.*

The fact that the definition of an accident must make reference to something outside of the accident was seen by Aristotle not simply as affording a convenient, quasi-formal way of distinguishing the definitions of accidents from those of substances, but rather as a sort of genuine embarrassment for an accident. For there is pressure both to include and not to include the subject in which the accident inheres in the accident's definition. On the one hand, since the subject is a distinct being, separate from the accident and external to it, it would seem that the subject ought not to be included in the accident's essence; on the other hand, if the definition is to reveal the accident's nature as a dependent being, it must at least make mention of the subject in which the accident inheres.[7] Because of an accident's imperfect state of being it can have a definition only in a secondary (or analogical) sense. Since substances are fully definable and accidents are definable only in a secondary sense, and then only through definitions that ultimately make reference to the substances in which they inhere, substances are prior to accidents in definition.

This issue concerning the definability of an accident makes itself felt in Aristotelian thinking about essential or *per se* predication. One kind of essential predication is where part of the definition of a substance or accident, such as a genus or species, is predicated of the substance or accident, as when, for example, *rational* is predicated of *human being* or *color* of *white.* As rational is part of what it is to be a human being and color is part of what it is to be white, such essential predications are virtually identity statements. A second sort of essential or *per se* predication is tied to the peculiar character of the definition of accidents. We just noted that the definition of an accident must make reference to the subject in which the accident inheres: thus, *snub* is defined as a particular curvature of a nose and *risible* as a capacity for a sense of humor in a human being. Since the predication of an accident of its proper subject, such as *snub* of *nose* or *risible* of *human beings,* follows from the accident's definition, this sort of predication is also essential or *per se*. However, this latter kind of essential predication lacks the character of identity found in the first kind. *Snub* and *nose* are distinct beings, each with its own essence. Thus, when *snub* is predicated of *nose,* the relation of one being to another is affirmed, not the identity of the same being with self. Accordingly, Aristotelians kept the first sort of essential or *per se* predication distinct from the second; and the two types of predication became known in scholastic philosophy as the first and second modes of *per se* predication, respectively.[8]

Now, if we look carefully at Spinoza's treatment of the dichotomy we can discern a surprising degree of faithfulness to the Aristotelian conception of the substance/accident distinction just outlined. Consider, to begin with, Spinoza's definitions of substance and mode:[9]

> By substance I understand what is in itself and is conceived through itself, i.e., that whose concept does not require the concept of another thing, from which it must be formed. (ID3; Curley, 408; Geb. II, 45)

> By mode I understand the affections of a substance, or that which is in another through which it is also conceived. (ID5; Curley, 409; Geb. II, 45)

Each definition contains two contrasts: a mode is in another, whereas a substance is in itself; and a mode is conceived through the subject in which it is, whereas the concept of a substance "does not require the concept of another thing, from which it must be formed."

The relation of these two contrasts has inspired much commentary.[10] The first contrast, concerning inherence, reflects the Aristotelian thesis that substances are ontologically prior to accidents. What about the second contrast, concerning conceptual dependence? As others have suggested, Spinoza's view that a mode is conceived through its subject owes something to Descartes's view that modes are conceived through the principal attributes of the substances in which they inhere.[11] What is less frequently noted is that Descartes's view is not completely novel: his claim that modes are conceived through the principal attributes of substances reflects the traditional view that substances are prior to accidents "in definition," which means, as we saw above, that a full characterization of an accident has to make reference to an entity external to the accident, namely, the accident's subject. This is why Descartes, in his *Comments on a Certain Broadsheet,* after writing that "it is part of the nature of a mode that, although we can readily understand a substance apart from a mode, we cannot *vice versa* clearly understand a mode unless at the same time we have a conception of the substance of which it is a mode," feels entitled to add that "all philosophers are agreed on this point" (AT VIIIB, 350; CSM I, 298). In short, the two clauses in Spinoza's definitions of modes reflect the Aristotelian theses that substances are prior to accidents in being and in definition.

Not only does the way in which Spinoza introduces the distinction between mode and substance reflect Aristotelian thinking, but so does the way in which he subsequently reasons about it. Consider, for example, the demonstration of IP5. In that proposition Spinoza argues that substances cannot be individuated by their modes or affections. For, Spinoza argues, if two or more substances are distinguished from one another: "then since a substance is prior in nature to its affections (by P1), if the affections are put to one side and [the substance] is considered in itself, i.e. (by D3 and A6), considered truly, one cannot be conceived to be distinguished from another" (Curley, 411; Geb. II, 48). Commentators have puzzled over exactly what entitles Spinoza to put the affections of a substance to one side,[12] but Spinoza's reasoning is quite plain. Spinoza is simply appealing to the thesis—part and parcel of the traditional conception of the dichotomy between substance and accident—that a substance is ontologically prior ("prior in nature") to its accidents. As would have been obvious to a contemporaneous reader of the *Ethics,* to make a substance depend on its accidents for its individuation would be to make a substance depend on its accidents for its existence, a dependence that is incompatible with its status as a substance.

Let's consider a third and final way in which Spinoza's handling of the distinction between substance and mode is beholden to the Aristotelian tradition. We noted above the ambivalence of the Aristotelians concerning the inclusion of an accident's subject in the definition of the accident's essence. This issue carries over into Spinoza's metaphysics as a question about whether God belongs to the essences of produced things. And, in fact, if we turn to Spinoza's discussion of essence in IIP10CS, we find that he addresses this technical Aristotelian issue. In that scholium, he considers the apparent involvement of God in the essence of produced things, brought about by IP15's claim that God is the subject of all created things. Spinoza puts the problem thus:[13] "But in the meantime many say that anything without which a thing can neither be nor be conceived pertains to the nature of the thing. And so they believe either that the nature of God pertains to the essence of created things, or that created things can be or be conceived without God—or what is more certain, they are not sufficiently consistent" (IIP10CS; Curley, 455; Geb. II, 93). Clearly something has to give here. Spinoza suggests that the Aristotelian requirement that a thing's essence include everything that the thing depends on, or that its definition include everything through which that thing is conceived, ought to be dropped, as (in his view) this requirement had already been tacitly discarded by the tradition anyway. In its place, he suggests, it should be required that in order for *B* to be included in *A*'s essence, it must be the case both that (i) if *A* is posited, *B* is also posited, and *vice versa* that (ii) if *B* is posited, then *A* is also posited, or, what Spinoza regards as equivalent, both that (i′) *A* can neither be nor be conceived without *B* and that (ii′) *B* can neither be nor be conceived without *A*.

It is clear enough how Spinoza's response is supposed to work with respect to (i′) and (ii′). Whereas a mode is in and is conceived through its subject, a substance is neither in nor conceived through its modes. But what about (i) and (ii), which have to do with what Spinoza calls "positing?" Why is it the case that (i) a mode *M* cannot be posited unless God is? And how can it be the case that (ii) God can be posited without *M*'s also being posited, in view of Spinoza's position that all things (besides God) necessarily follow from him? These puzzles are solved once we recognize that Spinoza is using "positing" here as equivalent to the Aristotelian idea of essential or *per se* predication discussed above. If *M* is a mode of God, then God enters *M*'s definition as *M*'s subject, so there is an "essential" route from *M* to God (we are, in effect, relying on the second mode of essential or *per se* predication here). By way of contrast, even if the existence of *M* should in some way necessarily follow from God's existence,[14] it remains the case that *M* lies outside God's essence, so there's no "essential" route from God to *M*. That is, since a substance's definition does not include anything external to it, when one posits a substance one does not posit its modes.

Finally, to prevent misunderstanding, I point out that in claiming that Spinoza's conception of modal dependence is fundamentally the same as the traditional conception of inherence, I am not suggesting that Spinoza's views surrounding modal dependence are not innovative. To take but one example of Spinoza's novelty, consider how he under-stands the definitional priority of substance. If we think of attributes as definitions of essence, then his claim in IP10 that each attribute of substance is conceived through itself amounts to the idea that essences are conceptually independent (as thought and extension might be held to be). This involves a rather striking departure from a traditional Aris-totelian picture of the definitions of substances, where definitions of the essences of substances conceptually overlap, as in the definitions of *horse* and *human being,* each of which includes the genus *animal.*[15] My point is that Spinoza's thinking about modal dependence is suffi-ciently informed by traditional thinking about inherence (and related ideas, such as essence and definition) that an account of Spinoza's thinking must begin with the tradition. To paraphrase Austin, even if the tradition does not have the last word on interpreting Spinoza's views on modal dependence, it ought to have the first word. Indeed, even the appreciation of Spinoza's novelty often requires a firm grasp of traditional medieval Aristotelianism.

2. Curley's Objections

Spinoza's thinking about modal dependence reflects in obvious and subtle ways Aristotelian thinking about inherence. This suggests that Spinoza understands modal dependence in fundamentally the same way as the Aristotelians understood inherence. However, Edwin Curley has offered a number of interesting arguments against taking Spinoza's thesis that produced things are modes in this way.[16] Three of these arguments come from Bayle, which I will consider in the next section. Curley offers considerations of his own. In *Behind the Geometrical Method,* Curley argues that produced things cannot inhere in God because they are caused by God: "And one question which . . . we ought to ask ourselves is: how can a subject cause itself to have the properties it has? how can the relation of inherence which a property has to its subject be anything like the relation an effect has to its cause?" (BGM, 36).[17] Perhaps Curley's most important and influential objection is that finite things are simply of the "wrong logical type" to be modes: "Spinoza's modes are, prima facie, of the wrong logical type to be related to substance in the same way Descartes's modes are related to substance, for they are particular things (*E* IP25C), not qualities. And it is difficult to know what it would mean to say that particular things inhere in substance. When qualities are said to inhere in substance, this may be viewed as a way of saying that they are predicated of it. What it would mean to say that one thing is predicated of another is a mystery that needs solving" (SM,18).

This objection paves the way for Curley's own constructive interpretation of modal dependence in Spinoza. In Curley's view, two elements are involved in the traditional distinction between substance and mode, "a distinction between independent and dependent being" and "a distinction between subject and predicate" (SM, 37). According to Curley, while Descartes and others assumed that these two elements more or less coincide, for Spinoza they are separate: "If I understand him correctly, Spinoza, in classifying particular things as modes, was intent on emphasizing the fact that the two distinctions do not coincide, that what is the subject of predication is not an independent entity. He did not intend to say that the relation of particular things to

God was in any way like the relation of a predicate to its subject" (SM, 37). The substance/accident (mode) dichotomy, then, becomes simply the distinction between independent being and dependent being. Curley urges that this distinction, in turn, be understood in terms of causation:

> When Spinoza does undertake to characterize the relation between modes and substance—beyond saying that they exist in it and are conceived through it—the terms he uses are quite different. He says that God is the cause of the things that are in him (*E* IP18D), that he has produced them (*E* IP24), that he has determined them (*E*IP26), or that they follow from him (*E* IP28D). And since he identifies substance and attribute, he is just as likely to say that the modes are determined by, or produced by, or follow from an attribute of God, or the absolute nature of an attribute of God (*E* IP21–23; *E* IP28D). This terminology . . . does not in the least suggest inherence in a subject. What it does suggest is merely some kind of causal dependence. (SM, 19)

(By "merely some kind of causal dependence" Curley has in mind what, speaking very broadly, might be called a relation of *efficient* causation, as is clear from his subsequent interpretation of causation in Spinoza—see SM, ch. 2.) In Curley's eyes, Spinoza's initially striking thesis that things (besides God) are modes of God collapses into the rather more familiar thesis that things (besides God) are (efficiently) causally dependent on God.

To my mind, such a reading disappointingly flattens Spinoza's position. Curley's interpretation requires that we see Spinoza as assimilating modal dependence—an important traditional category often allied with material causality[18]—to efficient causal dependence.[19] But is such an assimilation under way in the *Ethics?* We may textually sharpen the question. In IP15 ("Whatever is, is in God, and nothing can be or be conceived without God") Spinoza establishes that all things (besides God) are modes of God; in IP16 Spinoza establishes that all things (besides God) are efficiently caused by God, as is evident from the proposition's first corollary ("From this it follows that God is the efficient cause of all things which can fall under an infinite intellect"). Does Spinoza see IP15 and IP16 as establishing (or elaborating) the same kind of dependence of things (other than God) on God? A survey of the relevant texts suggests not. For example, the arguments given for the two propositions are quite different: the argument of IP15 is based on the exhaustiveness of the substance/mode dichotomy, coupled with monism; the argument for IP16 concerns the extent of the reality or power expressed by the divine essence.[20] Further, Spinoza never refers to IP15 and IP16 in a way that suggests that they are interchangeable; in particular, he keeps their deductive consequences distinct.[21] Curley's interpretation effaces a distinction that is, prima facie, deeply etched in Spinoza's text, namely, the distinction between *A*'s depending on *B* in such a way that *A* must be in and be conceived through *B* and *A*'s depending on *B* in such a way that *A* is efficiently caused by *B.*

Do the reasons Curley provides really warrant such strong medicine? Let's look again at his primary objection against understanding modal dependence as inherence: "Spinoza's modes are, prima facie, of the wrong logical type to be related to substance in the same way Descartes' modes are related to substance, for they are particular things (*E* IP25C), not qualities. And it is difficult to know what it would mean to say that particular things inhere in substance. When qualities are said to inhere in substance, this may be viewed as a way of saying that they are predicated of it. What it would mean to say that one thing is predicated of another is a mystery that needs solving" (SM, 18). In this passage, Curley suggests Spinoza's modes are of "the wrong logical type" to be traditional modes because Spinoza's modes are particulars, whereas traditional modes are "qualities," and for a quality to inhere in a substance is "a way of saying that [it is] predicated of it." Viewed from the point of view of the sketch of Aristotle's *Categories* provided above, this seems to confuse the "can-be-said-of-a-subject/cannot-be-said-of-a-subject" distinction (the one that tracks the universal/particular distinction) with the "does-not-exist-in-a-subject/exists-in-a-subject" distinction (the one that tracks the substance/accident [mode] distinction). If we keep these distinctions separate, there is no immediate barrier to counting particular things as accidents: indeed, it seems to follow the scheme laid out above that there are both universal and particular accidents, just as there are both universal and particular substances.[22] Again, viewed against the background of the sketch given above, Spinoza's supposed insistence on "the fact that the two distinctions [i.e., the distinctions between independent being and dependent being and between subject and predicate] do not coincide" (SM, 37) is quite unnecessary, as Aristotle himself holds that the subject/predicate dichotomy is orthogonal to the dichotomy between what constitutes a (basic) subject and what depends on a subject for its existence.

Evidently, then, Curley rejects the sort of framework sketched above for understanding the substance/accident distinction. Why? There is, I believe, an unstated assumption that lies behind Curley's treatment of the topic, namely, the rejection of the idea of a particular accident. Jonathan Bennett, who is (up to a point) sympathetic to Curley's position, writes in § 23.3 (p. 94) of *A Study of Spinoza's "Ethics"*:[23]

> Some philosophers have postulated items—which might be called 'states' or 'modes'—which are at once particular and universal. As well as this box and the property of cubicness which it shares with other things, they have thought, there is *the cubicness of this box.* It is not the box, but only an aspect of it; but it is an aspect *of this box,* and is not to be identified with the cubicness of anything else. If Spinoza meant modes and states to be items of that kind, Curley and I would both be wrong. Curley's 'mystery' would have a solution, but not the one I propose for it. I am glad there's no direct evidence that Spinoza did believe in these particularized universals, for I think they are nonsense. I cannot prove him to be innocent of them; but I am willing to suppose that he was, since I can explain all the texts through an interpretation which allows modes and states to be honest universals.[24]

While Curley does not make his reliance on such a dismissal explicit, it is fairly clear that he does reject the notion of a particular accident. Thus, in a footnote on p. 161 of SM, n. 3, Curley argues against a reading of a passage from Arnauld and Nicole's *Port-Royal Logic* which, in Curley's words, "may suggest that modes are to be regarded as nonsubstantial particulars which cannot exist apart from their own subject." And in that same note Curley writes concerning the treatment of individual accidents in *Categories:* "The same difficulty, less easily resolved, arises there." But if one dismisses the notion of a particular accident (or if—which amounts to the same thing—one insists, as Bennett seems to, that all accidents are universal, so that a particular accident must be "at once particular and universal"), then one will find an account of accidents like the one sketched from the *Categories* untenable.

If I am not mistaken, then, there is a fundamental assumption—stated in the case of Bennett, unstated in the case of Curley—that plays a pivotal role in their interpretation of Spinoza's conception of modes, namely, the anathema of particular modes. Now, to be sure, the idea that Aristotle himself subscribed to the notion of an individual accident has been challenged in recent years, most prominently by G. E. L. Owen, in his well-known article "Inherence."[25] But Owen, in that article, is arguing against what he takes to be a "fashionable dogma," which he finds "hints of" in Porphyry and Pacius and in modern writers such as Ross, Jones, Anscombe, and Ackrill, all of whom interpret Aristotle as holding that there are accidents which are particular or individual in the sense of not being able to exist in more than one subject.[26] Clearly, Owen took the prevalent interpretation to be that Aristotle allows for particular accidents.

Now, if the notion of an individual accident or particular property were absurd on its face, then it would be desirable to keep Spinoza free of such entities. But although Bennett sometimes gives the impression that one can tell by a sort of metaphysical inspection that such entities are to be dismissed out of hand, it is not clear to me that this is really so: indeed, the notion of accident seems to me, of itself, empty enough that it is not obvious what is supposed to be at stake when the issue of whether individual accidents exist or not is taken in abstraction from the role that the notion of accident (and its correlate, substance) plays in larger metaphysical systems.[27]

As I've argued in Section 1, Spinoza inherits the distinction between mode and substance from the medieval Aristotelian tradition. So our question is more focused: Did that tradition recognize individual accidents? The answer is a resounding yes. The fundamental reason for this is that medieval Aristotelians regarded the distinction between substance and accident as a division within "real being."[28] Accordingly, they viewed accidents as "perfections" or "realities." But since they held further that any real being must be individual, they regarded accidents as individuals. Thus, for example, Aquinas takes the soul's powers, such as the intellect and the faculty of sensation, to be (proper) accidents of the soul, while maintaining (against Arabic interpreters of Aristotle) that these faculties are individual. Similarly, the medieval doctrine, mentioned earlier, that accidents are individuated through their subjects indicates how firmly individual accidents are ensconced in that tradition.[29]

Now, Martial Gueroult has argued that Descartes moved away from the Aristotelian tradition concerning modes. In particular, he has suggested that Descartes denies that modes are real things,[30] which might give cause for wondering whether Spinoza's views on accidents are continuous with medieval Aristotelianism in regard to the individuality of accidents. Without commenting on the specific merits of Gueroult's interpretation, whatever else one holds concerning Descartes's views on modes, it is clear that he, too, is committed to the existence of individual accidents or modes. In the letter to Mesland of 9 February 1645, Descartes tells us that a surface is "a mode, or manner of being" and goes on to discuss conditions under which "the surface remains always *numerically the same.*"[31]

I conclude that the objection that (unreconstructed) modes are of the "wrong logical type" to be particulars rests on an assimilation of inherence with predication and a closely related dismissal of the notion of an individual accident that are not supported by the medieval Aristotelian tradition's way of thinking about accidents, a way of thinking that is remarkably reflected in the fine structure of Spinoza's texts. Spinoza's handling of the Aristotelian substance/accident distinction ought to earn him a secure place among Owen's "dogmatists."

What about Curley's other objection, that there is a tension between the thesis that finite things are modes (or accidents) of God and the thesis that they are caused by God? To begin with (although this is not the point behind Curley's objection), we should observe that there is no incompatibility in the medieval Aristotelian tradition between something's being a property of a substance and its being efficiently caused by that substance. Aristotelians held that since a substance is a complete being in its own right, it is sufficiently external to its accident to support the intelligibility of its efficiently causing an accident. A good illustration is Aquinas's account of the relation of the powers of the soul to its essence. Aquinas characterizes this relation as one where the powers "flow from" *(fluant ab)* the essence of the soul, a relation that is causal in character: "But the subject is the cause of its proper accidents; whence also it is included in the definition of accident, as is clear from *Metaph.* vii (Did. vi. 4). Therefore the powers of the soul proceed from its essence as their cause" (ST I, Q. 77, A. 6). More precisely, the essence of the soul provides three of the four Aristotelian causes of the soul's powers—all but the formal cause, which is supplied, as in the case of any accident, by an accidental form: "The subject is both the final cause, and in a way the active cause, of its proper accident. It is also as it were the material cause, inasmuch as it is receptive of the accident. From this we may gather that the essence of the soul is the cause of all its powers, as their end, and as their active principle; and of some as receptive thereof" (ST I, Q. 77, A. 6, ad 2).

Now, Aquinas takes care to explain why the production of the soul's powers by its essence is not an unwelcome case of self-causation. Two features of the subject contribute to the intelligibility of such causation. On the one hand, the fact that a proper accident is an accident of the subject means that the accident is not a part of what it is to be the subject. The subject does not require the accident in order to be a complete being; accordingly, there is something metaphysically prior to the accident to do the causing. On the other hand, even though the subject does not require the accident for its completeness, the subject is open to the reception of the accident as a further perfection over and above what belongs to the subject as such. Thus, the subject of a proper accident is able both to produce and to receive its proper accidents: "Actuality is observed in the subject of the accidental form prior to its being observed in the accidental form; wherefore the actuality of the accidental form is caused by the actuality of the subject. So the subject, forasmuch as it is in potentiality, is receptive of the accidental form: but forasmuch as it is in act, it produces it" (ST I, Q. 77, A. 6).[32] According to Aquinas, then, a being is able to serve as the efficient cause of its properties.

On the medieval account just considered, the same entity—the essence of the soul—plays two distinct causal roles, that of a material cause and that of an efficient cause. So part of the answer to Curley's rhetorical question, "How can the *relation* of inherence which a property has to its subject be anything like the *relation* an effect has to its cause?" (my emphasis; BGM, 36), is that to claim that substance plays these two roles is not to claim that the roles themselves are the same. For Aquinas, to say that the (essence of) the soul serves as both the material cause and the efficient cause of its proper accidents is not to say that the two causal relationships are the same.

Curley would respond, I believe, by arguing that Spinoza identifies efficient causal independence too closely with substancehood, and efficient causal dependence too closely with modehood, for there to be two different relations here. Such a response is suggested by Curley's remark, made in the course of an elaboration of his objection, that "a substance is, by definition, something causally self-sufficient, and a mode is, by definition, something causally dependent on something else, ultimately on substance."[33] But the uses of "by definition" here are unjustified, since causal idioms do not appear in Spinoza's definition of substance and mode, and the propositions establishing the causal self-sufficiency of substance (IP6 and IP7) appear in the *Ethics* as *theorems,* indicating at least some room between substancehood and causal self-sufficiency. Further, if a relation of inherence is simply a relation of efficient causal dependence, then one would expect IP16 (affirming the efficient causal dependence of things on God) to be very closely related to IP15 (affirming the modal dependence of things on God). But, as we have already noted, this is not the case. Spinoza keeps the demonstration of IP15 and its consequences distinct from the demonstration of IP16 and its consequences, suggesting that those two propositions concern different relationships.

3. Bayle

Curley cites three arguments from Bayle as reasons for distancing Spinoza's views on modal dependence from a traditional conception of inherence. (Bayle, of course, presents his arguments as objections to the thesis that produced things are modes of God, and not as objections to interpreting Spinoza as straightforwardly holding the thesis.) First, Bayle argues that it follows from Spinoza's ontology that God is the subject of contradictory properties.[34] For example, George does not like broccoli, so God, the ultimate subject underlying George, does not like broccoli; but Michael likes broccoli, so God, the ultimate subject underlying Michael, likes broccoli; hence, God both does not like and likes broccoli.[35] Second, it follows that God is mutable. On a standard Aristotelian theory of change, a substance changes when it acquires or loses accidents. But if God is the subject of modes, and (some of) these modes come into or go out of existence, then God changes.[36] Third, it follows that God is responsible for evil. For on a traditional understanding of the substance/accident dichotomy, a substance is the ultimate agent that lies behind the activity of its accidents.[37] Therefore, if the Germans have killed ten thousand Turks, and the Germans are modes or accidents of God, then ultimately it is God who kills ten thousand Turks.

If Curley's own objections can be met by keeping in view the traditional conception of inherence that Spinoza inherited, the objections raised by Bayle are another story. In two cases at least, they raise substantive issues, issues that reveal part of what is at stake in Spinoza's claim that things (besides God) are modes of God.

One of Bayle's objections does rest on an unsympathetic treatment of the Aristotelian tradition, namely, his charge that Spinoza is committed to the position that the single substance of the universe, as the ultimate subject of predication, has contradictory predicates. To be sure, if some accident A inheres in a substance S, then, according to the tradition, it will be in some sense true that S is A.[38] But consider the traditional formulation of the principle of noncontradiction, as accurately reported by Bayle: " 'Opposita sunt quae neque de se invicem, neque de eodem tertio secundem idem, ad idem, eodem modo atque tempore vere affirmari possunt'. That is, two opposite terms cannot be truly affirmed of the same subject in the same respects, and at the same time" (XIII, 442; IV, 295). The clause "in the same respects" is important. As Bennett has in effect pointed out,[39] even if it is true that God in some way likes broccoli, this is compatible with its being true that God in some other ways does not like broccoli. Indeed, it seems to me that Spinoza often uses the Latin *quatenus* to mark out these different "ways" or "respects," as when, for example, he writes that a finite thing must "follow from God or from the attribute of God insofar as [*quatenus*] it is considered to be affected by some mode" (IP28; Curley, 432; Geb. II, 69) or, again, when he writes that "God, not insofar as [*quatenus*] he is infinite, but insofar as [*quatenus*] he is explained through the nature of the human Mind, or insofar as [*quatenus*] he constitutes the essence of human Mind" has a certain idea (IIP11C; Curley, 456; Geb. II, 94–95). Spinoza would reply, then, to Bayle, that God, the unique substance of the universe, *quatenus* he constitutes the essence of George's mind does not like broccoli, and *quatenus* he constitutes the essence of Michael's mind likes broccoli.[40]

Let's turn to Bayle's second objection, that giving God modes threatens divine immutability. Gauging Spinoza's position on this matter is of particular importance for understanding his relation to traditional conceptions of God. Historically, arguments for divine immutability are closely related to arguments for God's simplicity with respect to accidental composition. Both arguments trade on the idea that God is in his essence fully actual. Since there is no potentiality in God's essence, it is not open to the further perfection that an accident would afford;[41] hence, there can be no composition of substance and accident in God. Similarly, since there is no potentiality in God, and since change involves the movement from potentiality to actuality, God does not change.[42] Spinoza, too, links the claim that God is immutable to the claim that God does not have modes—although in the converse direction, from immutability to simplicity with respect to modal composition—in *Cogitata Metaphysica* (I, ch. 5): "That there is also in God no composition from different modes is sufficiently demonstrated from the fact that there are no modes in God. For modes arise from the alteration of substance" (Curley, 324; Geb. I, 258). On the basis of the tradition, then, one would expect God's immutability and God's simplicity with respect to modal composition to stand or fall together.

How does Spinoza handle this problem? Commentators are divided on this question. Those, such as Bennett, who take seriously the traditional notion of inherence read Spinoza as giving up divine immutability.[43] Those, such as Curley and Gueroult, who assimilate modal dependence to efficient causal dependence claim as an advantage for this reading that it preserves God's immutability.[44] One reason for this disagreement is that Spinoza is circumspect in the *Ethics* concerning God's immutability, something that is surprising in view of the traditional association (noted in the preceding paragraph) between immutability and simplicity with respect to modal composition. The one text that bears directly on this question is IP20C2: "It follows, secondly, that God, or [*sive*] all of God's attributes, are immutable." While those who interpret Spinoza as holding that God is immutable have emphasized this text,[45] it is a delicate piece of evidence. As the "or" here, *sive,* is the "or" of apposition, it is not obvious that Spinoza is claiming anything more than that God's attributes are eternal. And when we look to the demonstration of the corollary—"For if they [i.e., God's attributes] changed as to their existence, they would also (by P20) change as to their essence, i.e. (as is known through itself), from being true become false, which is absurd"—we find an argument that is ultimately based on the fact that God's essence is identical with his existence. Clearly, this argument tells us nothing at all about God's modes (in the traditional sense)[46] and, in particular, there is no suggestion here (or, for that matter, anywhere else in the text) of the maneuver envisioned by Curley and Gueroult: namely, that Spinoza, by reading out the notion of inherence at the center of the traditional notion of modal dependence, creates sufficient ontological distance between God and his modes so as to allow modes to change while God remains immutable.

How should we understand IP20C2, then? We might try to build on a point that Curley makes concerning IP29S, where Spinoza writes:

> Before I proceed further, I wish to explain here—or rather to advise [the reader]—what we must understand by *Natura naturans* and *Natura naturata*. For from the preceding I think it is already established that by *Natura naturans* we must understand what is in itself and is conceived through itself, or such attributes of substance as express an eternal and infinite essence, i.e. (by P14C1 and P17C2), God, insofar as he is considered a free cause.
>
> But by *Natura naturata* I understand whatever follows from the necessity of God's nature, *or* from any of God's attributes, i.e., all the modes of God's attributes insofar as they are considered as things which are in God, and can neither be nor be conceived without God. (Curley, 434; Geb. II, 71)

Although there is a tendency to identify God with nature taken as a whole, Curley rightly calls attention to the fact that in the first paragraph God is not identified with all of nature, but simply the *Natura naturans,* and that, moreover, there is a firm distinction in the second paragraph between God or his attributes and the modes that follow from them (BGM, 37).[47]

It is characteristic of Spinoza's use of the term 'God', I believe, to use the term, at least when in apposition with a phrase referring to the divine essence, to refer strictly to the universe's substance, as opposed to the composite of substance and accidents. In that case, IP20C2 ought to be understood as claiming not that the composite of God and his accidents is immutable, but rather that God qua substance is immutable.[48] Viewed from the Aristotelian tradition, such a claim is rather curious. It would be like claiming that Socrates qua substance is immutable. But since change in general involves the gain or loss of accidental perfections, what would it mean to claim that Socrates qua substance—that is, Socrates taken in abstraction from his accidents—is immutable? Well, there is one kind of change[49] that is not understood in terms of the gain or loss of accidental forms, namely, the generation or corruption of a substance. So to claim that Socrates qua substance is immutable appears to be tantamount to claiming that Socrates neither comes into nor goes out of existence, that is, that Socrates is eternal. And this is precisely the sort of change contemplated in Spinoza's argument for God's "immutability": he argues that the divine attributes cannot "change as to their existence," because, as the existence of a divine attribute is identical with its essence, this would imply a change in their essence.

On this interpretation, Spinoza does not defend divine immutability, if this is taken to mean, as it traditionally was, the immutability of God's entire being, including what accidents, if any, he may have.[50] But this, I think, was only to be expected in view of the close association in the tradition between the claim that God does not have accidents and the claim that God is immutable. The mutability of the entire composite of God and modes is an unavoidable cost of maintaining that God possesses modes. This is confirmed in a roundabout way by Curley's and Gueroult's interpretations, which are able to keep God immutable (in the traditional sense) only by, in effect, eradicating the thesis that God has modes.

Let's turn to the remaining objection that Curley draws from Bayle, concerning God's responsibility for evil. This objection turns on the idea that it is not modes that act, but rather the substances which they modify that act:

> But to affirm that men are only the modification of one and the same Being, that, consequently, God only acts, and that the same individual God being modified into Turks and Hungarians, there are wars and battles, is to advance a thing more monstrous and chimerical than all the deliriums of men shut up in mad houses. Take particular notice, as I have said before, that modes do nothing, and that substances only act and suffer. This phrase, "the sweetness of honey pleases the palate," is only true, as it signifies that the extended substance of which honey is made up pleases the palate. Thus, according to Spinoza's system, whoever says, "The Germans have killed ten thousand Turks," speaks improperly and falsely, unless he means God modified into Germans has killed God modified into ten thousand Turks. (Bayle, XIII, 444; IV, 298)

It is reasonable to take Bayle as objecting here that Spinoza's monism, coupled with traditional theses about substancehood and activity, implicates God in evil.[51]

From the point of view of traditional Aristotelianism, such an objection is well taken. Bayle's remark that the action of the sweetness of honey on the palate belongs not to the mode or accident *sweetness,* but rather to the modified substance, is reminiscent of the scholastic commonplace that it is not the active[52] accidental form *heat* that acts, but rather the substantial composite, the hot fire.[53] This is not to deny all efficacy to active accidental forms. Active accidental forms were considered to be the immediate causes of their effects; but the principal cause was held to be the substantial form in which the accidental form resided.[54] For this reason, active accidental forms were sometimes styled the "quasi-instruments" of substantial forms.[55] Further, the thesis that accidents are not the ultimate actors, but rather that the substantial composite is the principal actor, when coupled with Spinoza's holding that human beings are modes of God, does seem to involve God in human evil. Our inherence in God takes away from our autonomy as actors; it leaves less metaphysical space between God and our misdeeds than is found on a traditional view, according to which our substantiality stands between God and our actions. I do not think that Spinoza would for a moment deny this. Indeed, I take it to be a central feature of Spinoza's teaching that we are modes of God, that we are to surrender the autonomy that was accorded to us in traditional metaphysics—that we must surrender the idea, as he puts it in a well-known text from the introduction to Part Three of the *Ethics,* that human beings are in "nature as a domination within a domination" (Curley, 491; Geb. II, 137).

How does Spinoza respond to Bayle's difficulty? While there is no text that I know of where Spinoza directly responds to this problem, there is one where he takes up a related problem. Moreover, his treatment of that problem carries over to the present context. A correspondent, Willem van Blyenbergh, raised a difficulty concerning Descartes's views as exposited by Spinoza in *Descartes's "Principles of Philosophy"* and reiterated in his appendix, *Cogitata Metaphysica.* Blyenbergh's difficulty is based on the Cartesian conception of the divine conservation of the universe, according to which "God is the cause not only of the Soul's substance, but also of the Soul's every Motion or Striving, which we call will." He objects:

> From this assertion it also seems to follow necessarily, either that there is no evil in the Soul's motion or will, or else that God himself does that evil immediately. For the things we call evil also happen through the Soul, and consequently through such an immediate influence and concurrence of God. For example, Adam's Soul wants to eat the forbidden fruit. According to the proposition above, that will of Adam happens through God's influence—not only that [Adam] wills, but that he wills in this way, as will be shown immediately. So either Adam's forbidden act is no evil of itself, insofar as God not only moved his will, but also moved it in such a way, or else God himself seems to do what we call evil. (Letter 18, Curley, 356; Geb. IV, 82–83)

Blyenbergh charges that Spinoza's doctrines force the conclusion that God produces evil.[56] While Blyenbergh's and Bayle's objections have different metaphysical bases, they have in common the charge that Spinoza's views bring God and human beings together in a way that infringes on human autonomy. According to Blyenbergh, God's conservation of the actions of substances as well as the substances themselves unites God too closely to those actions for him to escape culpability for evil human actions; according to Bayle, Spinoza's claim that we are modes of God intimately links him to our activity in a way that brings blame for our misdoings back on him.

How does Spinoza reply to Blyenbergh's objection? He begins by observing: "But for myself, I cannot grant that *sins and evil are something positive, much less that something would exist or happen contrary to god's will. On the contrary, I say not only that sin is not something positive, but also that when we say that we sin against god, we are speaking inaccurately, or in a human way, as we do when we say that men anger god*" (Letter 19; Curley, 358; Geb. IV, 88). Blyenbergh had attempted to preempt the response that since evil is the absence of reality it does not need a cause: "Nor does it seem to me that either you or M. Descartes solve this problem by saying that evil is a *nonbeing,* with which God does not concur. For where, then, did the will to eat come from? Or the Devil's will to pride?" (Letter 18, Curley, 356; Geb. IV, 83).

Spinoza develops his conception of evil as negation by criticizing the teleological orientation of the traditional conception of essence, an orientation that he takes to lie behind Blyenbergh's misgivings.[57] Traditionally, a thing's essence implicitly contains standards of excellence for that thing. The essence of a human being, for example, brings with it the characteristic pattern of human flourishing; similarly, the essence of a given sort of human act implicitly contains the standards of excellence for an act of that sort. Such a conception allows us to say of a given thing—be it a substance or an act or whatever—whether it is perfect or imperfect. To this conception of essence, Spinoza opposes a conception where a thing's essence is just the reality that that thing contains, and carries no implicit standards of perfection: "For regarding the first [that sin and evil are not something positive], we know that whatever there is, considered in itself, without relation to any other thing, involves perfection, which always extends, in each thing, as far as the thing's essence does" (Letter 19, Curley, 358; Geb. IV, 88–89). But if essence is understood in this way, we will be unable to make out that a given thing is less perfect than it "should" be, because we will lack a canonical standard against which to measure that thing. Rather, we will be able only to compare the reality of that thing with the reality possessed by indefinitely many others, some of which it will exceed (and some of which it will not): "Therefore, we will be able to find no imperfection in Adam's decision, if we consider it in itself, without comparing it with others which are more perfect, or show a more perfect state. Indeed, we can compare it with infinitely many other things which are much more imperfect in relation to that, such as stones, logs, etc." (Letter 19, Curley, 358; Geb. IV, 89).

As Spinoza goes on to point out, this understanding of perfection involves the rejection of a distinction between privation and negation.[58] The distinction between privation and negation was particularly important in medieval Aristotelianism and is preserved, somewhat uneasily, in Descartes's metaphysics.[59] A negation is the simple absence of reality, such as a rock's inability to see. A privation, by way of contrast, is the absence of a reality or a perfection in a "subject in which the missing perfection is meant to be,"[60] as, for example, blindness in a human being. The distinction between privation and negation is linked to the teleological orientation of essence in that it is the essence which is supposed to tell us whether a given perfection "is meant to be there." For Spinoza, the two doctrines stand or, as he believes, fall together: "It is certain that privation is nothing positive, and that it is said only in relation to our intellect, not in relation to god's intellect. This arises because we express all the singular things of a kind (e.g., all those which have, externally, the shape of man) by one and the same definition, and therefore we judge them to be equally capable of the highest perfection which we can deduce from such a definition. When we find one whose acts are contrary to that perfection, we judge him to be deprived of it and to be deviating from his nature" (Letter 19, Curley, 359; Geb. IV, 91). Spinoza explains more fully in a subsequent letter to Blyenbergh that "Privation is nothing but denying something of a thing which we judge to pertain to its nature, and Negation nothing but denying something of a thing because it does not pertain to its nature" (Letter 21, Curley, 378; Geb. IV, 129). The reference to what "we judge" is deliberate, relativizing the distinction to human ways of thinking, particularly to human imagining; these ways of thinking have no standing from the point of view of "the divine Decree and intellect":

> I say, therefore, that Privation is, not the act of depriving, but only the pure and simple lack, which in itself is nothing. Indeed, it is only a Being of reason, or mode of thinking, which we form when we compare things with one another. We say, for example, that a blind man is deprived of sight because we easily imagine him as seeing, whether this imagination arises from the fact that we compare him with others who see, or his present state with his past, when he used to see. And when we consider this man in this way, by comparing his nature with that of others or with his own past nature, then we affirm that seeing pertains to his nature, and for that reason we say that he is deprived of it. But when we consider God's decree, and his nature, we can no more affirm of that man than of

a Stone, that he is deprived of vision. For at that time vision no more pertains to that man without contradiction than it does to the stone, *since nothing more pertains to that man, and is his, than what the Divine intellect and will attribute to him.* Hence, God is no more the cause of his not seeing than of the stone's not seeing, which is a pure Negation.

Similarly, when we attend to the nature of a man who is led by an appetite for sensual pleasure, we compare his present appetite with that which is in the pious, or with that which he had at another time. We affirm that this man has been deprived of a better appetite, because we judge that then an appetite for virtue belongs to him. We cannot do this if we attend to the nature of the Divine decree and intellect; for in that regard, the better appetite no more pertains to that man's nature at that time than it does to the Nature of the Devil, or of a stone. That is why, in that regard, the better appetite is not a Privation, but a Negation. (Letter 21, Curley, 377–78; Geb. IV, 128–29)

To pursue matters more deeply, *why* does Spinoza dismiss the Aristotelian conception of essence and the distinction between privation and negation, which was integral to medieval Aristotelianism? His reasons are connected with the changing picture of the universe brought about by Cartesian science and metaphysics. In the Aristotelian universe, individuals are constituted by form and matter. It is easier to view such individuals as fashioned from an archetype or mold in the divine understanding—a mold or archetype which they may exemplify more or less completely or perfectly. This picture of an individual is a good deal less natural in the Cartesian (physical) world of extension in motion. The forms or essences no longer have a fundamental standing. What God does is not to exemplify certain essences or patterns, but rather to produce matter in motion, which may or may not sort itself out into certain kinds. It is unnatural to view these sorts or kinds into which matter happens to be arranged as providing the standards of excellence for the relevant individuals. And so Spinoza offers this diagnosis of how the tradition goes wrong concerning essence: "*We would not do this* [judge Adam to be deprived of a more perfect act], *if we had not brought him under such a definition and fictitiously ascribed such a nature to him. But because god* does not know things abstractly, and does not make such general definitions, because he does not attribute more essence to things than the divine intellect and power endow them with, and in fact give them, it follows clearly *that that privation can be said only in relation to our intellect, not in relation to god's*" (Letter 19, Curley, 359; Geb. IV, 91–92). Kinds, such as *rational animal,* have no standing from God's point of view.[61] Hence they do not supply standards of perfection and imperfection in any absolute sense. The rejection of the distinction between privation and negation and the correlative theme that the (normative) "idea of man" is not something found in nature but a practical guide or model that we set up for ourselves hold an important place in the *Ethics* (see especially the preface to Part Four).

I have digressed somewhat from my central concern, which is Spinoza's conception of modes, because of what I take to be the intrinsic interest of his treatment of the problem of evil. For present purposes the key point is that since it is impossible to make local assessments of evil and perfection, it is impossible to pin responsibility for local evil on God, whether the basis of the charge is that God conserves modes as well as substances, or that God, as the subject in which the modes exist, is the principal actor behind the actions of his modes. This sort of reply does not involve distancing God from the actions of his modes. It does not provide a reason, then, for shrinking from Spinoza's thesis that things other than God are modes of God.

The arguments that we have considered do not afford good grounds for doubting that Spinoza's handling of the substance/mode dichotomy is profoundly indebted to Aristotelian thinking about the substance/accident distinction; or that when Spinoza claims that things other than God are modes of God he means roughly the same thing as a medieval Aristotelian would have meant by the thought that everything besides God is an accident of God. In particular, Curley's arguments do not provide a good reason for turning Spinoza's claim that we are modes of God into the comparatively uninteresting commonplace that we are (efficiently) caused by God. Rather, his considerations can be met by taking seriously the Aristotelian (especially the medieval Aristotelian) origins of the substance/mode dichotomy. Bayle's arguments (at least two of them) do raise important issues. But these questions—what Spinoza means by claiming that "God, *or* his attributes" are immutable and how Spinoza would respond to the difficulties posed by God's apparent involvement in evil—are to be explored and not deflected by refusing to attribute to Spinoza a view that he gives every indication of wanting to hold.

Notes

I would like to acknowledge the suggestions and criticisms of Edwin Curley, Paul Hoffman, Olli Koistinen, Susan Sauvé Meyer, and Margaret Wilson. I would also like to thank the editor of this journal and two anonymous referees for their helpful criticism and advice.

1. For ease of exposition, I am using *modal dependence* as a label for the dependence of modes on their subjects in Spinoza (whatever that dependence

may amount to) and *inherence* for the traditional idea of an accident's existing in a subject (whatever that may amount to).

2. Curley writes in *Spinoza's Metaphysics: An Essay in Interpretation* (Cambridge, MA: Harvard University Press, 1969), hereafter cited as "SM," p. 18: "When qualities are said to inhere in substance, this may be viewed as a way of saying that they are predicated of it."

3. As we shall see, questions have been raised in the middle part of the twentieth century about the fidelity of the following account to Aristotle's own views.

4. This is a bit rough from the point of view of medieval interpretations of Aristotle. Abelard, for example, seems to understand the discussion in the *Categories* in such a way that individuals can be predicated of themselves (see his "The Glosses of Peter Abailard on Porphyry," in Richard McKeon, ed. and trans., *Selections from Medieval Philosophers,* I, 221; a translation of Bernhard Geyer, ed., *Peter Abelards philosophische Schriften, Beiträge zur Geschichte der Philosophie des Mittelalters,* 21 [Münster i. W.: Aschendorff, 1919], I, 1–32), though not "of many." Again, while it is clear from chapters two and three of *De Ente et Essentia* (in Joanes Perrier, ed., *S. Thomae Aquinatis: Opuscula Omnia Necnon Opera Minora* [Paris: P. Lethielleux, 1949], I, 24–50) that Aquinas sees a close relation between universality and "agreeing with many," it is also true that he allows that there is a sense in which an individual, such as Socrates, can be predicated of something, as in "This white thing is Socrates" or "This human being is Socrates." See *In VII Metaph.,* lect. 2, n. 1273; trans. by John P. Rowan, *Commentary on the Metaphysics of Aristotle* (Chicago: Henry Regnery Co., 1961), II, 497; orig. lang. M.-R. Cathala *et al., S. Thomae Aquinatis: In Duodecim Libros Metaphysician Aristotelis* (Rome: Marietti, 1964), 321.

5. Aquinas makes reference to the individuation of accidents through their subjects in *On the Power of God,* Q. 9, A. 2 ad 8 (orig. lang. *Quaestiones Disputatae* [Rome: Marietti, 1949]), II, and ST I, Q. 29, A. 1 c. For the *Summa Theologica* (ST), I have used the translation of Fathers of the English Dominican Province, 4 pts. in 5 vols. (Westminster, Md.: Christian Classics, 1981; first published 1911); orig. lang. *Summa Theologiae,* 4 pts. in 5 vols. (Madrid: Biblioteca de Autores Cristianos, 1978).

6. See Marilyn McCord Adams, *William Ockham* (Notre Dame: University of Notre Dame Press, 1987), II, 672–73, and I, 14–15.

7. See especially *Metaphysics* VII. 4 and 5.

8. See *Posterior Analytics* I.73a34–b5, and *Metaphysics* V.1022a25–32; and Aquinas's commentaries on these passages, *In I Post. Anal.* lect. 10 (Leonine: Rome, 1882), I, and *In V Meta.,* lect. 19, nn. 1054–1057, especially nn. 1054 and 1055.

9. All citations of Spinoza are taken from Edwin Curley, ed. and trans., *The Collected Works of Spinoza* (Princeton: Princeton University Press, 1985), I; henceforth cited as "Curley," Original language references are to Carl Gebhardt, ed., *Spinoza Opera* (Heidelberg: Carl Winter, 1925), in 4 vols.; henceforth cited as "Geb."

10. See M. Gueroult, *Spinoza* (Hildesheim: Olms, 1968), I, 1, §§ 13 and 21, where he understands the two clauses as linked through the fact that, for Spinoza, "l'essence objective est rigoureusement conformé à l'essence formelle" (p. 58); Wolfson, *The Philosophy of Spinoza*, I, ch. 3; and SM, ch. 1, especially 14–16.

11. See AT III, 474–76 (Kenny, 123–24); VII, 444; VIII.2, 350, 355 (CSM I, 298, 301–302); and *Principles*, I, Arts. 53 and 61 ("CSM" refers to John Cottingham, Robert Stoothoff, and Dugald Murdoch, trans., *The Philosophical Writings of Descartes* [New York: Cambridge University Press, 1985], Vols. I and II). Wolfson discusses this interpretation in *The Philosophy of Spinoza*, I, 65, citing A. Léon, *Les éléments cartésiens de la doctrine spinoziste,* 85 in this regard; and Gueroult maintains that Descartes's claim that a mode must be conceived through the concept of the substance in which it exists influences Spinoza's account of modes in *Spinoza*, I, 61, but overestimates the discontinuity between Descartes's claim and the Aristotelian thesis that accidents are definitionally dependent on their proper subjects (see esp. *Spinoza*, I, 61, n. 171).

In SM, 15, Curley argues against relating Spinoza's definition of substance to Descartes on the ground that "for Descartes, though substance is supposed to exist in itself, it is conceived through another," an assertion that Curley repeats in *Beyond the Geometrical Method* (Princeton: Princeton University Press, 1988); hereafter cited as "BGM," 142, n. 10. The "other" that Curley has in mind is a substance's principal attribute. But this fails to take into account that Descartes holds that there is only a distinction of reason between a substance and its principal attribute (see *Principles*, I, arts. 62 and 63); although Descartes's views on the distinction are complex (see AT IV, 348–50, in Anthony Kenny, trans., Descartes, *Philosophical Letters* [Minneapolis: University of Minnesota Press, 1981], 186–88), there does not seem to be enough of an extramental difference between a substance and its principal attribute for the latter to count as "other" than the former.

12. See, e.g., BGM, 17–19; and Jonathan Bennett, *A Study of Spinoza's "Ethics"* (Indianapolis: Hackett, 1984), § 17, esp. § 17.3 and 4; Don Garrett, "Spinoza's Necessitarianism," in Yovel, ed., *God and Nature: Spinoza's Metaphysics* (New York: E. J. Brill, 1991), § III.1.

13. Spinoza treats the concern as a general problem for standard Western theology. According to standard Western theology, created things are never fully independent beings because they depend on God throughout their existence: "God is not only the cause of the coming to be of things, as they say, but also of their being" (IIP10CS; Curley, 455 [Geb. II, 93]; see also IP24C; Curley, 431 [Geb. II, 67]). However, Spinoza's move from God's conservation of creation, which is a form of efficient causal dependence, to God's being implicated in the definition of a finite thing, which involves a relation of modal dependence, is contentious.

14. For an account of the way in which modes "follow" from God see § 3 of my "Spinoza's Views on Necessity in Historical Perspective," *Philosophical Topics* 19 (1991).

15. I've been helped in thinking about this difference between Spinoza and

the Aristotelians by Marleen Rozemond's discussion of the structure of Cartesian essences in "Descartes's Case for Dualism," *Journal of the History of Philosophy* 33 (January 1995): 29–63. See especially § 5.

16. See especially SM, ch. 1.

17. Curley raises this question in the context of a discussion of whether Bennett's interpretation of modes can accommodate infinite modes; but obviously the question is of more general import. Curley expands on this objection in his contribution to the proceedings of the Jerusalem Spinoza Conference at Hebrew University in 1987, "On Bennett's Interpretation of Spinoza's Monism," in Yovel, *God and Nature,* the first volume of *Spinoza by 2000,* 48–49.

18. See, e.g., *De Principiis Naturae,* in Joannes Perrier, ed., *S. Thomae Aquinatis: Opuscula Omnia Necnon Opera Minora* (Paris: P. Lethielleux, 1949), I, 3–4; Eng. trans., "Principles of Nature," in Robert P. Goodwin, trans., *Selected Writings of St. Thomas Aquinas* (Indianapolis: Bobbs-Merrill, 1965), where Aquinas makes it clear that substances serve as the matter in which accidental forms come into being. And, he writes in ST I, Q. 77, A. 6 ad 2: "The subject [of an accident] . . . is . . . as it were the material cause [of its proper accident], inasmuch as it is receptive of the accident." The reason for the qualification "as it were" is that the passage concerns an immaterial subject, the essence of the human soul.

19. Martial Gueroult proposes a similar assimilation in *Spinoza,* I, 60–65. Gueroult writes of "la traduction des notions d'*in se* et d'*in alio* en termes de causalité" (I, 63) in Spinoza. Gueroult proposes this translation as a consequence of Spinoza's revision of Descartes's metaphysics. According to Gueroult, Descartes breaks with the Aristotelian conception of the substance/accident distinction by requiring not only that a substance not inhere in another thing, but also that it be clearly and distinctly perceivable through itself; similarly, a mode is something that not only inheres in another, but also must be conceived through another (I, 61). But Descartes limits the scope of his innovation (which, allowed free rein, would lead to the conclusion that only a completely independent being, God, qualifies as a substance) by permitting the parts of a thing and all particulars to count as substances, reserving the category of modes for manners of being instead of real things (ibid.). Spinoza, by way of contrast, holds that individual minds and bodies are modes; and so modes, notwithstanding the fact that they are not substances, are real things. And this, Gueroult thinks, requires the translation of the notions of *in se* and *in alio* into the terms of causality (I, 63).

It is not clear that such a translation is really necessary. If by "real thing" Gueroult means what the scholastics would have called a *res,* then there is no incompatibility between something's being a *res* and its being an accident. If by "real thing" Gueroult has something stronger in mind, say the ability to exist apart from a subject, then there is indeed an incompatibility between something's being a real thing and its being a mode; but there is no reason to believe that Spinoza holds produced things to be real things in this stronger sense. Rather than seeing Spinoza as abandoning the substance/accident dichotomy in favor of an efficient cause/effect dichotomy, it is simpler and accords better with the texts to read him as embracing a fairly traditional version of the substance/mode dichotomy, which is, after all, supposed to mark off a division within "real being."

Moreover, Gueroult does not, for example, explain why the substance/mode distinction and cause/effect distinction appear to function as independent dichotomies in Spinoza's text. Indeed, it is not obvious how complete this "translation" is in Gueroult's own mind: for example, in his discussion of the third demonstration of IP11, he relies on his observation that "l'instrument de sa preuve est, non le rapport de cause à effet, mais celui de substance à mode" (I, 197) and distinguishes between two forms of divine immanence with respect to things, one having to do with God's essence and the other with divine causality (I, 222-23).

20. The demonstration of IP16 is discussed in detail in § 3 of my "Spinoza's Views on Necessity in Historical Perspective."

21. IP25, "God is the efficient cause, not only of the existence of things, but also of their essence," is instructive in this regard because Spinoza offers two demonstrations for it, one based on IP15 and one based on IP16. The IP15 demonstration runs through the idea that if God did not cause modes, their essences could be conceived without God, contradicting their modal status; the IP16 demonstration runs through the idea that divine essence has sufficient reality to produce the essence as well as the existence of things. These are clearly very different arguments.

The demonstration of IP18 affords another example of Spinoza's keeping the meaning of IP15 and IP16 distinct: both IP15 and IP16C1 are invoked in that demonstration, to advance different steps of the argument.

22. Although this has been challenged in twentieth-century Aristotle exegesis. See below.

23. Bennett agrees that the "wrong logical type" objection presents a serious obstacle to taking the thesis that finite things are modes of God in an unreconstructed manner. In response to this problem, Bennett undertakes to present, on Spinoza's behalf, a "field metaphysic." See ch. 4 of his book.

24. See also § 15.2 (p. 57): "It may be objected: 'In saying that the redness doesn't need this face, you are taking the redness to be a universal which can be equally present in several particulars. But there is a property-instance that needs this particular face; if this face didn't exist, this *case* of redness wouldn't exist'. Such an objection presupposes that in addition to the face and the redness, there is something called a redness-instance which is particular like the face and yet is a property rather than a substance. I deny that there is any such item: the only sense I can attach to 'instance of redness' is that of 'red thing'; and then the instance of redness doesn't depend on the face because it is the face."

25. Originally published in *Phronesis* 10 (1965): 97–105; rpt. G. E. L. Owen, *Logic, Science, and Dialectic* (London: Duckworth, 1986). Curley refers to this article in n. 3 on 161 of SM.

26. "To say that vink is a particular colour is to say that it, or its name, cannot be predicated: it is not to say that it cannot be found in more than one

subject. Any particular shade of colour is of course reproducible. Any bit of linguistic knowledge can of course lodge in more than one head. Aristotle does not for a moment contemplate denying this. His commentators saddle him with the denial, and this is the dogma I set out to examine" (254 [*Logic, Science*, 99]).

27. Indeed, particular accidents have been taken seriously in modern times. See, e.g., D. C. Williams, "The Elements of Being" in his *Principles of Empirical Realism* (Springfield, Ill.: C. C. Thomas, 1966); Keith Campbell, "The Metaphysics of Abstract Particulars," in Peter A. French *et al.*, eds., *Midwest Studies in Philosophy* 6 (1981), 477–88 (I am grateful to Olli Koistinen for these references). Jonathan Bennett points out in correspondence that he, too, now defends particular accidents in *Events and Their Names* (Indianapolis: Hackett, 1988).

28. See, e.g., Aquinas, *De Ente et Essentia*, ch. 1.

29. See, e.g., *On the Power of God*, Q. 9, A. 2 ad 8; and ST I, Q. 29, A. 1 c.; III, Q. 77, A. 2; cf. A. 1. See also Marilyn Adams, *Ockham*, I, 179.

30. See n. 19 above.

31. Charles Adam and Paul Tannery, eds., *Oeuvres de Descartes* (Paris: J. Vrin, 1973–1982, augmented ed.; orig. pub. 1897–1913), IV, 164; trans. Anthony Kenny, *Descartes: Philosophical Letters* (Minneapolis: University of Minnesota Press, 1981), 155. Henceforth cited as "AT" and "Kenny" respectively. The italics are owed to Kenny's practice of italicizing Latin words in a French context.

32. The priority that Aquinas refers to in this passage is not, of course, to be understood temporally. Since a proper accident necessarily accompanies its subject, there is no time at which the subject lacks it.

33. "On Bennett's Interpretation of Spinoza's Monism," 48. Curley cites the following passage of *The Emendation of the Intellect* to support his claim that "Spinoza *does* gloss his definition of substance in terms of causal self-sufficiency": "If the thing is in itself, *or*, as is commonly said is the cause of itself, then it must be understood through itself alone; but if it is not in itself, but requires a cause to exist, then it must be understood through its proximate cause" (§ 92; Curley, 38–39; Geb. II, 34). It is not obvious, however, that this passage should be read as an account of substance, because it is not clear that existing in itself is being opposed to existing in another here. There is no suggestion, for example, that something which is not "in itself" must be in another (although Curley seems to suggest otherwise, BGM, 142, n. 10). Indeed, this passage does not make clear what "the other" would be: after all, it is hard to see how a thing (e.g., a circle) could be a mode of its proximate cause (e.g., the process of rotating a line about a fixed endpoint). Moreover, it is not clear how to understand the "commonly [*vulgo*]" on Curley's reading. The most obvious precedent would be Descartes's characterization of substance in the *Principles*, I, 51. But, first, it is not clear that Descartes's views are prevalent enough to justify the "commonly." And, second, as it quickly emerges (see § 97) that only uncreated things qualify as being *in se*, the view expressed in § 92, taken as a complete account of substance, seems sufficiently

remote from Descartes's own views (who, after all, makes room for created substances) to make it doubtful that Spinoza would appeal to his precedent without elaboration. I'm inclined to follow Wolfson (II, 142), who takes *in se* here to mean simply an uncreated thing.

Finally, even if we accept Curley's reading of § 92 of TdIE, it still is the case that the *Ethics* keeps causal notions out of the definitions of mode and substance. For example, Gueroult, who seems to read § 92 in the way that Curley does (see *Spinoza,* I, 41, n. 77), argues that in the *Ethics* being *causa sui* is only a *propria,* and not a part of the essence, of God or substance (see *Spinoza,* I, i, §§ 10–11 and 13). There may, indeed, be some fairly quick routes from being a substance to being causally independent (as, for example, the alternative demonstration to IP6C testifies), but we shouldn't lose sight of the fact that there is distance to be traveled.

34. See *Dictionnaire historique et critique de Pierre Bayle* (Paris: Desoer, 1820), XIII, 443. I have used the translation found in *A Historical and Critical Dictionary, Selected and Abridged from the Great Work of Peter Bayle* (London: Hunt and Clarke, 1826). Hereafter cited as "Bayle," where the first page reference is to the French original and the second to the English translation.

35. Bayle concludes: "It is therefore God who at the same time forms an act of will, and does not form it with respect to the same object. And therefore, two contradictory terms are true of him, which overthrow the first principle of metaphysics" (XIII, 443; IV, 296).

36. Bayle, XIII, 441; IV, 293; see also XIII, 443; IV, 297.

37. Bayle, XIII, 444; IV, 298–99.

38. This thesis is based on a view about language reflecting the way the world is: What makes "*S* is *P*" true is either that *P* constitutes *S* (i.e., is a part of *S*'s essence) or that *P* inheres in *S.* This suggests, in turn, that if some *P* inheres in some *S,* there ought to be a predication corresponding to this fact (although, to my knowledge, not much explicit attention was given to the inference in this direction). Spinoza seems uninterested in the relationship between predication and modal dependence. In the *Ethics,* he does not move from the claim that *M* is a mode of *S* to *S* is *M,* nor does he tell us what he things of such an inference.

One should not confuse this comparatively peripheral view about predication with the substance/accident distinction itself. (Spinoza can be very interested in the latter without being especially concerned with the former.) Similarly, subscription to the linguistic thesis mentioned above does not involve conflating Aristotle's dichotomies between, on the one hand, what can be said of a subject and what cannot be said of a subject and, on the other hand, between what does not exist in a subject and what exists in a subject: indeed, since the distinction between what constitutes *S* and what does not has to be in place before one determines whether "*S* is *P*" is to be "analyzed" as an essential or accidental predication, the metaphysics is prior to the linguistic thesis. (See also the citation from Aquinas, *In VII Metaph.,* in n. 4 above, where he allows that there is a way in which an individual can be predicated.)

39. See Bennett, *A Study,* § 23.5.

40. This point was suggested to me by Michael Della Rocca's unpublished manuscript, "Predication and Pantheism in Spinoza."

41. Cf. Aquinas's argument concerning the essence of the soul and its powers sketched on pp. 259–60 above.

42. Cf. *Cogitata Metaphysica,* I. 4: "Let us, therefore, go on to ask whether there is any change in God from God himself. We do not concede that there is such a change in God—indeed, we deny it completely. For every change which depends on the will occurs in order that its subject may change into a better state. But this cannot occur in a most perfect being. Also there is no change except for the sake of avoiding some disadvantage or acquiring some good which is lacking, neither of which can occur in God. So we conclude that God is an immutable being" (Curley, 322; Geb. I, 256–57). This argument is similar to one in the text in that it presents God's perfection as the principal obstacle to his changing himself. It differs in the role given to the divine will in the explanation of why God's perfection precludes self-change. The resulting argument is reminiscent of IP7ff. in Spinoza's *Descartes' "Principals of Philosophy."*

43. See Bennett, *A Study,* § 49.3–5.

44. See Curley, BGM, 34; Gueroult, *Spinoza* I, i.23 (p. 64); but see also I, ap. iii, p. 446, n. 80, which might be taken to suggest that Gueroult thinks that Spinoza changed his mind over the issue of divine immutability from the *Cogitata Metaphysica* to the *Ethics.*

45. See SM, 13; BGM, 34.

46. Indeed, by depriving Spinoza of a genuine conception of a mode, Curley and Gueroult leave the *Ethics* silent as to whether God possesses accidents in the traditional sense of accidents.

47. In n. 53 (p. 150), Curley credits Lachièze-Rey with this interpretation. Michael Della Rocca points out in "Predication and Pantheism in Spinoza" that IP29S does not provide clear evidence against identifying God with the whole of nature, since Spinoza is talking there only about God "insofar as he is considered a free cause." Spinoza's view might be then that if this condition were removed—that is, if God were considered *simpliciter*—God would be all of nature, that is, *natura naturans* and *natura naturata.*

48. Cf. Bennett, *A Study,* § 49.3: "Some things in [Spinoza's] work tend that way [i.e., toward 'denying the reality of change'], especially the tendency to regard God as a subject only of necessary truths and never of contingent ones, i.e., to identify God with what I call 'God as seen from above'. I think that explains the statement that 'God, or all of God's attributes, are immutable' (1p20c2), and the implication that God is 'immutable and eternal' in 5p20s." Bennett includes more under the heading of 'God seen from above' than God's essence and attributes, namely, the infinite and eternal modes (see § 28.3–6).

49. Technically, a *mutatio* as opposed to a *motus.*

50. Incidentally, Bayle's complaint suggests that he reads IP20C2 in the same way. Bayle writes: "Observe, that the Proteus mentioned by the poets, their Thetis, their Vertumnus, who were images and examples of inconstancy, and which occasioned the proverbs whereby the oddest fickleness of men was de-

noted, would have been immutable gods, if the god of the Spinozists were immutable; for it was never pretended that there happened any alteration in their substance, but only new modifications" (XIII, 441; IV, 293). Bayle's charge is that for Spinoza to hold "there [never] happened any alteration" in God's "substance" is not enough to show that God is immutable.

51. It must be admitted that Bayle could be clearer as to the precise nature of his objection(s). In particular, while this passage occurs in a section ostensibly concerned with showing Spinoza's doctrine to be "an execrable abomination if it be considered with regard to morality" (XIII, 443; IV, 297), it is not obvious whether Bayle has in view God's apparent implication in evil or some more general worry about the dignity of God in Spinoza's metaphysics. The cited passage continues: "And therefore all the phrases made use of to express what men do one against another have no other true sense than this: God hates himself; he asks favours of himself and refuses them to himself; he persecutes himself, kills himself, eats himself, calumniates himself, executes himself, &c. This would be less incomprehensible, if Spinoza had represented God as a collection of many distinct parts; but he reduces him to the most perfect simplicity, to a unity of substance, to indivisibility" (Bayle, XIII, 444; IV, 298–99). But it is hard to see how the denial of divine simplicity would serve to extricate God from the evil committed by his modes. At any rate, Bayle may well have had several objections in view, and it does no harm, as far as I can see, to take him to be raising the problem concerning God's implication in evil, as the problem is an interesting one.

52. For a helpful discussion of active accidental forms, see Anneliese Maier, in Steven D. Sargent, ed. and trans., *On the Threshold of Exact Science: Selected Writings of Anneliese Maier on Late Medieval Natural Philosophy* (Philadelphia: University of Pennsylvania Press, 1982), 43–44.

53. See, e.g., Aquinas, ST I, Q. 77, A. 1, ad 3: "Action belongs to the composite [of substance and accident], as does existence; for to act belongs to what exists. Now the composite has substantial existence through the substantial form; and it operates by the power which results from the substantial form. Hence an active accidental form is to the substantial form of the agent (for instance, heat compared to the form of fire) as the power of the soul is to the soul."

54. See Maier, *On the Threshold of Exact Science,* 44-45.

55. "Sed oportet ut forma accidentalis agat in virtute formae consubstantialis, quasi instrumentum ejus, alias non induceret agendo formam substantialem," Aquinas, in James H. Robb, ed., St. Thomas Aquinas, *Quaestiones de Anima* (Toronto: Pontifical Institute of Mediaeval Studies, 1968), Q. 12.

56. Strictly, Blyenbergh's query concerns Descartes's positions, as interpreted by Spinoza. He writes to Spinoza: "Both in the *Principles* and in the *Metaphysical Thoughts* you generally maintain—whether as your own opinion or to explain M. Descartes, whose Philosophy you were teaching . . ." (letter 18; Curley, 355; Geb. IV, 81–82). But Spinoza does not distance himself in his response from the position that Blyenbergh criticizes. Moreover, what particularly concerns Blyenbergh—the claim that God (efficiently) causally determines

the manner in which substances act, as well as conserving the being—is endorsed by Spinoza in the *Ethics* (see PI26 and 27).

It must be remarked that from the point of view of the high scholastic tradition, Blyenbergh's focus on God's role in conserving the manner in which substances act is curious. No serious medieval theodicy traded on exempting certain activities of created substances from the need of divine concurrence. One may speculate that perhaps Descartes's views of the laws of motion, which seem to locate all the agency of the universe in the way God conserves the universe, made Descartes's views on divine conservation seem suspect to Blyenbergh. (At any rate, Spinoza's untraditional response to Blyenbergh's objection is distinctive and instructive.)

57. There are other ways in which Spinoza's treatment deviates from the tradition. In keeping with the antiteleological thrust of his later works, Spinoza presents evil as an absence of *reality* or perfection, not as an absence of *good*. In the tradition, being and good are viewed as "convertible," so that a thing occupies the same place on the scale of goodness as it does on the scale of reality, whereas Spinoza denies that good has the same sort of metaphysical standing as reality or perfection (he explicitly rejects the medieval conception of good as a transcendental, or general, affection of being in *Cogitata metaphysica,* I, 6). I take up Spinoza's views on good and perfection in my unpublished paper "Spinoza on Teleology and Agency."

58. Spinoza's views on privation and negation are helpfully discussed by Joachim in *A Study of the Ethics of Spinoza,* 109–11. If there is a point of disagreement between Joachim's treatment and my own, it is that he seems to treat Spinoza's views on negation and privation as an original doctrine rather than (as I see it) fundamentally the repudiation of a traditional doctrine. See also Raphael Demos, "Spinoza's Doctrine of Privation," in S. Paul Kashap, ed., *Studies in Spinoza: Critical and Interpretive Essays* (Berkeley: University of California Press, 1972), 276–88. I discuss Spinoza's treatment of the doctrine of privation further, in connection with texts from the *Ethics,* in my unpublished paper "Spinoza on Teleology and Agency."

59. Descartes makes use of the distinction between privation and negation in his intellectual theodicy in the Fourth Meditation (AT VII, 54–56). In general, Descartes is moving away from a conception of essence or nature which underwrites the distinction, as is clear from his discussion, in the Sixth Meditation, of whether a sick human body, any more than a broken clock, is "unnatural." But Descartes also allows: "Admittedly, when I consider the purpose of the clock, I may say that it is departing from its nature when it does not tell the right time; and similarly when I consider the mechanism of the human body, I may think that, in relation to the movements which normally occur in it, it too is deviating from its nature if the throat is dry at a time when drinking is not beneficial to its continued health" (AT VII, 85; CSM II, 58–59). Descartes immediately warns the reader that this teleological sense of nature, where assessments of what is natural and unnatural are informed by some background purpose (telling time; health), is very different from the sense of 'natural' where 'natural' means obeying the laws of nature.

60. Aquinas, Perrier, *De Principiis Naturae,* 5–6; Eng. trans., Goodwin, "Principles of Nature," ch. II, Goodwin, *Selected Writings,* 11 (see also the texts cited by Goodwin in n. 19 on that page).

61. This suggestion is corroborated by the fact that Spinoza is willing to employ the notion of privation with respect to things whose essences do have standing from God's point of view in ways in which he is not with respect to the "fictitious" man-made essences of finite things—see letter 36 and Gueroult's discussion of it in *Spinoza* I, 228–29.

7

Spinoza's Argument for the Identity Theory

Michael Della Rocca

> It seems evident that *any* success in understanding Spinoza is gong to require working one's way through a thicket of intensionality of which only the bare outlines have so far been discerned.
>
> —Margaret D. Wilson[1]

1. Introduction

Does Spinoza hold an identity theory of the mind-body relation? He certainly seems to. Consider these passages:

> The mind and the body are one and the same thing, which is conceived now under the attribute of thought, now under the attribute of extension. (3p2s)

> A mode of extension and the idea of that mode are one and the same thing, but expressed in two ways. (2p7s)[2]

The second passage entails mind-body identity because for Spinoza the body is a mode of extension and the mind is the idea of that mode (see 2p13). It seems difficult not to interpret such passages as directly committing Spinoza to a numerical identity between the mind and body. After all, to be one and the same thing is, it seems, to be numerically identical.

I accept this literal interpretation, which I will call the numerical identity interpretation. In this paper, I will continue a project of defending this reading of Spinoza. In a previous paper, I showed that a numerical identity position is not, contrary to what some have thought, incompatible with certain basic features of Spinoza's system (see my 1991). However, even if Spinoza can consistently hold a numerical identity position and even if this literal interpretation of Spinoza is correct, the proponent of this interpretation faces a challenge concerning its significance. That Spinoza consistently holds an identity theory would not in itself be of much interest unless there is in Spinoza an interesting and important way of *arguing* for an identity theory. We need to be given good reasons to hold that a numerical identity position grows out of, and is not simply superadded to, Spinoza's system.[3] In what follows, I provide such reasons.

It might seem that the claim of numerical identity follows from Spinoza's view that the thinking substance and the extended substance are identical.[4] For Spinoza, there is only one substance, God, and this substance has infinitely many basic features or attributes, including thought and extension.[5] Thus for Spinoza the one thinking substance is identical with the one extended substance. The modes of thought, which include all the particular, finite thinking things, and the modes of extension, which include all the particular, infinite extended things, are not themselves substances, but are somehow dependent on the one substance. When Spinoza introduces his claim about identity of modes, he seems to be drawing an inference from the identity of the thinking substance and the extended substance to the identity of modes of thought and modes of extension:

> The thinking substance and the extended substance are one and the same substance, which is now comprehended under this attribute, now under that. So also [*sic etiam*] a mode of extension and the idea of that mode are one and the same thing, but expressed in two ways. (2p7s)

However, it is not clear whether Spinoza intends to be drawing an inference here. Bennett, for one, thinks that Spinoza's '*sic etiam*' signals merely an analogy and not an inference (1984, 142). And even if Spinoza is drawing an inference here, it is not clear whether such an inference would be valid. Bennett expresses some doubts on this point: "Mind-body identity is not entailed by the thesis that thought and extension are attributes of a single substance. Why should not a thinking and extended substance have details under one attribute which are not also details under the other?" (1984, 142).

To resolve these issues would require an investigation of Spinoza's notion of attribute and of his claim that the thinking substance is identical with the extended substance. I intend, however, to avoid that cluster of difficult issues here since I think we can approach our topic from a separate and perhaps more promising angle. Independently of any particular understanding of the notion of the attributes of substance, I will show how Spinoza could support the claim of numerical identity. I will focus on some explicit and some less than explicit considerations at work in the text. In particular, I will argue that Spinoza regards certain causal contexts as referentially opaque. With the help of what I will call the Opacity Transmission Principle, we can see that the opacity of these contexts in Spinoza shows that he also would accept the opacity of a wide variety of other contexts—ones involving the attributes of thought and extension. This broad range of opaque contexts in Spinoza is the key to the Spinozistic argument for the claim of numerical identity that I will present. Not only will I show that this argument is one that Spinoza could provide, but I will also show that there is evidence that Spinoza is actually relying on such an argument in making his claim of numerical identity. In the final section of the paper, I will question Spinoza's reasons for holding that so many contexts are opaque.

2. Opacity in Spinoza[6]

The best way to introduce the elements of Spinoza's argument for the Identity Theory is to neutralize an important objection to interpreting Spinoza as holding that mind and body are identical. The objection, which comes from R. J. Delahunty, goes as follows:[7] If my mind is identical with my body and if my body causally interacts with another body, say mode of extension A, then it follows that my mind causally interacts with mode of extension A. But such interaction goes against Spinoza's oft-repeated ban on causal interaction between attributes. For example, Spinoza says, "The body cannot determine the mind to thinking and the mind cannot determine the body to motion, to rest or to anything else (if there is anything else)" (3p2; see also the second half of 2p7s). Thus Delahunty concludes that Spinoza cannot coherently accept mind–body identity.

This objection works only if Spinoza takes certain causal contexts to be referentially transparent, for the objection relies upon the validity of the inference

1. My body causally interacts with mode of extension A.
2. My body = my mind.
So
3. My mind causally interacts with mode of extension A.

However, there is good reason to think that Spinoza does *not* regard the relevant causal contexts as transparent.

Spinoza recognizes two different kinds of causal relation: immanent and transitive. Transitive causation occurs between different finite things. Immanent causation occurs between God, the one substance, and finite things. Spinoza says quite clearly that whether it's true to say that God is the (immanent) cause of a finite mode depends on how God is conceived. Thus: "The modes of each attribute have God for their cause only insofar as he is considered under the attribute of which they are modes, and not insofar as he is considered under any other attribute" (2p6). This suggests that for Spinoza

(a) The thinking substance causes mode of thought 1

is true, while

(b) The extended substance causes mode of thought 1

is false. The fact that Spinoza sees (a) as true and (b) as false, despite the identity of the thinking substance and the extended substance, shows that for Spinoza contexts involving immanent causation are referentially opaque. Specifically, this shows that the position within such sentences for the term picking out the immanent cause is referentially opaque. Spinoza thinks that the truth value of certain immanent causal claims is sensitive to the way in which the immanent cause is described.

Spinoza's basis for holding that the truth value of certain immanent causal claims is sensitive to the way in which the immanent cause is described shows that he would also be committed to treating certain transitive causal claims as involving referential opacity.

Here is Spinoza's basis in 2p6d for holding that the truth value of certain immanent causal claims is sensitive to the way the immanent cause is described:

> Each attribute is conceived through itself without any other (by 1p10). So the modes of each attribute involve the concept of their own attribute, but not of another one; and so (by 1ax4) they have God for their cause only insofar as he is considered under the attribute of which they are modes, and not insofar as he is considered under any other.

1ax4, which Spinoza relies on here, is the important claim: "The knowledge of an effect depends on, and involves, the knowledge of its cause." 1ax4 is relevant to this proof since, for Spinoza, the claim that the idea of the effect depends on and involves the idea of the cause entails that the effect is conceived through the cause (see, e.g., 1p3d, 1p6cd2). Thus Spinoza is saying here that if mode of thought 1, say, were immanently caused by the extended substance, then mode of thought 1 would be conceived through the extended substance. This, Spinoza claims, would violate the conceptual separation of the attributes.

A similar proof could be provided for the conclusion that a given mode has another mode for a cause only insofar as the latter mode is considered under the attribute of which the first mode is a mode.[8] This would be a claim of the opacity of transitive causal contexts. The proof would go as follows:

Each attribute is conceived through itself without any other (by 1p10). So a mode of a particular attribute involves the concept of its own attribute, and not that of any other. Therefore (by 1ax4) it has another mode for its cause only insofar as that other mode is considered under the attribute of which the first mode is a mode and not insofar as that other mode is considered under any other attribute.[9]

Just as 2p6d indicates that Spinoza would regard (a) as true and (b) as false, despite the identity of the thinking substance and the extended substance, the analogous proof just given suggests that Spinoza would regard

(c) Mode of extension A causally interacts with mode of extension B

as true, and

(d) Mode of thought 1 causally interacts with mode of extension B

as false, even if mode of extension A = mode of thought 1. Such a position would amount to the referential opacity of certain causal contexts.

Thus, Spinoza's basis for saying that certain immanent causal contexts are opaque shows that he would have the same basis for saying that certain transitive causal contexts are opaque. The point here is not that the opacity of certain transitive causal contexts is entailed by the opacity of certain immanent causal contexts,[10] but rather that Spinoza's basis for asserting the opacity of the latter contexts shows that he is committed to a similar basis for asserting the opacity of the former contexts.

This opacity of certain transitive causal contexts in Spinoza shows that the numerical identity interpretation can successfully avoid Delahunty's objection. Given this opacity, Spinoza can affirm an identity of modes of thought and modes of extension even while maintaining that there is no causal interaction across attributes.

The same considerations suggest that Spinoza would regard the following contexts as referentially opaque:

> '. . . is caused by the extended substance'
> '. . . is caused by the thinking substance'.

These are immanent causal contexts where the position for the term picking out the *effect* of the immanent cause is opaque. By contrast, 2p6, as I claimed above, is a statement to the effect that in sentences concerning immanent causation, the position for the term picking out the immanent cause itself is referentially opaque.

The fact that for Spinoza certain causal contexts are opaque implies that for him a vast number of other contexts are opaque as well. This underappreciated fact about the extent of opacity in Spinoza's system is essential to understanding his argument for the Identity Theory. These additional kinds of opaque contexts involve the attribution of mental or physical properties to an object.

Spinoza holds that each thing is caused by God (1p25). But, as Spinoza claims in a passage I quoted earlier, modes that are extended are caused by God only insofar as God is considered as the extended substance and modes that are thinking are caused by God only insofar as God is considered as the thinking substance (2p6). It follows that

> (e) mode x is extended only if mode x is caused by the extended substance

and

> (f) mode x is thinking only if mode x is caused by the thinking substance.

Earlier I noted that the context '. . . is caused by the extended substance' is, for Spinoza, opaque. Given the dependence, which (e) reveals, of the property of being extended on the property of being caused by the extended substance, and given the opacity of the context '. . . is caused by the extended substance', it follows that the context '. . . is extended' is also opaque. One way of bringing this conclusion out is as follows. (e) shows that whether a mode is extended depends on whether it is caused by the extended substance. But, as we saw earlier, whether a mode is caused by the extended substance depends on how that mode is conceived of or described. Thus, by the transitivity of this dependence relation, whether a mode is extended depends on how that mode is conceived of or described. This conclusion, however, is just the claim that the context '. . . is extended' is opaque. A similar line of reasoning would show that the context '. . . is thinking' is also opaque. This line of reasoning would rely upon the entailment (f) above.

My point here can be made more formally with the help of the Opacity Transmission Principle.[11]

If
   (i) for any term 't', 'F(t)' entails 'G(t)'
   (ii) there are possible situations in which G(t), t = t*, and −G(t*) and
   (iii) in at least some of those situations F(t),
   then
   there are possible situations in which F(t), t = t*, and −F(t*).

Condition (ii) is just the claim that the context 'G(. . .)' is opaque and the conclusion is just the claim that the context 'F(. . .)' is opaque. Thus the principle says that in the case of an entailment of the form 'F(t) → G(t)', if the position for 't' in the entire context of the consequent is opaque and if condition (iii) is also met, then the position for 't' in the entire context of the antecedent is opaque.

The proof of the principle is straightforward. Consider a possible situation in which G(a), a = b, and −G(b) and in which F(a). Conditions (ii) and (iii) assert that there is such a situation. Since a = b, 'a' and 'b' are coreferring terms. Now let's say that substitution of coreferring terms within the context 'F(. . .)' is legitimate. If we allow such substitutions, then we can substitute 'b' for 'a' in that context and thus we arrive at the claim 'F(b)'. But now recall condition (i): For any term 't', 'F(t)' entails 'G(t)'. From this and the claim 'F(b)' we reach the conclusion that in this situation 'G(b)' is true. But, ex hypothesi, this is a situation in which −G(b). Thus given the initial description of this situation we reach a contradiction once we make the further assumption that we can validly substitute for coreferring terms in the context 'F(. . .)'. Thus we must conclude that given conditions (i)–(iii), we cannot validly substitute within the context 'F(. . .)' and thus that that context is opaque. In this way, under the conditions (i)–(iii), opacity would be transmitted from the context 'G(. . .)' to the context 'F(. . .)'.

These three conditions are met for the context from Spinoza we are considering, namely the context '. . . is extended'. For Spinoza the following claims are true:

   (i′) For any term 't', 't is extended' entails 't is caused by the extended substance'.

(ii′) There are possible situations in which t is caused by the ex-
        tended substance, t = t*, and it is not the case that t* is caused
        by the extended substance.

(iii′) In at least some of those situations t is extended.

(i′) simply follows from claim (e) above:

(e) Mode x is extended only if mode x is caused by the extended
      substance.

Spinoza would regard (ii′) as true since his view that certain causal
contexts are referentially opaque commits him to the view that it is
possible that a mode, under a physical description such as 'mode of
extension A', is caused by the extended substance, but that same mode,
under a mental description such as 'mode of thought 1', is not caused
by the extended substance.[12] This also leads to the claim that for Spinoza (iii′) is true. The possible situations which make (ii′) true are
ones in which a mode, under a physical description such as 'mode of
extension A', is caused by the extended substance. Thus the relevant
term 't' in those situations is 'mode of extension A' or some similar
physical term. Now 'mode of extension A is extended' is trivially true
for Spinoza as long as we are considering a situation in which there is
a mode referred to by that description (or by a similar physical description). Thus in those situations that make (ii′) true, 't is extended' is
also true and so condition (iii′) is also met.

Since the above three conditions are met for the context '. . . is
extended', the Opacity Transmission Principle applies here and thus,
for Spinoza, the context '. . . is extended' is opaque. A parallel application of the principle would show that '. . . is thinking' is opaque. Since,
for Spinoza, thought and extension are attributes, I will call these contexts "attribute contexts."

The opacity of attribute contexts enables us to obviate another objection to the interpretation of Spinoza as holding that mind and body are
identical. The objection is based on the fact that while Spinoza holds
that modes of thought are thinking and modes of extension are extended, he also holds that modes of extension are *not* thinking and
modes of thought are *not* extended.[13] This disparity between modes of
thought and modes of extension might seem to preclude any mode of
extension from being identical with a mode of thought. But such a
conclusion is not warranted since, for Spinoza, the contexts '. . . is
thinking' and '. . . is extended' are opaque. The opacity of these contexts would mean that from the fact that a given mode of extension is
extended and a given mode of thought is not extended we cannot val-

idly infer that that mode of extension is not identical with that mode of thought.

I will call a property an *intensional* property when (and only when) contexts involving the attribution of that property to objects are opaque. I will call all other properties *extensional* properties. Thus the properties of being thinking and being extended are intensional properties since attribute contexts are opaque. If the general properties of being thinking and being extended are intensional, then so too are all the more particular properties that presuppose one or the other of these general properties. The proof of this point relies upon the Opacity Transmission Principle. Take a particular property that presupposes the general property of being extended, for example, being five feet long. Notice that 't is five feet long' entails 't is extended'. Since, for Spinoza, the latter context is opaque (and since nothing seems to preclude the possibilities that in some of those situations in which t is extended, t = t*, but t* is not extended, it is also true that t is five feet long) it follows, by virtue of the Opacity Transmission Principle, that the former context, '. . . is five feet long', is also opaque. The same holds for any other particular property that presupposes extension or for one that presupposes thought (such as "being a thought about the Olympics"). Thus all these particular properties, like their general counterparts, are intensional. In effect, for Spinoza, all physical and all mental properties, as well as the causal properties mentioned earlier, are intensional. But what properties then, if any, are extensional? Spinoza's system seems to leave no room for transparent contexts. There is, however, a small, but important class of extensional properties—important because, as we will now see, these properties enable Spinoza to argue for mind-body identity.

3. The Argument for Identity

With this background concerning the prevalence of opaque contexts in Spinoza, the argument for the claim of numerical identity can proceed. I will start by introducing an intuitively appealing principle of identity (often called "Leibniz's Law"):

a = b iff a and b have all their properties in common.[14]

As Leibniz himself and others have recognized, however, this principle does not hold in complete generality.[15] There are certain kinds of properties that are such that the fact that a has a property of that kind and b does not does not by itself undermine the claim that a = b.

These properties not included within the scope of the above principles are, of course, the intensional properties. Since intensional properties are not covered by Leibniz's Law, we can formulate a version of Leibniz's Law that is exceptionless:

a = b iff a and b have all their extensional properties in common.[16]

Throughout the rest of this paper, I will use the label "Leibniz's Law" for this version of the principle.

Does Spinoza hold Leibniz's Law? 1p4 shows that he accepts the right-to-left half of this principle. In 1p4 he says:

> Two or more distinct things are distinguished from one another, either by a difference in the attributes of the substances or by a difference in their affections.

Part of what 1p4 involves is the assumption that there must be a way of distinguishing two distinct things. There must be some difference between them by which they can be distinguished.[17] That this assumption is at work here is made clear by 1p4d, where Spinoza says that there must be something "outside the intellect through which a number of things can be distinguished from one another." This assumption amounts to the right-to-left half of Leibniz's Law. Spinoza does not here explicitly restrict this principle to extensional properties, but, given his implicit reliance on the notion of intensional and extensional properties, this is a restriction that he is committed to accepting.

Spinoza does not argue for the claim that there must be a way of distinguishing two distinct things. 1p4 takes this claim for granted and merely goes on to argue that the difference between two distinct things must come down to either a difference in attributes or a difference in modes. What, then, entitles Spinoza to this claim behind 1p4? Although Spinoza does not address this issue explicitly, it is not hard to see how he would argue here.

Consider what would be the case if the above assumption were false, that is, if there could be two distinct but qualitatively identical things, a and b.[18] Of such a situation, Spinoza would ask: what *accounts for* the fact that a is not identical with b? What *makes* a distinct from b? It seems that there could be no answer to these questions. If a and b are qualitatively identical, yet numerically distinct, then there would be no way to explain their distinctness. A difference in properties is precisely the kind of thing needed to provide a foothold for an explanation of their distinctness. Without such an explanation, we would be forced to the conclusion that it is simply a brute fact that a is distinct from b: a would be distinct from b but there would be no way to explain this fact or make it intelligible. Such a conclusion, however, is one that Spinoza would reject. Spinoza strongly adheres to the Principle of Sufficient Reason (see 1p11d2 and Garrett 1979, 202–3) and so he would not tolerate such a brute fact.[19]

Thus Spinoza does clearly state in 1p4 and 1p4d that there must be a way of distinguishing distinct things. And there seems to be good reason within Spinoza's system for holding this view, which, as I noted, amounts to the right-to-left half of Leibniz's Law.

Does Spinoza accept the other half: the claim that if a = b, then they have all their extensional properties in common? This claim is far less controversial than its converse. Indeed, it is trivially true: for an extensional property is, by definition, a property that a thing has under any description. So it could not be the case that a = b, a has extensional property F, and b does not. Spinoza does not explicitly discuss this principle, but given its triviality, it seems legitimate to attribute this principle to him. We could not, I think, coherently see Spinoza as denying this principle.

Thus we have a good basis for saying that Spinoza holds Leibniz's Law. Armed with this principle we can construct the Spinozistic argument for the claim of identity. I will first show that this argument is one that Spinoza is committed to accepting. At the end of this section, I will provide evidence that such an argument is not only one that Spinoza is committed to, but also one that is actually at work in Spinoza.

According to Leibniz's Law, we can determine whether a mode of extension and the idea of that mode are numerically identical by determining whether they have all their extensional properties in common. Intensional properties are irrelevant in deciding the issue of identity. Thus since Spinoza regards the properties of being extended and being thinking as intensional, these properties can be left to the side for the purposes of my argument here, and so can all the particular properties that presuppose one or the other of these general properties. Any conclusion about the identity of a mode of thought and a mode of extension will have to be reached on the basis of a relatively impoverished class of properties.

The properties in this class must all be neutral. A neutral property is one that does not presuppose that the item with that property is of a particular attribute. Thus, for example, being extended and being five feet long are non-neutral properties since they presuppose that the item that has these properties is extended. Since all non-neutral properties are intensional, the class of extensional properties, the class of those properties relevant to the issues of identity and distinctness, must be drawn from the class of neutral properties.

I will present the Spinozistic argument for the identity of mind and body in the following way. Since all extensional properties must, for Spinoza, be neutral, I will investigate what kinds of properties Spinoza would regard as neutral. By eliciting these neutral properties, it will become evident that for Spinoza mind and body share all their neutral properties. From this fact, it follows that mind and body share all their extensional properties and are thus identical. Throughout this section, Spinoza's parallelism helps us to see what properties are neutral and why mind and body share them. Thus parallelism provides the basis for concluding that mind and body are identical.

Spinoza states the thesis of parallelism in 2p7: "The order and connection of ideas is the same as the order and connection of things." Part of what this thesis entails is that there is a one-to-one correspondence between ideas and extended things.[20] But parallelism goes well beyond such a claim. For Spinoza, the fact that the order and connection within the two series is the same entails that certain neutral properties are shared by parallel modes. To see what kinds of neutral properties are covered in this way, let's turn to some of the ways Spinoza applies the thesis of parallelism.

The notion of the same order and connection suggests immediately that the causes and effects of a mode of extension and a parallel mode of thought are themselves parallel to one another. This is implicit throughout Spinoza's discussion of parallelism in 2p7s (see also Bennett 1984, 127). From this it follows that if a mode of extension has a certain number of immediate effects (say, five immediate effects) then the parallel mode of thought will have the same number of immediate effects and these effects of the mode of thought will be parallel to the effects of the mode of extension. So, an example of a neutral feature that is shared by parallel modes is the feature 'having five immediate effects'. Each mode will have very many neutral features of this kind— features that specify the number of causes or effects a given mode has at a certain remove. All of these neutral features are, by virtue of parallelism, shared by each mode and its parallel counterpart. Since these neutral properties are covered by parallelism—the thesis that the order and connection in the two series are the same—we can say that these neutral properties contribute to the order and connection within each of the two series.

For Spinoza, neutral temporal properties are also covered by parallelism. Neutral temporal properties are properties of the kinds: "began to exist at t1," "exists at t2," "ceases to exist at t3," etc. Spinoza thinks that parallel modes share all the same neutral temporal properties:

> When singular things are said to exist, not only insofar as they are comprehended in God's attributes, but insofar as they are said to have duration,

their ideas also involve the existence through which they are said to have duration. (2p8c)

The meaning of this claim becomes clear when we see how Spinoza applies it to the case of the human mind and the body that is parallel to it: "we do not attribute duration to [the mind] except while the body endures" (5p23d). This claim, which depends on 2p8c, indicates that the mind and body (and parallel modes generally) endure for the same period of time and thus share all the same neutral temporal properties.[21] This sharing is guaranteed by parallelism since 2p8c follows solely from 2p8, which in turn follows solely from the statement of parallelism in 2p7. Spinoza obviously sees the neutral temporal properties of modes as contributing to the order and connection of series of modes.

Another neutral property that modes can have is the property of being a complex individual. For Spinoza, certain collections of modes unite to form a single individual. This phenomenon occurs both in the realm of extension and in the realm of thought and thus the property of being a complex individual is neutral. Further, Spinoza thinks that if a mode of one attribute is a complex individual, then the parallel mode of another attribute must also be a complex individual. When Spinoza makes this claim in 2p15d, he relies on 2p7, the statement of parallelism. This indicates that Spinoza sees the fact that certain modes unite to form a single individual as an aspect of the way in which a series of modes is ordered and connected.[22]

So Spinoza explicitly claims that parallelism guarantees that modes of extension and modes of thought share a wide range of neutral properties. Since these neutral properties are covered by parallelism, we can say that they contribute to the order and connection of a series of modes. Given the emphasis in Spinoza's account of parallelism on neutral properties that contribute to order and connection, I think we can say that for Spinoza, parallelism guarantees in general that any neutral property that contributes to the order and connection of a series of modes is shared by parallel modes.[23] If a neutral property that contributes to order and connection is not shared by a particular mode of extension and a particular mode of thought, then there would be grounds for saying that these modes are not parallel to one another.

But this is not to say that *all* neutral properties are covered by parallelism. Can we give a general criterion by which to tell whether a given neutral property contributes to order and connection and is thus covered by parallelism? Spinoza's broad use of the parallelism thesis to show that certain neutral properties are shared indicates that he would accept a certain general principle. This principle makes use of the claim that for each mode of a certain attribute there is a point that it occupies in the chain of modes of that attribute and for each such point there is a different mode. I will say that a property F appears at a certain point in a chain of modes if the mode at that point in the chain has that property. The principle is as follows:

> If the fact that neutral property F appears at a certain point in the chain of modes of a certain attribute is explained by the fact that a certain feature appears at another point in that chain, then F is a neutral property that contributes to order and connection.

We can see why this is so in the following way. Let's say that F is a neutral property that appears at a certain point in the chain of modes of extension and that the fact that F appears at that point in the chain is explained by the fact that a certain feature appears at another point in the chain of modes of extension.[24] Since the fact that F appears at a certain point in the chain is explained by the fact that a certain feature appears at another point in the chain, it follows that neutral property F contributes to the way in which the modes at those two different points are connected. To say that the fact that F appears at one point in the series of modes of extension is explained by a feature that appears at another point is to say that there is a respect in which the mode at the former point depends on the mode at the latter point. The neutral property F that the first mode has plays a crucial role in this relation of dependence. Thus F contributes to the kind of connection there is between the two modes and so contributes to the order and connection that obtains in the series of extended modes generally.

Since neutral property F of a certain mode of extension contributes to the order and connection of the extended series, there must be a parallel mode of thought that also has property F. The fact that F appears at this point in the chain of modes of thought must be explained by the fact that a certain feature appears at another point in the chain of modes of thought. If there were no parallel mode of thought that had feature F or if the fact that feature F is present at that point were not explained by a certain feature of another mode of thought, then the order and connection of the mental series would be different in a certain respect from the order and connection of the physical series. This would be a violation of parallelism. Thus any neutral property of a given mode that is explained by a feature of a different mode contributes to the order and connection of a given series and is thus shared by parallel modes.

The legitimacy of this general principle is confirmed by the fact that the neutral properties that Spinoza explicitly regards as covered by parallelism meet the condition laid down in the above principle. For example, consider the property of being a complex individual. The fact that the mode at a certain point in the chain of modes of extension is a complex individual depends on features of other modes, in particular features of the modes that constitute it and also features of other modes that provide the setting for such a complex individual to appear. Thus the feature of being a complex individual is covered by the above principle. Similar points would apply to the other neutral properties already discussed.

Thus all neutral properties of modes that enter into explanatory relations in this way with other modes are covered by parallelism. Are there any neutral properties not covered by parallelism? A neutral property F that appears at a certain point in the chain of modes of extension would not be covered by parallelism only if one of the following two scenarios were the case: (1) The fact that F appears at that point has no explanation at all. (2) The fact that F appears at that point, although explainable, is not explained by facts concerning other modes.

We can see right away that the former scenario is illegitimate. This is because, as we have seen, Spinoza holds the Principle of Sufficient Reason and thus, for him, every fact must be explainable.

Are there any neutral properties that conform to the second scenario? This would be the case only if the fact that F appears at that point, though explainable, is not explained by any facts concerning modes other than the mode that occupies that point in the chain. In such a case, the fact that F appears at that point would be explanatorily restricted to the mode of which it is a feature. In general, for a neutral property to fail to be covered by parallelism, the fact that that property appears at that point must be explanatorily isolated in this way from other modes.[25]

An example of such an isolated feature would be the feature of not-(existing at t2 while also not existing at t2). This feature appears at each point in the chain of modes of extension. For each such point, there is an explanation of why the feature appears at this point. But this explanation does not require citing facts about what is the case at other points in the series. To explain why this feature appears at a given point, we do not appeal to other modes, we simply appeal to the necessary truth that nothing can instantiate incompatible properties.

In general, the neutral properties that are explanatorily isolated in this way from other modes are, like not-(existing at t2 and not existing at t2), necessarily universal. If a neutral property is not necessarily universal, if it is not guaranteed to be instantiated by everything, then there must be an explanation of *why* it appears at some particular point in the causal chain (and not at another). To know why a thing with this property appears at this juncture, we need to know other facts about the situation that allow for and require the existence of a thing with that feature. Such facts will include facts about other modes. And thus the neutral property in question will not be explanatorily isolated. It will be a feature that contributes to the order and connection of a series, and thus it will be shared by parallel modes.

So the only neutral properties that are, potentially, *not* covered by parallelism are the necessarily universal neutral properties. But this fact does not affect the ability of parallelism to help us show that mind and body are identical. This is because the universal neutral properties are, by virtue of their universality, irrelevant to deciding questions of identity. Since all things have them (whether the things are thinking or extended), it follows that the fact that X and Y have them goes no distance toward showing that X = Y. The universal properties also cannot be used to determine nonidentity, since there could not be a case in which one object had a particular universal neutral property and another did not.

Thus we can safely ignore these properties when deciding issues of identity. The only neutral properties that could be relevant to identity are the ones that are not necessarily universal and, as we have seen, parallelism guarantees that these are shared by parallel modes. So, although parallelism may not itself guarantee that all neutral properties are shared by parallel modes, the ones it might not cover are necessarily shared. Thus a mode of extension and the parallel mode of thought share all their neutral properties.

For this sharing of all neutral properties to guarantee that parallel modes are identical, we need to show that the neutral properties encompass all the extensional properties. We saw earlier that if there are to be any extensional properties at all, they must be neutral. So, since mind and body share all their neutral properties, they share all their extensional properties, *if* there are any extensional properties to be shared. But are there any extensional properties? Spinoza's commitment to Leibniz's Law shows that there must be. If there were no extensional properties at all, that is, if all properties were intensional, then there would be no way to determine that one mode is not identical with another. This is because the nature of intensional properties is such that a difference between a and b in intensional properties does not show that a≠b. Thus, if all properties were intensional, there would be no legitimate way to distinguish nonidentical things. This would be intolerable to Spinoza since he clearly thinks that there are nonidentical things and he is clearly committed to there being a basis for such nonidentity in each case. Thus there must be some extensional properties. Since all extensional properties are neutral and since parallel modes share all their neutral properties, it follows that the body and the idea of the body, that is, the body and the mind, share all their extensional properties and, hence, are identical.

Let me approach from a different angle the claim that at least some neutral properties are extensional. Consider the causal property, discussed earlier, of having five immediate effects. We would expect Spinoza to regard this property as extensional for the following reason. When Spinoza relies on the notion of the opacity of certain causal contexts, he is concerned about those causal contexts that, we might say, are vulnerable to attribute mismatch. These are causal contexts that can be completed in such a way that in the resulting sentence the cause is represented as being of one attribute and the effect of another.[26] '. . . causes mode of thought 1' is such a context. If this context is completed with the term 'the extended substance', the resulting sentence, 'The extended substance causes mode of thought 1', contains an attribute mismatch in a causal context. As 2p6d indicates, it is because of such a mismatch that Spinoza regards this sentence as false even though it is true that the thinking substance does cause mode of thought 1 and that the thinking substance = the extended substance.

This kind of mismatch is not possible with the neutral causal context '. . . has five immediate effects'. No substitution here would result in a claim that something extended is causally related to something thinking. Since such neutral causal contexts are not vulnerable to attribute mismatch, and since Spinoza seems primarily concerned with such mismatch when he relies on the claim that certain contexts are opaque, it seems likely that for him the neutral causal contexts are transparent and thus that the neutral causal properties are extensional. Similar points would apply to most, if not all, of the other neutral properties we have discussed.[27] And thus, once again, we have a Spinozistic basis for the conclusion that there are at least some extensional properties.

So the argument, in brief, is this: Parallelism helps us to see that mind and body share all their neutral properties. Since all extensional properties are neutral and since there must be some extensional properties, it follows that mind and body share all their extensional properties. By Leibniz's Law, we can, therefore, conclude that mind = body.

An immediate objection, however, arises. Let's grant that there are some extensional properties. Let's even grant that *all* neutral properties are extensional. Even so, how can we be sure that the fact that mind and body share all their neutral properties and extensional properties provides a sufficient basis for saying that they are identical? The sharing of all these properties would not provide such a sufficient basis if it is possible for two distinct, non-identical things to have all the same neutral properties and hence all the same extensional properties.

The worry here is that the class of neutral properties might not be rich enough to guarantee that there are no duplications of sets of neutral properties. To see the force of this problem, consider neutral temporal properties which are a subset of the neutral properties and which, let us assume, are extensional. Now from the fact that mode X and mode Y share all their neutral temporal properties, we would not want to conclude that mode X and mode Y are identical. This is because it seems quite possible that two distinct things share all their neutral temporal properties. Such a scenario is especially plausible if we include, as Spinoza does,[28] events among things. The same kind of objection would arise in the case of neutral properties generally: how can we be sure that two distinct things cannot have *all* their neutral properties in common?

Spinoza would answer by again invoking what I have called Leibniz's Law. If two distinct things shared all their neutral properties and extensional properties, then there would be no legitimate way to distinguish them. We could not turn to the non-neutral properties since these are intensional and thus do not provide an appropriate basis for distinguishing things. So we would be left without a way to distinguish the two distinct things and this would violate Spinoza's commitment to the intelligibility of all facts, including the intelligibility of the distinction between two distinct things. Thus Spinoza is committed to the view that no two distinct things share all their neutral properties.

The above argument for the identity of mind and body is a Spinozistic one that proceeds from Spinoza's acceptance of Leibniz's Law, from his central thesis of parallelism, and from his commitment to the view that non-neutral properties are intensional. So far, all I have claimed is that Spinoza is committed to this argument. This is in itself an important fact since it shows that Spinoza's claim of identity is not a mere addition to his system, but instead is a position that grows out of what we can now see as the rich resources of that system.

Still, I think we can go further. There is evidence for seeing Spinoza not merely as committed to the above argument, but as actually relying on such an argument. This evidence emerges from a single passage— the crucial 2p7s—but it should not surprise us that there is only one passage that provides evidence on this point. Spinoza, after all, says very little about his identity position.

The passage in question is this:

> Whether we consider nature under the attribute of extension, or under the attribute of thought, or under any other attribute, we shall find one and the same order, or one and the same connection of causes, i.e. [*hoc est*] that the same things follow one another.

Here Spinoza seems to regard the thesis of parallelism as equivalent to the claim of trans-attribute mode identity. Stating such an equivalence is exactly what we would expect Spinoza to do if he were relying on an argument like the one I gave above. For by means of that argument, we can see that such an equivalence holds. The argument contends that given other aspects of Spinoza's system, the fact that parallelism holds entails that the idea of a given mode of extension is identical with that mode of extension. And, of course, this entailment works in the other direction as well: identity of modes across attributes entails sameness of order and connection. (Recall that the features having to do with order and connection are neutral and, it seems, extensional. Hence they would be shared by identical modes.) Thus the argument I have given helps to show that, for Spinoza, the thesis of parallelism is equivalent to the claim of trans-attribute mode identity, and this is precisely what Spinoza says in 2p7s.

Further, and more significantly, Spinoza can assert such an equivalence *only if* he is relying on something like the above argument. Parallelism guarantees that a mode of extension and the idea of that mode share certain neutral properties. For Spinoza to treat parallelism as entailing the identity thesis, he would have to see the sharing of these neutral properties as a sufficient basis for determining that these modes are identical. If Spinoza did not regard the sameness of order and connection as providing a sufficient ground for the claim of identity, then his assertion of the equivalence in 2p7s would be unjustified. So, in asserting that equivalence in 2p7s, Spinoza is, in part, claiming that the neutral properties covered by parallelism show that the modes in question are identical. And this is precisely how the Spinozistic argument that I have presented proceeds.

The points in the previous two paragraphs indicate that the above argument is not only a Spinozistic argument, but also that it may actually be Spinoza's.

4. Why Opacity?

Spinoza's argument for the Identity Theory turns upon his view that mental properties and physical properties are intensional. I established that for Spinoza these properties are intensional by showing that he accepts the following entailments:

(e) Mode x is extended only if mode x is caused by the extended substance.

(f) Mode x is thinking only if mode x is caused by the thinking substance.

Because Spinoza regards the latter context within each conditional as
opaque, he is committed to seeing the former context within each conditional as opaque as well. The opacity is transmitted from the causal
contexts to the attribute contexts. Thus one way to defend the view
that attribute contexts are opaque is to support both the claim that the
relevant causal contexts are opaque and the claim that the entailments
(e) and (f) hold.

I have doubts on both of these points. I don't think that Spinoza
gives sufficient justification for regarding the relevant causal contexts
as opaque. It is fairly commonplace in current philosophy to regard
causal contexts as referentially *transparent*.[29] The intuition here is that
whether or not it's true to say that one item causes another is not
dependent on how those things are described. This seems right; there
are, though, some demurrals. According to Mackie (1974, chap. 10)
and Anscombe (1981), at least some causal contexts are opaque. The
basis for their views is the notion that the truth of certain causal claims
requires that those claims have explanatory value. These causal claims
must, in order to be true, explain *why* the effect occurred. Now it is
widely agreed that explanatory contexts are opaque. Searle gives a clear
example of the failure of the principle of substitutivity in the context of
explanation:

> If Jones's eating the poisoned fish causally explains his death and the
> event of Jones's eating the poisoned fish is identical with the event of his
> eating rainbow trout with sauce béarnaise for the first time in his life, it
> does not follow that his eating rainbow trout with sauce béarnaise for the
> first time in his life causally explains his death. (1983, 117)

Since explanatory contexts are opaque, if, as Mackie and Anscombe
hold, certain causal claims must count as explanations in order to be
true, then those causal claims will contain opaque contexts.

Spinoza may also hold that certain causal claims must count as explanations in order to be true, and I suspect that such a link between
causation and explanation is importantly connected with what commentators often see as Spinoza's assimilation of causal and logical relations. That Spinoza holds that certain causal claims must have explanatory value in order to be true is evident from the fact that Spinoza
accepts the following conditional:

(g) If x is caused by y then x is conceived through y.[30]

The claim that x is conceived through y is plausibly seen as a claim about the explanation of x. This is indicated by the second half of 2p7s where Spinoza says that when we perceive effects through their causes, we are explaining the order of nature. Spinoza sometimes uses 'perceives' and 'conceives' interchangeably in these contexts (see, e.g., 2p38d), so we can say that for him when we conceive effects through their causes we are explaining the order of nature. This shows that Spinoza regards claims about conceiving one thing through another as claims about the explanation of one thing by another (see also 2p5). Thus the above conditional indicates that Spinoza sees certain causal claims as entailing explanatory claims. If Spinoza does link certain causal claims with explanatory claims in this way, then, we can see why, for him, certain causal contexts would be opaque as well. This is because *if* (g) is true and if conceptual or explanatory contexts are opaque, then, by virtue of the Opacity Transmission Principle, it follows that certain causal contexts are opaque.

Unfortunately, although Spinoza's acceptance of (g) may account for his acceptance of the opacity of certain causal contexts, I see no argument in Spinoza for this conditional, and thus I do not see any argument in Spinoza for the view that certain causal contexts are opaque. Let's assume that the relevant conceptual contexts are opaque. On this assumption, if 'x is caused by y' does entail 'x is conceived through y', then the context '. . . is caused by . . .' would be opaque. But why should the entailment hold? Even if x is conceived through y only under particular descriptions of x and y, why can't it be the case that *under any* descriptions of x and y it is true to say that x is caused by y? Even if being conceived through something else depends on how the relevant things are described, I see no reason why it should follow that simply being caused by some other thing also depends on how the things are described. So Spinoza has not shown us why we should think that (g) holds and thus why we should think that since the relevant conceptual contexts are opaque, then so too are certain causal contexts.

For a similar reason, I also think that Spinoza fails to show that the entailments (e) and (f) hold. Let's assume, as Spinoza must, that the relevant causal contexts are opaque. On this assumption, if 'x is extended' does entail 'x is caused by the extended substance' then the context '. . . is extended' would be opaque. (Again, this follows by virtue of the Opacity Transmission Principle.) But why should this entailment hold? Even if being caused by the extended substance depends on how things are conceived or described, I see no reason why it should follow that simply being extended also depends on how things are described. So, Spinoza has not shown us why we should think the entailment holds and thus why we should think that if the relevant causal contexts are opaque then so too must be the contexts '. . . is extended' and '. . . is thinking'.

There is, in principle, another way to demonstrate the opacity of attribute contexts. If Spinoza were justified in holding that it is *possible* for a mental thing to be identical with a physical thing, then he could be justified in holding that attribute contexts are opaque. This opacity in turn would, as we have seen, help to establish that mental things are actually identical with physical things. So we would be relying on the possibility of trans-attribute identity of modes to establish the actuality of such identity.

The possibility of trans-attribute identity of modes would lead to the conclusion that attribute contexts are opaque in the following way. We would be convinced that the context '. . . is extended' is opaque if an inference of the following form were invalid:

4. Mode of extension A is extended.
5. Mode of extension A = mode of thought 1.
Therefore,
6. Mode of thought 1 is extended.

This kind of inference would, of course, be invalid if there is a possible situation in which the premises are true and the conclusion false. This would show that the premises do not entail the conclusion. The first premise, 'mode of extension A is extended', is necessarily true since it follows from the notion of a mode of extension that each such mode is extended. The conclusion, 'mode of thought 1 is extended', is false, according to Spinoza, and I think necessarily so. Thus if it is merely *possible* for a mode of extension to be identical with a mode of thought, then it would be possible for both premises to be true and the conclusion false. This is because if it is possible for (5) to be true, then there is a possible situation in which a mode of thought is identical with a mode of extension. In that situation (4) would also be true and (6) would be false. This is because (4) is necessarily true and (6) is necessarily false. Thus if it is possible for (5) to be true, then there is a possible situation in which both premises are true and the conclusion false. But this is just to say that the argument is invalid. But if the argument is invalid then the context '. . . is extended' would be opaque.

A similar line of reasoning would show that the context '. . . is thinking' is opaque.

This would be a legitimate way to show the opacity of attribute contexts, but is it available to Spinoza? It would be available only if Spinoza were to provide a reason for holding that trans-attribute identity of modes is possible. This is something that Spinoza cannot just *assume,* especially in light of the fact that Descartes, to whom Spinoza is to a large extent responding here, has a famous argument for the conclusion that such identity is *impossible.* What then could justify belief in this possibility?

One potential justification is the following. Spinoza holds, as we have seen, that the extended substance is identical with the thinking substance. Now although the substance and the modes of that substance belong to distinct ontological categories for Spinoza, they are each in some broad sense things or individuals (see 2p1 and 2p2 and 2lemma7s). Thus the fact that, according to Spinoza, the extended substance is identical with the thinking substance shows that it is at least possible for a thinking thing to be identical with an extended thing. This possibility might give us confidence in holding that it is possible for a thinking *mode* to be identical with an extended *mode.* Thus, on this line of thought, the identity of the thinking substance and the extended substance would lead to the *possibility* of trans-attribute identity of modes. This possibility would lead to the opacity of attribute contexts and this opacity in turn would undergird Spinoza's argument for the *actuality* of trans-attribute identity of modes. Thus substance identity would lead to a claim of mode identity and, in particular, mind–body identity. Whether we can be persuaded of the mode identity claim on this basis depends in part on whether Spinoza has good reasons for his claim of substance identity. This is an issue I will not explore here.

At the beginning of this paper, I noted that Spinoza may be drawing an inference from substance identity to mode identity. Now, in investigating the basis for the opacity of attribute contexts, I have again arrived at the issue of the connection between substance identity and mode identity. So, in one sense, we are back where we started. But I believe our journey has not been fruitless. I have defended the numerical identity interpretation of Spinoza from some important objections and I have uncovered an intriguing argument for mind-body identity that may be at work in Spinoza. Equally important, perhaps, is the fact that throughout this process I have taken some steps toward discerning the structure of what Wilson calls Spinoza's "thicket of intensionality."

References

Spinoza's Works

Curley, Edwin, ed. and trans. 1985. *The Collected Works of Spinoza,* vol. 1. Princeton: Princeton University Press.

Gebhardt, Carl, ed. 1925. *Spinoza Opera,* vols. 1 and 2. Heidelberg: Carl Winter.

Other Works

Allison, Henry E. 1987. *Benedict de Spinoza: An Introduction.* New Haven: Yale University Press.
Anscombe, G. E. M. 1981. "Causality and Extensionality." In *The Collected Philosophical Papers of G. E. M. Anscombe,* vol. 2. Minneapolis: University of Minnesota Press. (Originally published 1969.)
Aquila, Richard E. 1978. "The Identity of Thought and Object in Spinoza." *Journal of the History of Philosophy* 18:271–88.
Bennett, Jonathan. 1984. *A Study of Spinoza's Ethics.* Indianapolis: Hackett.
Black, Max. 1952. "The Identity of Indiscernibles." *Mind* 61:153–64.
Curley, Edwin. 1988. *Behind the Geometrical Method.* Princeton: Princeton University Press.
Davidson, Donald. 1980. *Essays on Actions and Events.* Oxford: Oxford University Press.
Delahunty, R. J. 1985. *Spinoza.* London: Routledge and Kegan Paul.
Della Rocca, Michael. 1991. "Causation and Spinoza's Claim of Identity." *History of Philosophy Quarterly* 8:265–76.
Feldman, Fred. 1970. "Leibniz and 'Leibniz' Law'." *Philosophical Review* 79:510–22.
Freeman, Eugene, and Maurice Mandelbaum, eds. 1975. *Spinoza: Essays in Interpretation.* LaSalle, Illinois: Open Court.
Garrett, Don. 1979. "Spinoza's 'Ontological' Argument." *Philosophical Review* 88:198–223.
———. 1990. "*Ethics* 1p5: Shared Attributes and the Basis of Spinoza's Monism." In *Central Themes in Early Modern Philosophy,* ed. J. A. Cover and Mark Kulstad. Indianapolis: Hackett.
Hampshire, Stuart. 1971. "A Kind of Materialism." In his *Freedom of Mind and Other Essays,* 210–31. Princeton: Princeton University Press.
Jarrett, Charles. 1982a. "Materialism." *Philosophy Research Archives* 8:457–97.
———. 1982b. "On the Rejection of Spinozistic Dualism in the *Ethics.*" *Southern Journal of Philosophy* 20:153–75.
———. 1991. "Spinoza's Denial of Mind-Body Interaction and the Explanation of Human Action." *Southern Journal of Philosophy* 29:465–85.
Leibniz, G. W. 1989. *Philosophical Essays.* Ed. and trans. Roger Ariew and Daniel Garber. Indianapolis: Hackett.
Mackie, J. L. 1974. *The Cement of the Universe.* Oxford: Oxford University Press.
Mates, Benson. 1986. *The Philosophy of Leibniz.* Oxford: Oxford University Press.
Matson, Wallace I. 1975. "Spinoza's Theory of Mind." In Freeman and Mandelbaum, 49–60.
Odegard, Douglas. 1975. "The Body Identical with the Human Mind: A Problem in Spinoza's Philosophy." In Freeman and Mandelbaum, 61–83.

Searle, John. 1983. *Intentionality: An Essay in the Philosophy of Mind.* Cambridge: Cambridge University Press.

von Leyden, Wolfgang. 1968. *Seventeenth Century Metaphysics.* New York: Barnes and Noble.

Wilson, Margaret. 1975. Review of Thomas Carson Mark, *Spinoza's Theory of Truth. Journal of Philosophy* 72:22–25.

Notes

An earlier version of this paper was delivered at Brown, Ohio State, the University of California at Berkeley, and the University of Texas at Austin. I would like to thank the audiences at each of these philosophy departments for their warm reception and helpful comments. Janet Broughton, Wallace Matson, and David Schmidtz read the paper at various stages and offered important advice. The editors of the *Philosophical Review* and their outside reader made comments that led to many improvements in the paper.

1. Wilson 1975, 24–25.

2. See also 2p21s. Translations from Spinoza are from Curley's *The Collected Works of Spinoza,* vol. 1. Quotes from Spinoza's Latin are from Gebhardt. I have followed Curley's system of numbering passages from the *Ethics.*

3. Commentators have not, I believe, handled this issue adequately. Although many have recognized that Spinoza holds some form of an identity position, these interpreters have often failed to investigate in any detailed way how he might argue for this position. See, for example, the otherwise helpful accounts by Allison (1987, chap. 4, pt. 1), Hampshire (1971), Matson (1975), and Odegard (1975). Those who do attempt to spell out a Spinozistic argument fail in various ways. Jonathan Bennett, for example, presents an intricate characterization of, and argument for, some version of an identity position that he finds in Spinoza. Unfortunately, among other difficulties, Bennett's interpretation attributes to Spinoza some highly anti-Spinozistic claims. For example, Bennett attributes to Spinoza the view that the infinite intellect of God misconstrues God's own essence (see Bennett 1984, 139–51). I intend to present my criticisms of Bennett in a future paper. Richard E. Aquila also presents a subtle interpretation according to which Spinoza's claim of identity "follows in a certain way from principles central to his philosophy" (1978, 285). However, the kind of identity between mind and body that Aquila's Spinoza winds up with is something short of the numerical identity that Spinoza seems to emphasize (see especially 1978, 282). Throughout his article, Aquila employs scare quotes when talking about the identity of Spinozistic modes of thought and modes of extension. Finally, Curley claims that he is able to show why Spinoza affirms a numerical identity position (1988, 68). But the reasons Curley offers in the immediately following passage at most show that a mode of extension cannot exist without the idea of that mode and vice versa. As Curley himself admits (69), this falls short of a claim of identity. Curley also asserts that Spinoza "came to see [the identity thesis] as providing a metaphysical explanation,

not only of the mind's awareness of and concern for the body, but also of its dependence on the body for its knowledge of other things" (159 n. 18; see also 62). But Curley does not make clear how an identity of mind and body, as opposed to mere necessary correlation, provides such an explanation.

4. Curley endorses something like this interpretation (1988, 153 n. 13). See also von Leyden 1968, 21; Allison 1987, 85–86; Aquila 1978, 272–73.

5. There is, of course, a debate as to whether when Spinoza says that substance has infinitely many attributes he means that substance has a literal infinity of attributes (in our sense of 'infinite') or that substance simply has all possible attributes. This issue does not affect my interpretation or arguments in this paper.

6. Charles Jarrett, in several stimulating papers which I saw only after completing the initial versions of this paper, also emphasizes the importance of referential opacity in understanding Spinoza's position on the mind-body problem (see the three papers by Jarrett listed among the references). However, his development of this theme differs from mine, and he does not employ the notion of referential opacity as I do later in the paper to show how Spinoza might argue for his version of the Identity Theory.

7. See Delahunty 1985, 197. My response to Delahunty stems from section 1 of my "Causation and Spinoza's Claim of Identity."

8. Spinoza allows that modes are considered under attributes—see, for example, 2p21s.

9. 1ax4 plays a similar role in this proof as in 2p6d itself. If mode of thought 1 were caused by a mode of extension, then, since (according to 1ax4) effects are conceived through causes, mode of thought 1 would be conceived through a mode of extension. Such a conclusion, however, would go against Spinoza's conceptual separation of the attributes.

10. We will see shortly cases in which the opacity of one context *does* entail the opacity of another context.

11. I am indebted here to Jamie Dreier's extremely helpful comments.

12. In the last section of this paper, I will explore ways in which Spinoza might support this view.

13. For the claim that a mode of thought is thinking, see 2def3 where Spinoza calls the mind (which, according to 2p11, is a mode of thought) a thinking thing (*res cogitans*). I see no reason why Spinoza would not make a parallel claim about modes of extension.

Spinoza's attack against Cartesian interactionism is premised on the claim that mental and physical things have nothing in common and thus that, in particular, mental things are not physical and physical things are not mental. See Spinoza's critique of Descartes in the preface to part 5. Many other passages also indicate that Spinoza holds this view. See *Short Treatise,* book 2, appendix 2 (Gebhardt 1:118) where Spinoza says that the object of an idea (for example, a mode of extension) "has nothing of thought." In the *Treatise on the Emendation of the Intellect,* para. 58, he says that the idea that a soul (a particular mode of thought) is extended is fictitious. See also para. 33, 74, and *Ethics* 2p49s (Gebhardt 2:132).

14. For this formulation of Leibniz's Law, see Mates 1986, 123, and Feldman 1970, 510. Feldman, however, does not attribute this version of the principle to Leibniz himself.

15. For an illuminating discussion of Leibniz's awareness of this point, see Mates 1986, 130–32.

16. This principle must, in order not to be trivial, include further restrictions. In the right-to-left direction, the above biconditional would be trivially satisfied if we count "being identical with a" as a property. I think that the proper restrictions can be formulated, but I will not go into such complications here. On this kind of problem, see Black 1952, 153–55.

17. Although in 1p4 and the surrounding passages Spinoza is primarily interested in the issue of the identity and distinctness of *substances,* the general term 'thing' (*res*) in 1p4 and its demonstration shows that his claim would apply to modes as well as substances. (See Garrett 1990, 99–100.) This broad application is significant because of my focus on the issue of *mode* identity.

18. Again, we are omitting properties such as being identical with a—a and b obviously do not share this property.

19. Leibniz also derives the claim that there must be a difference between distinct things from the Principle of Sufficient Reason. See Leibniz's Correspondence with Clarke in Leibniz 1989, 327, 333, 334.

20. The thesis also entails that for each mode of an attribute besides extension there is an idea of that mode and vice versa. Since we are interested here in the relation between thought and extension in particular, we will pass over this important ramification of parallelism.

21. This commitment on Spinoza's part may or may not be compatible with his views on the eternity of the mind. I will not explore this matter here.

22. A related neutral property is the power of a mode of extension or of a mode of thought. Spinoza thinks that the power of the mind and the power of the body rise and fall together. See 3p11, which relies on the parallelism of 2p7.

23. For this characterization of parallelism, see Bennett 1984, 360.

24. For our purposes, it is irrelevant whether the other feature is neutral or not.

25. This is a necessary condition for a neutral property to fail to be covered by parallelism. It may not be sufficient. That is, it could well be the case that even a neutral property that is explanatorily isolated in this way is still covered by parallelism.

26. Spinoza would also be concerned about certain noncausal contexts that are vulnerable to attribute mismatches.

27. There may be reasons (independent of a concern about attribute mismatches) for thinking that *some* neutral properties *are* intensional. For example, one might argue that temporal properties are intensional since we could have a case in which the ring = the piece of gold, the ring ceases to exist at t1 (because it is crushed and destroyed), but the piece of gold does not cease to exist at t1 (since it survives the crushing). If in such a case the ring really is identical with the piece of gold, then we might have reason to see certain

neutral temporal properties as intensional. However, Spinoza does not give any indication as to whether he would say that in such a case the ring is identical with the piece of gold, and so we cannot be sure as to whether Spinoza would, on this basis, hold that neutral temporal properties are intensional. (The above example is adapted from Jarrett 1982a.)

28. See 2p12, where Spinoza speaks of things that happen (*contingit*) in the body.

29. See, for example, Davidson's "Actions, Reasons, and Causes," "Causal Relations," and "Mental Events," in Davidson 1980.

30. See 1p3d and 1p6cd2.

8

Spinoza's Causal Axiom (*Ethics* I, Axiom 4)

Margaret D. Wilson

Treatments of causality in seventeenth-century philosophy present the interpreter with a peculiar problem. On the one hand, the notion of causality is central to the period's major positions and disputes in metaphysics and epistemology. On the other hand, few of the most prominent figures of the period enter into detailed or precise accounts of the relation of causal dependence or causal connection. As a result, one is often left with only the most exiguous materials for dealing with some of the most important and far-reaching interpretive issues.

Spinoza is an interesting case in point. Most of the best-known, most characteristic features of his system—the conception of substance as *causa sui,* the thorough-going determinism, the distinction between *Natura naturans* and *Natura naturata,* the denial of mind–body interaction, the doctrine of thought–matter parallelism, the theories of perception and knowledge, the doctrine of the passions and the account of freedom—are all firmly centered on notions of causal order and dependence. Yet Spinoza says very little to elucidate directly the concept or concepts of causality he relies on.

The treatments of Spinoza's conception of causality that appear in the literature—most of them quite brief—typically focus on his use of geometrical analogies to indicate that causal necessity is truly ineluctable, and in some manner essential, as in the following, often-cited passage:

> from God's supreme power or infinite nature . . . all [things] have necessarily flowed forth [*effluxisse*], or always follow with the same necessity, in the same way, as from eternity and to eternity it follows from the nature of a triangle that its three angles are equal to two right angles (EIp17s).[1]

According to a number of commentators, such passages indicate that Spinoza assimilates or conflates the causal relation with the relation of logical entailment, or of "ground" and "consequent."[2] There are plenty of objections that might be made to this interpretive claim, beginning with the observation that its meaning isn't very clear. One thing it might mean is that Spinoza holds that the conjunction of the assertion of the cause and the denial of the effect, under some sort of canonical descriptions of each, will yield a formal contradiction. Or it might mean that, on Spinoza's view, physical things or facts somehow literally *logically entail* each other. Or perhaps some combination of these two notions is intended. Each of these readings goes well beyond anything actually present in the text, however, and all of them involve formidable conceptual difficulties.[3] In the passages quoted (and elsewhere) Spinoza himself offers no direct clarification of the notion of essential consequence involved in the triangle analogy—or the "necessity" that it exemplifies.[4]

In the present essay I wish to widen interpretive discussion of causality in Spinoza's system by turning from the geometrical analogies and the issues they bring to mind to systematic consideration of an axiom that has been characterized as a "definition of cause," axiom 4, *Ethics* I,[5] which reads:

> Effectus cognitio a cognitione causae dependet, & eandem involvit.

"Cognitio" is normally translated "knowledge." Although some have raised objections to this practice, I propose to continue it here, but with the understanding that the concept in question may be only loosely connected with the normal connotations of "knowledge" in modern English.[6] So I translate this axiom as:

> Knowledge of an effect depends on knowledge of the cause, and involves it.[7]

This axiom plays a key role in the development of a number of the central Spinozist doctrines mentioned above, and others as well.

Axiom 4 has not been wholly neglected by Spinoza scholars. For example, among recent and relatively recent commentators, Martial Gueroult, Louis Loeb, and Jonathan Bennett have each devoted a few pages to it; and Harold Zellner has published a short article focusing on the axiom.[8] The variety of views and suggestions about the axiom advanced in just these few brief treatments is rather astonishing. Unfortunately, however, little of what has been proposed really stands up to scrutiny when one looks closely enough at a range of actual applications of the axiom. Although I will not attempt here to discuss in detail all the argumentative uses of EIax4 in the *Ethics,* I will discuss several important applications. These include, first, its intimate connection with the mode–attribute relation in the early parts of the *Ethics*; second, Spinoza's exploitation of this connection in setting up his case against Cartesian interactionism; third, his use of the axiom at the beginning of *Ethics* II to establish the proposition that the modes under the different attributes are "connected" in the same way; and, finally, its role in Spinoza's remarkable and peculiar theory of perception of external bodies.

Each of these contexts, as I will try to show, contributes elements and constraints to the interpretation of the axiom. In light of them I will argue that various proposals found in the literature are either utterly untenable or (in some cases) at least highly misleading. I will be particularly concerned to show that *"cognitio"* in axiom 4 cannot be restricted to adequate knowledge, as Gueroult insists. I shall also dispute certain other readings, connected with the sense of *"cognitio,"* proposed by Loeb and Bennett. I will try to show that—contrary to a suggestion found in Bennett—the axiom is not a straightforward expression of "causal rationalism," of an assimilation of the cause–effect relation to that of logical ground and consequence. I will present a reason for rejecting Zellner's thesis that the axiom should be read as the expression of a "transmission" view of causality. I will argue that the axiom must be sharply distinguished from Descartes's causal principles. (Bennett and Zellner touch on the possible relation of these to Spinoza, though without definite commitment.) And I will question the reasoning behind Bennett's claim that Spinoza moves from a "logical" to a "psychological" interpretation of the axiom when he draws on it to establish the Thought-Extension "parallelism" thesis at EIIp7.

Besides addressing specific misconceptions, my discussion will provide support for the view that the significance of the particular terms of the axiom, and of the whole proposition, cannot really be understood in isolation from the actual contexts in which it plays a role and the highly original doctrines which it is used to develop. Not only *"cognitio,"* but also *"causa"*—and perhaps *"dependet"* and *"involvit"* as well—take on peculiar technical significance as the axiom becomes entwined with the unfolding of Spinoza's system. Having noted the importance of contextual factors in interpreting the axiom, one is still confronted with problems of intelligibility and consistency in its various uses in the *Ethics.* I will briefly address one of these toward the end of the paper. (I will not otherwise be very much concerned here to assess the cogency of demonstrations that rely on the axiom, however.)

Before proceeding to direct consideration of Spinoza's arguments, I will sketch a little more fully some of the claims or suggestions about axiom 4 with which I will later take issue.

On first acquaintance, axiom 4 presents an appearance of paradox. For it appears incompatible with both common sense and ordinary forms of scientific inquiry. Surely we often know what's happened without at all knowing what brought it about; and it certainly seems that scientific research customarily begins with known effects and attempts to discover their initially unknown causes. Such reflections already suggest that the terms in Spinoza's axiom need to be interpreted with care, if the axiom is not to be regarded as denying the obvious. At the very least one would like to have a reading that would make it possible to understand its appeal *for Spinoza*. The range of readings that have been proposed at least partly reflects such systematic and philosophical concerns.

One reading, versions of which have been proposed by several commentators, renders the axiom virtually tautologous in Spinoza's system, by imposing an extremely restrictive reading on *"cognitio."* Probably the most uncompromising version of the restrictive approach is found in Gueroult. He writes: "l'*Axiome 4* et le parallélisme qu'il implique entre l'ordre des idées et l'ordre des causes ne sauraient valoir pour les idées inadéquates. . . . *L'Axiome 4* ne concerne . . . que les idées vraies."[9] And as he also explains, no true knowledge will be acquired as long as "all the causes are not known,"

> that is as long as [*tant que*] the idea of the thing is not total or adequate, the adequate idea being that which includes in itself the integral knowledge of the causes of its object. In other words, since any singular thing is such only through the infinity of causes which it envelops, an idea which does not include this infinity in itself only knows the thing partially, mutilates it, does not conform to it, and, consequently, is false.[10]

Loeb's account of the axiom, while expressed in less peculiarly Spinozist terminology, has elements in common with Gueroult's. Loeb claims that in axiom 4 Spinoza is employing a special technical sense of "knowledge" such that one doesn't have knowledge of something *unless* one knows about its causal history.[11] (It is thus his view that axiom 4 is not intended *generally* to rule out the possibility of knowledge of an effect—say "by acquaintance"—which does not include knowledge of the cause.) He further explains that one will lack *perfect* knowledge in the sense at issue as long as one fails to know "the entire or complete causal history of the entity."[12]

It is not entirely clear whether Loeb ultimately means to hold that the *"cognitio"* of axiom 4 must be interpreted as perfect causal knowledge. It seems that this probably is what he means, though: for he goes on at once to stipulate that he will use the expression "SP-knowledge" just to mean perfect knowledge in the sense defined; and he subsequently discusses EIax4 in terms of this expression. Similarly, it is not entirely clear whether Loeb's "perfect causal knowledge" is to be understood as something like Gueroult's "adequate idea." The use of the term "perfect," and Loeb's indication that this knowledge is a special sort of knowledge, do seem to suggest such a restrictive notion, however.[13]

The most decisive evidence against taking axiom 4 to concern only adequate knowledge of a thing, or knowledge of its whole causal history, is found in Spinoza's use of the axiom to develop his theory of sense perception in *Ethics* II. But the development of other implications of the axiom, from the very beginning of *Ethics* I, also shows the untenability of any such restrictive reading. It turns out, in fact, that *all* forms of "knowledge," *all* "ideas," are taken to satisfy the axiom.

At one point, Bennett, too, entertains the possibility that, in enunciating EIax4, "Spinoza is thinking of some stratospherically high standard of cognitive perfection—some sort of utterly comprehensive knowledge—which we cannot have of a thing unless we have just as good knowledge of its cause."[14] But elsewhere Bennett provides a nice example of an extremely weak and commonsensical reading, according to which the axiom only means "that one's intellectual grasp on any item is weakened by one's ignorance of its cause."[15] This reading is, he suggests, most likely to yield a plausible axiom if understood in terms of instances like the following: "I would have a better grasp of the French Revolution if I knew more about what led up to it."[16] But this bland reading has little connection with any of the roles the axiom is given to play in the *Ethics*.[17] I will try to make this clear shortly, in connection with the contexts I consider. If I am right, then interpreting *"cognitio"* weakly in terms of an ordinary "intellectual grasp" (such as I might have of the French Revolution) is no sounder than restricting it to "adequate" or perfect causal knowledge.

Zellner avoids the problem of interpreting *"cognitio"* in the axiom by treating EIax4 as essentially a metaphysical, rather than an "epistemological," principle. He construes axiom 4 as expressing a "transmission theory of causality"—as "saying that" the cause and effect "share" a property which the cause transfers to the effect.[18] Zellner defends his interpretation by complex reasoning which I won't attempt to assess in detail. It does seem though, that his reading is unsatisfactory insofar as it renders the actual phrasing of the axiom—in terms, precisely, of *"cognitio"*—so far out of accord with what he thinks it is meant to "say."[19] In any case, I think it can be shown that axiom 4 cannot be expressing a "transmission" theory, in virtue of some of the same considerations that tend to undercut Gueroult's view. (Without doubt, though, it is quickly *tied in with* some form of "causal likeness principle," the relevance of which Zellner advocates more plausibly.) Indeed, I think it can be shown that Spinoza did not hold a transmission theory of causality, in any general form, in the *Ethics*.[20]

According to another viewpoint EIax4 is an expression of Spinoza's "deductive" conception of causality. Bennett appears more or less to exemplify this viewpoint, too. He says that EIax4 must be read in a "logical" way in all its uses, except at EIIp7, where a "psychological" reading is required. Setting aside the issue of a "psychological" reading (which I'll return to later), one may ask what Bennett means by a "logical" reading of the axiom. He writes: "If 1a4 is read in a logical way, it says that if x causes y then there is a conceptual link between them, this being a version or a part of causal rationalism" (p. 127). "Causal rationalism," he has earlier explained, is the view that "a cause relates to its effect as a premise does to a conclusion which follows from it."[21] It is hard to guess what Bennett means by "a version or a part" of causal rationalism. Thus it is hard to know whether he means to imply that axiom 4 represents *cognitio* of an effect as requiring *cognitio* of a cause, such that the latter logically entails the former. But there is at least the suggestion of this view in his wording.

I earlier indicated reservations about the "logical entailment" interpretation of Spinoza's conception of causality. Even setting those aside, though, one may still dispute a reading of the axiom that construes it as an expression of a "deductivist" conception of the cause–effect relationship.[22] Although the axiom quickly becomes implicated in *some* assumptions about "conceptual relations" between cause and effect, these appear to go in the opposite direction than that required by "causal rationalism" as Bennett defines it. For, in some uses of the axiom, it appears that the "knowledge" of the cause is supposed to follow from "knowledge" of the effect (but, perhaps, not vice versa). Or, to express the point epistemically, knowledge of the effect is sufficient for knowledge of the cause (but not vice versa).

In the next section I will try to establish some of these points by examining Spinoza's development of the implications of his axiom in the early propositions of *Ethics* I and some of the middle propositions of *Ethics* II, with particular reference to the attribute–mode relation. Afterward I will show how this development underlies his repudiation of mind–body interaction, while also indicating the importance of sharply distinguishing axiom 4, on its Spinozist interpretation, from Cartesian causal principles. Subsequent sections will be concerned with Spinoza's unique applications of axiom 4 to support Thought–

Extension parallelism, and to explain the possibility of sense perception without inter-attribute causation.

I

One thing that emerges at once, with respect to this axiom, is that Spinoza seems to take the following as equivalent formulations: "the knowledge of B depends on and involves the knowledge of A"; "the concept of B depends on and involves the concept of A"; and "B is understood through A." One can see this by considering EIax5, and the way that Spinoza employs it in conjunction with EIax4. Axiom 5 reads:

> Things that have nothing in common with each other, also cannot be understood by means of each other, or the concept of the one does not involve the concept of the other. [Quae nihil commune cum se invicem habent, etiam per se invicem intelligi non possunt, sive conceptus unius alterius conceptum non involvit.]

The "understanding" and "conceptual involvement" of this axiom are then merged with the *"cognitio"* of EIax4 in the proof of EIp3:

> If things have nothing in common between them, one of them cannot be the cause of the other.

The short proof goes:

> If they have nothing in common with each other, then (by Axiom 5) they cannot be understood through each other, and thus (by Axiom 4) one cannot be the cause of the other.

Similarly, the definition of substance as "conceived through itself" is combined with axiom 4 to yield a proof of EIp6: "One substance cannot be produced by another substance." Thus, axiom 4 must be read as asserting—or at least implying—that the *concept* of an effect depends on the *concept* of a cause, and involves it.[23] (Spinoza's use of axiom 4 in *Ethics* II expands the list of substitutions for *"cognitio"* to include *"idea"* and even *"perceptio,"* as further explained below.)

But does this not mean that the "knowledge" of an effect (by the implications here ascribed to axiom 4) always follows logically from that of its cause? The answer, I think, is "No." To understand this point one needs to consider the relation between the "conceptual dependence" asserted by axiom 4, and the conceptual dependence of modes on substance, which is built into the definition of modes.

A substance, by definition, is that which

> is in itself, and is conceived through itself: that is that, the concept of which does not need the concept of another thing, from which it must be formed (EIdef3).

A mode, however, is an affection of substance,

> or that, which is in another, through which also it is conceived (EIdef5).

This definition of "modes" appears quite harmonious with the Cartesian notion. As Descartes says of the distinction between modes and substances (*Principles of Philosophy*, I, §61):

> we can clearly perceive substance apart from the mode which we say differs from it, but we cannot, conversely, understand that mode without the substance. Thus figure and motion are modally distinguished from corporeal substance, which they are in [*cui insunt*]; so also affirmation or recollection [are modally distinguished] from the mind.[24]

Of course, the modes of body and of mind pertain to separate substances for Descartes, whereas Spinoza recognizes only one substance. There is, nevertheless, an analogous dualism in the order of modes for Spinoza. For modes pertain to substance just insofar as it is understood under a particular attribute, as one can see from EIp25c:

> Particular things are nothing but affections of the attributes of God, or modes, which express the attributes of God in a certain and determinate way.

Or, as the point is expressed even more explicitly in EIp28:

> besides substance, and modes, there is nothing . . . , and modes are nothing except affections of the attributes of God.[25]

But attributes are "really distinct" from each other (EIp10). And however exactly we interpret Spinoza's position on unknown attributes, Thought and Extension are, as Bennett says, the only specific ones relevant to the *Ethics*.[26]

The coherence of the Cartesian system certainly requires that the relation of causal dependence *not* be conflated with the conceptual dependence of modes on substances (or their attributes). Thus God causes motion, but motion is a mode of *res extensa,* which is entirely distinct from God. Similarly, the human mind, through the volitions which are *its* modes, causes changes in brain states, or modes of body. Spinoza, however, definitely runs together the conceptual dependence of modes on substance and the conceptual "involvement" of effect and cause.

This point can be briefly established by considering the proof of EIp25: "God is the efficient cause not only of the existence of things but also of their essence." The core of the proof goes as follows:

> If you deny this, then God is not the cause of the essence of things; and so (by Axiom 4) it is possible to conceive the essence of things without God: but this (by Prop. 15) is absurd.[27]

And the relevant part of the proof of EIp15 is simply:

> Modes however (by Def. 5) cannot be, nor be conceived, without substance.

This intimate connection between axiom 4 and the mode–attribute relation is further reflected in EIIp45. Because substance is God, and an attribute is just "what intellect perceives of substance, as constituting its essence" (EIdef4), Spinoza can reason as follows:

> singular things (by Prop. 15, p. I) cannot be conceived without God; but because . . . they have God for a cause, insofar as he is considered under the attribute, of which the things themselves are modes, the ideas of them (by Axiom 4, p. I) must necessarily involve the concept of their attribute, that is . . . the eternal and infinite essence of God.[28]

(This passage exemplifies the point mentioned above, that in Part II *"idea"* joins *"conceptus"* as an evidently equivalent substitute for *"cognitio"* in axiom 4; *"perceptio"* is employed in place of *"idea"* in certain contexts of *Ethics* II.[29] It follows, Spinoza thinks, that *"each* idea of *every* body, or singular thing, existing in act, necessarily involves the eternal and infinite essence of God" (EIIp4; emphasis added).

These passages, which stress the "involves" component of axiom 4, indicate that the *cause* is conceptually included *in the effect.* Thus, if an "entailment" relation figures here at all, it is an entailment of the cause by the effect—not a "deduction" of effect from cause. Thus the axiom cannot rightly be construed simply as an expression of "causal rationalism."

Notice too that the application of the axiom at EIIp45 is readily intelligible as long as a more or less Cartesian understanding of the mode–

attribute relation is assumed. For on this understanding there is no longer much mystery in the claim that we *don't* "know" *anything*—even in the sense of "know by acquaintance"—without having some knowledge of its cause. It is, after all, very easy to see why someone who believes that all "effects" are either mental or physical might consider it evident that all effects "depend on and involve knowledge" of either Thought or Extension. While I may not know just what occurrence brought about the stain on the rug—so that the specific nature of that occurrence forms no part of my conception of the stain—I wouldn't deny that in conceiving of the stain I conceive it *as extended.* Similarly, while I might be quite perplexed about what made my fantasies take a certain form, I have to admit that I can't really conceive of them without conceiving of them *as thoughts.*

We see already why axiom 4 cannot be restricted to adequate knowledge. Admittedly, Spinoza holds that all knowledge of God's essence, through our knowledge of particular things, is adequate. ("Those things which are common to all, and which are equally in the part and in the whole, can only be conceived adequate"; EIIp38; cf. EIIp47.) But the *knowledge of modes/effects* through which we possess such adequate knowledge of substance/cause is *not* itself adequate. It is the human mind's ideas "from which it perceives itself, . . . its own Body, and . . . external bodies as actually existing" (EIIp47d) which establish (by EIIp38) its claim to possession of adequate knowledge of God's essence. But such ideas are not adequate in the human mind. We have, for instance, "only completely confused knowledge of our Body" (EIIp13s). (Later, in discussing Spinoza's account of perception of external things, I will show that both occurrences of *"cognitio"* in the axiom can be satisfied by inadequate knowledge.)[30]

Of course I do not mean to deny that *"cognitio" encompasses* adequate knowledge. In EIIp47 Spinoza in fact goes on to link our possession of adequate knowledge of God's essence with the possibility of achieving the "third kind of knowledge," which "proceeds from an adequate idea of the formal essence of certain attributes of God to adequate knowledge of the essences of things" (EIIp40s2). He comments in EIIp47s:

> since all things are in God, and are conceived through God, it follows that from this knowledge [*ex cognitionem hac*] we can deduce many things [*nos plurima posse deducere*], which we know adequately [*quae adaequate cognoscamus*], and thus form that third kind of knowledge, of which we spoke in Scholium 2 of Proposition 40 of this Part.

But for present purposes "can" is a key word in the passage just quoted. By virtue of our adequate knowledge of God's essence, we are *able* to form the third kind of knowledge; but the use of axiom 4 to show that we have adequate knowledge of God's essence does not construe *cognitio* of the effect as itself of this kind.

Neither do I mean to deny that EIax4 is in some ways connected with the view that finite modes are "deducible" from the attributes that are their "causes"—however exactly this "deducibility" relation is to be understood. That Spinoza holds such a view is evident from the passage just quoted, as well as from others concerned with *scientia intuitiva*. This view is the cognitive mirror of the claim at EIp16 that all things "must follow from the necessity of the divine nature" (which is explicated through the triangle analogy at EIp17s).[31] EIp16 and EIax4 are joined in the proof of EVp22, "In God . . . there necessarily is an idea, which expresses the essence of this and that human Body under the form of eternity." (Because God is the cause of such essences, they must—by EIax4—be conceived through him, "with a certain eternal necessity (by Prop. 16, p. I)"; a later proposition is then adduced to establish that the ideas of such essences "must be in God.") Rather, I have simply been trying to show that EIax4 plays a broader role in the *Ethics:* that it is not restricted to contexts where the *cognitio* is assumed to be adequate, or the manner in which effect "follows from" cause is assumed to be evident.

We are now in a position to see some reasons for the untenability of some of the other readings mentioned above. Consider Zellner's suggestion that Spinoza held a "transmission" view of causality, and that axiom 4 should be read as an expression of this position. I believe that the application of the axiom I have just traced rules out this interpretation. Insofar as axiom 4 covers the relation of substance to its modes (as we have just seen that it does), it cannot be interpreted in terms of the transmission of a property from one thing to another. The model of a quantity of motion being transferred from a moving to a previously stationary billiard ball (Zellner's example)[32] simply fails to apply when the cause is God or substance—an immanent, not a transitive cause, by EIp21—and the effect is an affection or expression of an attribute of God. There appears in this case to be no *transmission* at all, and certainly not a transmission of a *property* from one entity to another distinct one. In fact, the dependence of modes on attributes seems basically to consist in the fact that modes have no being apart from their respective attributes.

Finally, one may also see from this application of EIax4 that the axiom need have little to do with "improving one's intellectual grasp" of a thing or event, by expanding one's knowledge of the causes in the conventional sense. Causes, in the conventional sense, do not come into the picture; and in the case of "knowing" the attribute through the mode, one's intellectual grasp is any case *always* "adequate."³³

II

Although I deny that axiom 4 is just an expression of "causal rationalism" as defined by Bennett, I of course agree with Bennett that, in light of the propositions immediately following it, axiom 4 must be interpreted as indicating connections of some kind between the concepts of the cause and of the effect. (In my view, then, it is important to distinguish the "conceptual involvement" notion from the claim that "knowledge" of the cause logically entails "knowledge" of the effect.) This requirement of conceptual connection is the basis of Spinoza's repudiation of the Cartesian assumption of mind–body interaction, and the Cartesian view that God, an immaterial entity, is the creative cause of a substance of a different nature (the material universe). To clarify the significance of Spinoza's axiom, it is important to see its role in these anti-Cartesian arguments. I will now focus on the former of these. I particularly want to emphasize the difference between axiom 4, as Spinoza employs it, and the restrictions on causality espoused by Descartes, with which it is sometimes too uncritically compared. As mentioned above, the Cartesian must certainly repudiate Spinoza's partial conflation of the dependence of effect on cause with the relation of dependence between substance (or attributes) and modes. The Cartesian also must reject axiom 4 as Spinoza interprets it. Consideration of the relation between Descartes's causal principles and EIax4 helps show that he is in a position to do so consistently.³⁴

Spinoza's "refutation" of mind–body interaction begins with his definitions of "substance" and "attribute." An attribute is (just) what intellect perceives of substance, "as constituting its essence." In EIp10 Spinoza makes clear that he takes the latter clause to mean that an attribute must conform to the definition of substance, in respect of being "conceived through itself" (and not through another). (Spinoza of course indicates that, unlike Descartes, he does not permit an inference from such independent conception to independent *entities,* i.e., distinctness of *substance.*) According to EIIp1 and EIIp2 thoughts (or "ideas") and bodies are just "modes expressing the nature of God in a definite and determinate way" (by EIp25c).

Therefore [in the case of thought] there belongs to God (by Def. 5, p. I) an attribute, the concept of which all singular thoughts involve, and through which they are conceived. Therefore Thought is one of the infinite attributes of God. (EIIp1d)

Similarly, for body or extension, mutatis mutandis. But the status of Thought and Extension as attributes is then sufficient to show—by EIax4—that thoughts (or ideas) and bodies, as modes of the respective attributes, never stand in causal relation to each other:

neither can the Body determine the Mind to think, nor can the Mind determine the Body to motion, nor to rest, nor to anything else (if such there is) (EIIIp2).

For it follows from the conceptual independence of the attributes that

the modes of any attribute involve the concept of their attribute, but not of another; and so (by Axiom 4, p. I) have God for a cause, insofar only as he is considered under that attribute, of which they are modes, and not insofar as he is considered under another (EIIp6d; cf. EIIIp2d).

Q.E.D.[35]

The primary Cartesian argument for mind–body distinctness of course relies on the independent conceivability of (oneself as) a thinking thing, on the one hand, and *res extensa* on the other hand. Further, Descartes seems committed to the view that there is in *some* sense a conceptual connection between cause and effect: he holds that one cannot conceive a (total) cause as having less reality or perfection than is contained in the effect; or, indeed, as failing itself to contain the effect, "formally or eminently."[36] Some have held that this principle— sometimes called a "causal likeness principle"—is inconsistent with the postulation of mind–body interaction. Some have held, in fact, that Descartes himself saw an inconsistency in maintaining mind–body interaction. Bennett, while acknowledging that Descartes "freely allowed" mind–body interaction in "some of his works," claims that

usually, however, Descartes was uneasy about allowing causal flow between thought and extension.[37]

Bennett goes on to relate Descartes's followers' rejection of mind–body interaction to the causal principle of *Meditations* III, interpreted as indicating that an effect cannot receive a property not possessed by the cause. (It is not entirely clear whether Bennett means to suggest that Descartes's own "uneasiness" had something to do with his causal principle.)

In fact, however, Descartes decisively rejected any claim that the postulation of mind–body interaction involves inconsistency. As he writes to Clerselier, it is a "false" supposition, "which cannot in any way be proved,"

> that if the soul and body are two substances of different nature, that prevents them from being able to act one upon the other.[38]

It is perfectly credible, moreover, that this position is compatible with Descartes's causal principle (or principles). The key points are (1) that Descartes initially states his causal restriction in terms of "reality or perfection"; and (2) that he permits "eminent" containment (of effect in cause). The "reality" aspect of the principle rules out only the causation of the more perfect by the less perfect; thus it absolutely does not rule out the causation of matter by God, or of a physical mode by a mental one. Even the requirement that the cause must "contain" the effect does not rule out cross-attribute causation per se, precisely because "eminent containment" is allowed. Admittedly, there is some problem in reconciling Descartes's restrictions with *body–mind* causation, on the assumption that mind is more perfect than body. One move by which Descartes might cover this point—and perhaps one which he does actually make—is to hold that a bodily state is never more than a partial cause of a mental state (amplified by further causes which are themselves mental).

If one takes Descartes's causal principle(s) to imply that the concept of the effect "involves" the concept of a cause with equal or greater perfection, one might conclude that, in a marginal sense, Descartes accepts a version of EIax4. But he does not accept EIax4 as Spinoza interprets it. As the statement to Clerselier in effect shows, Descartes sees no difficulty in the notion that conceptually distinct substances can satisfy such conceptual conditions as exist on causation: the distinctness of *res cogitans* from *res extensa* does not prevent the substances or their modes being suitably comparable in terms of degrees of reality or perfection. Unlike Spinoza, Descartes does not accept a specific identification of the conceptual restriction on causation with the conceptual involvement of attribute in mode: and there seems to be no obvious "inconsistency" in his position.

One may still ask, however, whether Spinoza's argument against interactionism from axiom 4 has intrinsic plausibility. On the one hand, the popularity over the centuries of the view that mind–body interaction is *somehow* "inconceivable" would seem to suggest that Spinoza has *some* sort of intuition on his side. On the other hand, it does not seem that the exact nature of the alleged problem has ever been made very clear; and it is certainly doubtful that Spinoza's argument does very much to clarify it. For there seems to be no great difficulty, for Cartesians or others, in rejecting EIax4 on its Spinozist interpretation: as requiring that the concept of an effect "involve" the concept of a cause in a way that presupposes identity of attribute between the two.[39]

In summary, the main points I have so far made about EIax4 are the following. First, Spinoza takes the mode–attribute relation to satisfy the axiom. Insofar as an attribute is considered as cause, knowledge of an effect is sufficient for knowledge of the cause (and it is not too hard to see why this should be so). Second, the knowledge of the effect involves knowledge of the cause, under the mode–attribute interpretation, even when the former is inadequate. Third, Spinoza views the "conceivability" relation between effect and cause indicated by EIax4 as ruling out inter-attribute causality: for he construes it as inconsistent with the conceptual distinctness that obtains between attributes. (I have also held that the Cartesian can coherently resist the latter move, without totally denying the spirit of EIax4, because his causal principle requires only a more abstract, less restrictive condition on causal conceivability.)

I turn now to Spinoza's use of axiom 4 in connection with certain positive doctrines about mode–mode causality. Of greatest interest are its roles in grounding the "parallelist" thesis developed in *Ethics* II, and in underpinning the crucial theory of external perception presented later in the same part. I will take these up in order.

III

Perhaps the most striking use of EIax4 occurs in the proof of EIIp7, one of the foundation stones of Part II, and subsequent sections of the *Ethics*. The proposition reads:

> The order, and connection of ideas is the same, as the order, and connection of things.

The demonstration is stunningly simple:

> This is evident from Axiom 4, p. I. For the idea of whatever is caused depends on the knowledge of the cause, of which it is the effect. [Patet ex Ax. 4. p. I. Nam cujuscunque causati idea a cognitione causae, cujus est effectus, dependet.]

It is here that the transition occurs to the use of *"idea"* as a substitution for *"cognitio."* In addition, "depends" is here the operative verb, whereas the arguments previously considered (and one to be considered later) rely on "involves." What is the significance of these changes?

Bennett holds that in this application of EIax4 *"idea"*/*"cognitio"* must be understood as a "mental" or "psychological" term (as opposed to the "logical" interpretation that he considers appropriate to other contexts).[40] It seems to follow that the appeal to EIax4 is specious, for a *different* "axiom" must really be involved: one concerned with the relation of "mental" items, as opposed to an expression of the relation of "logical" items, or concepts. Bennett's reason for this view is that Spinoza soon begins identifying "the human mind" with "the idea of" the human body. He is able to find, however, no satisfactory account of the new "axiom."[41]

There are a number of reasons to reject Bennett's view. For one thing, Spinoza has just defined an idea as a concept: "a concept of the Mind that the Mind forms insofar as it is a thinking thing" (EIIdef3). Admittedly, one may object to Spinoza's combining this definition with the identification of minds *with* ideas; but the definition does rather clearly indicate that Spinoza sees no sharp break between terms that Bennett considers "logical" and those that he considers "psychological." Further, it is at best misleading to construe the term "idea" in the *Ethics* as "psychological" or "mental." Bennett seems to take for granted that the meaning of "mental" or "psychological" at least is clear: but this is something one emphatically must not take for granted in dealing with Spinoza.[42] Finally, up to EIIp7 Spinoza has been talking exclusively of ideas *in God.* Making sense of the claim that there actually exists an ordered series of "ideas," in one-to-one correspondence with the series of things, really depends on thinking of "ideas" in this way, as bits of God's omniscience. (At any rate, one could hardly make sense of the claim if one thought of ideas as items just of human—and perhaps other higher animal—awareness.) Thus, EIIp3, which provides necessary background for EIIp7 (though not explicitly invoked in the "demonstration"), reads:

> In God there is necessarily the idea both of his essence, and of all things that necessarily follow from his essence.[43]

I conclude that, since the need for interpretation of Spinoza's terminology in relation to ordinary usage extends to the term *"idea"* itself, and to *"mens"* as well, it is misleading to insist that EIax4 takes on a new, "psychological" sense when introduced in the proof of EIIp7.[44] Of course this observation does not settle the question whether the axiom is susceptible of a single interpretation in all of its applications; and does not conflict with the point that EIax4 turns out to have important connections with Spinoza's *theory* of "the human mind."

Whatever significance one attaches to the substitution of "idea" for "knowledge" at EIIp7, one should recognize that this application of the axiom also includes a different shift, which truly is important: the switch from "involves" to "depends on." Whereas "involves" connotes a relation of internal conceptual inclusion, "depends" connotes a sort of external relation between ideas or items of knowledge. This distinction between internal and external causal and cognitive relationships is in fact the basis for Spinoza's distinction between adequate and inadequate knowledge, between "God insofar as he is affected by the human Mind," and "God insofar as he is considered as affected by other ideas" (EIIp28d). That Spinoza is able to make such a distinction shows something important about EIax4: that the "involvement" of cause in effect is somehow limited. For, if all ideas in the human mind involved the full chain of their causes without limit, then, it seems, there could only be adequate knowledge, or knowledge that contains the "premises" as well as the "conclusions" (EIIp28d). Spinoza in fact stresses that the human mind knows things only insofar as they relate to its body; whereas God knows things in all their relations, and specifically (by EIIp7 itself) knows them as effects of causes that are "prior in nature" (EIIp25).[45] This is the point at which the dual occurrence of "*cognitio*" in the axiom appears to create problems, though. For it appears to tie knowledge of anything, in *any* mind, to knowledge of the whole regress of causes: by the terms of the axiom, to have knowledge of anything is to have knowledge of *its* cause.

This consideration may well lie behind Gueroult's claim that the axiom concerns only adequate knowledge. (Certainly the wording of his discussion of the axiom suggests that he had its use at EIIp7 prominently in mind.) I have shown already that Gueroult's claim cannot be sustained, however; and I will strengthen my refutation in the next section. Thus, the problem of interpreting the axiom for inadequate knowledge must be faced. I will return to it in the next section.[46]

There is one other important point about the interpretation of EIax4 that emerges from its use in the demonstration of EIIp7: namely, that the dependence relation between ideas is *the same as* the relation that holds between material causes and effects. This is clear from the fact that the axiom is supposed to support the *idem* of EIIp7: the order and connection of ideas is *the same as* the order and connection of things. Further, Spinoza actually begins speaking of the order of *ideas* as *causal* in EIIp9d:

> the order and connection of ideas (by Prop. 7 of this part) is the same as the order and connection of causes [or things].[47] Therefore, the cause of

one singular idea is another idea, *or* God, insofar as he is considered to be affected by another idea . . . and so on, to infinity.[48]

Thus it is clear that Spinoza does not distinguish (from the theocentric point of view) between the relation of necessary determination that holds among physical things and that which obtains among *cognitiones.* There may actually be less information here than appears to meet the eye, however. To tell us that the same relation holds among physical causes that holds among bits of God's omniscience does not really tell us all that much about the relation. In particular, it does not directly tell us that the relation in question should be construed as "logical entailment." For in order to tell us this, it would have to make clear—as it does not—that the envisaged relation among *ideas* is one of logical entailment.

IV

The final application of EIax4 that I will consider occurs at EIIp16. This proposition is concerned with our knowledge of external bodies, i.e., bodies external to our own bodies. To understand the problem of external perception as it presents itself to Spinoza, it will be helpful again to consider Descartes's position briefly for purposes of contrast.

Descartes uses a causal argument to justify his belief that there are bodies, starting from the solipsistic viewpoint of the thinking self. His causal-containment principle yields, he insists, the conclusion that the cause of his sensory ideas of bodies must contain as much reality as is contained in the ideas themselves, considered as ideas *of bodies.* But to obtain conclusions that the causes of these ideas must be *physical,* Descartes introduces further premises about both his "disposition to believe" that the ideas are caused by bodies, and God's veracity. After he has obtained this general conclusion that "corporeal things exist," Descartes proceeds to conclude, more specifically, that he "has" a body and feels sensations according to its needs; and, further, that there are other bodies which exist around his body, and can do it good or harm.

Subsequently in the *Meditations*—and also in such other works as the *Dioptrics* and the *Principles*—Descartes explains the process of sense perception more concretely. Motions transmitted from bodies form impressions in the brain, there giving rise to sensory ideas in the mind, according to a "natural convention," or system of regular correlations, established by God. These ideas in turn may lead the mind to make judgments about external things. Because the ideas tend to be confused, the judgments are very likely to be mistaken unless carefully subordinated to reason.

A number of aspects of Spinoza's *general* position underlie the fundamental differences between his position on the perception of bodies and that of Descartes. Among them are the fact that Spinoza eschews the Cartesian solipsistic starting point, in favor of a theocentric one; that he accords little epistemological priority to the mental; and (most important in the present context) that he repudiates causal interaction between mind and body. According to Spinoza, the human body is that "existing thing" which (by EIIp11, citing EIIp7) is the "object" of the idea which "constitutes the being of the human Mind." Thus, according to EIIp13,

> the object of the idea constituting the human Mind is the Body, *or* a certain mode of Extension actually existing, and nothing else.

Hence it follows, Spinoza says, "that man consists of Mind and Body, and the human Body, as we sense it [*prout ipsum sentimus*] exists" (EIIp13c).

One thing we know about this mysterious "object of" relation is that it is non-causal: the mind's objects are *never* causes of it or of (the formal being of) its subsidiary ideas. Thus, as Spinoza says in EIIp5,

> the ideas both of God's attributes and singular things do not admit as their efficient cause the objects [*ideata*] themselves, or the things perceived, but God himself, insofar as he is a thinking thing.

Yet EIax4 does enter into Spinoza's account of sense perception in a crucial way.

Descartes, as mentioned above, uses a causal argument to establish the existence of body, reasoning in a general way from ideas of sense; he then moves specifically to claims about his own body and external bodies. Spinoza first establishes the existence of the human body as the "object," but not cause, of the human mind. But he then faces the problem of providing an account of the "perception" of *external* bodies (i.e., bodies external to the human body), given that he takes "perception" to be strictly mental, and that he denies any physical–mental causality. If the relation between sense perception and thing perceived cannot at all be explained in terms of a causal relation between the two, how are we to understand it? In addressing this problem Spinoza again enlists the aid of EIax4.

Important in the analysis is EIIp12:

> Whatever happens in the object of the idea that constitutes the human
> Mind must be perceived by the human Mind, or there necessarily is given
> in the Mind the idea of this thing. That is, if the object of the idea consti-
> tuting the human Mind is a body, nothing can happen in this body which
> is not perceived by the human Mind.

Thus, the idea or knowledge of any change of state in the body will
occur in the mind, of which the body is the "object." But, when the
change of state is the effect of an external body, then it would seem to
follow directly by EIax4 that knowledge of this change of state "involves" knowledge of its cause, i.e., that in virtue of having knowledge
of the bodily changes, the mind also has knowledge of, or perceives,
the external bodies which cause them.

This is in fact *roughly* the line that Spinoza does take, but two points
of mild complication need to be noted. First, in developing his theory
of sense perception, Spinoza relies on the following additional
"axiom," presented as Axiom l' in the midst of the lemmata about bodies that follow EIIp13:

> All the modes in which any body is affected by another body follow from
> the nature of the affected body, and at the same time from the nature of
> the affecting body.

Such modes, in other words, have as causes both the affected and the
affecting bodies. So, by EIax4, the ideas of these modes will involve the
knowledge or ideas of the affected, as well as the affecting bodies. This
enables Spinoza to conclude that sense perception reflects the nature
of our own body as well as external bodies, a view which he relates to
the subjectivity of sense perception.[49]

Second, Spinoza's phrasing of the key proposition about sense perception fails to reflect the phrasing of EIax4 in a puzzling way, despite
the explicit citation of the axiom in its demonstration. "Knowledge of
an effect . . . knowledge of the cause" is altered to "knowledge of an
effect . . . *nature* of the cause." Thus, EIIp16—which has as its first
corollary the claim that "the human Mind perceives the nature of a
great many bodies together with the nature of its own body"—reads
as follows:

> The idea of any mode in which the human Body is affected by external
> bodies must involve the nature of the human Body, and at the same time
> the nature of the external body.

For (according to the demonstration), the idea of such a mode will (by
EIax4) necessarily involve the nature of both the bodies from which

(by the special lemmata axiom) the mode follows: the human body itself, and the external body.

I see no great significance in the omission of the second *"cognitio"* (or *"idea"*) in EIIp16, and shall not comment on it further.[50] But the fact that our perceptions of the states by which we know external bodies at the same time reflect the nature of our own bodies connects with a point on which I want particularly to insist. Both the ideas of the affections of the human body and the ideas of external bodies with which EIIp16 is concerned manifestly include *confused or inadequate* ideas. Since the derivation of EIIp16 turns on EIax4, then, we see again that the latter cannot be construed as restricted to adequate ideas.

Spinoza directly asserts at EIIp25:

> The idea of any affection of the human Body does not involve an adequate knowledge of the external body.

The proof of EIIp25 depends on the claim that (by EIIp7) God has knowledge of any external body, not merely insofar as it affects the human body, but also insofar as he has an idea of something *outside* the human body—from which point of view the knowledge must thus be inadequate. Again, Spinoza maintains at EIIp28:

> The ideas of the affections of the human Body, insofar as they are related only to the human Mind, are not clear and distinct, but confused.

Now, EIIp16 is of course not *restricted* to "ideas of the affections of the human Body, insofar as they are related only to the human Mind." But it must be taken to *encompass* ideas considered in this way: otherwise the crucial inference from EIIp16 to its first corollary would be incomprehensible. Hence the ideas of the affections of the human body, and the perceptions of external bodies which (by EIax4) they "involve," include inadequate and confused ideas. In other words, the axiom is supposed to be satisfied under conditions where *both* occurrences of *"cognitio"* denote *inadequate* knowledge.

Axiom 1' from the lemmata section is not formally involved in the proof of the inadequacy of the ideas which (by EIIp16) we have of external bodies. It is clear, though, that Spinoza does connect the claim that our ideas of external things involve the nature of our own body as well as (indeed, by EIIp16c2, more than) the nature of external bodies with the error of confusing our own physiological responses with actual properties of objects. For this is precisely the point of the examples he cites at EIIp16c2. Thus Spinoza appears to explain the "inadequacy" or "confusion" of our perception of external things through their effects on our bodies in two ways. On the one hand, he holds that adequate ideas of the things require knowledge of them through "things prior in nature" (or prior "in the order of nature"), and not merely through their effects. On the other hand, he indicates that our ideas of external bodies are thoroughly contaminated with "the nature of our own bodies," through which we perceive them.

Beside refuting the view that EIax4 applies only to *"idées vraies,"* its use in the proof of EIIp16 also tells strongly against any attempt to construe the axiom as an expression of "causal rationalism," as explained by Bennett. The notion that we know or perceive external things confusedly through their effects on our bodies is perhaps consistent with the notion that the effects are "logical consequences" of the causes (assuming one can make any sense at all of the latter view). But, certainly, no such deductivist view is involved in the account of knowledge that Spinoza goes on to describe as "confused" and "mutilated" (EIIp28d and EIIp29c,s).[51]

Earlier I suggested that the notion that "knowledge of an effect involves knowledge of a cause" is susceptible to an obvious and commonsensical interpretation, once one notes that attributes count as "causes" of their modes (assuming a more or less Cartesian conception of attributes). I now want to suggest that it is possible to interpret, in commonsensical terms, the "involvement" of knowledge of cause in knowledge of effect that might be at issue in EIIp16—as long as one is ready to follow Spinoza in saying that the mind "knows" its body. For if one thinks of sense perception as an "effect" of external things, it is hard to see how to avoid thinking of it as an effect that "involves the nature" of its cause or its causes. Even if one restricts oneself, as Spinoza's system requires, to intra-attribute causation, the notion of "involvement" makes obvious sense. One need only think of retinal images, let alone of the impressions of external objects lodged in the center of the brain, on standard Cartesian theory. The internal states do not merely follow on external stimuli—do not only follow *with necessity* from external stimuli: they in some sense incorporate the external entity (or so it seems).

It would be a mistake to rely too far, though, on this homely view of Spinoza's application of EIax4 in developing his theory of our perception of external bodies: at best, it constitutes a sort of partial interpretation. I have already mentioned in passing Spinoza's claim that the human mind perceives *everything that happens in the human body.* What we must now acknowledge is that his use of axiom 4 in EIIp16 and its corollaries appears to commit him also to the view that we perceive *everything that causes any change whatsoever in our body.* Retinal images (or for that matter the cortical mappings of contemporary perceptual theory) can have no favored status as effects relevant to external perceptions, as opposed, for instance, to X-rays transmitted through one's hand, odorless and colorless gasses that have subtle metabolic effects, and so on.[52] (Such considerations are also sufficient to show what a very technical sense *"cognitio"* has taken on by the middle of *Ethics* II; we are far indeed from such routine illustrations as "improving our intellectual grasp on the French revolution by learning more about its causes.")

I return, finally, to the problem sketched toward the end of the last section: that of reconciling the cognitive regress implicit in EIax4 with the claim—essential to the notion of inadequate knowledge—that we have only limited knowledge of the causal chains that impinge on our bodies. As recently noted, the proofs of EIIp24 and EIIp25 lay some emphasis on the notion that God's possession of adequate knowledge of external things consists in the fact that he knows them through his ideas of things "prior in the order of nature" to them. One might take this to mean that God, "insofar as he is affected with other ideas," has ideas of the *causes* of external things, whereas God, "insofar as he constitutes the nature of the human mind," has ideas only of their *effects*. It does not seem, however, that Spinoza can categorically deny, consistently with EIax4, that *our* causal knowledge, too, in some sense extends to infinity.

Perhaps the problem of reconciling inadequate knowledge with EIax4 can be more satisfactorily resolved by focusing on another theme prominent in these passages: the observation that we know things only in relation to our *own* body, whereas God knows them in *all* their relations with *all* bodies—and in the correct, "internal" order. Thus (one might propose) it does not really matter how *many* cause-ideas are somehow "involved" in the idea that constitutes the human mind; the knowledge will remain inadequate and partial as long as each of these presents its object only in its limited relation to us. (Whether this is a *completely* satisfactory solution—one consistent with other aspects of Spinoza's treatment of adequate and inadequate knowledge—I will not attempt to determine here.)[53]

Conclusion

I have tried to show how several attempts to explain or interpret EIax4 fail to fit well with—or are actually contradicted by—some of the most important uses of the axiom in the *Ethics*. One moral I draw from all this is, of course, that there is not much point in trying either to explain or to justify the axiom in an off-the-cuff manner, without considering in detail what Spinoza does with it. This moral applies to attempts to interpret the axiom in terms of other Spinozist doctrine (such as the theory of adequate ideas); to attempts to give commonsensical readings; to efforts to relate it to previous or contemporary causal theories. It applies as well to attempts to connect the axiom with "causal rationalism" (or more specifically) the "logical entailment" view of causality supposedly expressed in EIp16–17, and elsewhere in Spinoza's work. I have also argued that Bennett's claim, that the axiom has a different sense at EIIp7 from its other applications, fails to take adequate account of the context of that proposition, and of the oddities of Spinoza's use of "mental" terms. I have not claimed that the axiom is used in a consistent and univocal way throughout the *Ethics*, though. Indeed, the fact that the "involves" component figures essentially in certain contexts, while "depends" does the work in others, shows at least that appeal to "EIax4" does not come to exactly the same thing in all cases. Further, the fact that the axiom unquestionably applies *across* the distinction between adequate and inadequate knowledge introduces additional interesting complications into the interpretive problem.[54]

Notes

1. Sometimes Spinoza speaks in similar terms of the determination of one finite mode by another: "These [human dispositions] follow from this [human] affect as necessarily as [it follows] from the nature of a triangle that its three angles are equal to two right angles" (EIVp57s).

Translations throughout the paper are substantially my own. Translations of Spinoza are based on the Gebhardt edition. I have, however, consulted Shirley's and Curley's versions of most passages.

2. Henry E. Allison, *Benedict de Spinoza* (Boston: Twayne, 1975), p. 71; G.H.R. Parkinson, *Spinoza's Theory of Knowledge* (Oxford: Clarendon Press, 1954), p. 64; Jonathan Bennett, *A Study of Spinoza's Ethics* (Indianapolis: Hackett, 1984), p. 30. For a relatively detailed discussion, see E.M. Curley, *Spinoza's Metaphysics* (Cambridge, Mass.: Harvard University Press, 1969), pp. 45ff.

3. Curley's exposition of the "logical entailment" interpretation, while not entirely clear, is the clearest I know. (For reference, see n. 2.)

4. At EIp33s1 Spinoza offers an "explanation" of how "necessary" should be understood. This turns out to consist of explaining that things are "necessary" either by reason of their essence or by reason of their cause! The account he offers here of impossibility is perhaps slightly more suggestive: a thing is said to be impossible "either because its essence or definition involves a contradiction, or because no external cause is given, determined to produce such a thing." (See Curley, chap. 3, for some other passages relevant to this issue from the *Ethics* and other works.)

5. Charles Jarrett has said of the axiom in question that it "might in fact be taken as a definition of 'cause' "; "The Logical Structure of Spinoza's *Ethics*," *Synthese* 37 (1978):29. This suggestion derives support from Spinoza's definition of "adequate cause" and "inadequate cause" at the beginning of *Ethics* III.

6. Among those who have objected to translating *"cognitio"* as "knowledge" are Jonathan Bennett (*Study,* p. 127) and Alan Donagan (in conversation). I prefer to use "knowledge" because the one likely alternative, "cognition," sounds so strained and contrived as to be distracting. The term employed in EIax4 is the same used by Spinoza in EIIp40s2, where he expounds (what are usually known in English as) the three kinds of knowledge. Later I will emphasize that *"cognitio"* in EIax4 is not restricted to adequate knowledge, i.e., to knowledge of the second or third kinds.

Spinoza, of course, also uses the term *"scientia,"* which has a more restricted sense for him than *"cognitio."* Thus, in EIIp40s2, the third kind of knowledge is identified as *"scientia intuitiva."*

7. I see no justification for the practice followed by most English-language translators—including both Curley and Shirley—of simplifying the structure of the axiom by incorporating *"et eandem involvit"* into the first clause: "The knowledge of an effect depends on, and involves, the knowledge of its cause" (*The Collected Works of Spinoza,* ed. and transl. E.M. Curley (Princeton: Princeton University Press, 1985), vol. I, p. 410; see also Spinoza, *The Ethics and Selected Letters,* transl. Samuel Shirley, ed. Seymour Feldman (Indianapolis: Hackett, 1982), p. 32). Although this move does not change the literal sense of the axiom, it does create a slight shift of emphasis away from *"involvit,"* as a distinct relation. But as I shall show, this is really the operational term in most of the important applications of the axiom, and the distinction between *"involvere"* and *"dependere"* is genuinely significant. (By contrast, Louis Loeb maintains that *"involvit"* does not figure essentially in any application, and accordingly "simplifies" axiom 4 by dropping the term; *From Descartes to Hume* [Ithaca: Cornell University Press., 1981], p. 102.) I take it that the antecedent of *"eandem"* is clear on either reading.

8. See vol. I of Gueroult's *Spinoza, Dieu* (Paris: Aubier-Montaigne, 1968), pp. 95–98; Loeb, *From Descartes to Hume,* pp. 102–103, and 167 ff.; Bennett, *Study,* p. 50 and 127 ff.; Zellner, "Spinoza's Causal Likeness Principle," *Philosophy Research Archives* 9 (March 1986): 453–462.

9. "Axiom 4, and the parallelism between the order of ideas and the order of causes that it implies, does not hold for inadequate ideas. . . . Axiom 4 concerns nothing but true ideas." Gueroult, *Spinoza,* I, pp. 96–97.

10. Ibid., p. 96. It will turn out that "including in itself the integral knowledge of the causes of its object" may not be a sufficient condition of adequate knowledge for Spinoza: confused and inadequate ideas, by virtue of EIax4, contain knowledge of their causes, considered in certain relations.

11. Loeb, *Descartes to Hume,* p. 102.

12. Ibid., pp. 102–103. (Loeb cites a relevant passage on knowledge of effects from the *Treatise on the Emendation of the Intellect.*)

13. Ibid., pp. 103, 175. As indicated in note 10, above, I will suggest later that, *in a sense,* all ideas may have to involve infinite causal knowledge. This result derives from the double appearance of *"cognitio"* in the axiom, which of course suggests a regress: if the cause is itself an effect, then *cognitio* of it will require *cognitio* of *its* cause, and so forth. This consideration seems to underlie the longer passage quoted from Gueroult. His error, in my view, is to assume that the regressive aspect of the axiom ties it exclusively to the domain of adequate knowledge.

14. Bennett, *Study,* p. 129. Bennett notes that on such an understanding the axiom would require "an infinite mental embrace—a cognition of something, and of its cause, and of *its* cause, and so on." (At this point he is considering what he takes to be the "psychological" version of the axiom; unsurprisingly, then, he considers it less than evident that on this strong interpretation there will exist a "cognition" that satisfies it.)

15. Ibid., p. 179. Bennett is here discussing EIIp16, and hence assuming what he calls the "logical" understanding of EIax4; see ibid., pp. 127–128, and p. 128, n. 1.

16. Even on this understanding, Bennett doesn't seem to think the axiom is especially plausible, though it's hard to see why not.

17. Bennett does not say it does. In fact, on p. 179 he is indicating that, on its most "plausible" reading, the axiom cannot help with the problem at hand: of explaining why inadequate ideas are "mutilated." His approach throughout is to generate freely possible "meanings" of the axiom, evaluating each one in terms of (1) whether it is "plausible," and (2) whether it produces a valid argument in the context under discussion. (It appears that none of the readings of the axiom that he considers in connection with particular arguments passes both tests.) My approach here, by contrast, will be to try to get a better understanding of Spinoza's conception of the axiom by close consideration of its use.

18. "Spinoza's Causal Likeness Principle," pp. 453–456.

19. *"Cognitio"* also appears prominently in EIax5, discussed below, which Zellner regards ad providing a partial interpretation of axiom 4.

20. Bennett, like Zellner, interprets a remark that Spinoza makes in correspondence with Oldenburg (Letter 4) as indicating a "transfer" view of causality, which would rule out mind–body interaction. He expresses agnosticism, however, about "[w]hether this line of thought was at work in [Spinoza's] later years, encouraging his view that if one thing has nothing in common with another it cannot be its cause" (p. 50).

The gist of the comment to Oldenburg is that an effect must have something in common with its cause; otherwise "whatever the effect had, it would have from nothing" (Letter 4; G4/10–11; Curley transl., vol. I, p. 172). I do not think this comment actually establishes a transfer view of causality. (It is compatible as well with, for example, a "copy" view of causality.) The passage from Spinoza's exposition of Descartes's *Principles,* which Zellner also cites in this connection, seems to me even less strongly indicative of a transfer or transmission view.

21. Bennett, *Study,* pp. 29–30.

22. It of course cannot be assumed that a philosopher influenced by Descartes understands "deduction" as a formal relation.

23. This point seems to be generally accepted in the literature; cf., e.g., Jarrett, "Logical Structure . . . ," p. 32; and Bennett, *Study,* p. 127.

24. *Oeuvres de Descartes,* ed. Charles Adam and Paul Tannery, 12 vols. (Paris: Cerf, 1897–1913; reprinted Vrin 1957–1958), vol. VIII-1, p. 29.

25. See also EIIp45d: "[Particular things] have God for their cause, insofar as he is considered under the attribute, of which the things themselves are modes."

26. Bennett, *Study,* pp. 75–79.

27. As Jarrett remarks ("Logical Structure . . . ," p. 29), the respective uses of EIax4 in EIp3 and EIp25 show that it must be interpreted as a biconditional. In the former, Spinoza takes it that x causes y only if knowledge of y depends on knowledge of x. In the latter, the operant assumption is that knowledge of y depends on knowledge of x only if x causes y. A less charitable view is taken by Bennett (*Study,* p. 128, n. 1), who accuses Spinoza of an "illegitimate conversion" of the axiom at EIp25.

28. EIIp45d. The omissions indicated by the ellipses are references to EIIp6 and EIdef6, respectively.

29. Given the transition from *"cognitio"* to *"conceptus"* at the beginning of *Ethics* I, the substitutability of *"idea"* appears to be licensed by the definition of that term at the beginning of *Ethics* II.

30. Because the attributes are "self-caused," the knowledge of them does not require any further knowledge under EIax4; and a regress problem does not emerge at this point. The use of EIax4 in connection with external perception—where both cause and effect are finite modes—does present such a problem, though. I will return to this issue in Section IV.

31. I have tried to demonstrate the integral connection between EIp16 and "the third kind of knowledge" in "Infinite Understanding, *Scientia Intuitiva,* and *Ethics* I.16," *Midwest Studies in Philosophy VIII,* ed. Peter A. French et al. (Minneapolis: University of Minnesota Press, 1983), pp. 181–191.

32. Another example that Zellner mentions is that of transfer of heat from one body to another.

33. See EIIp46.

34. The discussion in this section owes a considerable debt to Loeb's vigorous arguments in *Descartes to Hume,* chaps. 3 and 4.

35. The proposition Spinoza derives at EIp3 with the aid of EIax4—"if two things have nothing in common, one cannot be the cause of the other"—no doubt qualifies as a causal likeness principle. But this proposition is largely an idle part, and plays no role in the formal "refutation" of mind–body interaction. On this point, see Loeb's excellent discussion in *Descartes to Hume,* pp. 186–190.

36. Adam and Tannery, vol. VII, pp. 40–41; cf. the French version, vol. IX-1, p. 32. This principle figures both in Descartes's first argument for the existence of God and his later proof of the existence of bodies.

37. Bennett, *Study,* pp. 49–50.

38. Adam and Tannery, vol. IX-1, p. 213; Descartes goes on to observe (in the same sentence) that others don't hesitate to affirm that "accidents" like heat and weight can act on a body; yet, he says, there is "more of a difference" (*plus de différence*) between accidents and substance than between two substances.

On this point and related ones about Descartes's position, I largely follow Loeb's work and contributions by Robert Richardson and Eileen O'Neill. See especially Richardson, "The 'Scandal' of Cartesian Interactionism," *Mind* 91 (1982):20–37; and O'Neill, "Mind–Body Interaction and Metaphysical Consistency: A Defense of Descartes," *Journal of the History of Philosophy,* 25:2, pp. 227–245. O'Neill's interpretive position is developed more fully in *Mind and Mechanism: An Examination of Some Mind–Body Problems in Descartes' Philosophy* (unpublished Ph.D. thesis, Princeton University, 1983).

39. These points are cogently urged by Loeb, pp. 171–190.

40. Bennett, *Study,* pp. 127–131.

41. Ibid., p. 129: "I have done nothing to make 1a4 believable on a psychological reading, and that task is too much for me. It is hard even to suggest reasons for Spinoza's finding it plausible. He may have been influenced by its plausibility when read logically."

42. For a detailed defense of this claim, see my paper, "Objects, Ideas, and 'Minds': Comments on Spinoza's Theory of Mind," in *The Philosophy of Baruch Spinoza,* ed. Richard Kennington (Washington: Catholic University of America, 1980), pp. 103–120.

43. Bennett stresses the importance of EIIp3 for the "parallelism" thesis. But his treatment of EIax4 in connection with EIIp7 is rendered very confusing by his failure to consider the relevance of EIIp3 until after he has defended the need for a "psychological" reading for several pages, and raised objections to Spinoza's position read in this way.

44. One could even say that, in a sense, EIIp7 requires a *less* "psychological" reading of EIax4 than the other uses considered in this paper. The uses considered previously involve *"cognitiones"* of mind and body that are (on *one* interpretation of the mode–attribute relation, anyway) directly and consciously accessible to the human mind; the one to be considered last has to do with human sense perception.

45. See also EIIp24.

46. It is true, of course, that the use of EIax4 at EIIp7 has an important connection with the concept of adequate knowledge. The dependence relation among ideas with which proposition 7 is concerned is, precisely, the system of ideas *in God;* and "All ideas . . . insofar as they are related to God, are true . . . and . . . adequate" (EIIp36d). It does not follow, though, that truth or adequacy is presupposed as a *condition* on *"idea"/"cognitio,"* even in its application at EIIp7. For EIIp36d bases the claim about adequacy directly on EIIp7c, and the claim about truth on EIIp32, which is itself based on appeal to the same corollary (together with EIax6, "A true idea must agree with its object"). In other words, claims about truth and adequacy are posterior to this application of the axiom.

47. See Curley's note in his translation of Spinoza's works, vol. I, p. 453.

48. See also EIIp6c: "[T]he objects of ideas follow and are inferred [*consequuntur, & concluduntur*] from their attributes in the same way, and with the same necessity as we have shown ideas to follow from the attribute of Thought."

49. Indeed, according to EIIp16c2, our ideas of external bodies indicate the nature of our own body *more* than of external bodies. It is doubtful that Spinoza is strictly entitled to *this* conclusion by his preceding argument: see Curley's edition, vol. I, p. 463, n. 42.

50. Cf. Gueroult, *Spinoza,* vol. II, pp. 194–195, for a different view (which I think is mistaken).

51. It is perhaps worth mentioning that, inasmuch as EIIp16 is specifically concerned with *external* causes, its reliance on EIax4 implicitly rules out an attempt to interpret the axiom strictly in terms of *constituent* causes (where "knowing the effect" would be understood as knowing the *nature* of the effect, and knowing the nature of the effect would mean knowing its molecular structure, underlying chemical processes, or other microstructural factors). I do not discuss such an interpretation in the body of the paper because it does not seem to have been advocated by publishing scholars, though I have occasionally heard it proposed in both seminars and informal discussion.

52. This consequence is indeed more fundamental to Spinoza's account of perception than the claim that the human mind perceives everything that happens in the human body. See n. 49, above.

53. At one time I believed that the axiom's assertion of "involvement" actually came into conflict with the assertion of "dependence," since ideas of affections have to *depend on* ideas of remote causes, but (given the existence of inadequate knowledge) could not generally *involve* the ideas of remote causes. The solution I now propose in effect allows one to say that ideas of effects do generally involve ideas of remote causes, but only in a limited or partial way, working outward from effects, rather than "concluding" to effects from causes.

54. A confused and mutilated earlier version of this paper was presented at a Philosophy Department colloquium at the University of Pittsburgh, as well as at the Jerusalem Spinoza Conference. I'm grateful to the participants on both occasions, and especially to Annette Baier, for helpful and constructive comments. Work on the paper was undertaken during a year of leave, with support, from Princeton University, for which I also wish to express my thanks.

9

Phenomenalism and Corporeal Substance in Leibniz

Robert Merrihew Adams

The most fundamental principle of Leibniz's metaphysics is that "there is nothing in things except simple substances, and in them perception and appetite" (G II,270/L 537). This implies that bodies, which are not simple substances, can only be constructed out of simple substances and their properties of perception and appetite. ('Constructed' is our word for it. Leibniz commonly says that bodies or phenomena "result" from single substances and their modifications; but resulting is not what we would call a causal relation in this context.)[1]

How, according to Leibniz, are bodies constructed out of simple substances and their properties? Two theses frequently asserted by Lcibniz—that bodies are phenomena and that bodies are aggregates of substances—have been thought to represent incompatible theories of the construction of bodies. Interpreters have spoken of a vacillation in Leibniz or have tried to document a change of mind, assigning the different theories a predominant role in different periods of the philosopher's career.[2] I was once inclined to do that myself, but I have now become convinced that Leibniz did not vacillate or change his mind on this point. To be sure, he is often careless or imprecise, saying things in ways that ignore aspects of his views that he does not want to present at the moment. But if there are two theories here, Leibniz believed (rightly or wrongly) that they are consistent, and he held both of them throughout the mature period of his thought (say, from 1686 on).

In this paper I will try to show how he wove the theses that bodies are phenomena and that they are aggregates of substances into a single, phenomenalistic theory, which seems to me to be reasonably coherent. In section 3 I will try to explain why Leibniz thought that, precisely *as* aggregates of substances, bodies are only phenomena; and in section 4 I will examine the distinction between real and imaginary bodies in his system, which is the principal point at which he might be suspected of using two or more mutually inconsistent constructions. First, however, I must try to explain what Leibniz does and does not mean by calling bodies "phenomena." Section 1 will be devoted to this topic, which contains (in my opinion) some of Leibniz's most valuable contributions to metaphysics.

In order to understand Leibniz's views about corporeal aggregates, it will be important to know something about the relation between a simple substance, or "monad," and "its" body. This relation, which is the topic of section 2, is fundamental to the structure of what Leibniz calls a "corporeal substance." And this brings us to another theme, which I think Leibniz was not so successful in harmonizing with the rest of his philosophy. He held that a corporeal substance, composed of a monad (something like a soul) and its organic body (an aggregate or phenomenon), is one per se as no aggregate can be. As I will argue in my fifth and final section, the nature of this unity is puzzling and Leibniz himself seems to have been troubled about it during the last years of his life; he has left us, indeed, more evidence of vacillation on this point than on any other part of his philosophy of matter. In this connection I will examine the notorious conception of a substantial bond (*vinculum substantiale*) that appears in his letters to Des Bosses.

Thus, this paper will be concerned with three Leibnizian theses about the physical world that seem at first glance to be flatly inconsistent with each other: (1) that bodies are phenomena, (2) that bodies are aggregates of substances, and (3) that there are corporeal substances that, though composite, are one per se. And I will be arguing that Leibniz held all three of them at once and was reasonably successful in integrating the first two of them with each other, but not with the third.

1. Phenomena

Leibniz's phenomenalism is quite different from the sorts of phenomenalism with which English-speaking philosophers are likely to be most familiar. It is, therefore, important to clear our minds of preconceptions when we consider what Leibniz meant by calling bodies phenomena. 'Phenomenon' is a Greek word that means 'appearance', or more literally 'thing that appears'. Things that appear are objects of awareness. The first thing that I want to say about phenomena, as Leibniz conceives of them, is that they are *intentional objects*.[3] Bodies, as phenomena, may be thought of as the objects of a story—a story told or approximated by perception, common sense, and science. In calling them phenomena Leibniz means that they have their being in the awareness that perceivers have of this story.

Leibniz spoke of phenomena as "*objects* of limited minds" (G VII, 563, my emphasis). This should not be taken to imply that he thought of phenomena as fully distinct from the acts or properties of our minds by virtue of which we are aware of them, for he also said that "phenomena are nothing but thoughts" (G II, 70/L-A 86) and that the "phenomena" that are always produced in us when we see bodies "are simply new transitory modifications of our souls" (G VI,591/L 626). On the other hand, it is difficult to accept that Leibniz simply identified bodies, as phenomena, with perceptions; for the properties he ascribes to these two sorts of entities are quite different. For example, he ascribes size, shape, and motion to bodies but not to modifications of the mind as such. And, conversely, bodies are not said to be distinct or confused, although those are salient properties of perceptions of bodies for Leibniz.

I believe the solution to this problem is that, when Leibniz speaks of material things as phenomena, he usually thinks of those phenomena as qualities or modifications of a perceiving substance *considered only in a certain respect.* Specifically, corporeal phenomena are perceptions considered with regard to their objective reality or representational content or insofar as they express some nature, form, or essence.

Here I am extrapolating from things Leibniz says about "ideas." His notion of idea is by no means the same as his notion of phenomenon. The latter notion is more closely connected with perception than the former, and some phenomena are transitory, whereas ideas in general are not. But ideas, like phenomena, are both properties and objects of the mind; and Leibniz gives much fuller discussion to the relation between ideas and the mind than I have found him to give to the relation between phenomena and the perceiving substance.

A famous controversy between Malebranche and Arnauld provides the starting point for much of Leibniz's thought about ideas. Malebranche held that ideas of bodies are objects of awareness distinct from the modifications of our minds by which we are aware of them. He had to regard them as distinct, since he held that the ideas are in God's mind and not in ours. Arnauld maintained not only that we have ideas of bodies in our own minds but also that they are modifications of our minds. Leibniz declared himself for Arnauld in this debate: "It suffices to consider ideas as Notions, that is to say as modifications of our soul. That is how the school, M. Descartes, and M. Arnauld take them" (G III,659; cf. G IV,426/L 294).[4]

This declaration does not fully reflect the complexity of Leibniz's position, however. In the first place, he agreed with Malebranche that, *if* ideas are taken "as the immediate external object of our thoughts, it is true that they could not be placed in God, since there is nothing but God that can act immediately upon us" (RML 317, cf. 490). And in conciliatory moods he was prepared to say that "it can very well be maintained in this sense that we see everything in God" (RML 490). But Leibniz insists that we also have an immediate *internal* object of our thought (RML 317). "I hold, however, that there also is always something in us that corresponds to the ideas that are in God as well as to the phenomena that take place in bodies" (RML 321f.). In this sense we have our own ideas in our own minds (DM 28-29), and our ideas are modifications of our minds, or relations of correspondence to God's ideas, which are included in those modifications (RML 490).

In the second place, Leibniz's calling ideas modifications of the souls should not lead us to suppose that he identified them with conscious episodes. In section 26 of the *Discourse on Metaphysics,* he distinguishes two senses of 'idea':

> Some take the idea for the form or difference of our thoughts, and in this way we have the idea in our mind only insofar as we think of it, and every time we think of it anew, we have other ideas of the same thing, although similar to those that went before. But it seems that others take the idea for an immediate object of thought or for some permanent form which remains when we do not contemplate it.

Leibniz prefers the second of these conceptions. An idea, properly speaking, is a "quality of our soul," but a permanent quality and not a transitory modification (DM 26). It manifests itself in distinct successive modifications when we think of it consciously; and even when we are not thinking of it, there remains in us a property (*habitudo*) that expresses the content of the idea (G VII,263/L 207). The concrete reality of the idea in our minds is thus quite different at different times.

In the third place, it is only considered in a certain respect that modifications or qualities of the soul are ideas. If we ask what it is that is permanent in an idea that takes such different forms as the conscious and the unconscious at different times, the answer is first that the representational content, or in Cartesian terms the objective reality, of the idea is constant and second that the mind always has in it a certain potentiality for making that content conscious, "the quality," as Leibniz puts it, "of representing to itself whatever nature or form it is, when the occasion arises for thinking of it" (DM 26). Leibniz himself, in the passage quoted, connects the permanence of the idea with its character as object of thought. We may say that the idea is a permanent quality of the mind considered with regard to its objective reality or representational content; Leibniz says, "This quality of our soul *insofar as it expresses some nature, form, or essence,* is properly the idea of the thing, which is in us, and which is always in us, whether we think of it or not" (DM 26, my emphasis). "An idea is that in which one perception or thought differs from another by reason of the object" (RML 73).

Similarly, I believe that when Leibniz speaks of material things as phenomena he usually thinks of those phenomena as qualities or modifications of the perceiving substance considered with regard to their objective reality or representational content or insofar as they express some nature, form, or essence. Adapting Cartesian terms, one can say that, in their objective reality or as phenomena, perceptions have properties that they do not have in their formal reality or as modifications of the mind, and vice versa. Among the most important of these properties, for Leibniz, are causal properties, for they are the basis of the preestablished harmony between body and soul. Many philosophers have wondered what the things are that need to be harmonized, if bodies are phenomena and phenomena are modifications of the soul. Leibniz holds that corporeal phenomena as such are caused mechanically by preceding corporeal phenomena, whereas modifications of the soul as such are to be explained teleologically by preceding appetites (Mon. 79, 87; GV IV,391/L 409f.; C 12). God preestablishes a harmony between soul and body by so programming perceptions that, while their formal reality follows from the formal reality of previous perceptions and appetites of the same substance by laws of teleological explanation, their objective reality follows from the objective reality of previous perceptions by laws of mechanical explanation.

In spite of these fundamental differences between perceptions as phenomena and perceptions as modifications of the perceiving substance, Leibniz will resist any attempt to treat them as fully distinct entities. The point of his saying that phenomena are modifications of our souls is that as a conceptualist about all sorts of abstract entities and merely intentional objects, he does not believe that phenomena have any being except *in* the existence or occurrence of qualities or modifications of perceiving substances. The existence of a phenomenon must consist in the occurrence of certain perceptions.

Nonetheless, Leibniz distinguishes, among phenomena, between *real* and merely imaginary material objects and holds that some stories in which the real ones figure are *true.* The task of Leibnizian phenomenalistic analysis is to explain what this reality and truth consist in. It is not to analyze the content of the true stories. I can discover no phenomenalistic analysis in Leibniz that does not *presuppose* the concept of spatially-extended-objects-appearing-to a perceiver. There is no attempt to break that down into supposedly more primitive concepts of sensory impressions. This is a principal difference between Leibniz and many other phenomenalists.

This point may be pursued by asking whether the objective reality of perceptions must *result,* in Leibniz's sense, from their formal reality. Must phenomena be constructible, by sufficient conditions, from the nonintentional properties of the relevant perceptions? One might expect Leibniz to answer this question in the affirmative, and perhaps he would if pressed; but I have not found that he did. He is committed, I think, to the view that the objective reality of a perception must be *expressed* by the formal reality of the perception (cf. RML 321f.); but that is not clearly more than a *necessary* condition on a perception's having a certain objective reality. For one thing to express another, according to Leibniz, is for there to be a one-to-one mapping from elements of the latter to elements of the former according to appropriate rules. (See, for example, G VII,263f./L 207f.) This appears to be a transitive and symmetrical relationship, which does not provide a *sufficient* condition for perception. Since any two actual substances (Ronald Reagan and Leonid Brezhnev, for example) are expressions of the same universe, according to Leibniz, it would seem they must also express each other, and my perception of Reagan must express Brezhnev as well as Reagan—by virtue of the transitivity and symmetry of the expression relation. Yet, I doubt that Leibniz would be willing to say that my perception of Reagan is a perception of Brezhnev, too.

So far as I know, Leibniz neither demands nor promises nor begins to give an account of sufficient conditions for a perception's having a certain objective reality, in terms of its formal reality. I think his philosophy is best interpreted as one that treats the objective reality or representational content of a perception as a primitive feature of that perception, at least for all purposes that actually arise in the philosophy. Leibniz provides at least one analysis of the notion of the *reality* of a corporeal universe that appears to us (as we will see in section 4, below). But he provides no *analysis* of the notion of a corporeal universe's appearing to us (as opposed to something else appearing to us). He thus treats the notion of a corporeal universe's appearing to us as conceptually prior to the notion of such a universe's being real.

For further exploration of the distinctive features of Leibniz's conception of phenomena, let us turn to his explicit disagreements with Berkeley. His best-known comment on Berkeley, in a letter of 15 March 1715 to Des Bosses (G II,492/L 609), suggests that Leibniz failed to realize the strength of Berkeley's desire to be found in agreement with common sense and overlooked Berkeley's efforts to define a sense in which bodies can be called "real." Other evidence does not contradict these suggestions but does make clear that Leibniz actually read Berkeley and saw more than he is commonly thought to have seen of the similarities as well as the differences between Berkeley's views and his own. This evidence is provided by the following comments that Leibniz wrote on the last page of his copy of Berkeley's *Treatise Concerning the Principles of Human Knowledge*:

> Much here that's right and agrees with my views. [*Multa hic recte et ad sensum meum.*] But too paradoxically expressed. For we have no need to say that matter is nothing, but it suffices to say that it is a phenomenon like the rainbow; and that it is not a substance, but a result of substances; and that space is no more real than time, i.e. that it is nothing but an order of coexistences as time is an order of subexistences. The true substances are Monads, or Perceivers. But the author ought to have gone on further, namely to infinite Monads, constituting all things, and to their preestablished harmony. He wrongly or at least pointlessly rejects abstract ideas, restricts ideas to imaginations, despises the subtleties of arithmetic and geometry. He most wrongly rejects the infinite division of the extended; even if he is right to reject infinitesimal quantities.[5]

Leibniz did not fail to see that he and Berkeley were fundamentally on the same side. He thought much of their disagreement was in presentation, style, and tactics. Berkeley "expressed" their common beliefs "too paradoxically." Several substantial disagreements are reflected in Leibniz's critique, however. I will discuss three of these.

(1) The perceptual atomism of Berkeley's construction of physical objects evokes Leibniz's strongest protest. Berkeley "most wrongly [*pessime*] rejects the infinite division of the extended." For Berkeley, extended things are ideas or collections of ideas, and these ideas in turn are composed of parts that are finitely small because they cannot be smaller than the mind in which they exist can discriminate (*Principles,* § 124). In dividing any extended thing, therefore, we come eventually to parts that are still extended but so small that they cannot be divided any further; and Berkeley maintains that there are no distinct parts within these smallest discernible parts, on the ground that as an idea exists only in the mind, "consequently each part thereof must be perceived" (ibid.).

For Leibniz, on the other hand, it is of the very essence of the extended as such to be continuous and therefore infinitely divisible. Because there are indefinitely many ways in which it can be divided in parts (G VII, 562) and no parts in it that cannot themselves be divided in parts, it has no parts of which it is ultimately composed as Berkeleyan extended things are ultimately composed of the smallest percep-

tible parts of ideas. There may indeed be indivisible, unextended substances that are in some sense "in" an extended thing, but the
extended thing cannot be composed of them precisely because a continuous quantity cannot be composed of elements that have no parts.
"Just as a part of a line is not a point, but a line in which the point is,
so also a part of matter is not a soul but the body in which it is" (FC
322; cf. G VII,268/L 536). This is one of the reasons why the extended
as such can only be a phenomenon. "From the very fact that a mathematical body cannot be analyzed into first constituents, it follows that
it is not real at all, but something mental and designating nothing but
the possibility of parts, not something actual" (G II,286/L 535f.). Another inference that Leibniz draws from his thesis that an extended
whole has, as such, no first constituent parts is that it is not constructed
out of its parts at all but is prior to them. "In the ideal or continuous
the whole is prior to the parts, as the Arithmetical unit is prior to the
fractions that divide it, which can be assigned arbitrarily, the parts being
only potential; but in the real the simple is prior to the groups, the
parts are actual, are before the whole" (G III,622; cf. G VII,562; G
II,379). Here, therefore, is another way in which bodies as phenomena
are not constructed according to Leibniz.

(2) Leibniz can take this position only because he also thinks Berkeley is wrong to "restrict ideas to imaginations"—or, in other words,
because he rejects the sensationalism of Berkeley's theory. If bodies
are phenomena for Leibniz, these phenomena are objects of the intellect as well as of sensation. Both faculties play a part in our perception
of corporeal phenomena.

The intellect's part is particularly important and includes both mathematics and physics. Berkeley was right in insisting that no sensory
image is infinitely divisible into parts that are still sensory images. Leibniz would certainly grant that the lines without breadth by which a
continuous surface can be divided into parts indefinitely small can neither be imagined nor perceived by sense. We conceive of them, rather,
by mathematical reason. Hence, body as an infinitely divisible phenomenon is "mathematical body" for Leibniz.

Among the features of phenomena that are not directly perceived by
sense at all are *forces.* Force is characteristic of monads, but there are
forces that are properties of phenomena. "As matter itself is nothing
but a phenomenon, but well founded, resulting from the monads, it is
the same with inertia, which is a property of this phenomenon"
(G III,636/L 659; Cf. G II,275f.). Certainly, Leibniz did not think we have
a sensory image of inertia. (Cf. G VII,314f.) We perceive it or conceive
of it only by rudimentary or sophisticated scientific thinking. Indeed, I
believe that for Leibniz the universe of corporeal phenomena is primar-

ily the object not of sense but of science. The *reality* of corporeal phenomena depends, as we will see in section 4, on their finding a place in the story that would be told by a perfected physical science.

Leibniz may well be committed to regarding corporeal phenomena as objects of a third faculty, unconscious perception, as well as of sensation and intellect. But the notion of an unconscious perception having a representational content is difficult to understand, and Leibniz does little to explain it. I will not take the time to speculate about it here but instead will pass now to a third disagreement.

(3) Part of Leibniz's point in saying that extended things as such are phenomena is to claim that they have their existence only in substances that perceive them, and in this he agrees with Berkeley. But there is also something else going on in Leibniz's talk of phenomena, something that is reflected in his comment that Berkeley "ought to have gone on further, namely to infinite Monads, constituting all things." 'Phenomenon' contrasts not only as intramental with 'extramental'; it also contrasts as apparent with 'real'. Part of what is going on in Leibniz is that he does assume that in our perception of bodies we are at least indirectly perceiving something that is primitively real independent of our minds, and he is asking what sort of thing that may be. His answer is that it is "infinite Monads," whose harmonious perceptions are the "foundation" of corporeal phenomena.

This answer, however, does not adequately represent the interplay of appearance and reality in Leibniz's thought. Like almost all modern philosophers, Leibniz thought that good science requires us to suppose that there are very considerable qualitative differences between bodies as they appear in naive sense perception and bodies as they exist independent of our minds—if they do exist independent of our minds. In the corporeal world as described by modern science, there is, in a certain sense, no part for colors and the other so-called "secondary qualities" to play. And, on the other hand, modern science postulates vast numbers of motions of minute particles in portions of matter that appear to our senses to be perfectly quiescent internally. This was true of what Leibniz viewed as modern science, and it is true of what we think of as modern science.

Many among us respond to this situation by supposing that, whereas what we perceive naively by our senses is only an appearance, what is described by science—or what would be described by a perfected science—is reality. Leibniz has a fundamental reason for rejecting this thesis of scientific realism—a reason for not expecting science to give us knowledge of reality as it is in itself. Scientific knowledge, as Leibniz sees it, is relatively distinct but buys its distinctness at the price of studying a mathematical idealization. Reality, he thinks, is infinitely complex, intensively as well as extensively. It is not just that there are infinitely many objects in infinite space; even when we perceive a body of limited extent, such as the body of a human being, Leibniz believes that the reality represented by our perception is infinitely complex and that all of that infinite complexity is relevant to the explanation of some of the salient features of the body's behavior. Human minds are finite, however; and the definitive mark of finite minds is that they cannot distinctly know an infinite complexity. So, if science is distinct knowledge, the only sort of science that is possible, even in principle, for human beings will have as its immediate object a finitely complex representation of the infinitely complex reality. At least to this extent, the objects of scientific knowledge will be phenomena. Leibniz's opinion, that the object of scientific knowledge is not reality as it is in itself but a mathematical abstraction from its infinite complexity, is plausible enough in its own right, I think; but it is also rooted in other aspects of his metaphysics, which need not be rehearsed in detail here—in his theory of free action and infinite analysis conception of contingency, for example, and in his doctrine that each thing expresses the whole universe.

Leibniz's treatment of the relation of the primary and secondary qualities to reality can be understood in this light. In section 12 of the *Discourse* on Metaphysics, he wrote:

> It can even be demonstrated that the notion of size, shape, and motion is not so distinct as is imagined, and that it includes something imaginary and relative to our perceptions, as are also (though much more so) color, heat, and other similar qualities of which it can be doubted whether they are really found in the nature of things outside us.

Many similar statements are found in other places in his work. It seems to be implied here that the secondary qualities are even less real than the primary, although both are apparent rather than ultimately real. The primary are more real only in the sense that they represent reality more distinctly than the secondary qualities. The primary qualities "contain more of distinct knowledge" than the secondary, although they both "hold something of the phenomenal" (G II,119/L-A 152).

According to Leibniz, the perception of secondary qualities, as they appear to us, is a confused perception of minute motions or textures—a confused perception of primary qualities that are too small for us to perceive them distinctly by sense (NE II,viii,13, 21). We might put this by saying that the secondary qualities are appearances *of* primary qualities—and as such are appearances of appearances. I do not know that Leibniz ever said exactly that, but in the last letter that he wrote to

Des Bosses (29 May 1716) he did suggest relating secondary qualities to the corresponding primary qualities as "resultant phenomena" to "constitutive phenomena." Thus, the "observed perception" of white and black results from tiny, unobservable bumps and depressions that reflect and trap rays of light, respectively; but these geometrical textures themselves are still only phenomena (G II,521; cf. C489).

Even within the realm of primary qualities there are veils behind veils of appearance between us and reality in the Leibnizian universe. Inspect the leg of a fly with the naked eye and under a microscope; you will see rather different shapes. Yet Leibniz would surely say that what you see with the naked eye is a confused representation of the more complex shape that appears under the microscope and that the latter is still not complex enough to be more than an appearance. This is indeed one of Leibniz's reasons for holding that shape is only a phenomenon.

> For even shape, which is of the essence of a bounded extended mass, is never exact and strictly determined in nature, because of the actual division to infinity of the parts of matter. There is never a sphere without inequalities, nor a straight line without curvatures mingled in, nor a curve of a certain finite nature without mixture of any other—and that in the small parts as in the large which brings it about that shape, far from being constitutive of bodies, is not even an entirely real and determined quality outside of thought. (G II, 119/L-A 152; cf. G VII,563)

One of the reasons, I take it, why Leibniz thought that finitely complex shapes cannot be "entirely real outside of thought" is that they cannot express a relation to every event in an infinitely complex universe as the qualities of a real thing ought to. "There is no actual determinate shape in things," he wrote, "for none is able to satisfy infinite impressions" (C 522/L 270). The conclusion Leibniz draws is not that real shapes are infinitely complex (though some things he says might leave us with that impression) but rather that shape as such is only a phenomenon. I suppose that an infinitely complex shape would involve a (finite) line segment that changes not merely its curvature but also the direction of its change of curvature infinitely many times and that Leibniz would have thought that an absurd and impossible monstrosity. What I assume he would say, instead of postulating infinitely complex shapes, is that for every finitely complex shape that might be ascribed to a body there is another still more complex that more adequately expresses reality. Every shape in the series of more and more adequate expressions, however, will still be only finitely complex and for that reason among others will still be an appearance, qualitatively different from the reality expressed, which is infinitely complex and does not literally have a shape at all.

Bodies—organic or living bodies in particular—are appearances of monads.[6] A monad is represented by its body; we perceive it by perceiving its body. This is possible because the monad and its body express each other; the body is the expression of the soul. We have just seen, however, that a body as a phenomenon having a certain definite extension, shape, and motion is not complex enough to be an adequate expression of any real thing, according to Leibniz. It is not complex enough to express something that expresses the whole universe as a monad does. It is a mathematical abstraction. Perhaps the body that adequately expresses a monad is an infinite series of such abstractions, each more complex than its predecessors.

This discussion of bodies as appearances *of* monads has already led to questions about the relation of monads to "their" bodies. These are questions about the structure of Leibnizian corporeal substances. It is time to examine that subject more closely.

2. Corporeal Substance (I): Monadic Domination

"I call that a *corporeal substance*," says Leibniz, "which consists in a simple substance or monad (that is, a soul or something analogous to a Soul) and an organic body united to it" (G VII,501). The corporeal substances are "bodies that are animated, or at least endowed with a primitive Entelechy or . . . vital principle"; they can, therefore, be called "living" (G II,118/L-A 152). When Leibniz says that corporeal substances are living things and that "all nature is full of life" (PNG 1), he emphatically does not mean that every material object is alive. He rejects the view of "those who imagine that there is a substantial form of a piece of stone, or of another non-organic body; for principles of Life belong only to organic bodies" (G VI,539/L 586). Here, as in many other places, Leibniz uses the Aristotelian term 'substantial form' to signify the soul, or that which is analogous to a soul, in any corporeal substance.) He adds that

> it is true (according to my System) that there is no portion of matter in which there is not an infinity of organic and animated bodies; among which I include not only animals and plants, but perhaps other sorts as well, which are entirely unknown to us. But it is not right to say, on account of that, that every portion of matter is animated—just as we do not say that a lake full of fishes is an animated body, although the fish is. (G VI,539f./L 586)

Stones and lakes, then, are not corporeal substances. "Each animal and each plant too is a corporeal substance" (G III,260); I believe that they are the only corporeal substances of which Leibniz claims empirical knowledge, if we include among animals and plants the tiny living things whose discovery under seventeenth-century microscopes so excited Leibniz (G II,122/L-A 156). In a lake full of fishes the water between the fishes is not a corporeal substance, but it is composed of corporeal substances, which may be very different from the things that we know as animals and plants (Mon. 68). In particular, they may be even smaller than microscopic organisms; there is indeed no minimum size for corporeal substances.

Still, all corporeal substances are alive, in a broad sense. And Leibniz seems to have assumed that we can detect the presence or absence of life in bodies large enough to be distinctly perceived by our senses. He speaks of a study of nature that would enable us to "judge of the forms [of corporeal substances] by comparing their organs and operations" (G II,122/L-A 155f.).

The principal characteristic of living bodies that Leibniz mentions as distinguishing them from other portions of matter is that they are "organized" or "organic." There is . . . no animated body without organs" (G II,124/L-A 159); "I restrict corporeal or composite substance to living things alone, or exclusively to organic machines of nature" (G II,520). I have found little explanation in Leibniz of what distinguishes organic from inorganic bodies. It is not a radical difference in the kind of causality that operates in them. Leibniz always insists that everything can be explained mechanically in organic as well as in inorganic bodies. There is no need to refer to the substantial forms or souls of corporeal substances in explaining their physical behavior (e.g. G II,58, 77f./L-A 65f., 96). "And this *body* is *organic* when it forms a kind of Automaton or Machine of Nature, which is a machine not only as a whole but also in the smallest parts that can be noticed" (PNG 3; cf. G III,356). Presumably, an organic body is one so organized mechanically that it continues over time to cohere and retain a sort of unity in physical interactions. But stones have that property, too; so it is not enough to distinguish organic bodies from others.

Perhaps the best account that can be given of the notion of organism here is that an organic body is a body so structured mechanically that it can be interpreted as always totally expressing and being expressed by the perceptions and appetites of a soul or something analogous to a soul. We recognize living things by observing that their behavior can be interpreted as a coordinated response to their environment on the basis of something like perception of the environment together with a tendency toward something like a goal—though Leibniz would insist, of course, that their behavior can *also* be explained mechanically. This account fits animals better than plants, but it is clear in any case that Leibniz's principal model of corporeal substance is the animal; he mentions plants only occasionally and seems favorably disposed toward the suggestion that they "can be included in the same genus with animals, and are imperfect animals" (G II,122/L-A 156).[7]

Leibniz's fullest statement about the structure of a corporeal substance is in a letter of 20 June 1703 to De Volder:

> I distinguish therefore (1) the primitive Entelechy or Soul, (2) Matter, i.e. prime matter, or primitive passive power, (3) the Monad completed by these two, (4) the Mass or secondary matter, or organic Machine, for which countless subordinate Monads come together [*ad quam . . . concurrunt*], (5) the Animal or corporeal substance, which is made One by the Monad dominating the Machine. (G II,252/L 530f.)

The first three of these items can be discussed quite briefly here. The monad (3) is "a simple substance . . . ; *simple,* that is to say without parts" (Mon. 1). The primitive entelechy and prime matter must not, therefore, be conceived as *parts* that compose the monad, but rather as aspects or properties of the monad. In particular, prime matter (2) is not to be understood here as a substance or an extended stuff. It is the primitive passive power that is a fundamental property of the monad. 'Entelechy' (1) is sometimes used by Leibniz (as in Mon. 62–64) as a synonym for 'monad' or 'simply substance'; but here the entelechy clearly is not the complete monad, but a property of it. Since it goes together with primitive passive power to form the monad, the entelechy here is presumably the monad's primitive active force. Leibniz held that "the very substance of things consists in the force of acting and being acted on" (G IV,508/L 502; cf. G II,248f./L 528). The properties possessed by monads as such are perceptions and appetites, or analogous to perceptions and appetites, as Leibniz often says. As properties of monads, therefore, "primitive forces manifestly cannot be anything but internal tendencies of simple substances, by which according to a certain law of their nature they pass from perception to perception" (G II,275). As we saw in section 1, Leibniz also spoke of certain forces as properties of bodies, but this is not the place to try to understand the connection he saw between forces as properties of bodies and forces as properties of monads.

My present purpose demands a fuller discussion of the mass, or secondary matter (4), which combines with the monad to form the complete corporeal substance. This mass is, as Leibniz says here, an organic machine or, as he more often says, the organic body of the monad. Not every mass of secondary matter is an organic body; inorganic bodies are also masses of secondary matter. But only an organic body combines with a single monad to form a corporeal substance. No mass of secondary matter, organic or inorganic, is in itself a substance. The organic body, "taken separately, that is, apart from the soul, is not one substance but an aggregate of several" (G IV, 396). "And *secondary matter* (as for example the organic body) is not a substance, but for another reason; it is that it is a heap of several substances, like a lake full of fishes, or like a herd of sheep, and consequently it is what is called *One per accidens*—in a word, a phenomenon" (G III,657). The mass of secondary matter that, as an organic body, combines with a monad to form a corporeal substance is thus merely a phenomenon *because* it is an aggregate of substances. The connection between being an aggregate and being a phenomenon will be the topic of section 3; for the present, I must simply note that the organic body, apart from its "soul" or dominant monad, is characterized both as an aggregate and as a phenomenon.

According to Leibniz, *every* created monad has an organic body of this sort with which it combines to form a corporeal substance (G IV,395f.; G VII,502, 530; cf. Mon. 62–63). The monad *always* has its body, and hence the organic body is an enduring object permanently attached to its dominant monad (G II,251/L 530). Even in death, it does not cease to exist, it does not cease to be organic; it just undergoes a sudden, drastic reduction in size and a change in its operations (e.g., PNG 6). The parts of an organic body do not belong to it permanently, however. "It is true that the whole which has a true unity can remain strictly the same individual even though it loses or gains parts, as we experience in ourselves; thus the parts are immediate requisites only for a time" (G II,120/L-A 153). The substances that are included in an organic body can be replaced with other substances so long as the body retains the necessary organs and the same dominant monad (Mon. 71–72).

In the outline I have been following, Leibniz clearly distinguishes the corporeal substance (5) both from its organic machine and from its dominant monad. It is something formed by the combination of those two. This appears to rule out one tempting interpretation. Cassirer identified corporeal substance with the monad itself "insofar as it is endowed with a particular organic body, according to which it represents and desires."[8] Cassirer added that this corporeal endowment is "only a determination of the *content of the consciousness*" of the monad. On this reading, the corporeal substance is a substance because it is a monad and corporeal because it is endowed with an organic body.

This conception of corporeal substance agrees admirably with other aspects of the philosophy of Leibniz and is suggested (though I think not unambiguously asserted) by some passages of his writings (G VII, 314; G IV,499, 395f.). It would provide the simplest explanation of the per se unity of a corporeal substance. Unfortunately, the weight of the evidence is against Cassirer's interpretation. Leibniz seems, at least usually, to have thought of a corporeal substance as including a mass or organic body as well as a dominant monad. We have seen that he defined a corporeal substance as consisting "in a simple substance or monad . . . and an organic body united to it" (G VII,501). In other passages, he speaks of "the complete corporeal substance, which includes the form and the matter, or the soul with the organs" (G VI,506/ L 551), or of "corporeal substance" as "composed of the soul and the mass" (G VI,588/L 624), and says that "a true substance (such as an animal) is composed of an immaterial soul and an organic body, and it is the Composite of these two that is called *One per se*" (G III,657). The corporeal substance is formed by the coming together of the subordinate monads with the primary monad (G II,252/L 530).

The corporeal (or composite) substance thus formed is not an aggregate, but one per se, according to Leibniz. Hence, it is not a mere phenomenon; corporeal substance is regularly contrasted with the phenomenal (G II,77/L-A 95; G VII, 314, 322/L 365; G III,657; C II,435/L 600). But corporeal substance certainly is not simple, as monads are. How then can it be one per se? Leibniz stated to De Volder that the corporeal substance "is made One by the Monad dominating the Machine" (G II,252/L 531). This statement gives rise to at least two questions: (a) how does a monad "dominate" its organic body or "Machine"? (b) How does this domination make the corporeal substance one per se? The second of these questions, as the center of the gravest difficulties and instabilities in Leibniz's theory of the physical world, will be reserved for the final section of this paper. But the first question will be discussed now. I think it can be answered in terms of the perceptions of monads in a way that is consistent with Leibniz's phenomenalism. This answer will be important in section 3 for understanding why Leibniz thought that corporeal aggregates, as such, are phenomena.

In what sense, then, does a monad "dominate" or rule its organic body? In what sense does it dominate or rule the subordinate monads, as Leibniz more often says?

In a letter of 16 June 1712 to Des Bosses, Leibniz says, "The domination, however, and subordination of monads, considered in the monads themselves, consists in nothing but degrees of perfection" (G II,452/L 605). Clearly, the dominant monad must be more perfect than the monads subordinate to it. And perfection of monads, for Leibniz, is measured by distinctness of perceptions; so the dominant monad must perceive some things more distinctly than the subordinate monads.

What must the dominant monad perceive more distinctly than the subordinate monads? Everything that happens within its body, suggested Bertrand Russell. But that does not adequately explain the sense in which Leibniz thought the dominant monad rules the body. In particular, the sufficient condition for domination that Russell seems to propose is not plausible. He says:

> If, then, in a certain volume, there is one monad with much clearer perceptions than the rest, this monad may perceive all that happens within that volume more clearly than do any of the others within that volume. And in this sense it may be dominant over all the monads in its immediate neighborhood.[9]

But suppose that a certain volume of air immediately adjacent to my right eye contains no monad that perceives anything in that volume or in my body as distinctly as I do. By Russell's criterion, if I dominate as a monad over my body, I will dominate also over all the monads in that adjacent volume of air, and it will presumably form part of my body. The incorporation of such volumes of air in my body would surely be an unacceptable consequence for Leibniz. He might try to avoid it by insisting that in any such space there would always be a monad that perceived something in the space as distinctly as I. But I would expect him to base his strategy more directly on the offensive feature of the example, which is that the volume of air does not seem to be part of the organic structure of my body.

In a letter to De Volder, Leibniz says, "Nay rather the soul itself of the whole would be nothing but the soul of a separately animated part, were it not the dominant soul in the whole *by virtue of the structure of the whole*" (G II,194/L 522, emphasis mine). I believe that a correct understanding of Leibniz's conception of monadic domination depends on the relation of the dominant monad to the structure of its organic body no less than on the superior distinctness of the dominant monad's perceptions. There are two main points to be discussed here.

(1) In a preliminary draft of his *New System*, Leibniz says that the perceptions of a monad correspond "to the rest of the universe, but particularly to the organs of the body that constitutes its point of view in the world, and this is that in which their union consists" (G IV,477). Every monad expresses everything in the whole universe, according to Leibniz; but each monad expresses, and is expressed by, its own or-

ganic body in a special way. A monad and its organic body both *contain* expressions of an infinity of things; but each *is,* as a whole, an expression of the other, and this relationship of mutual expression is peculiarly direct. An organic body stands in this relation to its dominant monad alone, not to the subordinate monads in it—though they do, of course, contain expressions of it. This is an important part of the structural relationship between a monad and its organic body by which monadic domination is constituted.

An organic body is an expression of its soul or dominant monad. Leibniz has less to say about this than about the soul's expressing its body, but expression as he understands it is a relation of one-to-one mapping, which will normally be symmetrical. So, if each monad is an especially good expression of its body, the organic body will be, reciprocally, an especially good expression of its dominant monad. I believe that in the most natural development of Leibniz's system this explains how one perceives another monad. There is only indirect textual support for this interpretation, but how else would Leibniz think that we perceive other monads?

Suppose I see a kitten jumping off a chair to pounce on a piece of string. Leibniz will surely say that I perceive certain internal properties of the kitten's soul: its seeing the string and intending to seize it. And how do I perceive those psychological properties? By far the most plausible answer is that I read them off certain properties of the kitten's body: its structure, posture, spatial position, and movements.

According to Leibniz, the subordinate monads in the kitten's body also have internal properties analogous to the seeing and intending in the kitten's soul. And since I perceive everything, at least unconsciously, I must perceive these perceptions and appetitions of the subordinate monads. But it would not be plausible to say that I perceive them by perceiving physical properties of the whole body of the kitten. Rather, I perceive the subordinate monads by perceiving *their* organic bodies, which most directly express their perceptions and appetitions. Perhaps I do not usually perceive them consciously; but with a suitable microscope, for example, I might observe one of the kitten's white blood cells reacting to a bacterium in its vicinity. In this case, I may be taken as perceiving a perception of the bacterium and an appetition for its obliteration that are present (confusedly, no doubt) in the dominant monad of the white corpuscle. And I would be reading these internal properties of the monad off movements and other physical properties of the cell. If I understand Leibniz correctly on this point, each monad is perceived by perceiving *its* organic body, and perception of an organic body directly yields perception of its dominant monad but not of its subordinate monads.

My claim that for Leibniz one perceives a monad by perceiving its body is somewhat speculative, but he explicitly holds that each created monad expresses and perceives everything else *by* expressing and perceiving its own organic body.

> Thus although each created Monad represents the whole universe, it represents more distinctly the body which is particularly assigned to it and of which it constitutes the Entelechy; and as this body expresses the whole universe by the connection of all matter in the *plenum,* the Soul also represents the whole universe in representing this body, which belongs to it in a particular way. (Mon. 62; cf. G II,90f., 112f./L-A 113f., 144f.; G II,253/L 531; G IV,530ff., 545; NE II,vii,21; C 14; G VII, 567)

The Leibnizian harmony is a system of infinitely many models—or even a system of systems of models. Each model perfectly, if perhaps obscurely, expresses all the others; but some express each other with a special closeness or directness. Perhaps Leibniz would explain this special closeness in terms of distinctness of perceptions; I find it a point of obscurity in his philosophy. One system of models occupies a peculiarly central role, although it does not have a high status ontologically. This is the universe of organic bodies, considered as phenomena and continuously extended in space and time. They are involved in all of the modeling in the whole harmony; for each of the ultimately real models, the monads, stands in a direct modeling relationship only to its own organic body. The organic body, however, is also a model of the whole universe of organic bodies. Leibniz thought that in a physical universe with no empty space every physical event would have some effect on each infinitely divisible organic body and that each such body would, therefore, always bear in itself traces from which, in accordance with the mechanical laws of nature, an infinite mind could read off all past, present, and future events in the spatiotemporal universe. Since my organic body expresses in this way the whole corporeal universe and also expresses me as its dominant monad, I perceive the whole corporeal universe in perceiving my own body. And, since the other organic bodies in the universe express their own dominant monads and since each finite monad is expressed by its own body, I perceive each monad by perceiving its organic body and I perceive the whole system of finite monads by perceiving the whole system of organic bodies. And I perceive all of this by perceiving my own organic body. (So far as I can see, the thesis that I perceive other monads by perceiving their bodies is needed here if the idea that I perceive *everything* by perceiving my body and the effects of other bodies on it is to be carried through.)

Obviously, I do not consciously perceive all these things. Because I am finite, I perceive most of them much too confusedly to be conscious of them, Leibniz would say. His scheme is at least initially less plausible if we attend mainly to conscious perceptions. When I am reading a page, do I really perceive the letters on the page by perceiving what is going on in my eye? It seems that I can see perfectly well what is on the page without consciously knowing anything at all about what is going on in my eye (and without even being able to become conscious of the inner workings of my eye by paying attention to them). If my perception models what is going on in my eye more *directly* than it models the surface of the page and if conscious perceptions are always more *distinct* than perceptions that cannot even be brought to consciousness by attending to them,[10] then this case shows that Leibniz cannot consistently explain directness of the expression and perception relations wholly in terms of distinctness of perceptions. Perhaps directness and indirectness of perception in such a case are founded on explanatory relations rather than on degrees of distinctness. I perceive what is going on in my eye more directly than what is on the page because the psychophysical laws that correlate corporeal phenomena with what happens in monads relate visual perceptions more directly to events in the eye than to events at a distance.[11] The distant events are related to visual perceptions by virtue of their connection, under mechanical laws, with events in the eye.

The task of providing a satisfactory account of the relation of directness of expression will not be pursued further here, but clearly it is an important problem. The idea that each monad and its organic body express each other with a unique directness plays a pivotal role in Leibniz's philosophy. As we have seen, it is used to explain how every monad perceives everything else. I think it plays an essential part in determining which monad has, or dominates, which organic body. That is my present concern; in addition, I will argue in section 3 that the spatial position, or "point of view," of a monad depends in turn on which organic body it has, while any aggregation of monads to form bodies depends on their spatial position. Thus, a great deal depends directly or indirectly on the relation of directness of expression.

(2) Leibniz does imply that a dominant monad perceives some things more distinctly than the monads subordinated to it do. What remains to be explained here about monadic domination is how the greater distinctness of the dominant monad's perceptions is related to the structure of the organic body and why these relationships should be expressed by an idea of domination, that is, of rule or control. The hypothesis I propose to answer these questions is that what the dominant monad as such perceives more distinctly than any other monad

in its body is an appetite or tendency for perceptions of the normal organic functioning of the body. I call this a hypothesis because I have not found any place in which Leibniz explicitly asserts it, but it seems to me to provide the best explanation of much that he does say.

In developing the hypothesis, I begin with a passage of an early draft of section 14 of the *Discourse on Metaphysics*:

> It is sure above all that when we desire some phenomenon which occurs at a designated time, and when this happens ordinarily, we say that we have acted and are the cause of it, as when I will that which is called moving my hand. Also when it appears to me that at my will something happens to that which I call another substance, and that that would have happened to it in that way even if it had not willed, as I judge by frequent experience, I say that that substance is acted on, as I confess the same thing about myself when that happens to me following the will of another substance.

I believe that these statements reveal the intuitive origins of the idea that activity and passivity can be explained in terms of distinctness of perceptions. Voluntary agency provides the paradigm of activity. It is characterized by consciousness of a tendency or appetite that has a certain event as its goal. The goal is described by Leibniz here as a "phenomenon," a certain event as perceived by the voluntary agent. The whole passage is stated very much in terms of what appears to the agent; that Leibniz was thinking in those terms is confirmed by the fact that he initially wrote "perception" where "phenomenon" stands in the text as I quoted it and that he initially wrote "when I will that it appear to me" in describing the willing of a motion of his hand. A substance that is conscious of an appetite for a perception of a certain event is active in producing the event, if the appetite does indeed produce the perception; whereas other substances involved in the event are acted on if they are not conscious of such an appetite for their perceptions of the event. According to Leibniz's philosophy, they must have had appetites for those perceptions, but they were not conscious of them; that is, they were much less distinctly aware of them than the active substance was of its corresponding appetite. I believe that for Leibniz activity and passivity in the production of an event consist in more and less distinct perception of a monad's own appetite for perceptions of the event, although this distinctness does not reach consciousness in most cases as it does in the case of voluntary action.

My hypothesis is that Leibniz saw the dominant monad as active, in this way, in the normal functioning of its organic body, the functioning that fits the body constantly to be the direct expression of the dominant monad. This is connected with Leibniz's speaking of the monad as the "soul" or "substantial form" of the body or of the corporeal substance. He was consciously and professedly adopting or adapting Aristotelian and scholastic terminology here, and he explicitly took a position, in the famous scholastic dispute about the unit or plurality of substantial forms, for those who held that there is only one substantial form or soul in each substance. He considered himself to be in agreement with theological authority on this point (Gr. 552), and to Queen Sophia Charlotte he wrote:

> I have read the sheet that Your Majesty was kind enough to send me on the subject of my letter. It is very much to my taste, when it says that the immaterial is active, and that the material is passive. That is exactly my idea. I also recognize degrees in activities, such as life, perception, reason, and thus believe that there can be more kinds of souls, which are called vegetative, sensitive, rational, as there are kinds of bodies which have life without sensation, and others which have life and sensation without reason. I believe, however, that the sensitive soul is vegetative at the same time, and that the rational soul is sensitive and vegetative, and that thus one single soul in us includes these three degrees,[12] without its being necessary to conceive of three souls in us, of which the lower would be material in relation to the higher; and it seems that that would be to multiply beings without necessity. (G VI,521)

Two points in this text are important for my present purpose: that I am the vegetative and sensitive soul of my body, as well as a rational soul, and that the functions of a vegetative and sensitive soul are the activities of life and sensation. If I am the vegetative soul of my body, that is presumably because I am active in the nutritive functioning of my body—for example, in particular events of sugar metabolism in the cells of my body. And, if I am active in those events, that is because I perceive my preceding appetite for my perception of them and that perception, though unconscious, is more distinct than the perception any other monad in my body has of its corresponding appetite.

This hypothesis allows, but does not require, that the dominant monad perceives *all* events in its body more distinctly than any other monad in the body does. All that is required is that it have more distinct perceptions of its appetites for all events of *normal* functioning of the body. I see no reason why the soul must be similarly active with respect to traumas of disease or injury in the body. In fact, I suspect Leibniz would deny that it is. His fullest discussion of the soul's role in the production of such traumas is in response to a criticism by Bayle. Bayle had asked how the theory of preestablished harmony could explain the sudden transition from pleasure to pain in a dog that is struck unexpectedly by a stick while eating (G IV,531). What is the previous state of the dog's soul from which the sudden pain results, according to Leibniz? Leibniz replies:

> Thus the causes that make the stick act (that is to say the man positioned behind the dog, who is getting ready to hit it while it eats, and everything in the course of bodies that contributes to dispose that man to this) are also represented from the first in the soul of the dog exactly in accordance with the truth, but weakly by little, confused perceptions, without apperception, that is to say without the dog noticing it, because the dog's body is also only imperceptibly affected. And when in the course of bodies these dispositions finally produce the blow pressed hard on the body of the dog, in the same way the representations of these dispositions in the dog's soul finally produce the representation of the blow of the stick. Since that representation is distinguished and strong, . . . the dog apperceives it very distinctly, and that is what makes its pain. (G IV,532)

This explanation, according to which perceptions produce one another in the soul by virtue of their representing corporeal events that follow from one another by the laws of the corporeal universe, is reminiscent of Spinoza's version of psychophysical parallelism. But what I want to emphasize in this text is that the soul's prior tendency to have the pain that is its perception of the trauma in its body is based on its unconscious perception of events outside its body.[13] It perceives these events indirectly by perceiving its own body; I cannot see that Leibniz is committed to saying that the soul perceives those external events more distinctly than the subordinate monads do. At any rate, a more distinct perception of external events, or of the causes of traumas, is not obviously connected with the functions of a vegetative soul.

This hypothesis about the nature of the rule that the dominant monad bears in its body confirms and illuminates my interpretation of the nature of organism in Leibniz. An organic body is one of many of whose operations, in its parts of all sizes, can be explained not only mechanically but also *teleologically,* as directed in accordance with the active appetites of a soul that is at least vegetative and may also be sensitive and rational. And the active appetites of a vegetative soul are for states that contribute to the maintenance of the body as a direct expression of a monad and a perfect expression of the whole corporeal universe, according to certain laws of nature.

3. Aggregates

Leibniz says that "the body is an aggregate of substances" (G II,135/L-A 170). We may be tempted to think this contradicts the thesis that bodies are phenomena, but Leibniz did not think these views inconsistent. He speaks of masses as "only Beings by aggregation, and *therefore* phenomena."[14] (G II,252/L 531, my emphasis: cf. G VII,344). In order to understand this doctrine—frequently asserted by Leibniz—that precisely as aggregates of substances, bodies are phenomena, we must first consider how these aggregates are constituted. There are two questions here: of what sort of substances are bodies aggregates, and what is the principle of aggregation that determines which substances are grouped together to form a particular aggregate?

Leibniz is commonly read as holding that bodies are aggregates of *monads.* A question naturally arises: how could an aggregate of those ultimately real substances be only an appearance? But it is not directly clear that he did think of bodies as aggregates of monads or simple substances. There are indeed places in his works where he speaks of a corporeal mass as aggregated from "unities" (G II,379) or, more clearly, as "a result or assemblage of simple substances or indeed of a multitude of real unities" (G IV,491; cf. G VII,561; G III,367; G II,282/L 539; G III,622). I think there are more texts, however, that support the view that "a mass is an aggregate of *corporeal* substances" (G VII,501, my emphasis; cf. III,260; G IV,572; G II,205f.; G VI,550; C 13f.; L-W 139). We have seen that, according to Leibniz, a corporeal substance is composed of a monad and the organic body of that monad and that in his opinion the organic body is a phenomenon (G III,657). This might suggest to us that Leibniz thought corporeal masses are phenomena *because* they are aggregates of corporeal substances that are partly composed of phenomena.

This explanation of Leibniz's belief in the phenomenality of corporeal aggregates is unacceptable, however, for at least four reasons. (1) If masses are phenomena because they are composed of corporeal substances that are partly composed of phenomena, the corporeal substances themselves should also be phenomena because they are partly composed of phenomena; but Leibniz did not hold that corporeal substances are phenomena. (2) So far as I know, Leibniz never says that corporeal aggregates are phenomena because they are partly composed of phenomena; but he often says they are phenomena because they are aggregates. (3) Indeed, a vicious-looking circle would arise if Leibniz tried to explain the phenomenality of corporeal aggregates on the ground that they are partly composed of organic bodies that are phenomena, for he explains the phenomenality of organic bodies on the ground that they are aggregates. (4) Leibniz did write to De Volder that "accurately speaking, matter is not composed of" monads "but results from them" (G II,268/L 536). Elsewhere, however, it seems that the treatment of bodies as aggregates of *corporeal* substances is not meant to exclude the claim that at bottom they are entirely reducible to *simple* substances or monads, related in certain ways. Thus, Leibniz can say that every body is "an aggregate of animals or other living and therefore organic things or else of concretions or masses, but which also themselves are finally analyzed into living things"—where I take the living things to be corporeal substances; but he adds immediately that "the last thing in the analysis of substances is simple substances, namely souls or, if you prefer a more general word, *Monads,* which lack parts" (C 13f.). For all of these reasons, I think we must try to understand why Leibniz would have thought that aggregates as such cannot be more than phenomena even if they are aggregates of *simple* substances.

First, however, we have to consider what is the principle that determines how substances—simple or corporeal, as the case may be—are grouped together to form a body. Although Leibniz does not give much explanation on this point, I think it is fairly clear that a body will be an aggregate of all or most of the substances whose positions are within some continuous three-dimensional portion of space. What portion of space that is, and which substances are members of the aggregate, may change over time, of course. This spatial togetherness is a necessary condition for any corporeal aggregation, but it is presumably not a sufficient condition for even the accidental unity that Leibniz ascribes to a stone. For such unity, additional, quasi-causal conditions on the way in which the members of the aggregate change their positions relative to each other will also be necessary.[15]

If the aggregation of substances into bodies depends on the positions of the substances, the next thing we will want to know is what determines the positions of the substance in space. It is not hard to answer this question if it is about *corporeal* substances. A corporeal substance is composed of an organic body and the dominant monad of that body. The position of the corporeal substance will surely be the position of its organic body. The organic body is a phenomenon, spatial position is a phenomenal property, and the spatial position of the organic body is *given* in appearance. The spatial position of a corporeal substance is thus the one it appears to have, or perhaps the one it *would* appear to have in a perfected science.

If we think of bodies as aggregates of *simple* substance, we will need to have spatial positions for the simple substances as well as for corporeal substances. But this can be accomplished by assigning to each simple substance the spatial position of its organic body (cf. G II,253/L 531), for, according to Leibniz, each simple substance is the dominant monad of an organic body.

This construction of bodies as aggregates of either corporeal or simple substances has the metaphysical peculiarity that the grouping of the substances into aggregates depends on the spatial appearance of the bodies. Those who seek a less phenomenalistic reading of Leibniz might wish to find a construction of corporeal aggregates that is independent of such phenomenal properties of bodies. I once thought I had discovered such a construction. It starts with Bertrand Russell's statement that for Leibniz "places result from points of view, and points of view involve confused perception or *materia prima.*"[16] In this construction, all spatial relations are to be defined in terms of the points of view of monads. These points of view will be the positions of the monads and will be conceptually prior to the positions of bodies. The points of view of monads will be positions determined by comparison of the degree of confusion of their perceptions of each other, in accordance with the principle that, if monad A's perception of monad C is more obscure than monad A's perception of monad B, then monad A is closer to monad B than to monad C.

William Irvine[17] has persuaded me that this construction is mathematically possible. That is, if we are given a monad corresponding to every point of space, plus, for every triple of monads, A, B, and C, the information whether the distance AB is greater or less than, or equal to, the distance AC, that will suffice for the construction of all spatial relations. Furthermore, Leibniz often indicates that distance is correlated with obscurity of perception. Nevertheless, I have not found this construction in Leibniz, and I have come to believe that it does not correspond to his intentions, for several reasons.

(1) It is not plausible to suppose that we always perceive nearer things more distinctly than anything that is farther away, and Leibniz does not seem to have believed it. In response to a related objection by Arnauld, he wrote that in distinctness of perception "the distance of some is compensated for by the smallness or other hindrance of others, and Thales sees the stars without seeing the ditch in front of his feet" (G II,90/L-A 113). In other places, he says that the things a monad perceives distinctly are "some that are nearer *or more prominent, accommodated to its organs*" or "the nearest, *or the largest* with respect to each of the Monads" (C 15, Mon. 60, my emphasis). Thus, distance and obscurity of perception are not always directly proportional to each other, and it is not clear that degrees of obscurity of perception will provide enough data for a mathematically satisfactory construction of spatial relations.

(2) In order to make the points of view of monads completely prior to bodies, I was trying to define them in terms of monads' perceptions *of each other,* rather than in terms of their perceptions of bodies. But I have not found any indication that Leibniz thought that any monad,

except God, ever perceives any other monad directly. In section 2, I have argued for an interpretation of his system according to which I perceive every other created monad by perceiving, more or less distinctly, its organic body.

(3) The construction of all spatial relations, and therefore of bodies, from the points of view of monads depends on assigning to each monad a point in space as its precise position. Leibniz noted in 1709, however, that, although he had once "located Souls in points," that was "many years before, when his philosophy was not yet mature enough" (G II,372/L 599). In the last decades of his life, he seems to have thought that the only spatial position that could correctly be assigned to monads is that of "the whole organic body that they animate" (G II,371/L 598; cf. G IV,477; NE II,xxiii,21; G III,357).

I conclude that the first construction I gave of the spatial positions of simple and corporeal substances is the one intended by Leibniz. These positions and, therefore, the aggregation of substances into bodies are dependent on the apparent position of bodies as phenomena. Having come to this conclusion, I am ready to try to explain why Leibniz would have thought that corporeal aggregates cannot be more than phenomena even if they are aggregates of simple substances. There are two sorts of reason to be considered here: Leibniz has (1) a reason for thinking that *all* aggregates as such must be merely phenomena and (2) a special reason for ascribing phenomenal status to *corporeal* aggregates.

(1) The reason that he usually gives for thinking that aggregates as such are only phenomena is that they are not one per se. "Finally, bodies are nothing but aggregates, constituting something that is one *per accidens* or by an external denomination, and therefore they are well founded Phenomena" (G VII,344). The unity of an aggregate comes to it by an "external denomination"—namely, by relation to a mind that perceives relationships among the things that are aggregated. And, since Leibniz adhered to the Scholastic maxim that 'being' and 'one' are equivalent ["*Ens et unum convertuntur*" (G II,304)], he inferred that aggregates that have their unity only in the mind also have their being only in the mind.

This reasoning is clearly expressed in Leibniz's long letter of 30 April 1687 to Arnauld.

> To be brief, I hold as an axiom this identical proposition which is diversified only by accent, namely that what is not truly *one* being [*un* estre] is not truly a *being* [un *estre*] either. It has always been believed that these are mutually convertible things. . . . I have believed therefore that I would be permitted to distinguish Beings of aggregation from substances, since

those Beings have their unity only in our mind, which relies on the relations or modes of genuine substances. (G II,97/L-A 121)

Leibniz's claim is that aggregates have their unity and, therefore, their being only in the mind and that this is true even of aggregates of real things.

Why did Leibniz think that aggregates have their unity only in the mind? Another passage in the same letter to Arnauld reminds us that Leibniz is a conceptualist about abstract objects in general and also about relations (G II,438), believing that they have their being only in the mind (especially in the divine mind). (Cf. NE II,xii,3–7.) The same treatment is to be accorded to the unity of an aggregate and, hence, to the aggregate itself.

> Our mind notices or conceives some genuine substances which have certain modes; these modes include relations to other substances, from which the mind takes the occasion to join them together in thought and to put one name in the accounting for all these things together, which serves for convenience in reasoning; but one must not let oneself be deceived into making of them so many substances or truly real Beings. That is only for those who stop at appearances, or else for those who make realities out of all the abstractions of the mind, and who conceive number, time, place, motion, shape, sensible qualities as so many separate beings. (G II,101/L-A 126f.)

In Leibniz's ontology, the only things that have being in their own right are particular "substances, or complete Beings, endowed with a true unity, with their different successive states" (ibid.). Everything else, including universals and also including aggregates, "being nothing but phenomena, abstractions, or relations" (ibid.), is at best a being of reason (*ens rationis*), existing in the mind and dependent on being thought of.

(2) There is another reason for assigning the status of appearances to *corporeal* aggregates in particular. "Mass is nothing but a phenomenon, like the Rainbow," wrote Leibniz to Des Bosses (G II,390). The rainbow provides Leibniz with a favorite example of a phenomenon to which he frequently likens bodies. His treatment of the example is not perfectly consistent. At least once (G II,58/L-A 66), he contrasts the rainbow with aggregates, but more often it is presented as something that is a phenomenon because it is an aggregate (e.g., G II,306). "The rainbow," Leibniz says, "is an aggregate of drops which jointly produce certain colors that are apparent to us" (Gr. 322). "The rainbow is of diminished reality under two headings," Leibniz says, "for it is a Being by aggregation of drops, and the qualities by which it is known are

apparent or at least of that kind of real ones which are relative to our senses" (Gr. 322). The first of these reasons for the diminished reality of the rainbow is simply Leibniz's general thesis of the phenomenality of aggregates; it is the second reason that we must now develop.

This reason has to do with the perceptual relativity of colors. Colors, Leibniz indicates in the same text, are "apparent qualities" in the sense that they are "not in things absolutely, but insofar as they act on us; thus the same water will seem cold or tepid or hot according to the disposition of my hands. Yet this is real in it, that it is naturally apt to produce this sensation in me when I am thus disposed" (Gr. 322). Colors in general are apparent qualities in this sense, according to Leibniz; but he neglects to emphasize that the colors of the rainbow are even more than ordinarily relative to perception. Any particular aggregate of drops of water will be colored as a rainbow only relative to perceptions from a particular place. And, on the other hand, Leibniz thinks that spatial properties, too—such as size, shape, and position—are not in monads absolutely but can be ascribed to monads or aggregates of monads in a derivative sense defined in terms of the way the organic bodies of the monads are perceived. Because the aggregation of drops in a rainbow, and of monads in a body, is based on properties that are relative to perception in this way, he infers that the rainbow and the body are phenomena and have diminished reality.

It is misleading, I think, that Leibniz says in presenting this argument that the qualities by which the rainbow is *known* or recognized (*noscitur*) are apparent or relative to our senses. What is crucial here is not that we know or recognize the rainbow by merely apparent qualities. We know or recognize other monads generally by properties of their bodies that are merely apparent, according to Leibniz, and the monads are not less real for that. The crux of the argument is that the *existence* of the aggregate depends on properties that are relative to our perceptions. The relation to perception provides the principle of grouping that defines the aggregate. If we think of a rainbow as an aggregate of drops, what is it that picks them out from all the other drops of water in the sky and groups them as an object that we call a rainbow? It is their relation to the color perceptions that an observer (in one place but not in others) would have. It is only in appearance that there is more reason to aggregate these drops together than to form any other group from the drops in the sky. Likewise, the aggregation of monads as belonging to a single corporeal mass depends entirely on their bodies' *appearing* to occupy contiguous or overlapping spaces.

Suppose through a cleverly contrived network of glass fibers the images of a thousand different people walking, talking, and gesturing on a thousand different streets of a hundred different cities were combined to give you an image of an angry mob. This "mob," we might say, is an aggregate of real human beings, but the reality of the individual persons does not keep the mob as such from being a mere phenomenon. This is because the existence of an aggregate (in the Leibnizian sense) depends on relations among its members in a way that the existence of a set does not. If sets exist at all, the existence of all the members of a set suffices for the existence of the set. But that Leibnizian paradigm of an aggregate, a pile of wood, ceases to exist when the logs in it are scattered, even though the logs are not destroyed. A pile or mob exists only while its members are grouped by a certain proximity. In the case that I described, the mob is a mere phenomenon because its grouping is merely apparent and exists only in the image presented to you by the optical apparatus. This would be an apt example for Leibniz, because in his opinion the aggregation of monads by spatial relations, to form bodies, is no less dependent on perception since monads do not have spatial properties in their own right but are spatially represented in our perceptions (Cf. G III, 623). "And the aggregates themselves are nothing but phenomena," Leibniz says, "since besides the monads that enter into them, the rest is added by perception alone, by the very fact that they are perceived together" (G II, 517).

Doubts may remain, nevertheless, as to whether this conception of bodies as aggregates and therefore phenomena is completely consistent with the account I gave in section 1, according to which bodies, as phenomena, are perceptions considered with regard to their objective reality or representational content. Several questions arise here. (1) Does Leibniz think that aggregates of monads, or of corporeal substances, as the case may be, are perceptions or modifications of the mind (considered with regard to their objective reality or representational content)? Yes, he seems to be saying that in his conceptualism about aggregates. (2) If bodies as phenomena are the objects of stories told by perception, by common sense, and especially by science, as I suggested earlier, can they also be aggregates of substances? Certainly they can also be aggregates, for, according to Leibniz, it is part of the story told by science, and less clearly also by common sense and perception, that every extended thing is composed of parts into which it could be divided; and that is enough to make extended things aggregates in Leibniz's book. On the other hand, it does not seem to be part of the story told by perception, common sense, or science that extended things are composed of *monads,* nor perhaps even that they are composed of *substances* at all. To this I think Leibniz might say that those stories do not *exclude* the thesis that bodies are aggregates of substances. It is at least vaguely part of the stories told by common sense and science that the appearances of bodies have or may have some further foundation in reality. But no hypothesis of the nature of that foundation is part of the stories of Leibnizian science and common sense; it is left to metaphysics to consider what the foundation might be.

(3) Can aggregates of substances possess the physical properties that bodies have in the story told by science? It might seem, in particular, that an aggregate of *simple* substances would not be *continuous* because it is composed of parts that cannot be divided again into parts and that do not adjoin or overlap each other. Leibniz seems to say as much himself in his last letter to De Volder (G II,282/L 539); but that passage is a difficult one in which he also appears to have forgotten his doctrine that aggregates, even aggregates of real things, are phenomena.[18] We could say, however, that, though monads may be *elements* of corporeal aggregates, the relevant *parts* of the aggregate are not monads but subaggregates containing infinitely many monads. The aggregate will be divisible in indefinitely many and various ways into subaggregates of this sort, which will themselves be similarly divisible into subaggregates and which may overlap each other in their membership or may share a common "boundary" of monads. In this way, the aggregate as such can have the mathematical structure of continuity. This distinction between the role of monads and the role of subaggregates in the composition of corporeal aggregates seems to me to be approximately what Leibniz was after when he wrote to Fardella, in March 1690:

> Meanwhile it should not therefore be said that an indivisible substance enters into the composition of a body as a part, but rather as an essential internal requirement. Just as a point, although it is not a component part of a line, but something heterogeneous, is still necessarily required, in order for the line to be and to be understood. (FC 320; cf. G II,436/L 600)

Just as the parts of a line are not points but lines, so the parts of a corporeal aggregate are not monads but (I suggest) subaggregates.

Continuity is not the only physical property, of course, but there are natural enough ways of assigning other physical properties to any aggregates of monads that might constitute bodies. Although monads do not have any primitive spatial properties, Leibniz assigns them, in a derivative sense, the spatial positions occupied by their organic bodies. I have argued, further, that the principle of aggregation by which Leibniz thinks monads are grouped to form a corporeal mass provides that the monadic membership of a particular corporeal mass at any given time includes all or most of the monads whose spatial position at that time, in this derived sense, is within a certain region of space. And it seems natural to say that the size and shape of such an aggregate are the size and shape of the space in which the member monads have their positions. The positions are resultant or constructed properties of the monads, but the size and shape are constitutive properties of the aggregate. That is indeed one reason why the aggregate is only a phenomenon, since size and shape are phenomenal properties. Motions can be ascribed to corporeal aggregates on an analogous basis.

I am guilty of some oversimplification here, however. It was pointed out at the end of section 1 that for Leibniz the spatial representation of a monad is defined, not by any single shape, but by an infinite series of increasingly complex shapes. Presumably, the same will be true of aggregates of monads; instead of a single determinate shape, they will have an infinite series of shapes that increase in complexity as they increase in accuracy.

4. The Reality of Phenomena

Phenomenalists and idealists do not generally leave us without a systematic difference between the physical objects that appear to us in normal experience and those that appear to us in dreams and hallucinations. In Leibniz's thought, there is a distinction between "real" phenomena and "imaginary" (G VII,319/L 363) or "apparent" or "false" phenomena (Gr. 322). As I stated in section 1, it seems to be part of Leibniz's projects to analyze this distinction in a way that he does not attempt to analyze the *content* of physical phenomena.

His principal account of what it is for phenomena to be "real" or "true" is classically phenomenalistic in the sense that it is in terms of the contents of perceptions and their agreements with other perceptions. "Matter and motion are . . . phenomena of perceivers, whose reality is located in the harmony of perceivers with themselves (at different times) and with other perceivers" (G II,270/L 537). This account can be found in works of all periods of Leibniz's thought—in the Paris years,[19] in 1686 in section 14 of the *Discourse on Metaphysics,* in criticisms of Descartes about 1692 (G IV,356/L 384), in a letter to De Volder in 1704 (G II,270/L 537), and in a sketch of his metaphysics prepared for Remond in 1714 (G III,623), to mention only a few texts.

The criteria for reality of phenomena are most fully spelled out in an essay, "On the Method of Distinguishing Real from Imaginary Phenomena" (dated to 1684 by Hochstetter).[20] They are similar to criteria proposed by other early modern philosophers. The internal marks of a real phenomenon are that it is *vivid, complex,* and *harmonious (con-gruum).*

> It will be vivid if qualities such as light, color, heat appear intense enough. It will be complex if they are varied, and suited for setting up many experiments and new observations, for example if we experience in the phenomenon not only colors but also sounds, odors, tastes, tactile qualities, and that both in the whole and in various parts, which we can investigate again according to various causes. (G VII,319f./L 363)

These first two marks do not usually figure in Leibniz's formulations about the reality of phenomena, but *harmony* is stressed repeatedly. Internally, "a phenomenon will be harmonious when it is composed of several phenomena for which a reason can be given from each other or from some sufficiently simple common hypothesis" (G VII,320/L 364).

The main external mark, and the most important mark, of the reality of a phenomenon is also a sort of harmony:

> if it keeps the custom of other phenomena that have occurred to us frequently, so that the parts of the phenomenon have the same position, order, and outcome that similar phenomena have had. . . . Likewise, if a reason for this [phenomenon] can be given from those that precede, or if they all fit the same hypothesis as a common reason. The strongest proof, however, is surely agreement with the whole series of life, especially if most other [people] affirm that the same thing agrees with their phenomena. . . . But the most powerful proof of the reality of phenomena, which even suffices by itself, is the success of predicting future phenomena from past and present ones. (G VII,320/L 364)

The notions of complexity and harmony are clearly connected here with notions of causal order. Real phenomena are those that form part of a *causally* coherent, *scientifically* adequate story that appears all or most of the time, at least in an obscure or fragmentary way, to all or most perceivers. That is the story that would be told by a perfected physical science. Imaginary phenomena are those that do not fit in this story.[21]

There is a problem about how Leibniz can admit imaginary phenomena in this sense at all, for he holds that every monad always perceives the whole universe. It follows that the true physical story appears at *all* times to *all* perceivers, not just to most of them at most times. How then can there be any false phenomena? I have not found Leibniz dealing explicitly with this problem, but we can conjecture what his answer might have been. In the first place, I think he believed that all perceptions of every monad do express something that is in the monad's organic body. Suppose I seem to see a pink rat. Leibniz would say that this perception expresses, and is a perception of, some event in my body. As a perception of that event it is a true, not a false, perception, and the event is a real, not an imaginary, phenomenon. What appears to me consciously, however, is not the event in my body, but a pink rat. In this case, I think Leibniz has to say that my perception has two different objective realities or representational contents. The first, an event in my body, is a phenomenon that certainly coheres with the story told by a perfected physical science. The second, a pink rat, may or may not cohere with that story; it is real if it does and an hallucination if it does not.

There are many passages in which Leibniz seems to say that internal and external harmony, supplemented perhaps by vividness and complexity, is a sufficient condition for the reality of a phenomenon. In the essay "On the Method of Distinguishing Real from Imaginary Phenomena," however, he speaks more cautiously. The marks of reality are presented as epistemic criteria by which we may tell when a phenomenon is real; it is not asserted that they define what the reality of a phenomenon consists in. Indeed, it is virtually implied that a phenomenon could possess the marks of reality and yet not be fully real. "It must be admitted that the proofs of real phenomena that have been adduced thus far, even taken in any combination whatever, are not demonstrative." They have "the greatest probability," or "moral certainty," but not "Metaphysical" certainty; there would be no contradiction in supposing them false. "Therefore it cannot be absolutely demonstrated by any argument that there are bodies; and nothing keeps certain well ordered dreams from being the object of our mind, which we judge to be true and which are equivalent for practical purposes to true things because of their mutual agreement." Leibniz rejects Descartes's claim that in such case God would be a deceiver. "For what if our nature happened not to be capable of real phenomena? Surely God should be thanked rather than blamed in that case; for by causing those phenomena at least to agree, since they could not be real, he has furnished us with something equally as useful, for all of life, as real phenomena" (G VII,320f./L 364; cf. G I,372f.; NE IV,ii,14).

It has been thought that Leibniz vacillated or changed his mind about the sufficiency of the harmony and agreement of phenomena for their reality, but it seems to me more probable that he used 'real' in stronger and weaker senses in expressing different aspects of a fairly constant system of opinions. A statement in the previous paragraph of the same essay is particularly revealing: "Indeed even if it were said that this whole life is nothing but a dream, and the visible world nothing but a phantasm, I would call this dream of phantasm real enough if we were never deceived by it when we used our reason well," that is, if predictions reasonably based on past experience generally succeeded so far as future experience is concerned (G VII,320/L 364). To say that this whole life is a dream is presumably to say that its phenomena lack a kind of reality that phenomena could have, but Leibniz indicates another sense in which our phenomena would still be "real enough," provided only that our experience had all the internal marks of reality.

This helps to explain the fact that Leibniz seems to offer two other accounts of what the reality of bodies consists in. These accounts, I suggest, should be seen as stating additional conditions that harmonious phenomena must satisfy in order to be real in the fullest sense, although their harmony is sufficient for their reality in a weaker sense that is enough for all practical purposes. It must be admitted, however, that all three accounts—the one in terms of the harmony of perceptions as well as the other two—are usually presented as if they were completely independent.

One of the other accounts is theological. In a study for a letter to Des Bosses, Leibniz wrote:

> If bodies are phenomena and are evaluated on the basis of our appearances, they will not be real, since they appear differently to different people. Therefore the reality of bodies, space, motions, and time seems to consist in their being God's phenomena, or the object of intuitive knowledge [*scientia visionis*]. (G II,438)

This is an exceptional text in two respects. In the first place, it seems to deny that there is enough agreement among human perceivers for their phenomena to satisfy the intersubjective harmony condition for reality. Elsewhere Leibniz seems to assume that the required agreement does exist (DM 14), especially if unconscious perceptions are taken into account. Even in writing to Des Bosses just a few months later, Leibniz says that on the hypothesis that there is nothing outside of all souls or monads, "when we say that Socrates is sitting, nothing else is meant than that those things by which we understand Socrates and sitting are appearing to us and to others who are concerned" (G II,451f./L605), which surely implies enough agreement in the perceptions of those "who are concerned" to distinguish a real from a merely apparent sitting of Socrates.

In the second place, the explanation of the reality of phenomena in terms of God's phenomena is rare in Leibniz's work. It occurs in other letters to Des Bosses (G II,474, 482/L 607f.), but I have not found it elsewhere. There are many unanswered questions, also, about what God's corporeal phenomena would be.[22] For these reasons, I will largely ignore this second, theological account of the reality of phenomena.

The third account applies chiefly to aggregates as such and says that their reality consists in the reality of the substances that enter into them. Aggregates "have no other reality than that which belongs to the Unities that are in them" (G II,261; cf. G VII,314). Given that Leibniz says that bodies *are* aggregates of substances, indeed, it is hard to see how he could fail to think that their reality consists at least partly in the reality of the substances that are aggregated in them. And this thesis plays a part in the argument for monads. It is partly because an aggregate "has no reality unless it is borrowed from the things contained" in it that Leibniz "inferred, therefore there are indivisible unities in things, since otherwise there will be in things no true unity, and no reality not borrowed" (G II,267).

There are several reasons for thinking that this is not a completely independent account of the reality of bodies, that it does not conflict with the account in terms of harmonious perceptions but supplements it and even depends on it. (1) Leibniz seems to have regarded the two accounts as consistent. He sometimes gives both of them in the same document. I have quoted expressions of both of them from his letter of 30 June 1704 to De Volder (G II,267, 270/L 537). And in a single two-page piece written in 1714 Leibniz says both that bodies *are* assemblages of monads and that material things "have their reality from the agreement of the perceptions of apperceiving substances" (G III,622f.).

(2) I think Leibniz believed that the two accounts are at least materially equivalent—that there is a true scientific story that is always at least unconsciously perceived by all monads, that most of what appears consciously to conscious perceivers fits at least approximately into that story, that there are infinitely many monads whose properties are expressed by organic bodies that would figure in a sufficiently detailed extension of the true scientific story, that aggregates of these monads (or of the corporeal substances that they form with their organic bodies) can, therefore, be regarded as the bodies that figure in the true scientific story, and thus that the bodies of the true scientific theory are real according to both accounts, both as coherent phenomena and as aggregates of real things.

(3) The claim that the reality of bodies consists in the reality of the substances that are aggregated in them presupposes that substances *are* aggregated in them, and this aggregation presupposes the harmony of perceptions. As I argued above, the grouping of substances into corporeal aggregates depends on the spatial positions their organic bodies appear to have. If a single system of aggregates of substances is to be real, as opposed to any others, which may be imaginary,

it is surely not enough that the substances that belong to the real aggregates be real; it is also required that the aggregates themselves represent the *true* grouping of the substances. In particular, the true grouping of the substances can hardly depend on the positions the substances' organic bodies appear to have just a little of the time to just any perceiver. Rather, it depends on the positions the organic bodies have in a coherent system of phenomena that are represented by most of the perceptions of all perceivers—or else perhaps by all the perceptions of a single authoritative perceiver (God). In order for there to be corporeal aggregates that are real by virtue of the reality of the substances aggregated in them, they must appear as material masses in this coherent system of phenomena and, therefore, they must satisfy the harmonious perceptions condition for reality—or else the theological condition, but the latter usually seems to play no role in Leibniz's thought.

Considering all these reasons (and ignoring the theological account), I think we find in Leibniz, not two competing analyses of the reality of corporeal phenomena, but one analysis in two layers. Phenomena are real, in a weak sense, if and only if they fit into a single scientifically adequate system of harmonious phenomena of all perceivers.[23] Those phenomena—and only those—that are real in this weaker sense are also real in a fuller sense to the extent that there exist real monads that are appropriately expressed by organic bodies belonging to the system of phenomena that is at least weakly real.

5. Corporeal Substance (II): Principles of Unity

There are many texts in which Leibniz says that corporeal substances are distinguished from mere aggregates by a profounder sort of unity. Writing to Arnauld late in 1686, he said, "if there are no corporeal substances, such as I wish, it follows that bodies are nothing but true phenomena, like the rainbow," for on account of the infinite divisibility of the continuum, "one will never come to anything of which one can say, 'Here is truly a being,' except when one finds animated machines of which the soul or substantial form constitutes the substantial unity independent of the external union of contact" (G II,77/L-A 95). This statement implies, first, that there cannot be a corporeal substance without a "substantial unity" stronger than the unity that many aggregates have by the bodily contact of their members with each other and, second, that such a substantial unity is somehow provided by the dominant monad. And this is only one of a number of texts in which the dominant monad, or perhaps sometimes the active entelechy in the dominant monad, is characterized as the principle of unity of the corporeal substance. A corporeal substance is "actuated by one Entelechy, without which there would be in it no principle of true Unity" (G II,250/L 529); "the Monad dominating the Machine makes [the corporeal substance] One" (G II,252/L531; cf. G. II,120/L-A 154; L 454; G III,260f.; G II,314; PNG 3).

It may be doubted, however, whether on Leibniz's showing the dominant monad gives to the composite that it forms with the organic body a unity fundamentally different in kind from the unity of an aggregate. As Leibniz himself said, monadic domination and the unity that springs from it consist at bottom only in certain relations among the perceptions of monads. "The agglomeration of these organized corporeal substances which constitutes our body is not united with our Soul except by that relation which follows from the order of the phenomena that are natural to each substance separately" (G IV,573). Aggregates, too, are united (accidentally, Leibniz says) by relations among the perceptions of monads. So at bottom it would seem that the unity of an aggregate and the unity of a corporeal substance are of the same kind.

To be sure, the perceptual relations involved in monadic domination are more direct, in a puzzling sense that I have discussed in section 2, and they play a more basic part in explanation in the Leibnizian system than those that constitute aggregates. They also give rise to interesting properties of a corporeal substance; Leibniz mentions indivisibility, natural indestructibility, and the property of completely expressing its whole past and future, as distinguishing a corporeal substance from a mere aggregate (G II,76/L-A 94). But these properties belong to the organic body, which is not a substance, as well as to the corporeal substance; and they merely result, for Leibniz, from the fact that the organic body, as a phenomenon, is a perpetual perfect expression of the dominant monad, which possesses analogous properties. Given Leibniz's doctrine that "there is nothing in things except simple substances, and in them perception and appetite" (G II,270/L 537), there is no way for the unity of a corporeal substance to be anything over and above the system of relations among the perceptions of monads. By stipulation, of course, Leibniz would be free to define a difference between unity and accidental unity in terms of different patterns of relations among perceptions. But does this add up to such a fundamental metaphysical difference as Leibniz seems to wish to assert between corporeal substances and aggregates?

There is evidence that Leibniz himself worried about this issue, at least in the last ten or twelve years of his life. This evidence is connected with his correspondence with the Jesuit Fathers Tournemine and Des Bosses. Leibniz wrote a note for Tournemine, probably in

1706, in which he acknowledges that his preestablished harmony could not account any better than the Cartesian philosophy for "a true Union" between the soul and the body. He excuses himself from giving such an account:

> I have tried to give an account only of Phenomena, that is to say, of the relation that is perceived between the Soul and the Body. But as the Metaphysical Union that one adds to it is not a Phenomenon, and as an intelligible Notion has not even been given of it, I have not taken it upon myself to seek the explanation of it. I do not deny, however, that there is something of that nature. (G VI,595)

It is hard to interpret this statement. It certainly does not constitute an affirmation that there is, over and above the relations of perceptions of monads provided by the preestablished harmony, a metaphysical union of soul and body. In fact, Leibniz plainly denies that such a union is part of his philosophy. But is he tactfully muffling his belief that it is an unintelligible absurdity? Or is he more straightforwardly acknowledging that there may be something in the universe that cannot be understood in his philosophy?

The more cynical reading of the text is supported, in my opinion, by the last letter he wrote to De Volder, dated 19 January 1706, in which he reports an interchange with Tournemine. What he wrote to De Volder agrees closely in substance with what he wrote for Tournemine but is noticeably less respectful and more ironic in tone. It is introduced with the remark, "The scholastics commonly seek things that are not so much beyond this world [*ultramundana*] as Utopian. An elegant example was recently supplied to me by the Jesuit Tournemine, an ingenious Frenchman" (G II,281/L 538). The "example," stigmatized as "Utopian," is Tournemine's demand for an account of a union, different from agreement, between body and soul. By itself, therefore, the interchange with Tournemine is not much evidence that Leibniz had serious misgivings about his own philosophy.

The evidence of Leibniz's correspondence with Des Bosses, however, cannot be disposed of so easily. That correspondence is voluminous and in large part devoted to the nature of the union between soul and body. It is in writing to Des Bosses, probably in 1712, that Leibniz introduced the notorious concept of a *substantial bond (vinculum substantiale)*. The substantial bond is "a certain union, or rather a real unifier superadded to the monads by God"; it is "something absolute (and therefore substantial)" (G II,435/L 600). It "will not be a simple result, or will not consist solely of true or real relations, but will add besides some new substantiality or substantial bond; and it will be an

effect not only of the divine intellect but also of the divine will"
(G II,438)—or, as we might say, it will not be a mere logical construct
out of monads and the relations of their perceptions. A substantial
bond never unites spatially scattered monads; it unites only "monads
which are under the domination of one, or which make one organic
body or one Machine of nature" (G II,438f.; cf. G II,486/L 609). And
each substantial bond is permanently attached to a single dominant
monad (G II,496/L 611). It is only by the order of nature, however, and
not by absolute necessity, that the substantial bond thus requires the
dominant monad and its organic body. Supernaturally and miraculously, God can separate the bond from the monads (G II,495f./L 610f.)
and perhaps does so in transubstantiation, in the Eucharist.

The conception of the substantial bond includes some of the properties that Leibniz previously ascribed to the dominant monad. It is "the
very substantial form of the composite" (G II,516; cf. G II,504/L 614)
and apparently "consists in the primitive active and passive power of
the composite" (G II,485f./L 609). "This bond will be the source [*principium*] of the actions of the composite substance" (G II,503/L 613). It
is to the substantial bond that the properties of the composite substance are to be ascribed; "it will be necessary that the accidents of the
composite be its modifications" (G II,486/L 609).

Unlike any monad, however, the substantial bond is metaphysically
acted on by other finite things. It does not change anything in the
monads (G II,517; cf. G. II,451/L 604), for that would be contrary to
their nature. But it unites them by being influenced by them (G II,496/
L 611).

"If that substantial bond of monads were absent, all bodies with all
their qualities would be nothing but well founded phenomena, like the
rainbow or the image in a mirror" (G II,435/L 600). But, if there were
substantial bonds, then corporeal substance would be "something
making phenomena real outside of Souls" (G II,451/L 604; cf. G II,515f.,
519). Among phenomena made real are not only bodies but their qualities of continuity and extension. "Real continuity cannot arise except
from a substantial bond" (G II,517).

The question of the extent to which Leibniz personally accepted this
theory of substantial bonds is extremely controversial. Some interpreters have taken the theory straightforwardly as a part of his philosophy
in its final form. I believe the majority view, however, is typified by
Russell's statement, "Thus the *vinculum substantiale* is rather the
concession of a diplomatist than the creed of a philosopher."[24]

Several reasons can be given for not taking the substantial bond very
seriously as a part of Leibniz's thought. (1) The most important reason
is that it is blatantly inconsistent with other parts of his philosophy.

The theory of substantial bonds postulates something ultimately real in things besides "simple substances, and in them perception and appetite" (cf. G II,270/L 537). It also postulates a continuous extension that is not a phenomenon but is real. Both of these positions are emphatically rejected in many other places in Leibniz's writings, late as well as early (e.g., in G III,622f. and E 745f., written in 1714 and 1716, respectively).

(2) Russell says that "nowhere does Leibniz himself assert that he believes" the doctrine of substantial bonds.[25] This could be disputed. In a letter of 16 January 1716, he refers to "the primitive passive and active powers of the composite" and says to Des Bosses, "the complete thing resulting from them I really judge to be that substantial bond which I am urging" (G II,511). This certainly looks like an endorsement of this doctrine. It could be read, however, as a statement only of what Leibniz thinks should be said about primitive passive and active powers *if* they are ascribed to a composite substance as such. And it is true that Leibniz more commonly speaks of substantial bonds in a more tentative way that seems to leave open the alternative hypothesis that bodies are in fact only phenomena. He even explicitly expresses to Des Bosses some preference for the phenomenalistic view (G II,461).

(3) A particularly important indication of Leibniz's intentions is found in a passage, cited by Russell, from Leibniz's letter of 30 June 1715 to Des Bosses:

> Whether my latest answer about Monads will have pleased you, I hardly know. I fear that the things I have written to you at different times about this subject may not cohere well enough among themselves, since, you know, I have not treated this theme, of Phenomena to be elevated to reality, or of composite substances, except on the occasion of your letters (G II,499).

The theme (*argumentum*) mentioned in this text is certainly the doctrine of substantial bonds. Leibniz is telling Des Bosses, in effect, that he has not thought enough about it and does not have the ideas clearly enough in mind to be confident that he has been consistent in what he has said about it from one letter to another. Whatever may have seemed plausible to Leibniz in those hours that he spent writing to Des Bosses, a theory that he did not "treat" except in this correspondence, that he did not keep clearly in mind, and that is blatantly inconsistent with important doctrines that he asserted in many other places and continued to assert during this period of his life, cannot be counted as a part of his philosophy.

There is quite a range of attitudes, however, that a philosopher may have toward ideas that are not a part of his philosophy. He may be sure they are false. He may be afraid they may be true or wish they were true. He may think they present an intriguing or perhaps even a promising alternative to some of his own views. He may be playing more or less seriously with the thought of trying to incorporate them into his philosophy. He may be completely confident of the correctness of his own theories; but, if he is worried about their adequacy in some respect, that will affect his interest in alternative theories.

In trying to discover Leibniz's attitude toward the theory of substantial bonds, we must form some assessment of his motives in discussing it with Des Bosses. Russell's claim that the *vinculum substantiale* is "the concession of a diplomatist" reflects a cynical assessment. It is based on the idea that the theory "springs from Leibniz's endeavour to reconcile his philosophy with the dogma of transubstantiation." Not that he meant at this stage in his life to accept the dogma. As a Lutheran, he was quite frank with Des Bosses that he did not accept it (G II,390). But "he was extremely anxious to persuade Catholics that they might, without heresy, believe in his doctrine of monads," suggests Russell.[26]

There are at least four reasons for regarding Russell's explanation of Leibniz's motives as implausible. (1) Leibniz was certainly capable of concealing part of his position in order to make the rest of it more palatable to others. He has even left behind some indication that he believed in doing so.[27] But one at least must wonder why he would be interested in selling to Catholics what is left of the theory of monads after abandoning the claim that the world is constituted by monads alone.

(2) I must record my own impression that Leibniz strikes me as comparatively candid, rather than cautious, in his correspondence with Des Bosses. His very inability to remember exactly what he had said to Des Bosses supports the suggestion that he was not carefully shaping diplomatic missives but rather was freely and casually playing with ideas in letters to a good friend. It is worth noting that the more phenomenalistic aspects of Leibniz's thought find much fuller expression in his letters to Des Bosses than they do in his publications and his letters to most correspondents, though Leibniz withheld from Des Bosses a full endorsement of phenomenalistic views that he did endorse in writing to some others.

(3) The doctrine of the substantial bond was proposed by Leibniz, not forced on him by Des Bosses, although the term 'bond' (*vinculum*) in this context does have resonance with Jesuit metaphysics of the seventeenth century.[28] Indeed, Des Bosses showed a rather persistent preference for accidental or modal bonds, against which Leibniz

had to defend his substantial bonds. And Des Bosses did not react with horror to the phenomenalistic alternatives offered by Leibniz. If the *vinculum substantiale* was a concession, it was not in any simple way a concession to Des Bosses.

(4) Except in one of Leibniz's letters, neither he nor Des Bosses seems to have believed that the doctrine of transubstantiation could not be accommodated without the substantial bonds. Leibniz did once say that he could hardly see how the dogma could be "sufficiently explained by mere monads and phenomena" (G II,460). But he subsequently proposed two different theories of transubstantiation based on the assumption that only monads and their phenomena exist (G II,474/ L 607f.; G II,520f.), and the availability of these theories did not seem to diminish his interest in substantial bonds.

Des Bosses also proposed to Leibniz a theory of transubstantiation based on "the Hypothesis of bodies reduced to Phenomena" (G II,453–55). He did not endorse this theory, but he liked it better, in one way at least, than Leibniz's substantial bond theory of transubstantiation. In Leibniz's theory, the substantial bonds of the sacramental bread and wine, or of the corporeal substances contained in them, are miraculously destroyed, but the monads of the bread and wine endure and are miraculously united to the substantial bonds of the body and blood of Christ. Des Bosses objected to the survival of the monads of the bread and wine as inconsistent with "the dogma of the Church . . . that the whole substance of the bread and wine perish" (G II,463; cf. 474, 480). In Des Bosses's theory based on monads and phenomena alone, the monads of the bread and wine are destroyed and the monads of the body and blood of Christ take their place. Leibniz was averse, of course, to the destruction of monads; but Des Bosses forced him to admit, in the end, that the destruction of substantial bonds would be just as unnatural (G II,481f.).

There is more than one alternative, of course, to a cynical reading of Leibniz's discussion of substantial bonds. He could largely have been playing, in a friendly discussion, with ideas that he did not believe for a minute. But there is something to be said for the view that Leibniz was influenced to some extent by worries about the adequacy of his philosophy to account for certain types of union.

I have already argued that he had reason to be uneasy about the adequacy of his account of the special unity that he wished to ascribe to corporeal substances. A few hints of such uneasiness may be found elsewhere (e.g., the mention of "metaphysical union of the soul and its body" in G III,658), but the major evidence for it is in the letters to Des Bosses.

This evidence is independent of the question whether Leibniz accepted the theory of substantial bonds. Even if he did not, he seems at least to have asserted to Des Bosses that without the bonds there would be no corporeal substances that would be one per se because the monads and their subordination would not be enough to constitute such composite substances (G II,435,444,511,517f./L 600,602). This is clearly inconsistent with Leibniz's oft-repeated claim that the dominant monad is the principle of unity that makes a corporeal substance one per se.

It would be neat and tidy if it could be shown that these statements to Des Bosses represent a change of mind on Leibniz's part. But, in fact, there seems not to have been a settled change in his views on this point. Even after he began to make these statements to Des Bosses, he wrote in *The Principles of Nature and of Grace* that the dominant monad of a composite substance "makes . . . the principle of its unicity" (PNG 3).[29] We have to do here with a vacillation, at most, rather than a change of mind.

I believe that Leibniz's deepest grounds for misgivings about the adequacy of his treatment of concepts of union were theological. The theory of substantial bonds is introduced under the condition, "if faith leads us to corporeal substance" (G II,435/L 600), though the allusion there may be more to Des Bosses's theology than to Leibniz's own. In any event, Leibniz alludes to problems about the relation of his philosophy to dogmas to which he was committed as he was not committed to transubstantiation, problems about the need for a strong concept of union or something similar. The Lutheran doctrine of the Eucharist, as he explained it to Des Bosses, does not involve transubstantiation but does involve a real "presence of the body of Christ," and he acknowledged that this presence "is something Metaphysical, as union is: which is not explained by phenomena" (G II,390/L615*n*8; cf. G VI,595f. and Gr. 449).

Still more important is a problem about the doctrine of the Incarnation. He wrote to Des Bosses:

> If an account could be thought out for explaining the possibility of your transubstantiation even with bodies reduced to phenomena alone, I would much prefer that. For that Hypothesis pleases in many ways. Nor do we need anything else besides Monads and their internal modifications, for Philosophy as opposed to the supernatural. But I fear that we cannot explain the mystery of the Incarnation, and other things, unless real bonds or unions are added. (G II, 461)

This is not the only text in which Leibniz suggests something like this about the Incarnation. There is an obscure but fascinating theological fragment, not addressed to any correspondent, in which he brings the Incarnation together with the union of soul and body: "Everything can be explained by adding one thing to those things which can be explained from phenomena—namely, by adding the *union* of God with the creature in the incarnation; of the soul with the body to make the human suppositum; of the monads among themselves to make the secondary substance or organic body" (RML 414, Leibniz's emphasis). I take it that the human suppositum and organic body mentioned here are the human nature and human body of Christ, but it is striking that the idea of a union of body and soul, and of monads, that cannot be explained in terms of phenomena is once more linked with the union of divine and human in Christ.

Perhaps there was a reason for this linkage. A long tradition has seen the relation of divine and human in the Incarnation as analogous to the union of body and soul in a human being. The so-called "Athanasian Creed" states, "For as the reasonable soul and flesh is one man, so God and man is one Christ."[30] The analogy was familiar to Leibniz. In a study for a letter to the Electress Sophia in 1702 he wrote, "For as an active thing joined to the animal makes the man of it, so the Divinity joined to the man makes of it the man that is God's [*l'homme à Dieu;* or the man-god (*l'homme-Dieu*) as Leibniz actually wrote to the Electress]" (G VI,521).

There are two reasons why Leibniz might have thought that the doctrine of the union of divine and human natures in the Incarnation requires another conception of union than that which monadic domination provides in his philosophy for the union of body and soul. The first reason is simply that, as we have seen, the union provided by monadic domination is not very strong. The second reason is that applying the Leibnizian conception of domination directly to the Incarnation leads to heresy. According to Leibniz, the dominant monad is the *sole* substantial form of a corporeal substance. If it is a rational soul, it is the sensitive and vegetative soul of its body as well. By analogy, if the second person of the holy Trinity were united with a human nature as a dominant monad in a corporeal substance, the divine nature would be the only substantial form or soul of that substance. It would take the place of the rational as well as the sensitive and vegetative souls. But that is an extension of the Apollinarian heresy. Orthodoxy requires, as Leibniz surely knew, that the single person of Christ include a complete human soul distinct from the divine nature.

If Leibniz believed, at the end of his life, that the doctrines that are most satisfactory in philosophy as such are not adequate for theology, that would not have been an unprecedented belief. It was held, before Leibniz, by many philosophers whose loyalty to Christianity was sincere. That would have been an uncomfortable position, however, for a philosopher who held in his *Theodicy,* in the "Preliminary Discourse on the Conformity of Faith with Reason" (§ 63), that "the Mysteries surpass our reason, . . . but they are not at all contrary to our reason." Leibniz would surely have preferred to think that the central dogmas of Christianity can be reconciled with the views to which a rational examination of the nature of substance would lead us. But it is not clear that he saw how that could be done to his own satisfaction.

Abbreviations

The works of Leibniz are cited by the following abbreviations:

C = *Opuscules et fragments inédits de Leibniz,* ed. by Louis Couturat (Paris: Alcan, 1903).

DM = *Discourse on Metaphysics,* as ed. by Henri Lestienne (Paris: Vrin, 1975) and trans. by P. G. Lucas and L. Grint (Manchester: Manchester University Press, 1953), cited by section number.

E = *Opera philosophica,* ed. by J. E. Erdmann (Berlin: G. Eichler, 1840).

FC = *Nouvelles lettres et opuscules inédits de Leibniz,* ed. by Foucher de Careil (Paris: Aug. Durand, 1857).

G = *Die philosophischen Schriften von Gottfried Wilhelm Leibniz,* ed. by C. I. Gerhardt (Berlin: Weidmannsche Buchhandlung, 1875–1890), cited by volume and page.

GM = *Leibnizens mathematische Schriften,* ed. by C. I. Gerhardt (Berlin: A. Asher, and Halle: H. W. Schmidt, 1849–1863), cited by volume and page.

Gr. = *Textes inédits,* ed. by Gaston Grua (Paris: Presses Universitaires de France, 1948).

L = Leibniz, *Philosophical Papers and Letters,* trans. and ed. by Leroy E. Loemker, 2nd ed. (Dordrecht and Boston: Reidel, 1969).

L-A = *The Leibniz-Arnauld Correspondence,* ed. and trans. by H. T. Mason (Manchester: Manchester University Press, 1967).

L-W = *Briefwechsel zwischen Leibniz und Christian Wolf,* ed. by C. I. Gerhardt (Halle: H. W. Schmidt, 1860).

Mon. = *Monadology,* cited by section number from Leibniz, *Principes de la nature et de la grace fondés en raison* and *Principes de la philosophie ou Monadologie,* ed. in one volume by André Robinet (Paris: Presses Universitaires de France, 1954).

NE = *New Essays Concerning Human Understanding,* cited by book, chapter, and section from G, V.

PNG = *The Principles of Nature and of Grace,* cited by section number from the same edition as Mon.

RML = André Robinet, *Malebranche et Leibniz: Relations personnelles* (Paris: Vrin, 1955).

All works are cited by page number unless otherwise noted above. Entries separated by a slash refer to the original and an English translation of the same passage. I take responsibility for the English translation of all quotations, although I have made some use of existing English versions.

Notes

Drafts of parts of this paper have been read to several scholarly gatherings, and the material has been discussed with my Leibniz class at UCLA. Many people have helped me with their comments. I am particularly indebted to Nicholas Jolley, Louis Loeb, J. E. McGuire, and the late Wallace Anderson for giving me written comments, which have been of great use for my revisions.

1. "In actual realities the whole," for example, "is a result of the parts" (G VII,562), but that does not mean that the parts are (efficient) causes of the whole. I think that if *b* results from *a* in Leibniz's sense, then *a* entails *b* and *b* adds nothing to reality over and above *a*. The data from which something "results" are jointly *sufficient* for the result. (L 699 seems to say that the "result" is *uniquely* determined by the data, which must, therefore, be sufficient for it. In the original Latin of this mathematical context [GM VII,21f.], however, the word whose meaning is explained is the unusual *'prostultare'*; and it is not clear to me whether what is said here implies anything about the meaning of *'resultare', 'resultatum'*, and *'resultat'*, which are more usual in metaphysical contexts. Even if this text is not directly relevant, I think it is most plausible to take Leibniz as supposing that the data must be sufficient for a "result" in metaphysics.) Perhaps the data will also be individually *necessary* for the result, but I doubt that that is implied in the notion of "result." Certainly, the result need not be capable of definition in terms of the data, in a finite language, for the data will commonly be infinite. Leibniz is not committed to the possibility of translating talk about bodies into talk about simple substances and their perceptions.

2. For example, Erich Hochstetter, "Von der wahren Wirklichkeit bei Leibniz," *Zeitschrift für philosophische Forschung*, Vol. 20 (1966), pp. 421–46 (see especially the references to Leibniz's "Schwanken," pp. 422 and 440); and Louis Loeb, *From Descartes to Hume* (Ithaca, N.Y.: Cornell University Press, 1981), pp. 299–309—to mention two works that I hold in high regard.

3. Cf. Montgomery Furth, "Monadology," *The Philosophical Review*, Vol. 76 (1967), p. 172.

4. On Leibniz's relation to this controversy, see RML 133ff. Even before seeing the documents, Leibniz wrote in a letter that "Mons. Arnauld writes with more judgment" than Father Malebranche (RML 150).

5. Published, with a full report of the discovery, by Willy Kabitz, "Leibniz und Berkeley," *Sitzungsberichte der preussischen Akademie der Wissenschaften*, Philosophisch-historische Klasse N. xxiv, (Jahrgang 1932), p. 636.

6. Here I disagree with Hochstetter, "Von der wahren Wirklichkeit bei Leibniz," p. 436. It must be granted to Hochstetter that Leibniz did not explicitly speak of phenomena as "appearances of monads."

7. In writing to Arnauld, Leibniz expressed some agnosticism, or at least some hesitation, about whether there are any "true corporeal substances" besides those that have "souls" or whether it is enough for them to have something analogous to a soul. (See G II,76f./L-A 95.) If sincere, this uncertainty seems not to have endured.

8. Ernst Cassirer, *Leibniz's System in seinem wissenschaftlichen Grundlagen* (Marburg: N. G. Elwert'sche Verlagsbuchhandlung, 1902), p. 408. Cassirer represents this phrase as a quotation from E 678, but he seems to me to be mistranslating and misapplying the text.

9. Bertrand Russell, *A Critical Exposition of the Philosophy of Leibniz*, 2nd ed. (London: George Allen and Unwin, 1937), p. 148.

10. I believe consciousness and distinctness were linked in this way in Leibniz's mind (see Mon. 19–24), but the question could be raised whether his theory of perception would not go better if distinctness and consciousness were allowed to be two dimensions in which perceptions can vary independently—distinctness being a feature of the structure of the perception and consciousness being, as it were, the light that is turned on it. (I am indebted to Jeremy Hyman for this image.) Separating these dimensions would give the theory more flexibility.

11. As Wallace Anderson has pointed out to me, it is also true that visual perceptions are *more fully* correlated with the eye than with the page. There are features of my visual perception that express features of my eye without expressing features of the page (e.g., the dots that are swimming across my image of the page).

12. The mention of "degrees" in the soul here might serve to place Leibniz more precisely in the complex Scholastic debate about the unity or plurality of substantial forms, but I will not pursue that historical relationship here.

13. Despite what Leibniz says here, it will be difficult for him to refuse to distinguish my perceiving my appetite for a certain event from my perceiving the corporeal causes of that event, for I may perceive the latter much more distinctly than the former, as when I perceive that I am falling and about to strike the ground with considerable force. (I owe this observation to Timothy Sheppard.)

14. I take these phrases to apply only to masses. Literally, Leibniz says this about "the rest" (*reliqua*) by contrast with "simple things." "The rest" might be taken to include corporeal substances (which are composite), but I find it hard to believe that Leibniz meant to say that corporeal substances are "only Beings by aggregation, and therefore phenomena," given other things that he says about corporeal substances.

15. For this last point I am indebted to Wallace Anderson. Cf. G II,100/L-A 126.

16. Russell, *A Critical Exposition of the Philosophy of Leibniz*, p. 147.

17. In unpublished papers written at UCLA.

18. A much earlier text in which there is at least a suggestion that aggregates of true substances might not be phenomena is G VII,322/L 365 (dated to 1684 by Hochstetter; see note 21).

19. See Hochstetter, "Von der wahren Wirklichkeit bei Leibniz," and Hector-Neri Castaneda, "Leibniz's Meditation on April 15, 1676 about Existence, Dreams, and Space," *Studia Leibnitiana, Supplementa,* Vol. XVIII (1978) (*Leibniz à Paris,* Tome II), pp. 91–129.

20. Hochstetter, "Von der wahren Wirklichkeit bei Leibniz," p. 431f. This dating presumably reflects the thinking of the staff of the Academy edition as of 1966.

21. This is a convenient way of talking. Leibniz's conceptualism might give rise to some problems about the ontological status of such a story, if we rely heavily on "would be told'.

22. In G VII,563, Leibniz seems to equate "phenomena" with "objects of limited spirits"—which could be taken as implying that God has no phenomena.

23. Perhaps Leibniz recognizes a still weaker sense in which phenomena are "real enough" if they belong to a scientifically adequate system of the harmonious phenomena of a single perceiver.

24. Russell, *A Critical Exposition of the Philosophy of Leibniz,* p. 152.

25. *Ibid.*

26. *Ibid.*

27. See Lestienne's edition of DM, p. 14*n,* in the 1952 or earlier edition (missing from the 1975 edition, in which a new introduction by Andre Robinet replaces some of Lestienne's introductory material).

28. A. Boehm, *Le "vinculum substantiale", chez Leibniz: Ses origines historiques* (Paris: Vrin, 1938)—a very useful book, though Boehm takes remarkably little note of the reasons for denying that the doctrine of the *vinculum* was part of Leibniz's philosophy.

29. Leibniz first wrote 'unity' (*'unité'*) and then changed it to 'unicity' (*'unicité'*). *'Unicité'* was an unusual word, but the best evidence I have found suggests that the change did not weaken the claim of unity but was meant to emphasize that the unity here is original rather than produced. (Cf. the *Oxford English Dictionary* on seventeenth-century use of 'unicity'.) I am indebted to Nicholas Rescher for a comment that helped straighten me out on this point.

30. H. Denzinger, *Enchiridion symbolorum, definionum et declarationum de rebus fidei et morum,* 11th ed. (Freiburg-im-Breisgau: Herder, 1911), p. 19; trans. in the (proposed) *Book of Common Prayer of the Episcopal Church* (1977), p. 865.

10

Leibniz and Spinoza on Substance and Mode

Christia Mercer

For decades, scholars have attributed forms of Spinozism to Leibniz. Because Leibniz heard about Spinoza's *Ethics* in the winter of 1675–76, because he uses Spinozistic terminology in essays of 1676, and because some of his comments reek of Spinozism, it has often been assumed that he was deeply influenced by the thought of Spinoza and it has sometimes been claimed that he was himself a Spinozist for a while in the 1670s. Ludwig Stein began the discussion in 1890 with his proposal that Leibniz went through a "Spinoza freundliche" period between 1676 and 1679.[1] In 1900, Bertrand Russell made the point with characteristic verve: Leibniz "tends with slight alterations of phraseology, to adopt (without acknowledgment) the views of the decried Spinoza."[2] More recently, Robert Adams has claimed that in 1676 Leibniz toyed with Spinozistic pantheism where the latter is taken to be the denial of "the ontological externality" of created things.[3]

In this paper, I argue that Leibniz was never a pantheist of any sort. While it is surely true that he was fascinated with the metaphysics of the *Ethics* and that he responded to the details of Spinoza's system for much of his long life, it is false that Spinozistic pantheism ever seriously tempted him. Once we place the essays of 1676 in their proper historical and philosophical context and once we consider all the relevant texts, the specter of pantheism dissolves and Leibniz's conception of the relation between God and creatures emerges as one in a long line of Platonist accounts. In section 1, I summarize the evidence that scholars have presented for Leibniz's so-called pantheism. In sections 2 and 3, I present the proper theological and philosophical context within which to compare the views of Leibniz and Spinoza. In section 4, I show that, once we place Leibniz's works of 1676 in this context, it is possible to discern for the first time exactly how he conceived the relation between God and creatures. In section 5, I reconsider some of the evidence offered for Leibniz's so-called Spinozistic pantheism and show that it implies neither pantheism nor anything else theologically unorthodox. Finally, in section 6, the substance–mode relation as used by Leibniz is briefly compared to that of Spinoza. Against the historical and philosophical background set in the previous sections, the radical difference between the two positions becomes clear. We can safely conclude that Leibniz was not tempted by Spinozistic pantheism.

1. Leibniz's 'Spinozistic Pantheism'[4]

Leibniz was introduced to the philosophy of the *Ethics* and to Spinoza himself in 1676. According to the standard story of Leibniz's philosophical development, the *earliest* signs of his metaphysics appear in 1679. Therefore, it has been reasonable to assume that a window of opportunity existed in the years 1676–79 within which Leibniz might have absorbed important aspects of Spinoza's thought *before* constructing his own philosophy.[5] The German editors of Leibniz's philosophical papers added significantly to the debate when they published for the first time in 1980 all the notes and papers surrounding Leibniz's first contact with Spinoza's *Ethics*.[6] During the four years Leibniz spent in France (1672–76), his intellectual energies were focused primarily on mathematical and technical problems. The results include the construction of a calculating machine that was successfully demonstrated in early 1675 and the development of the calculus in the autumn of that year. Also in the fall of that year, Leibniz met and became friendly with Ehrenfried Walther von Tschirnhaus, a young nobleman from Saxony, who had spent time in both England and the Netherlands. When Tschirnhaus arrived in Paris, he had a letter of introduction from Henry Oldenburg, the secretary of the Royal Society, to Leibniz; he also had a thorough familiarity with the philosophy of Spinoza, which he had acquired during a lengthy stay in Amsterdam.[7] When Leibniz met Tschirnhaus in September 1675, he found the young man intellectually promising and personally engaging. The two developed a friendly relationship and began working together on mathematical matters.[8] By early 1676, Tschirnhaus had gotten to know Leibniz well enough to trust him with an account of the *Ethics*, or at least an account of its salient features. The brief notes that Leibniz took on their discussion—probably from February 1676—constitute his first reference to that text and indicate that he had gotten the gist of Spinoza's metaphysics. Leibniz writes, for example, that "God alone is substance . . . Creatures are nothing but modes" (VI iii 385). Within days of writing these notes, Leibniz began to produce a number of philosophical essays to which the Academy editors have given the title *De summa rerum* and which cluster around the topic of God and God's relation to creatures. It is in these essays that Leibniz refers to Spinoza, uses Spinozistic terminology, and appears to embrace 'Spinozistic pantheism'.

It is striking that, since the publication of the *De summa rerum* papers, two Leibniz scholars have used them to argue for Leibniz's Spinozism. Independently of one another, Mark Kulstad and Robert Adams have adopted the term 'pantheism' and argued that, while Leibniz was always opposed to some elements in Spinoza's metaphysics, he was not opposed to others. It is interesting that Kulstad and Adams offer the same passages from the *De summa rerum* and related texts as evidence for Leibniz's 'Spinozistic pantheism'.[9] In particular, Leibniz makes three claims that strongly suggest an endorsement of Spinozism. For example, in October 1676, Leibniz took notes on some letters that Oldenburg had received from Spinoza. Leibniz writes: "It can surely be said that all things are one, that all things are in God, in the same way the effect is contained in its full cause [*causa sua plena*] and a property of any subject [is contained] in the essence of that same subject" (VI iii 370). Now, consider a related passage of April 1676, this time from the *De summa rerum* essays:

> It seems to me that the origin of things from God is of the same kind as the origin of properties from an essence; just as $6 = 1 + 1 + 1 + 1 + 1 + 1$, therefore $6 = 3 + 3$, $= 3 \times 2$, $= 4 + 2$, etc. Nor may one doubt that the one expression [unam expressionem] differs from the other, for in one way we think of the number 3 or the number 2 expressly, and in another way we do not; but it is certain that the number 3 is not thought of by someone who thinks of six units at the same time. It would be thought of, if the person were to impose a limit after three had been thought. Much less does someone who thinks of six units at the same time think of multiplication. So just as these properties differ from each other and from essence, so do things differ from each other and from God.[10]

In both of these passages, Leibniz claims that things are related to God as properties are related to essence. About texts like these, Adams asserts: "Leibniz is *not* moved to speak clearly of the world as an additional 'result' *outside* the divine being."[11]

As for the second claim, consider another passage of April 1676 also from the *De summa rerum* essays:

> There is the same variety in any kind of world, and this is nothing other than the same essence related in various ways, as if you were to look at the same town from various places; or, if you relate the essence of the number 6 to the number 3, it will be 3×2 or $3 + 2$ [*sic*], but if you relate it to the number 4 it will be $6/4 = 3/2$, or $6 + 4 \times 3/2$. So it is not surprising that the things produced are in a certain way different. (VI iii 523: Pk 83)

Although the text is not clear, the suggestion is that the divine essence is like a town in that it can be viewed variously and like a number in that it can be expressed in a variety of ways. It follows that, like the different mathematical expressions of the number 6 or the different views of the same town, each creature is different from the others and yet contains the same divine essence. The same point is made more clearly in another text from an essay of the same month:

> The essence of God consists in the fact that he is the subject of all compatible attributes. But any property or affection of God involves his whole essence. . . . But when all other things are related to any attribute, there result modifications [*modificationes*] in it. Hence it comes about that the same Essence of God is expressed wholly [*expressa sit tota*] in any kind of World. (VI iii 514: Pk 69–71)

Here the implication is that a world is a modification of God and thereby expresses or in some sense contains the divine essence.

Finally, most persuasive of all is the fact that Leibniz applies the substance–mode relation to God and creatures. He writes in an essay apparently composed in preparation for his meeting with Spinoza:

> It can easily be demonstrated that all things are distinguished, not as substances (i.e., radically) but as modes. . . . Therefore, the essence of all things is the same, and things differ only modally, just as a town seen from a high point differs from the town seen from a plain. If only those things which are separated are really different or which one can perfectly understand without the other, it follows that no thing really differs from another, but that all things are one, just as Plato argues in the Parmenides.[12]

As Adams reads this passage, "Leibniz flatly affirms the Spinozistic idea that finite things are only modes."[13] Kulstad concurs: "we can easily believe that Leibniz is saying here that God's essence is the essence of all things, and that it follows from this that [finite] things are not separate substances at all, but rather modes or properties of God, contained in God's essence."[14]

On the basis of these and other facts, the following developmental story has suggested itself: Leibniz arrived in Paris in 1672, a young whippersnapper from the (philosophical) backwoods of Germany, with lots of philosophical ideas, but no original system of his own. In Paris, he directed his formidable energies toward mathematical and physical problems. With the invention of the calculus in 1675, he was ripe to return to philosophy. When Tschirnhaus placed the metaphysics of Spinoza at his feet toward the beginning of 1676, Leibniz found it enormously enticing. On his way to Hanover in the autumn of that year, he made a pilgrimage to Amsterdam where he met and exchanged philosophical arguments with Spinoza himself. Over the next few years, Leibniz struggled with Spinozism and other philosophical positions until his own system was born in 1679. This is an impressive developmental story based on a number of well-documented facts.

But it is false. The first point to note is that there are some significant facts that conflict with this story. Perhaps the most damaging of these is that many of the core doctrines of Leibniz's metaphysics are in place in 1671–72.[15] Among these doctrines is the commitment to the self-sufficiency and activity of substance where the idea is that created substances have their own principle or source of activity and hence are metaphysically distinct from God. Once we recognize that Leibniz arrived in Paris with his core metaphysics in hand, it seems much less likely that Spinoza's system would have so overwhelmed him. Another fact that conflicts with our developmental story is that there are a number of passages throughout the Paris period that imply a distinction between God and creatures. As in his pre-Paris texts, Leibniz insists that each created substance has its own principle or source of activity in terms of which its actions can be explained and in terms of which it can be distinguished—as a substance—from God. For example, in an essay written sometime in 1673–75, he explains "that every substance acts [*agere*] and every acting thing [*agens*] is called a substance. Now we can show from the inner principles of metaphysics that what is not active does not exist, for there is not such a thing as mere potentiality to act." Leibniz continues:

> There are certainly many and important things to be said . . . about the principle of activity or what the scholastics called substantial form, from which a great light is thrown on Natural Theology and . . . the mysteries of faith. The result is that not only souls but all substances can be said to exist in a place only through the operation of their active principle, that souls can be destroyed by no power of body; and that every power of acting [*omnem agendi vim*] exists from the highest mind whose will is the final reason for all things, the cause being universal harmony; that God as creator can unite the body to the soul, and that in fact, every finite soul is embodied, even the angels are not excepted.[16]

There is much that is interesting here. What is most important for our purposes, however, is the fact that God creates substances so that, although their power ultimately depends on their divine source, nevertheless the substances have their own power of acting and therefore are distinct from their creator. Roughly, Leibniz's assumption seems to be that, because created substances have their own principle of activity and their own substantial form and because they are embodied in some bit of matter, they are in some obvious sense distinct from God. The texts of 1676 are strewn with evidence of a similar distinction between God and creatures. According to Leibniz, the active things in a world are mind-like substances which are "the true entities" and "are one."[17] He insists that each substance contains its own "principle of individuation" (VI iii 490: Pk 51) by means of which it is distinguished from every other substance (and presumably therefore from God). At times, Leibniz is explicit about the relation between God and creatures: "God does not form part of things, rather, he is their principle."[18]

On the basis of such facts, it is perfectly clear that our original developmental story contains serious mistakes. But these facts themselves do not preclude the possibility that Leibniz went through some sort of Spinozistic frenzy in 1676. While it is surely noteworthy that the young man arrived in Paris with his core metaphysics in tow and that there are signs of that metaphysics in 1676, it remains perfectly possible that, at the heady culmination of his work on the calculus, he found the grandeur of Spinoza's system enticing. Besides the texts that Kulstad and Adams highlight, there are a number of others that, though not exactly Spinozistic, blur the distinction between God and creatures. In fact, throughout 1676, Leibniz is happy both to offer the distinction noted above between the activity of God and that of creature and to blur that distinction. It is clear that, according to Leibniz, God is *in* created things. For example, as part of an account for the indestructibility of creatures, he argues that "*God* is indeed the form of life" so that whatever "participates in life is not able to be distinguished" (VI iii 295). In a related essay, he insists that "there is something divine in mind . . . and this is the same as the omniscience of God" (VI iii 391: Pk 43).

Nor is that all. There are other passages written in 1676 which are even more extreme. Leibniz writes:

> This [divine] mind, like a soul, exists as a whole in the whole body of the World; the existence of things is certainly due to this mind. It is the cause of itself. Existence is nothing other than that which is the cause of consistent perceptions. The reason [*ratio*] of things is the aggregate of all the requisites of things. God comes from God. The whole infinite is one.

Particular minds exist, in short, simply because the highest Being judges it harmonious that there should exist somewhere what understands, or is a certain intellectual mirror, or replica of the world. To exist is nothing other than to be Harmonious; the mark of existence is consistent perceptions. (VI iii 474: Pk 25)

For our purposes, it is particularly important that God is supposed to be *in* the world. When we combine comments like these with the passages taken from the *De summa rerum* and related texts quoted above, we are left with the strong impression that Leibniz's views about the relation between God and creatures are either confused or inconsistent. On the one hand, he suggests that God is distinct from created substances; on the other, he says that God is in creatures *and* that creatures are properties and modes of God. Is there any way of making sense of these claims?

The short answer is yes. I offer an explanation in sections 2 and 3 of how—for Leibniz and many other theists—God is in creatures and creatures are in God. In the process, I show that the query about Leibniz's pantheism is misguided. In fact, the assumption that a pantheist is someone who denies that finite things are "*outside* the divine being" is historically wrong-headed.[19] For the sake of convenience, I center my discussion of Leibniz's 'Spinozistic pantheism' around an analysis of the substance-mode relation as it applies to God and creatures, what I call *the divine substance-mode relation.* There are at least two assumptions at work in the discussions about Leibniz's 'Spinozistic pantheism': (1) the pantheist is someone who denies that created things are ontologically external to God; (2) to use the substance-mode terminology of the Spinozistic sort (that is, to use the divine substance-mode relation) is equivalent to denying the ontological externality of creatures. From these two assumptions it follows that, because Leibniz describes the relation between God and creatures in *De summa rerum* and related texts as that between substance and mode and because he implies that relation in other passages, he was tempted by Spinozistic pantheism, at least for a while. I argue below that both of these assumptions are false. Leibniz's acceptance of the divine substance–mode relation implies nothing about pantheism, of any variety. This becomes clear when we place his use of the substance-mode terminology within two philosophical traditions: Platonist theism and the important (but unnoticed) history of the substance-mode relation. Let's consider each of these in turn.

2. Pantheism, Ontological Externality, and Theism.

Against the history of Judeo-Christian theism, our first assumption seems odd and I believe that most medieval, Renaissance, and early modern philosophers would have taken it to be so. In fact, as far as I can tell, the theism of such thinkers *demanded* that everything depend entirely on God, that everything be *in* God, and that God be *in* everything. The New Testament is full of such demands. As Paul writes to the Ephesians, there is: "One God and Father of all, who is above all, and through all, and *in* you all" (Ephesians 4:6). Concerning the fact that everything is *in* God, consider this passage from Acts: "For in Him we live and move and have our being" (Acts 17:28); while Paul writes to the Romans: God is that "of whom all things are, through whom all things are, *in* whom all things are" (Rom. 11:36). These sorts of biblical passages encouraged early theists, whether the first-century Jew, Philo of Alexandria, or the fourth-century Christian, Augustine of Hippo, to believe that God was *in* everything and everything was *in* God. In brief, within the context of western theism, an insistence on the ontological externality of creatures simply seems wrong-headed. According to the greatest Jewish and Christian thinkers, there is *nothing* external to God and moreover the ontological *inclusion* of creatures *within* the divine is theologically exactly right. Consider these remarkable claims in the eleventh-century *Monologion* by Anselm of Canterbury. First, Anselm explains: "The supreme essence is in and through all things. All things are through and in—and out of—the supreme essence" (sect. 14). Lest we think that there is no distinction between God and creatures, Anselm insists: "This [divine] spirit exists unqualifiedly. Compared to it, created things do not exist" (sect. 28).[20] In the fifteenth century, Marsilio Ficino wrote a letter to a friend that contains a brief dialogue between God and the soul. In Ficino's dialogue, God explains:

> "I am both with you and within you. I am indeed with you, because I am in you; I am in you, because you are in me. If you were not in me you would not be yourself, indeed, you would not be at all." God continues: "Behold, I say, do you not see? I fill heaven and earth, I penetrate and contain them. . . . Behold, do you not see? I pass into everything unmingled, so that I may surpass all; for I am also able to enter and permeate at the same time, to enter completely and to make one, being unity itself, through which all things are made and endure, and which all things seek."

In brief, God exclaims: "in me are all things, out of me come all things and by me are all things sustained forever and everywhere."[21]

Nor were such theists either philosophically or theologically unsophisticated. They were perfectly aware of the grave theological problems that such views about the relation between God and creatures posed. As Augustine nicely makes the point, worrying aloud to God in the *Confessions*: "Without you, whatever exists would not exist. But does what exists contain you? I also have being . . . which I would not have unless you were in me. Or rather, I would have no being if I were not in you" (book I, sect. 2). For such theists, there were two closely related questions: how can creatures be in the transcendent God? and, moreover, how can the transcendent God be in its creatures? For inspiration, early Christians like Augustine turned to Plotinus and Philo, who themselves of course were thoroughly indebted to Plato, or at least their version of Plato. Although I can only sketch an answer to these questions here, let me do that. Concerning the first question, namely, how the creatures can be *in* the transcendent God, theists endorsed a distinction between the supreme Being as wholly independent and as that on which all else depends. Whereas the divinity is self-sufficient and exists independently of all its creatures, the creatures depend fully and constantly on it. In this sense, a creature can be said to exist in God just in case the whole being and nature of the creature depends continually on the divine. To use the language of these philosophers, a creature "exists in" God because the being and nature of the creature "flows from" the divine. The classic analogy is to the sun whose rays depend entirely on it while it depends on nothing.

As to our second question, namely, how the transcendent God is supposed to be *in* its creatures, the same problem occurs in the great Plotinus himself. According to him, the One or Supreme Being is "alone by itself" and simple, while it is also "everywhere" and "fills all things."[22] Before I present the Platonist answer to our second question, it is important to remember that for Philo, Augustine, and many theists, the Platonic Forms or Ideas were taken to be Ideas in the mind of God.[23] Many Renaissance and early modern Platonists considered these Ideas to be the attributes of God, where the basic point was that these attributes were the eternal simple essences which the divine mind conceives and then uses as models for the things of the world. Platonists like Augustine and Philo employed this account of the divine intellect to explain how the transcendent God can be said to be *in* creatures. The explanation depends on the Plotinian notion of emanative causation.[24] Oversimplifying somewhat, the basic assumption is that any product of God contains the divine essence but in an inferior way. If the perfect God has an attribute f, then God can emanate f-ness to a lower being or creature. In the emanative relation, God loses nothing while the creature comes to instantiate f-ness. God remains transcendent and pure, while the creature becomes an imperfect manifestation of the perfect f. The emanative process is assumed to be continual so that the creature will have f just in case God emanates f-ness to it. The point here may be summarized as follows: the *Theory of Emanative*

Causation claims that, for a being A that is more perfect than a being B, A can emanate its attribute f-ness to B in such a way that neither A nor A's f-ness is depleted in any way, while B has f-ness, though in a manner inferior to the way it exists in A. The emanative process is continual so that B will instantiate f-ness if and only if A emanates f-ness to it.

We are now prepared to explain how it is that the divine transcends its products and yet is in them. The perfection and transcendence of God remains unchanged while it continually emanates its attributes to its products, which then have those attributes in an imperfect and hence distinctive manner. Plotinus distinguishes neatly between the transcendent One and its products when he explains that the former "is like the things, which have come to be" except that they are "on their level" and "it [the One] is better" (*Enneads,* VI.8.14.33–34). To put it in non-Plotinian language, the Supreme Being is *in* the creatures in the sense that it emanates its attributes to them; it remains transcendent from them because it neither loses anything in the emanative process nor gives them any part of itself. In the *Confessions,* Augustine suggests that it was Platonists like Plotinus who helped him see the solution to the problem. As he confesses:

> I considered all the other things that are of a lower order than yourself, and I saw that they have not absolute being in themselves, nor are they entirely without being. They are real in so far as they have their being from you, but unreal in the sense that they are not what you are. For it is only that which remains in being without change that truly is. . . . [God] himself [remains] ever unchanged, all things [are made constantly] new. (VII, x–xi)

Here the 'exists in' relation is to be understood in terms of emanation where the basic idea is that attributes or Ideas of the divine emanate to its products and, in that sense, exist in them. The crucial point to understand however is that the attributes exist in the products in a manner *inferior* to the way in which they exist in the Divine. God has f perfectly; creature has it imperfectly. The f-ness of God is not equivalent to the f-ness of the creature. The f-ness of the creature is in Augustine's words "of a lower order." However undivine we may feel, each of us is an emanation of the divine attributes. It might be helpful to summarize the point in the following way: the *Creaturely Inferiority Complex* asserts that every product of the supreme being contains all the attributes that constitute the divine essence though the product instantiates each of those attributes in a manner inferior to the way in which they exist in the supreme being.[25]

Against this background of Platonist theism, we can offer a response to the assumption that pantheism consists in the denial of ontological externality. Unless we are prepared to attribute pantheism to the great theologians of the medieval and Renaissance eras, something is wrong with this account of pantheism. In brief, the moral that I want us to draw from this theistic tale is as follows: although it was a standard belief among Jewish and Christian thinkers that creatures very much existed *in* God (and that God existed *in* creatures), such thinkers nonetheless were able to distinguish between God and creatures. The distinction did not have to do with externality, but rather with inferiority: the creatures were less good in every conceivable way than God.

3. Substance–Mode Relation, Divine and Non-divine

The history of the substance–mode relation in Renaissance and early modern philosophy has not been thoroughly studied. Although much more research needs to be done before the details of this story are in place, here are the facts most relevant to our present concerns.

Fact One. The *divine substance–mode relation* does not exist before the Renaissance.[26] Neither medieval Platonists like Augustine nor scholastic philosophers like Scotus, Aquinas, and Ockham seem to apply the substance-mode terminology to the divinity and its products. While scholastic discussions embrace the view that everything depends on God and that the world is "a perfect likeness" of the divinity,[27] the schoolmen used the full battery of Aristotelian ammunition to distinguish between God and creatures.

Fact Two. With the grand rediscovery and reinterpretation of Platonism in Renaissance Italy, philosophers like Marsilio Ficino and Giovanni Pico della Mirandola began to Platonize Christian metaphysics more thoroughly than had the scholastics.[28] Neither Ficino nor Pico uses the divine substance-mode relation in anything like a technical sense. But in their texts we find the following three claims: (1) God is a substance, (2) there are grades of reality with God at the top, and (3) each grade is (somehow) a mode of the divinity. In Ficino's *Platonic Theology on the Immortality of the Soul,* composed between 1469 and 1474, he displays a hierarchy of being and calls each level a mode.[29] In his *Heptaplus* of 1489 Pico offers an analysis of Genesis and, as part of his account of creation, asserts that there are "five modes in which one thing can be related to another" and in terms of which the relation between God and each grade (*gradus*) of creation can be explained.[30] Although created things can be more or less perfectly related to God,

Pico insists that the divinity is "diffused through everything" and that "everything participates" in God.[31]

Fact Three. By the mid-seventeenth century there had come to be two distinct ways of thinking of the substance-mode relation. Although both assume that the mode exists in the substance and is a determination or modification of the substantial essence, they understand the limitation in different ways. The first, which was applied to the relation between God and creatures, which I have been calling *the divine substance-mode relation,* and which most philosophers believed to be Platonist, assumed that the mode was a limitation of the substantial essence in the sense that it was an inferior manifestation or instantiation of the essence. In this case, the mode is morally and metaphysically inferior to the substance. The second use of the relation, which was applied to created substances, assumed (roughly) that the mode was a determination of the substance in the sense that it was a specific variation or modification of the substantial essence. In the case of the *non-divine substance-mode relation,* the mode is not morally and metaphysically inferior to the substance; rather, it was just a determination or modification of it. Although scholastics like Francisco Suárez discussed the modes of substance, the central place that Descartes gave the relation in his metaphysics was especially influential.[32] For example, in the *Principles of Philosophy,* part 1, art. 64, he writes, "thought and extension may be taken as modes of a substance, in that one and the same mind is capable of having many different thoughts, and one and the same body, with its quantity unchanged, may be extended in many different modes" (AT VIII 31).

A survey of what the standard seventeenth-century philosophical lexicons have to say about *modus* provides a nice history of the substance-mode relation in the century. In the *Lexicon Philosophicum* of 1613, for example, Goclenius approaches his topic from the perspective of Renaissance Platonism. He begins his account of *modus* in the following way: "In the universe, so there might be Perfection, there are diverse grades and modes of things, distributed to them by God. . . . A mode however of a thing is a certain limitation. A mode is the limitation of the divine efficient potential [*divinae potentiae efficientis*]."[33] Goclenius suggests that he is following Plato, Paul, and Augustine in understanding the relation between God and creatures in the way that he does. Among other things, Goclenius claims that God contains "all things . . . eminently," that is, in the best and most excellent way while everything else exists in a "composite" and inferior manner (p. 697). Moreover, although "creatures are not the being [*esse*] of God himself, nonetheless they are in him. . . . [W]hatever is in creatures proceeds from God." According to Goclenius, God is "everything in all things.

. . . [and] is said to be in the things of the universe, that is, in all things and in each thing." We can "understand God through creatures. . . . Indeed, God thinks [*cognoscit*] creatures through his nature; we think God through creatures" (p. 704). Goclenius composed his *Lexicon* prior to Descartes's philosophical writings; it is significant that he does not emphasize the second use of the substance–mode relation. Although he notes that created things have modes and discusses the way in which a mode is a "determination" of the essence of the thing, the primary sense of *modus* in this lexicon concerns its use in describing God's creation of the world.

Now consider Micraelius' *Lexicon Philosophicum* of 1653. In his brief account, he begins by writing,

> A *mode* is the determination of a thing, by which a thing in one way or another obtains essence, e.g., actually or potentially. Therefore, a *mode* does not compose a thing, but distinguishes and determines it. . . . [T]here can be many modes of a single thing . . . so things that differ in modes are not diverse in essence.[34]

For Micraelius, the substance–mode terminology seems to apply both to created and divine substance. Assuming that creatures are modes of God, then it follows that they are "determinations" of the divine essence. They can be different from one another and nonetheless share the same essence. Micraelius goes on to explain that he is following Plato in offering "five modes of created things."[35] He writes: "The five modes, says Plato, are composed out of the *infinite* and the *terminus*" where the former is "the passive potential" of the created world and the latter is "the Platonic God . . . that is, pure act" (p. 667).

By the end of the century, the non-divine substance–mode relation had replaced the divine one in importance. Consider Stephan Chauvin's multi-volume *Lexicon Philosophicum* of 1713. Unlike his predecessors, Chauvin gives prominence to the non-divine substance–mode relation. He begins with an account of a mode as "determination toward fixed being" and then discusses the views of "the Cartesians" and other "recent philosophers." Eventually, Chauvin turns to the relation between God and creatures. After explaining that God "is most simple and perfect" and contains the attributes of "all things," he notes that created substances are subject to imperfection, variation, and change.[36]

Fact Four. Encouraged by their Renaissance Platonist predecessors, many early modern philosophers took themselves to be following the "divine Plato" in applying the substance–mode relation to that of God and creatures. It was common for seventeenth-century thinkers to con-

ceive the relation between God and creatures as that between substance and mode where the assumption was that creatures exist in the
divine essence and manifest that nature in an inferior way.

Consider two examples. Anne Conway distinguished clearly between
God and creatures and yet happily proclaimed that "God is present in
all things and immediately fills all things."[37] Or turn to a less well known
figure, Johann Adam Scherzer, who was professor of Hebrew and theology at the university in Leipzig at exactly the time when Leibniz studied
there. In the textbooks by Scherzer, we find a thorough discussion of
kabbalism and Renaissance Platonism. He refers to Plato, Plotinus,
Philo, Proclus, Augustine, and the Christian kabbalist Johann Reuchlin.
In his *Vade mecum*, Scherzer makes several points that are especially
relevant to our present discussion. He says that he is following Plato in
the second book of the *Republic* when he defines God as what "remains simple" while being "most beautiful . . . and most good." Embracing the causal doctrine of emanation, Scherzer claims that the supreme being is the principle of all things and their constant source: "in
acting . . . [God] is neither changed nor depleted" and yet "is that
through which things live." He claims to follow Marsilio Ficino and
other Platonists by conceiving of God as "the light itself . . . , the reason
of reasons, the fount and maker of all things, the uniform and omni-
form form . . . , the unity in the multitude." According to Scherzer,
the supreme being contains all things while remaining fundamentally
simple, and acts constantly to conserve creatures while "nothing in him
is changed, nor is it depleted."[38] Scherzer distinguishes between the
archetypal world and the created world, where the former is the Idea
of all possible things as they exist in the mind of God and the latter is
the coordinated aggregate of created things. Scherzer's conception of
the divine and its relation to the created world is clear. The mind of
God contains the Platonic Ideas or archetypes; the creatures of the
world are manifestations of these Ideas. The former are perfect, the
latter are not; yet the perfection of God is evident in the composition
and harmony of created things.[39] In sum, Scherzer accepts the Theory
of Emanative Causation and the Creaturely Inferiority Complex.

Fact Five. Many seventeenth-century authors consider the cosmol-
ogy of the Stoics to be the paradigm case of an unorthodox account of
nature. Although I have not found uses of the word 'pantheism', the
point is clear: the Stoics are those philosophers who do not distinguish
sufficiently between natural things and their source. The very Renaissance and early modern Platonists who happily use the divine substance-mode terminology insist that they are not like the Stoics in that
they (the Platonists) *do* distinguish sufficiently between God and nature.

In this context, consider Leibniz's *Doktorvater* in Leipzig, Jakob Thomasius. Although the standard accounts of seventeenth-century German philosophy describe Thomasius as a relatively conservative scholastic and although he was well known among his contemporaries as a defender of the Aristotelian philosophy, he was thoroughly conversant with the details of Platonism and had an impressive grasp of the other great ancient systems.[40] For example, his *Exercitatio* is an extended comparison of the philosophies of the Stoics, the Aristotelians, and the Platonists on a long list of philosophical and theological topics.[41] In his text, Thomasius refers to the whole range of pagan and Christian Platonic philosophers. One of his general conclusions is that Platonism is on the whole much less heretical than Stoicism, although he insists that all ancient pagan philosophers must be approached with caution. He agrees with Scherzer that God, who is thoroughly perfect and simple, is the source of all things.[42] Thomasius claims that the supreme being is "the fountain of features which flow into creatures" and he is happy to accept Augustine's conclusion that "God contains all things in himself," but he insists that this flowing or emanation be understood in the right way. For Thomasius, it is enormously important to understand that the flowing is controlled by God's will[43] and that the divine is properly transcendent. In short, Thomasius accepts the general features of the account of God and the relation between God and creatures offered by Scherzer, although he often goes into many more details than the latter does.

Thomasius's *Exercitatio* is an important work for our purposes. As an extended comparison between the philosophies of the Stoics, the Aristotelians, and the Platonists, it contains a careful explication of the relation between God and creatures. Explicitly drawing on the ideas of Plato, Plotinus, and later Platonists, Thomasius offers a fascinating variation on the Platonist theme of an hierarchy of dependence. Thomasius is concerned to explain in a thoroughly orthodox manner exactly how God is related to creatures and how creatures are related to one another and to God. In his discussion of these difficult topics he is keen to turn the Stoic notion of a World Soul, which he considers heretical, into something both theologically correct and metaphysically useful. Concerning the relation among creatures and their relation to God, Thomasius cites a number of authors who claim that the "essence of God permeates" the world so that there is an "effusion of vital spirit." He points out that some philosophers have wanted to identify "the Agent Intellect of Aristotle with the Platonic Soul of the World" and have claimed that "the Agent Intellect participates in divinity." Thomasius agrees with the basic assumptions here that the World Soul *permeates* all creatures and connects them all together and moreover that there is a close relation among creatures in that they all exist within "the living spirit" and "light of God."[44]

But Thomasius also insists that such claims smack of heresy and incoherence unless we clarify the notion of a World Soul and avoid the mistakes of the Stoics. Thomasius agrees with those philosophers who claim that "everything is God and God is everything," but he demands that we understand exactly the relation between God and nature. According to Thomasius, it is important to grasp that everything "is wholly part of the divine" and yet that God himself is not *in* nature. In other words, Thomasius also accepts the Theory of Emanative Harmony and the Creaturely Inferiority Complex; and he wants to distinguish clearly between creatures and God. He writes,

> Things are in God as in a fount and first cause, i.e., most eminently; secondly, they are in Mind as Ideas and form; thirdly, they are in Soul as reasons [rationes] placed in its essence; fourthly, they are in Nature as seeds, for nature is the seminal power effused in universal matter by the soul of the World. Fifth, they are in Matter, although as a shadow, through imitation and participation.[45]

The details of Thomasius's proposals are both fascinating and difficult. What is particularly worth our attention is the fact that the hierarchy here is such that what is more complicated and divisible is supposed to depend on and be explained by what is more simple and unified. He writes: "As Mind depends on God, [and] Soul on Mind, so Nature depends on Soul."[46] It is important to grasp the exact nature of this dependence relation. Thomasius says that the higher stratum is the principle of the lower and contains "eminently" what the lower stratum "participates in" or has "formally." Thomasius summarizes his point: "As mind receives Ideas from God, Soul receives reasons [*rationes*] from mind; so nature receives seeds from soul."[47] The dependence relation here assumes the Theory of Emanative Causation: each higher level in the hierarchy causes the next lower stratum and has more perfectly what the lower has in a less perfect way. Moreover, each higher stratum remains transcendent while also being immanent in the lower. In the same way that the Plotinian One contains everything perfectly, so does Thomasius's God; in the same way that each level in the Plotinian hierarchy contains less perfectly what the higher level contains more perfectly, so does each stratum in Thomasius's system.

But what about the substance–mode relation? According to Thomasius, the divine mind contains the Platonic Ideas which are "mental modes" of God and "the exemplars and archetypes" of things.[48] The Ideas are in a sense the ingredients of all other things; each level in the hierarchy is a mode of God, though each level is more inferior than the one just above it. So far, so good. But what exactly is "the World Soul"? According to Thomasius, "the reasons [*rationes*]" of the World Soul must contain the being of the Ideas though in a less perfect and less unified way. In other words, the Ideas must be transcendent from and yet immanent in the reasons in the World Soul. A fairly obvious way of making sense of this is to suppose that "the reasons [*rationes*]" are the complex essences or blueprints for the individuals in the created world. They are complex instantiations of the Ideas. In this case, the World Soul is the collection of such essences or blueprints; it is the fully articulated blueprint for the actual world. This interpretation of the World Soul successfully explains how it "depends on" Mind and how the seeds contain formally what the Ideas contained eminently. Moreover, this interpretation helps to explain Thomasius's account of nature. According to Thomasius, nature is "the power [*virtutem*] of the seeds infused into Matter by the World Soul."[49] The World Soul is God's plan for the actual world; nature is the instantiation of that plan in matter. Thomasius claims that there are great benefits to this account of the World Soul. In particular, he thinks that it helps to make sense of the relation between the Ideas of God and the world. According to Thomasius, he successfully explains how created things can be said to come from the supreme being and yet be distinct from it. He also avoids the problems which the theory of the Stoics faces because, unlike that account, his account does not conflate God and the World Soul. Rather, it makes it clear that the Ideas are not in matter, although the seminal powers are.[50] It is Thomasius's view that he successfully *explains* how created things can be said to depend on the supreme being and yet be distinct from it.[51] In fact, it is Thomasius's explanation of the difference between God and creatures that distinguishes him— and his precocious student Leibniz—from some other early modern Platonists. By telling a coherent story about how the Ideas or attributes of God are first manifested in a plan of the world which itself is then instantiated in the individual essences of the world, Thomasius makes sense of the claims that everything is contained in God and yet inferior to the divine nature.

Let's take stock of the facts of this section. As our story suggests, there were different ways to use the substance–mode terminology in the early modern period and moreover there were lots of Renaissance and early modern thinkers who made ample use of the divine substance-mode relation and yet drew a careful distinction between the divinity and its products. For our purposes here, it is especially important that many thinkers embraced the utter ontological dependence of creatures on God, described creatures as "modes" of God, and yet would have staunchly denied that they were in any way contaminated by (what twentieth century scholars have called) *pantheism*. Therefore, the use of the substance–mode terminology of the Spinozistic sort (that is, the application of the substance–mode terminology to God and creatures) need not imply pantheism or anything else unorthodox. It follows that the conclusion about Leibniz is shown to be unwarranted: that is, by describing the relation between God and creatures as that between substance and mode, it by no means follows that Leibniz is a pantheist.

4. Leibniz's Platonism

Well, if Leibniz wasn't a pantheist, then what *was* he and how exactly does he differ from Spinoza? Nearly from the beginning of his philosophical career, Leibniz accepted both the Theory of Emanative Causation and the Creaturely Inferior Complex. That is, as a young man, he believed that God continually emanates the divine essence to all creatures and he conceived of each creature as an inferior instantiation of that essence. Concerning the Theory of Emanative Causation, consider the following two very early texts. In the well-known *Dissertation on the Combinatorial Art* of 1666, Leibniz briefly turns to the topic of the relation between God and creatures. After the title page of the published text, Leibniz presents some "corollaries" which are supposed to follow from this combinatory art and which fall into four categories: logic, metaphysics, physics, and practical. One of the metaphysical corollaries is "God is substance; creature is accident."[52] Throughout the 1660s, Leibniz uses the Latin term (*accidens*) in a fairly standard scholastic way: an accident is a non-essential property that can be said "to flow" from the essence of the thing of which it is a property. Micraelius, for example, writes in his *Lexicon Philosophicum* that an accidental property "flows from the essential principles" although it is not "part of the essential constituents."[53] Leibniz's use of this term in describing the relation between God and creatures is important. It implies that creatures both flow from God's nature and reflect that nature, but do not do so necessarily. The text suggests that Leibniz had accepted the Platonic conception of God promulgated by his teachers. Or consider another early text, this time of 1668. For the very first time, Leibniz presents some of the details of the general relation between God and creatures. He proclaims his account to be similar to "Plato in the Timaeus about the world soul" and to "Aristotle in the Metaphysics and Physics about the agent Intellect." Like these other philosophers, he maintains that God is "diffused through everything."[54]

According to the Theory of Emanative Causation, the attributes of God constitute the metaphysical elements out of which individuals are made. According to Leibniz in 1676, when these attributes are combined or related to one another, modifications of them arise. In one of the passages from April 1676 that was quoted in section 1 and that is offered as evidence of his Spinozistic pantheism, Leibniz writes: "from the conjunction of simple possible forms there result modifications, that is, ideas, as properties result from essence" (VI iii 521: Pk 81). The point is that, when simple forms are combined, modifications of the essence of God result "just as properties result from essence." In another essay of April 1676, entitled *On forms or the attributes of God,* Leibniz elaborates. Concerning the creator, he makes it clear that "the essence of God consists in the fact that he is the subject of all compatible attributes." Concerning the products of God, Leibniz claims that "any property or affection of God involves his whole essence." For Leibniz, when God produces something, regardless of how small, it "involves" the divine nature (VI iii 514: Pk 69–71). He writes in a related essay, "modifications [*modificationes*] . . . are what result from all other forms taken together." They have an "infinite variety" which "can only result from an infinite cause" (VI iii 522: Pk 83). That is, modifications come about when divine attributes are combined; such combinations always contain all the divine attributes. Each modification is a product of the whole essence of God and therefore of all the divine attributes; it is in this sense that each modification of God will contain the whole divine essence.

When we piece together these and other clues, they yield a creation story that is very similar to Thomasius's account: the Platonic Ideas or attributes of God are combined so as to form blueprints of individual things; each of these blueprints is a "product" or "modification" of God and in that sense contains the divine essence. As Leibniz puts it in *On forms or the attributes of God,* when the attributes or "forms" of God are "related to one another, modifications result; hence it comes about that the same essence of God is expressed as a whole in any kind of world and, therefore, that God manifests himself in infinite ways [*modis*]" (VI iii 524: Pk 71). Moreover, according to Leibniz, individual substances result when these modifications are instantiated in an active subject. He exclaims: "It is a wonderful thing that a subject is different from forms or attributes. . . . Thought is not duration, but what thinks is something that endures. And this is the difference between substance and forms" (VI iii 514: Pk 69). That is, because substances are active things, they are not only the sorts of things that can endure, they can also instantiate properties. As he writes: "The correct way of considering the matter is that forms are conceived through themselves;

subjects, and the fact that they are subjects, are conceived through forms." In brief, "particulars result" when attributes or forms "are combined with a subject" (VI iii 514: Pk 69–71). According to Leibniz, a subject is that which has a mind or principle of activity. Each subject or substance will be a modification of divine attributes. God produces modifications through the combinations of the divine attributes or forms and then instantiates these in subjects. As Leibniz summarizes the point in a related essay: "I cannot explain how things result from forms other than by analogy with the way in which numbers result from units—with this difference, that all units are homogeneous, but forms are different" (VI iii 523: Pk 85). Since each subject is an instantiated modification and each modification is a combination of all the divine attributes, each substance will be an instantiation of the divine essence. Leibniz embraces this consequence. In a passage that was offered in section 1 as support of his pantheism, he writes: "It seems to me that the origin of things from God is of the same kind as the origin of properties from an essence; just as $6 = 1 + 1 + 1 + 1 + 1 + 1$, therefore $6 = 3 + 3, = 3 \times 2, = 4 + 2$, etc. Nor may one doubt that the one expression differs from the other. . . . So just as these properties differ from each other and from essence, so do things differ from each other and from God" (VI iii 518f: Pk 77). Each created substance is an expression of God's essence and in this sense each has the same essence.

An obvious question arises at this point. The Creaturely Inferiority Complex insists that each creature contains the divine attributes but in a manner inferior to their divine source. What exactly does Leibniz have to say about this topic? Although there is evidence that Leibniz endorsed the view as early as 1671, he is most explicit about it in the spring of 1676, that is, at exactly the time when he uses what is supposed to be the dreaded Spinozistic substance-mode terminology.[55] In 1676, he is clear about the fact that it is appropriate "to ascribe" the divine features to the things of the world. For example, he claims that a creature has the immeasurability of God if it can be said to be somewhere; it has the omniscience of God if it can be said to perceive. But he also insists that, strictly speaking, the absolute affirmative attributes of God are not *in* the world. For example, he writes in April that God "contains the absolute affirmative form that is ascribed in a limited way to other things." According to Leibniz, it is appropriate to ascribe the attributes of God to creatures, but it remains true that "God is not part of our mind" nor is the supreme being *in* any of the creatures which participate in the divine attributes.[56] In another essay of April, Leibniz writes, "all things are in a way contained in all things. But they are contained in a quite different way in God from that in which they are contained in things."[57]

5. Leibniz's Distinction between God and Creatures

Against the background set by Platonist theism in general and the history of the divine substance-mode relation in particular, the specter of Leibniz's Spinozistic pantheism dissolves. In fact, most Platonists in the history of philosophy would have found the demand for ontological externality bizarre. For them, there is *nothing* external to God and moreover the ontological dependence of creatures on God is theologically exactly right. In this context, we should remember that Leibniz's mentor, Jakob Thomasius, had written a long book in which he describes in detail the heresies of the Stoics and notes exactly how Platonist theism differs from it.[58] Leibniz was thoroughly acquainted with the dangers of Stoicism and fully aware of the significant differences between that philosophical option and the Platonist accounts of the relation between God and creatures. In short, to claim that these passages from Leibniz's Paris writings imply pantheism is to misunderstand a major tradition in the history of philosophy. Once we place Leibniz's comments within the Platonist tradition to which they belong, they prove to be no more pantheistic than similar passages in the texts of Augustine, Philo of Alexandria, Pico della Mirandola, Thomasius, Scherzer, and a hundred other philosophers who share Leibniz's Platonist leanings.

Furthermore, for every passage in Leibniz's writings that smacks of pantheism, there are several others (sometimes in the very same text) that suggest otherwise. An essay of March 1676, *Notes on Science and Metaphysics,* summarizes his position about the relation between God and creatures: "God does not form part of things, rather, he is their principle" (VI iii 392: Pk 45). For a more complicated example, let's return once more to a text that was offered in section 1 as support of Leibniz's pantheism and that was discussed in the preceding section. In *On Forms or the Attributes of God,* Leibniz writes, "any property or affection of God involves his whole essence. . . . When all the other attributes [of God] are related to any one of them, there result in it modifications, whence it happens that the same Essence of God is expressed as a whole in any kind of World, and so that God manifests himself in infinite modes" (VI iii 514: Pk 69). Adams has taken this passage as evidence of Leibniz's pantheistic tendencies. As he puts it: "What is striking here is that Leibniz is *not* moved to speak clearly of the world as an additional "result" *outside* the divine being."[59] But Leibniz could not have been so moved. Nor does *On Forms or the Attributes of God* leave the point unexplained. In the words that immediately follow the above quotation, Leibniz is explicit about exactly how he understands the ontological dependency between the divine essence and its products. He writes,

> Whatever is conceived per se, its cause cannot be understood. For an effect is conceived through its cause, from which it is evident that, if something exists through itself, and also if other things exist, then it exists. The correct way of considering the matter is that forms are conceived through themselves; subjects and the fact that they are subjects are conceived through the forms. But that whose modifications depend on the attributes of another, in which all its requisites are contained, is conceived through another. That is, it cannot be perfectly understood unless the other is understood. Those things are connected of which the one cannot be understood without the other. Requisites are those things which are connected with one another. (VI.iii.514–15: Pk 71)

In this passage, Leibniz offers a precise statement of the relation between an emanative cause and its product: the latter depends on the former, is conceived through the former, and cannot be understood without it. He also indicates exactly why this kind of relation is theologically good: if a creature were fully independent of God, then an understanding of its nature would not lead to an understanding of its divine cause.[60] For theists like Leibniz, the ontological inclusion of creatures in the divine is a *good* thing. As Augustine exclaims to God in the first lines of the *Confessions*: "I would have no being if I were not in you." Or, in Scherzer's words, God "is that through which things live" and "the unity in the multitude."[61]

6. Leibniz and Spinoza on Substance and Mode

This brings us to the real difference between Leibniz and Spinoza on substance and mode. Unlike Leibniz, when Spinoza applied the substance–mode model to God and creatures, he was doing something radical: he was not applying the divine substance-mode relation; rather, he was applying the non-divine one. For Spinoza, each mode is a limitation or variation of the divine nature, but it is not ontologically inferior to the divine nature, at least not in the way that it was for Leibniz: nowhere in Spinoza's account of individual created things do we find evidence either of the Theory of Emanative Causation or the Creaturely Inferiority Complex.[62] Leibniz, on the other hand, has in mind the divine substance-mode relation where God contains the divine attributes in an *entirely different manner* than do creatures. For Leibniz, there is a hierarchy of perfection, dependence, and explanation; for Spinoza, there is none of these things. When Spinoza took the non-divine substance–mode relation and applied it to the relation between God and the world, he was turning the Platonist tradition on its head. It is no wonder that his contemporaries were confused and upset. There is also little wonder that, after the publication of Spinoza's *Ethics*, the substance–mode terminology dropped out of common currency, even among Platonists. Philosophers like Leibniz, who accepted the divine substance-mode relation, wanted to distance themselves from the heretical views of this rash Dutchman. But, despite the fact that Leibniz changed his terminology, he did not change his views. As he wrote in the *Discourse on Metaphysics* of 1686: "Now, first of all it is very evident that created substances depend upon God, who preserves them and who even produces them continually by a kind of emanation, just as we produce our thoughts" (AG 46). And, at the end of his life, in his famous *Monadology,* he explains that "God alone is the primitive unity or the original simple substance; all created or derivative monads are products, and are generated so to speak by continual fulgurations of the divinity . . . limited by the receptivity of the creature, to which it is essential to be limited" (AG 219).[63]

Leibniz was not influenced by Spinoza in his use of the substance–mode relation, nor was he tainted by Spinozistic pantheism. Rather, Leibniz stood in a long line of illustrious Platonists in his conception of the relation between God and creatures. Spinoza, on the other hand, rejected that tradition and set out to do something very different.

Notes

1. See his *Leibniz und Spinoza* (Berlin: Georg Reimer, 1890), chapter V.

2. Russell, *A Critical Exposition of the Philosophy of Leibniz,* 2nd ed. (Northampton: John Dickens, 1967), p. 5.

3. See Adams, *Leibniz: Determinist, Theist, Idealist* (Oxford: Oxford University Press, 1994), p. 128.

4. It would be interesting to do a more thorough study of the use of the term 'pantheism' in the early modern period in general and in reference to Spinoza in particular. On the basis of somewhat cursory research, the following two points seem true: neither Spinoza nor his contemporaries use the term to refer to Spinoza's metaphysics; it was probably not until the eighteenth century that his metaphysics was described as pantheistic. Moreover, Edwin Curley has persuasively argued that Spinoza himself is not a pantheist if we take the term to refer to someone who identifies God with nature. In this context, I find it awkward to ask whether or not Leibniz was a 'Spinozistic pantheist'. However, because other scholars use this terminology, it seems unavoidable to employ it here. For the history of pantheism, see Michael Levine's *Pantheism,* p. 17; for Curley's views, see his *Behind the Geometrical Method: A Reading of Spinoza's*

Ethics (Princeton, N.J.: Princeton University Press, 1988), passim. On this topic, also see Y. Yovel's forthcoming *God and Nature.*

5. A. Robinet has made the most convincing case for the view that 1679 was a pivotal year in the development of Leibniz's philosophy. According to Robinet, it was in the summer of that year that Leibniz decided to "rehabilitate the substantial forms." Therefore, Robinet concludes that 1679 marks the birthdate of Leibniz's mature philosophy. See his *Architectonique Disjonctive Automates Systémiques et Idéalité Transcendantale dans L'oeuvre de G. W. Leibniz* (Paris: J. Vrin, 1986), sections 4.5; 5.9. Many subsequent scholars have accepted Robinet's conclusions. For example, Adams credits Robinet for the "pinpointing" of this "momentous decision." See Adams, *Leibniz,* 236, note 40. See also Paul Lodge, "When Did Leibniz Adopt Pre-established Harmony?" *Archiv für Geschichte der Philosophie,* forthcoming, sect. III. Kulstad is one of the few scholars who has worked on Leibniz's philosophy of the 1670s and yet does not accept Robinet's conclusions. Kulstad offers convincing alternative readings of the most important passages on which Robinet builds his point. See "Causation and Preestablished Harmony," in *Causation in Early Modern Philosophy,* ed. Steven Nadler (University Park: Pennsylvania State University Press, 1993), sections II–III.

6. I refer here to the Akademie der Wissenschaften edition of Leibniz's works whose full title is *G. W. Leibniz: Sämtliche Schriften und Briefe* (Berlin, 1923–). The essays relevant to Leibniz's relation to Spinoza's *Ethics* are in Series VI, vol. III. In the remainder of this paper, I refer to the Academy edition frequently. I abbreviate my references as follows: large roman numerals = series number, small roman numerals = volume number, arabic numerals = page number. For example, VI ii 44 = series six, volume two, page four hundred forty-four.

7. Mark Kulstad has written an interesting paper on the philosophical relations between Leibniz, Tschirnhaus, and Spinoza during this time. The paper, entitled "Leibniz, Spinoza, and Tschirnhaus: Philosophical Relations," was presented at the American Philosophical Association, December, 1998.

8. E.J. Aiton, *Leibniz: A Biography* (Bristol: Adam Hilger, 1985), 55f.

9. Although I disagree with his conclusion, I find the argument offered by Kulstad more subtle and convincing than the one put forward by Adams. See Kulstad, "Did Leibniz Incline toward Monistic Pantheism in 1676?" Internationaler Leibniz-Kongress, 1994, pp. 424–28.

10. VI iii 518f. For a fine English translation of some of the *De summa rerum* essays, see G. H. R. Parkinson, *G.W. Leibniz: De summa rerum: Metaphysical Papers 1675–76* (Yale University Press, 1992), p. 77. Hereafter, Pk.

11. Adams, *Leibniz,* p. 126.

12. VI iii 573: Pk 93–95. About the essay, see VI iii 571 as well as the editors' introduction, p. xxix.

13. Adams, *Leibniz,* p. 129.

14. Kulstad, "Did Leibniz Incline toward Monistic Pantheism in 1676?" p. 428.

15. For the complete argument to this conclusion, see my *Leibniz's Meta-*

physics: Its Origins and Development (New York: Cambridge University Press, 2000), especially chapters 6–9.

16. VI iii 158. This text is translated in P.P. Wiener, *Leibniz: Selections* (New York: Scribner and Sons, 1951), pp. 64–65.

17. VI iii 510: Pk 61. See also VI iii 393: Pk 49.

18. VI iii 392: Pk 45. Adams and Kulstad both acknowledge that this and some other passages have a non-Spinozistic ring.

19. Adams, *Leibniz*, p. 128.

20. *Saint Anselm: Basic Writings,* ed. by S. N. Deane (La Salle, Ill.: Open Court, 1982), pp. 60, 87.

21. *The Letters of Marsilio Ficino,* preface by P. O. Kristeller (Suffolk: Shepeard-Walwyn, 1975), vol. I, p. 36.

22. Plotinus, *Enneads,* III.8.4. The standard English translation is by A.H. Armstrong (Cambridge, Mass.: Harvard University Press, 1990).

23. Plotinus's notion of the realm of Ideas is more complicated, and I will just ignore it here.

24. It is not at all clear that Plotinus himself employs an emanative theory of causation. For our purposes, however, it is sufficient that many Renaissance and early modern Platonists came to think of the causal relation between God and creatures as emanative and that many took Plotinus to have proposed such a theory.

25. There is a more thorough discussion of this and related topics in Mercer, *Leibniz's Metaphysics: Its Origins and Development,* chapter 5. My account here partly developed out of the very helpful discussions in Eileen O'Neill's *"Influxus Physicus": Causation in Early Modern Philosophy,* ed. Steven Nadler (University Park, Pa.: Pennsylvania State University Press, 1993), pp. 27–55; and in Dominic J. O'Meara, "The Hierarchical Ordering of Reality in Plotinus," *The Cambridge Companion to Plotinus,* ed. Lloyd Gerson (Cambridge: Cambridge University Press, 1996), pp. 66–81.

26. As noted at the end of sect. 1, the *divine substance–mode relation* is the substance–mode relation as it applies to the relation between God and creatures.

27. See *Summa contra Gentiles* II, 45 [2–3] where Aquinas is happy to admit that there is more than "one grade of being" and that "the presence of multiplicity and variety among created things was necessary so that the perfect likeness of God might be found in things according to their manner of being."

28. For a general introduction to the thought of Ficino and Pico and to the vast literature on these important Renaissance figures, see Charles Schmitt and Quentin Skinner, *The Cambridge History of Renaissance Philosophy* (Cambridge: Cambridge University Press, 1988), passim; and see Charles Schmitt and Brian Copenhaver, *Renaissance Philosophy* (Oxford: Oxford University Press, 1992), passim. While it is true that Platonism was rediscovered in the Renaissance, it is also true that there is a significant amount of medieval Platonism extant in the thought of our scholastic heroes.

29. See e.g. *Theologia Platonica,* Book II, chpt. XI.

30. *Heptaplus,* VI, 2. The Latin of the quotation is: "quinque modos . . . ,

quibus coniungi aliquid alicui potest." See *De hominis Dignitate, Heptaplus, De Ente et Uno, e scritti Vari,* ed. Eugenio Garin (Florence, 1942), pp. 312–14. For an English translation, see *On the Dignity of Man, On Being and One, Heptaplus,* trans. by Charles G. Wallis, Paul J. W. Miller and Douglas Carmichael (Indianapolis: Bobbs-Merrill, 1965), pp. 141–42.

31. *Ibid.* VII, Proem; Garin, p. 328; Wallis, p. 148.

32. For some suggestive remarks about the difference between some scholastic accounts of mode and Descartes's conception, see Dennis Des Chene, *Physiologia: Natural Philosophy in Late Aristotelian and Cartesian Thought* (Ithaca, N.Y.: Cornell University Press, 1996), pp. 131–33. For some of Suárez's more succinct accounts of mode, see *Disputationes metaphysicae* (1597; repr. by Georg Olms Verlag, 1965), Disp. 7, sect. 1, 18.

33. Rodolph Goclenius, *Lexicon Philosophicum* (Frankfurt, 1613; reprinted by Georg Olms Verlag, 1980), p. 694.

34. Johann Micraelius, *Lexicon Philosophicum terminoruom Philosophis unitatorum* (Jena, 1653), p. 666.

35. Although Pico describes them differently, it is striking that he also offers five modes of created things. See Garin, p. 312–14; for an English translation, see Wallis et al., pp. 141–42.

36. Stephan Chauvin, *Lexicon Philosophicum,* 2nd ed. (Leovardia, 1713; reprinted by Stern-Verlag Janssen & Co, 1967), pp. 412–13.

37. Anne Conway, *Principia Philosophiae Antiquissimae & Recentissimae* (Amsterdam, 1690), book V, sect. 4. For the best English translation, see *The Principles of the Most Ancient and Modern Philosophy,* ed. A. Coudert and T. Corse (Cambridge: Cambridge University Press, 1996), p. 25.

38. Scherzer, *Vade mecum sive manuale philosophicum quadripartitum* (Leipzig, 1686), pp. 52–53. This textbook went through at least five editions; the one cited here is the fourth.

39. Scherzer, *Vade mecum,* p. 137. For a more complete discussion of Scherzer's views, see my "Humanist Eclecticism in Seventeenth-Century Germany," in *London Studies in the History of Philosophy,* ed. Jill Kraye and Martin Stone (London: Routledge, 1999), vol 1.

40. I have not come across any accurate account of Thomasius and his work in the secondary literature. For a more thorough account of his views and for citations to the little that has been written on him, see my *Leibniz's Metaphysics: Its Origins and Development,* passim.

41. We tend to think of Thomasius as an Aristotelian because that is how Leibniz described his illustrious teacher. E.g., At VI ii 426, Leibniz claims that Thomasius is the "most celebrated German Peripatetic." But Thomasius was much more than that. He wrote a number of books explicating and then comparing ancient philosophies. He was obviously well-versed in Stoicism, Platonism, and other ancient ideas. Although he tends to agree with Aristotle, he takes Platonism very seriously. The full title of the book that I here discuss is *Exercitatio de Stoica mundi exustione: cui accesserunt argumenti varii sed inprimis ad historiam Stoicae philosophiae facientes, dissertationes XXI,* 1676.

42. Thomasius, *Exercitatio*, p. 189.

43. Thomasius, *Exercitatio*, pp. 249–53.

44. Thomasius, *Exercitatio*, pp. 215–17.

45. Thomasius, *Exercitatio*, p. 188.

46. Thomasius, *Exercitatio*, p. 188.

47. Thomasius, *Exercitatio*, p. 190.

48. Thomasius, *Exercitatio*, p. 191.

49. Thomasius, *Exercitatio*, p. 190.

50. Thomasius, *Exercitatio*, pp. 190–91.

51. Thomasius, *Exercitatio*, pp. 190–91.

52. VI i 229: L 75. Scherzer defines accidental emanation as what follows "naturally from a subject as a result of its properties or modes." See Scherzer, *Vade mecum,* p. 67.

53. For a brief account of the scholastic notion, see Gracia, *Introduction to the Problem of Individuation in the Early Middle Ages,* 176. For some of Leibniz's uses, see VI i 13–16, 91, 483, 503.

54. Although part of the remainder of this provocative text is illegible, the gist of Leibniz's proposals seem clear. The relevant text in the Academy edition reads as follows (with the illegible bits in the text marked with dots by the editors): "Ipse Plato in Timeo animam mundi, Aristoteles in Metaphysicis et Physicis Intellectum agentem per omnia diffusum, Stoici Substantiam Mundi Deum statuentes, Averroes Aristotelis Intellectum . . . propagans, Fracastorius et Fernelius Originem Formarum . . . in hoc consentiunt omnes: Substantiam, naturam, principium. . . ." See VI i 511.

55. For the textual evidence that Leibniz was committed to the Creaturely Inferiority Complex as early as 1671, see VI i 485; for a lengthy discussion of this and related points, see my *Leibniz's Metaphysics: Its Origins and Development,* chapter 9, sect. 2.

56. VI iii 520: Pk 79f. For more details about the inferiority of creatures, see my *Leibniz's Metaphysics: Its Origins and Development,* chapter 10, sect. 3.

57. VI.iii.523: Pk 85. For a fuller account of Leibniz's conception of the relation between God and creatures, see my *Leibniz's Metaphysics: Its Origins and Development,* chapters 9–10.

58. Thomasius, *Exercitatio de Stoica mundi exustione: cui accesserunt argumenti varii, sed inprimis ad historiam Stoicae philosophiae facientes, dissertationes XXI,* Leipzig, 1676.

59. See Adams, *Leibniz,* 128; Adams's emphasis.

60. The most significant evidence offered for the thesis that Leibniz briefly flirted with Spinozistic pantheism in 1676 is the following passage from a text of November 1676, part of which was quoted in section 1: "It can easily be demonstrated that all things are distinguished, not as substances (i.e., radically) but as modes. This can be demonstrated from the fact that, of those things which are radically distinct, one can be perfectly understood without the other; that is, all the requisites of the one can be understood without all the requisites of the other being understood. But in the case of things, this is not so; for since the ultimate reason of things is unique, and contains by itself the aggregate of

all requisites of all things, it is evident that the requisites of all things are the same. So also is their essence, given that an essence is the aggregate of all primary requisites. Therefore, the essence of all things is the same, and things differ only modally, just as a town seen from a high point differs from the town seen from a plain. If only those things which are separated are really different or which one can perfectly understand without the other, it follows that no thing really differs from another, but that all things are one, just as Plato argues in the Parmenides" (VI iii 573: Pk 93–95). While there seems little doubt that Leibniz here uses Spinozistic terminology, the point seems fundamentally the same as that in the passage just discussed: creatures are not radically different from one another because they depend on God; because the Unity itself is immanent in each creature and in the totality of creatures, it follows (as the Theory of Emanative Harmony claims) that all things are one. For a more thorough consideration of this and related passages, see my *Leibniz's Metaphysics: Its Origins and Development,* chapter 10.

62. Scherzer, *Vade mecum,* 52–53.

63. I do not mean to suggest that individual things are not inferior to God, according to Spinoza. For example, individual things are finite and God is infinite. However, the inferiority here is not that of the Platonists: it is not an inferiority rooted in metaphysical and moral difference. For Spinoza's views about the relation, see especially the *Ethics,* Book I, passim.

64. AG here refers to *G. W. Leibniz: Philosophical Essays,* ed. Roger Ariew and Daniel Garber (Hackett, 1989). Notice that, in this quotation from the *Monadology,* we find an idea that was suggested in Micraelius's account of mode, namely, that it is the nature of created things to be inferior and that a creature will be more or less inferior depending on its "receptivity." For a discussion of this aspect of Leibniz's thought, see my *Leibniz's Metaphysics: Its Origins and Development,* chapter 9.

11

Natures, Laws, and Miracles: The Roots of Leibniz's Critique of Occasionalism

Donald P. Rutherford

Leibniz regarded his theory of preestablished harmony as offering the only plausible explanation of the remarkable agreement of the soul and the body: the agreement whereby physical stimuli give rise to appropriate sensory perceptions and volitions of the will terminate in appropriate bodily motions. According to his account, there is no real communication between the soul and the body, for neither is capable of exerting a real causal influence on the other. Instead, the soul and the body are to be conceived on the analogy of two perfectly synchronized clocks: each is responsible for the production of all its own states, yet the two nevertheless manage to agree or "harmonize" as a consequence of the consummate skill of the watchmaker who first set them in motion.

Since its conception, the theory of preestablished harmony has confronted the charge that it is at bottom indistinguishable from the doctrine of occasionalism.[1] Like preestablished harmony, occasionalism denies any causal influence of one created substance on another. By its account the only real causal agent is God, who causes thoughts to arise in the soul on the occasion of the appropriate motions in the body, and movements of the body on the occasion of the appropriate volitions of the will.[2] Now, fairly clearly, this is not a position to which Leibniz himself subscribes. Critics of preestablished harmony, however, are little moved by this fact. They allow that occasionalism may make a more direct appeal to divine action than does preestablished harmony; nevertheless, they contend that the two theories share the crucial feature that a prima facie natural phenomenon is ascribed to a supernatural cause: either God's immediate production of all the states of the soul and the body, or his creation of two substances that are programmed to instantiate just those states that will ensure their perfect agreement. From the critic's point of view, the similarities between occasionalism and preestablished harmony far outweigh their differences. Whether God actually deals the cards or merely stacks the deck, the result is the same.

In certain moods, Leibniz is happy to acknowledge the common ground that the theory of preestablished harmony shares with occasionalism. Despite his concessions on this point, however, he remains adamant that there are important problems with the doctrine of occasionalism that his theory avoids.[3] Among the most prominent objections he raises to it are the following: (1) occasionalism is inconsistent with the supposition of finite substances; (2) occasionalism presupposes the occurrence of "perpetual miracles"; and (3) occasionalism requires that God "disturb" (*déranger, troubler*) the ordinary laws of nature. The first of these objections has received considerable attention in the literature. It has generally been acknowledged that Leibniz faults occasionalists for transferring all power to God on the grounds that such a move leads inevitably to the denial of finite created substances, that is, to Spinozism. At issue here is the proper understanding of divine omnipotence, and of the relationship between the power of God and that of created things. In this essay, I will not be directly concerned with this topic, although in the next section I will sketch the main lines of Leibniz's argument. My focus instead will be on objections (2) and (3). I will argue that both of these objections derive from a particular conception of the intelligibility of nature, a conception to which Leibniz is firmly committed and that occasionalists like Malebranche no less firmly reject. I will further suggest that this division is rooted in a deeper disagreement about the correct interpretation of divine wisdom as it figures in the respective theodicies of Leibniz and Malebranche.

I

Leibniz's theory of substance is constructed around two main claims: first, any substance is endowed with an intrinsic force or power sufficient to determine all its own states or modifications; second, the determinations of this active power are in agreement or harmony with those of the active powers of all other substances. It is the first of these claims that bears directly on his critique of occasionalism, for it is the occasionalist view that created beings lack all activity and that God alone has the power to bring about things in the world. Nevertheless, it is at least worth noting here the significance of the idea of universal harmony that animates Leibniz's thought from his earliest days.[4] It is a fundamental thesis of his philosophy that harmony, or the unity and agreement of a multiplicity of diverse beings, is a defining characteristic of metaphysical perfection. Consequently, insofar as it is accepted that God has been motivated to select this world for existence on account of its superior perfection, such a harmony must be a key component in our understanding of the world. The doctrine of the preestablished harmony of substances is but a refinement of this basic theme.[5]

That any substance is endowed with an intrinsic force or power appears in many places as a necessary truth for Leibniz. Commenting on Locke's debate with the Bishop of Worcester in the Preface to the *New Essays,* he says unequivocally that "activity is the essence of substance in general" (NE 65). Similarly, in a letter to De Volder, he writes that it is "metaphysically necessary" that any substance possess an intrinsic activity (G II, 169; cf. G VI, 598/AG 207). Again, he writes to Bayle in 1702 that "[w]ithout an internal force of action a thing could not be a substance, for the nature of substance consists in this regulated tendency, from which phenomena are born in order" (G III, 58). As I read these remarks, they involve more than a mere stipulation on Leibniz's part. Rather than simply fixing what is to be called "substance," he is working from a complex, historically rooted conception of what it is to *be* a substantial being, and is subsequently arguing that these conditions can only be satisfied if substance is conceived as being by nature a principle of activity. We may see him as claiming that substance could not fulfill its prescribed metaphysical roles—as an ultimate explanatory principle, as a being that is dependent for its existence on no other created being, as a being that persists through change, and as a true unity—unless it is also conceived as a principle of activity: a source productive of changes in its states or modifications, which nevertheless persists as itself through those changes.

Now, the occasionalist response to this line of reasoning will be to reassert the essential dependence in Christian metaphysics of all created being on God. As Malebranche interprets this dependence, created beings are conserved in existence only because God continues to will their existence. Thus, while from the side of creatures there appears to be a difference between creation and conservation, "in reality, creation does not pass away, since in God conservation and creation are one and the same volition, which consequently is necessarily followed by the same effects" (OC XII–XIII, 157/D 153). The dependence of creatures on God, moreover, extends not only to the conservation of their existence but to the conservation of their particular modalities.

> [God] cannot will what cannot be conceived. Hence, He cannot will that this chair exist without willing at the same time that it exist in some place or other and without his will putting it there, since you are unable to conceive that this chair exists and that it does not exist in some place, there or elsewhere. (OC XII–XIII, 156/D 153)

The upshot of the occasionalist position is that creatures essentially dependent on God are *completely* dependent on him for the production of all their states and effects. They possess no power to bring such things about themselves.[6] This is the conclusion that Leibniz rejects, emphasizing instead the connection between the claim of substance to an existence that, while dependent, is nonetheless distinct from that of God and its status as a persisting principle of activity.[7] In the absence of such a connection, he argues, the occasionalist position comes dangerously close to Spinozism. If created beings are denied a persistent force capable of producing (with the concurrence of God) their own modifications, and if instead those modifications are ascribed exclusively to the action of God, it ceases to make sense to talk about the modifications as being *theirs* rather than God's. Without a force of some duration, Leibniz writes in the 1698 essay *De ipsa natura,*

> no created substance, no soul would remain numerically the same, and thus, nothing would be conserved by God, and consequently all things would be only certain vanishing or unstable modifications or phantasms, so to speak, of the one permanent divine substance. Or, what comes to the same thing, God would be the very nature or substance of all things. (G IV, 508–9/AG 160)[8]

Leibniz's first, and in many ways most compelling, response to occasionalism, then, is to claim that to deny causal activity to substances is to deny that they satisfy the conditions of persistence and independence constitutive of substantial being. Thus, rather than solving the problem of how two distinct substances like mind and body appear to communicate with one another, occasionalists eliminate the problem by, in effect, denying that there are two such substances.

In the essay *De ipsa natura* Leibniz offers a further argument for the intrinsic activity of substance. He is principally occupied in this text with criticizing the occasionalist view, defended by Johann Christopher Sturm, that the motion of bodies occurs solely "by virtue of the eternal law God once set up." As it stands, Leibniz argues, this claim may be interpreted in one of two ways. On the one hand, it may imply that the motions of bodies come about as the result of a single original "volition or command" on the part of God, or "a divine law that . . . bestowed a mere *extrinsic denomination* . . . on things." On the other hand, this volition or command may be understood to have "conferred some kind of enduring impression" on things: namely, "an inherent law [*legem insitam*], . . . from which both actions and passions follow" (G IV, 506–7/AG 158). Leibniz strongly attacks the first of these alternatives, which he associates with occasionalists like Sturm, on the grounds that it destroys any intelligible connection between God's original volition and the present effects of things:

> For, since that past command does not now exist, it cannot now bring anything about unless it left behind some subsistent effect at the time, an effect which even now endures and is now at work. Whoever thinks otherwise, in my judgment, renounces all distinct explanation of things; anything could equally well be said to follow from anything else if something absent in place or time could be at work here and now, without an intermediary. And so, it is not sufficient to say that God, creating things in the beginning, willed that they follow a certain definite law in their change [*progressus*] if we imagine this will to have been so ineffective that things are not affected by it and no lasting effect was produced in them. (G, IV 507/AG 158)

The only coherent way to understand the connection between God's volition and the present effects of things, he argues, is to suppose that God's action has left some permanent impression on them: an "inherent law" that is sufficient to account for the pattern of their particular effects that itself involves an intrinsic force.

> But if, indeed, the law God laid down left some trace of itself impressed on things, if by his command things were formed in such a way that they were rendered appropriate for fulfilling the will of the command, then already we must admit that a certain efficacy has been placed in things, a form or a force, something like what we usually call by the name 'nature,' something from which the series of phenomena follow in accordance with the prescript of the first command. (G IV, 507/AG 158–59).

This second argument provides a basis for rejecting at least one version of the occasionalist thesis and for recognizing in its stead the existence of beings endowed with an intrinsic force or activity. However, it is doubtful whether it proves telling against all versions of the doctrine. In criticizing Sturm, Leibniz begins from the assumption that God's will is exercised in the form of a single command prior to creation; from this he infers that such a command is either insufficient to account for the present effects of things, or that it issued in the creation of beings whose natures incorporate causal powers capable of producing the observed effects. An occasionalist might object, however, that Leibniz has omitted the possibility that God acts either by a continuous series of particular acts of will, intervening at each moment to secure a particular effect, or by an eternal or timeless will, which is sufficient to account for the effects of all things at all times, without the action of secondary causes. And, indeed, this latter view would seem to be the position of Malebranche, who writes in his *Dialogues on Metaphysics*: "From all eternity God has willed, and to all eternity He will continue to will—or, to speak more accurately, God wills unceasingly though without variation, without succession, without necessity—everything He will do in the course of time" (OC XII–XIII, 159/D 157).[9] Here, then, would seem to be a version of occasionalism that is at least prima facie resistant to Leibniz's charge that the doctrine assumes an unbridgeable gap between God's original volition and the present effects of things.

II

I turn now to Leibniz's second main criticism of occasionalism—his objection from the intelligibility of nature. The crux of his criticism here is that, regardless of the mode of God's willing (whether it be singular or successive, in time or eternal), occasionalism is to be rejected on the grounds that it assumes a natural order that is at odds with the *wisdom* God has exercised in selecting this world for existence. Thus, in addition to the objection that a world with no secondary causal powers would be a world in which there would be no persistent substances, and hence no distinction between God and creation, Leibniz claims that the occasionalist picture of God acting at each instant to secure the continued progression of the world, or acting timelessly to produce the totality of the world's effects, fails to support the idea that God has chosen to create this world, as the best of all possible worlds, because it best answers to the demands of his wisdom.

Essential to Leibniz's conception of this as the best of all possible worlds is that it is a world in which the principle of sufficient reason is observed, a world in which for anything that happens there is a reason that it happens thus and not otherwise. A further dimension of this requirement, however, which has not been widely recognized, is that within the "order of nature" it is not enough simply that there be some reason for anything to happen as it does; in addition, there must be what Leibniz calls a "natural reason": a reason that displays the effect in question as following in an intelligible manner from the nature or essence of some created being.[10] As Leibniz writes in the Preface to the *New Essays,*

> within the order of nature (miracles apart) it is not at God's arbitrary discretion to attach this or that quality haphazardly to substances. He will never give them any that are not natural to them, that is, that cannot arise from their nature as explicable modifications. (NE 66)

In attempting to account for the phenomena of nature, Leibniz argues, we may reject as insufficient any explanation that appeals either to supernatural causes or to unintelligible "occult qualities": forms or faculties that are postulated solely for the purpose of accounting for a particular phenomenon (e.g., gravity, magnetism), without an attempt being made to explain how such a quality follows from the nature of its subject. We must instead begin from the assumption that the properties of things can in general be conceived as modifications of attributes that partly define the natures of their subjects.[11] I will return later to the deeper motivations, associated with his understanding of divine wisdom, that attract Leibniz to this "principle of intelligibility." For the moment, I want to examine how it is applied in his critique of occasionalism.

We may begin with Leibniz's claim that occasionalism employs God as a deus ex machina, and that it consequently resorts to miracles in its attempt to account for the agreement of the body and the soul.[12] The first of these charges rests squarely on the principle just described. Espousing a conception of nature's order in which an explanation of the effects of any thing is always to be sought in that thing's intrinsic nature, Leibniz is hostile to all attempts to account for features of the natural world through appeal to divine action. A similar line of reasoning supports the claim that occasionalism transforms a natural circumstance like the agreement of the body and the soul into a "perpetual miracle." Pierre Bayle, who had commented on Leibniz's "New System" in his *Dictionnaire Critique et Historique* of 1697, argues that Leibniz had simply misunderstood the occasionalist position in bringing this objection against it.[13] According to Bayle, occasionalism does not require that the actions of God occur miraculously. For an occasionalist like Malebranche, God acts in the world, but he ordinarily acts only by "general volitions" or "according to general laws"; hence, the natural order of things does not amount to a continual miracle.[14]

In his 1698 reply to Bayle, Leibniz reiterates his charge against occasionalism, while taking care to distinguish his own understanding of the notion of a miracle from that assumed by Bayle:

[L]et us see whether the system of occasional causes does not in fact assume a perpetual miracle. Here it is said that it does not, because according to this system God would only act through general laws. I agree, but in my opinion this does not suffice to remove the miracles; even if God should do this continuously, they would not cease being miracles, taking this word, not in the popular sense of a rare and marvelous thing, but in the philosophical sense of what exceeds the powers of created things. It is not enough to say that God has made a general law; for besides this decree there must be a natural means of executing it; that is, it is necessary that what happens can be explained through the nature that God gives to things. (G IV, 520/L 494)[15]

In this passage, as in many others like it, Leibniz links his understanding of the miraculousness of events to his conception of the intelligibility of nature. What qualifies an effect as "extraordinary" or miraculous, he argues, is that it cannot be explained by the natures of created things. Occasionalism, in interpreting all change as the direct effect of God's action, denies that such explanations can be given for natural effects. Hence, it renders them miraculous. From Leibniz's perspective, it matters not whether occasionalists interpret God as intervening only in a regular manner or according to "general volitions." The point is that on their view God *does* intervene in the world, rather than granting created things natures sufficient to account for their effects.

In claiming that the system of occasional causes assumes a "perpetual miracle," then, Leibniz does not fault occasionalists for advancing a theory in which no provision is made for natural regularities. His objection is instead directed at how occasionalists account for such regularities. According to Malebranche, a law of nature exists just in case God wills that a certain sort of event should regularly follow another sort of event. On his account, God's nature places important constraints on the form that natural laws can take. Most significantly, such laws will always be simple and will guarantee the maximum uniformity of nature, since these qualities reflect the perfection of God's "ways."[16] Beyond this, Leibniz argues, occasionalists regard natural laws as products of divine convention. All things being equal, there is no reason that bodies should tend to move along a tangential path, rather than a circular one, except that God has decreed it to be so. Likewise, there is no reason that minds and bodies should not interact (in the occasionalist's sense), so long as God chooses that such a regularity should be observed in nature. It is precisely this suggestion of the potential arbitrariness of God's choice concerning the laws of nature that Leibniz finds objectionable.[17] For properties or events to be characterized as natural, it is not enough that they conform to lawlike generalizations. In addition, it must be possible to understand how such properties or events follow from the nature of their subject. The debate between Leibniz and the occasionalists thus comes down to the question of what it is to be a genuine law of nature (and, conversely, what it is to be a miracle or an exception to such a law). According to occasionalists, a law of nature exists just in case God wills, in a manner consistent with his nature, that a certain regularity should occur. According to Leibniz, for a generalization to qualify as a law of nature it must, in addition, be possible to conceive of the effcts it describes as "explicable modifications" of the nature of their subject. To put the point succinctly, for Leibniz, laws of nature are laws of *natures*: exceptionless sequences of events that are explainable by the intrinsic natures of *types* of being.[18]

The establishment of this point helps us to understand Leibniz's further charge that on the system of occasional causes God would be guilty of "disturbing" the respective laws of the soul and the body:

> [R]ather than saying with [occasionalists] that God has made it a law always to produce in a substance changes conforming to those of another substance, which disturbs [*troublent*] at every moment their natural laws, I would say that God has given to each of them from the start a nature whose own laws bring about its changes, in such a way that in my view the actions of souls neither increase nor decrease the quantity of moving force which is in matter, nor even change its direction, as M. Descartes believed. (G III, 122)

The basis of Leibniz's criticism in this case is not that occasionalists like Malebranche commit themselves to mistaken views about the laws of nature (e.g., they ignore the principle of the conservation of force). Nor does he take issue with their failure to acknowledge the existence in nature of certain types of causal sequences.[19] He is instead concerned with the tendency of occasionalists to conceive of God as arbitrarily imposing natural laws on created things otherwise undetermined in their effects, rather than giving each thing "from the start a nature whose own laws bring about its changes." The objection that God "disturbs" or "interferes with" the natural laws of things is just that on the occasionalist account natural laws are not conceived as the lawful expression of the natures of created things.[20]

Now, obviously, one of the principal points at issue here concerns the economy of power: whether God is to be accorded all power, or whether power is to be shared in some manner with finite created beings. On this question, there is a clear division between Leibniz and the occasionalists: he believes that there exist secondary causal powers, while occasionalists like Malebranche deny it.[21] The issue I want to emphasize, however, which in my view occupies at least as prominent a place in Leibniz's reasoning, concerns the provision made for the intrinsic intelligibility of the created world. On my reading, Leibniz faults Malebranche not simply for denying created things the power to produce their own effects but also for his failure to insist that created things be endowed with natures through which their properties and effects can be rendered intelligible. Extensionally, these objections might seem to amount to much the same thing, for it is plausible to think that the effects and properties of things will be explicable by their natures just in case their natures include powers sufficient to produce them. For two reasons, however, I want to resist the move to run these two lines of argument too closely together. First, they bear on what are manifestly different aspects of the created world: on the one hand, its intrinsic intelligibility; on the other, its degree of causal self-sufficiency.[22] Second, the intelligibility objection plays an important dialectical role in Leibniz's thought that is independent of the attribution of real causal powers. He deploys this objection in many contexts where it enjoys no obvious basis in a view about what sorts of created things are in fact endowed with force or activity. Instead, his point in these contexts is limited to the claim that, with regard to certain species or types of being, only certain effects can be conceived as following in an intelligible manner from their natures: namely, only those that can be conceived as "explicable modifications" of them.

This type of reasoning figures centrally in Leibniz's discussion of the soul-body relationship. He relies on it in attacking the Cartesian hypothesis of interaction on the grounds that it is impossible to conceive how a material thing could bring about changes in a mental thing, or vice versa.[23] As we have seen, he employs it in criticizing occasionalists: their account makes no attempt to explain divine action in a way that is consistent with the natures of created beings. Finally, he cites it as an advantage of his own theory of preestablished harmony that it ascribes to the body and the soul only those effects that can be understood as following from the nature of each being: material effects from material things, mental effects from mental things. In each of these cases, we find Leibniz arguing purely on the basis of considerations of intelligibility: within the "order of nature" it must be possible to conceive how any effect follows in an intelligible manner from the nature of its subject.

At another level, however, considerations of intelligibility do become closely linked in Leibniz's mind with the idea that any substance is by nature a principle of force or activity. Applying the principle of intelligibility to the *individual* nature of a substance, he infers that a substance must not only be *a* principle of activity, but a principle that is sufficient to account for the production of all its particular natural effects. Together, then, the claims of activity and intelligibility lead to the conclusion that it is of the very nature of the soul (and, in an extended sense, of the body)[24] to be causally responsible for the production of all its own states in the order in which they occur. Rather than one substance influencing the other, or God influencing both, each has been created from the start such that through the exercise of its own natural powers there follows the entire sequence of its effects.[25] We may conclude, then, that in his discussion of the problem of soul-body agreement Leibniz draws on the principle of intelligibility in two quite different ways: on the one hand, to insist that from any given being there follow just those effects proper to the type of being it is; on the other hand, to insist that the effects of any particular body or soul are determined by, and hence are explainable in terms of, its individual nature or causal power. Both of these considerations can be seen as contributing to the case he makes for the superiority of the theory of preestablished harmony over the Cartesian and the occasionalist positions:

> [S]ouls or vital principles, according to my system, change nothing in the ordinary course of bodies and do not even give God the occasion for doing so. Souls follow their laws, which consist in a definite development of perceptions according to goods and evils, and bodies follow theirs, which consist in the laws of motion; nevertheless, these two beings of entirely different kind meet together and correspond to each other like two clocks perfectly regulated to the same time. It is this that I call the theory of *pre-established harmony,* which excludes every concept of miracle from purely natural actions and makes things run their course regulated in an intelligible manner. Instead of this, the common system has recourse to absolutely unexplainable influences, while in the system of occasional causes God is compelled at every moment, by a kind of general law and as if by compact, to change the natural course of the thoughts of the soul in order to adapt them to the impressions of the body and to interfere with the natural course of bodily movements in accordance with the volitions of the soul. This can only be explained by a perpetual miracle, whereas I explain the whole intelligibility by the natures which God has established in things. (G VI, 540–41/L 587)

The interpretation of Leibniz's position I have so far developed leaves one point untouched. This is the question of what, if anything, the theory of preestablished harmony has to tell us about the apparent *communication* of the body and the soul. What we had expected to account for in the ordinary course of things, after all, was not simply the fact that material things give rise to material effects and mental things to mental effects; we were initially puzzled by the problem of how material things appeared to give rise to mental effects, and vice versa. What we seem to be missing to this point is any explanation of why the soul and the body appear to be joined in a functional union whereby it is reasonable to think of the two as communicating with each other.

In Leibniz's view, this impression that the soul is in immediate communication with the body—that it is capable both of influencing and being influenced by the body—is a phenomenon that can be explained in a way that is consistent with the assumption of nature's intelligibility. As he sees it, it is part of the soul's intrinsic nature to "represent" each and every state of its associated organic body.[26] To say that a soul is naturally representative of its body means, among other things, that it perceives itself as being located within a body that it identifies as its own, and that it perceives itself as interacting with other bodies via the instrumentality of this body.[27] Again, Leibniz takes this to be an essential property of any soul-like substance. To posit a soul acting without representing the state of its body, he suggests, would be to contravene the "order of nature." It would be to accept

> a metaphysical fiction, as when one assumes that God destroys a body in order to create a vacuum; the one is as contrary to the order of nature as the other. For since the nature of the soul has been made in such a way from the beginning as to represent successively the changes of matter, the situation which we assume could not arise in the natural order. (G IV, 519/L 493)

Presented with this position, a critic might well raise the objection that Leibniz has advanced what is fairly described as an ad hoc solution to the problem of the communication of the body and the soul. While rejecting as unintelligible the hypothesis that the two causally interact, as well as all appeals to a supernatural influence, he has failed to explain how it happens that two things as different as the body and the soul nevertheless appear to operate in complete agreement in the confines of a single human being. Leibniz's response seems to take us no further than: It happens because that's the sort of beings they are; God has created each from the start such that it appears to communicate with the other. Yet this seems uncomfortably like the notorious pseudoexplanation that opium sedates by virtue of its intrinsic dormitive power.

In answering the criticism that the system of preestablished harmony is in some way an ad hoc theory of the soul-body relation, what needs primarily to be stressed, I think, is the common methodology that informs the development of Leibniz's own system and his objections to occasionalism. In both cases, he is principally motivated by the requirement that it must always be possible to account for natural effects as intelligible consequences of the nature of some created being. As we have seen, in his discussion of the problem of soul-body agreement, he employs this principle in two quite different ways: sometimes critically, in order to undermine a given philosophical theory; at other times constructively, in formulating positive hypotheses about the natures of things. On the critical side, he draws on the idea of intelligibility in attacking a wide range of rival philosophical positions: the doctrines of interactionism and occasionalism, the supposition of atoms in a vacuum, the notion of a primitive force of attraction, and, in general, any hypothesis that invokes so-called occult qualities.[28] On the positive side, the assumption of intelligibility plays a complementary role in inspiring that part of Leibniz's philosophy that takes as its primary task the construction of a general theory of the natures or essences of created things. It is in this context, I think, that we can best understand the assertion that it is part of the nature of the soul both to be causally responsible for the production of its own internal states and to represent the states of its own body. We may see this claim as being in the first place a hypothesis about the intrinsic nature of any substantial being, which, consistent with the assumption of intelligibility, suffices to account for the apparent communication of the soul and the body.

Hypotheses about the natures of things are often defended by Leibniz on the grounds of their capacity to save the phenomena. Ultimately, however, such hypotheses end up being more than mere conjectures in his system, insofar as they are supported by the *a priori* consideration that the character of God's wisdom would in fact have inspired him to create a world that manifested just this sort of rational order. This brings us at last to the deepest level of Leibniz's disagreement with the occasionalist philosophy: what he sees as occasionalism's negative consequences for the project of theodicy.

III

We have seen how Leibniz's charge that occasionalism implies a "perpetual miracle" draws on the assumption of nature's intelligibility. In rejecting the demand for intelligibility, he argues, occasionalism promotes the elimination of any coherent distinction between the natural and the miraculous, and with it any notion of what Stuart Brown has called the "autonomy of nature."[29] For Leibniz, this is a result with profound consequences for the project of theodicy. As he sees it, the principle that the ordinary effects of things must always be explicable by the natures of those things stands in a critical relationship to God's wisdom.[30] As he writes in his 1709 response to Lamy: "the wisdom of God appears more clearly in the system of harmony, in which all is connected through reasons drawn from the natures of things, than in that of the occasionalists, in which everything is compelled by an arbitrary power" (G IV, 594).[31]

We can conceive of the relationship between God's wisdom and the intelligibility of nature as being established in the following way. We know that within Leibniz's theodicy there is an important connection between the character of this world as the best of all possible worlds and God's wisdom as the attribute determining his selection of this world for existence. If we now assume that the idea of nature's intelligibility plays an essential role in Leibniz's attempt to conceptualize the rational order that marks this as the best of all possible worlds, we may infer that any hypothesis that challenges the assumption of intelligibility also contains a concealed attack on the notion of God's wisdom. Given the capacity of occasionalism to pose just such a challenge, we may conclude that Leibniz's opposition to this doctrine is again ultimately motivated by theological concerns. In addition to placing in jeopardy the vital distinction between God and his creation, Malebranche's theory denies the condition of intelligibility by which the natural world is rendered compatible with God's wisdom, and thus worthy of his choice for creation.

At first sight this conclusion might seem a surprising one, for we know that Malebranche and Leibniz agree on the basic point that God has chosen this world for existence because its production represents, overall, the creative act of greatest possible perfection. There remains, however, a significant disagreement between them on the issue of how God's perfection is communicated in creation. Malebranche repeatedly asserts that it is not enough simply to look at the end of creation, the intrinsic perfection of the created world, but that it is also necessary to consider the means of God's volition. Accordingly, on his view, a world of greater perfection might have been created, but this would have required that perfection be sacrificed in the mode of God's willing. For Malebranche, God acts in ways that are "the most simple, the most general, the most uniform" (OC V, 28); and the result is a world in which there are intrinsic imperfections and evils, but in which the elimination of any of these imperfections would have interfered with the "simplicity of God's ways," that is, the general laws by which he brings about all that happens in the world.[32]

As Catherine Wilson has emphasized, Leibniz, particularly in his early writings, shows signs of being strongly influenced by Malebranche's approach to the theodicy problem.[33] Arguably, this is an influence that persists through the publication of the *Theodicy,* in the view that the metaphysical perfection of a world is to be regarded as a function of both the plenitude of its existence and the simplicity of its laws. Despite these points of contact between the views of the two philosophers, however, the fact remains that while Malebranche sees the perfection of God's creation as essentially dependent on the perfection of his "ways" or modes of willing (their simplicity, uniformity, etc.), Leibniz is concerned exclusively with the perfection that a world possesses by virtue of its own intrinsic nature. This is most immediately apparent in his image of God surveying the domain of all possible worlds, weighing their respective degrees of perfection, and only then choosing to create that world which is by its own nature the best of all possible worlds (cf. *Theodicy,* §225). Within this model there is no room for an independent weighing of the particular mode of God's willing. Instead, God brings into existence the possible world of greatest perfection by virtue of a "moral necessity, which constrains the wisest to do the best" (*Theodicy,* §367; G VI, 333/H 345).[34]

The conflict between the positions of Malebranche and Leibniz is not limited to this point alone. At bottom it extends to a set of basic disagreements concerning God's goal in creation and the character of the wisdom that he therein expresses. In Malebranche's view, God acts only for the sake of his own glory, and this he finds only if his work is sanctified by a divine person, Jesus Christ, the Incarnation of the Word.[35] "Separate Jesus Christ from the rest of creation," Malebranche writes in his *Traité,*

> and see if he who can only act for his glory, and whose wisdom has no limits, would not be able to carry out the plan of producing nothing externally. But if you join Jesus Christ to his Church, and the Church to the rest of the world, then you raise to the glory of God a temple so august and so holy that you will perhaps be surprised that its foundations have been set down so late. (OC V, 15)

We know, however, that for Malebranche the excellence of God's creation cannot be understood through its end alone; God must be honored both by his work and by his ways. It follows that while the Incarnation of the Word is the only end that justifies creation, insofar as it is the only end capable of ensuring God's glory, it is necessary that God also be glorified by the means he chooses to realize this end.[36] As Malebranche conceives them, the means God selects are chiefly distinguished by their being expressions of his unlimited wisdom.[37] To appreciate precisely how this wisdom is expressed in the created world, we must see Malebranche's theodicy from within the framework of his occasionalism. Within this framework, we have observed, there is no

significant distinction between creation and conservation: God's volition is a necessary condition for the existence of the world at each
and every moment. God's wisdom is expressed through his willing the
continued existence of the world according to those laws, or ways, that
are "the most simple, the most general, the most uniform" (OC V, 28).

On the basis of this brief account, we may see Malebranche's theodicy as defined by two basic commitments. The first is his concern to
uphold the tenets of orthodox Christianity—in particular the event of
the Incarnation, which he deems necessary for the creation of a world
worthy of God. The second is his determination to see God's wisdom
and providence as actively expressed in the world through the simplicity of his ways.[38] With respect to both of these commitments, his position is at odds with the main tendencies of Leibniz's thought. According to Leibniz, God's sole aim in creation is the production of the
maximum possible goodness; and this he conceives most basically as
metaphysical goodness: that is, perfection or reality.[39] Working from a
position that identifies goodness with being, Leibniz assumes that God
is naturally disposed to create something rather than nothing, and that
he is antecedently inclined to create any possible world in proportion
to its degree of goodness.[40] Within his scheme, the issue of the worthi-
ness of the created world vis-à-vis God receives a completely different
treatment than in Malebranche. Quite simply, we can say that the only
possible world worthy of God is that world which contains, in and of
itself, the greatest perfection or reality.

The notion of divine wisdom plays no less central a role in the theodicy of Leibniz than it does in that of Malebranche; however, again, this
wisdom is conceived very differently. Leibniz defines God's wisdom as
his "knowledge of the good" (L 564), which is to say his knowledge of
the perfection, or positive reality, that is contained in the eternal natures or essences of things.[41] In the context of creation, God's wisdom
is expressed in two principal ways. First, divine wisdom serves to determine God in his choice of which possible world to create. Motivated
by the supreme goodness of his will to create the best world possible,
God is informed by his wisdom, or knowledge of the good, as to which
possible world contains the greatest perfection.[42] Second, in willing
into existence a particular series of contingent events, God is constrained by his wisdom to act in accord with the principle of intelligibility, that is, to will only those events that can be explained by the natures
of created things. The reason for this constraint, crucial to Leibniz's
case against occasionalism, can be understood as follows. God's wisdom, according to Leibniz, is identical with his knowledge of what is
positive or unlimited in the natures of things. Thus, God is guided by
his wisdom insofar as he wills only those contingent events that can be

explained through "limitations" of the perfections definitive of those natures. These, we may assume, will be just those events that can be conceived as "explicable modifications" of the attributes of created beings.[43]

Although our survey of the theodicies of Malebranche and Leibniz has not been exhaustive, we have established grounds for seeing the conflict between occasionalism and preestablished harmony as predicated on a much deeper disagreement concerning the wisdom that guides God's will in creation. When Leibniz criticizes Malebranche for advancing a theory that is at odds with the principle of intelligibility, he is in effect calling into question Malebranche's understanding of divine wisdom and its relation to the perfection of the created world. While Malebranche conceives of God as bestowing activity on a world of otherwise passive creatures, and thereby realizing perfection through the exercise of his wisdom or the simple and uniform mode of his willing, Leibniz conceives of perfection as resident in the essences or natures that are themselves constitutive of the world. God exercises his wisdom in Leibniz's view by acting in ways that conform to his knowledge of the perfection of those natures. In addition to this specific point of disagreement, we have located a more general tension between the ways in which Malebranche and Leibniz each approach the problem of creation. Malebranche remains committed to constructing a metaphysics that is consistent with the fundamentals of Christian doctrine, one that acknowledges the central place of the Incarnation and the essential dependence of created beings on God. Leibniz, by contrast, develops his position largely under the influence of a conception of God as an infinitely skillful craftsman, one who is disposed to create that world which in and of itself contains the greatest possible perfection.

Given the theological distance that separates Leibniz from Malebranche, there is no easy way to judge the success of his critique of occasionalism. We can perhaps best see it as an attempt to push forward the program of rationalist metaphysics unencumbered by the demands of religious orthodoxy.[44] This is not to suggest that Leibniz rejects the significance of theological concerns—his philosophy is of course infused with them—but rather that his God is, to a more significant degree than Malebranche's, the God of a philosopher: the divine mathematician, the infinitely skillful artisan. Confronted with the occasionalist position, Leibniz will insist that in denying created things natures sufficient to account for their effects, Malebranche has effectively robbed God of the honor of having conceived and created that artifact which best displays his wisdom. Rather than being a worthy product of God's creative will, the world becomes no more than a continuous expression of God's personal power.[45]

Notes

I thank Thomas M. Lennon and Steven Nadler for their helpful comments on an earlier draft of this chapter.

1. This criticism was first made by Arnauld; see his letter to Leibniz of 4 March 1687 (G II, 84/LA 105–6).

2. As Leibniz himself notes, the occasionalist theory is not limited to an account of soul–body relations, but extends also to causal interactions among bodies: "since the communication of motions also seemed inconceivable to them, they believed that God imparts motion to a body on the occasion of the motion of another body" (G IV, 483/AG 143). For recent reassertions of this point, see Thomas M. Lennon, "Philosophical Commentary," in LO, 810, and Steven Nadler, "Occasionalism and the Mind-Body Problem," *Oxford Studies in the History of Philosophy* 2 (forthcoming).

3. For examples of Leibniz both affirming and qualifying the relation of this theory to the doctrine of occasionalism, see his letters to L'Hospital (30 September 16975; GM II, 299) and Remond (26 August 1714; G III, 625).

4. Leibniz's attachment to this idea can be traced to his early (c. 1663–66) acquaintance with the writings of Johann Heinrich Bisterfeld (see A vi.I; 151–61).

5. It is important to distinguish Leibniz's arguments *against* occasionalism from his arguments *for* preestablished harmony. In this essay, I am concerned solely with the former, which do not directly involve the doctrine of harmony. Arguments against occasionalism form an essential component of one of Leibniz's main defenses of preestablished harmony. Briefly, he contends that there are only three ways of accounting for the agreement of the soul and the body: interactionism, occasionalism, and preestablished harmony. Neither interactionalism nor occasionalism is tenable; preestablished harmony is possible; therefore, preestablished harmony must be accepted (cf. the "New System of the Nature and Communication of Substances" [G IV, 477–87/AG 138–45] and the Postscript to his 1696 letter to Basnage de Beauval [G IV, 498–500/AG 147–49]). In addition to this "argument from elimination," Leibniz also advances an *a priori* argument for preestablished harmony based on his concept of substance (cf. G IV, 494/P 126). Here the doctrine of harmony, or at least the weaker doctrine of universal expression, plays a central role in his reasoning. Starting from the premise that "God originally created the soul (or any other real unity) in such a way that everything must arise for it from its own depths, through a perfect *spontaneity* relative to itself, and yet with a perfect *conformity* relative to external things," he concludes in the "New System" that "[i]t is this mutual relation, regulated in advance in each substance of the universe, which produces what we call their *communication,* and which alone brings about *the union of soul and body*" (G IV, 484–85/AG 144). For a full discussion of both these arguments, see R. C. Sleigh, Jr., *Leibniz and Arnauld: A Commentary on Their Correspondence* (New Haven, Conn.: Yale University Press, 1990), pp. 161–80.

6. The above is not intended as a full account of Malebranche's arguments

for this last claim. See Lennon, "Philosophical Commentary," in LO, pp. 809ff.; and Robert C. Sleigh, Jr., "Leibniz on Malebranche on Causality," in *Central Themes in Early Modern Philosophy,* ed. J. A. Cover and Mark Kulstad (Indianapolis, Ind.: Hackett, 1990), pp. 161–93.

7. The precise nature of the dependence of created substances on God in Leibniz's philosophy—the content of his doctrine of divine concurrence—is a vexed issue. See Sleigh, *Leibniz and Arnauld,* pp. 183–85, and "Leibniz on Malebranche on Causality."

8. See also his letter to Lelong of 5 February 1712:

[F]orce is one of the principal perfections, which being removed there will remain nearly nothing of [substance], or soon nothing at all. And I dare to say that without force, there will be no substance; and one will fall, despite oneself, into the opinion of Spinoza, according to whom creatures are only passing modifications. It is necessary, therefore, to say that God gives the force, and that he does not replace it, in order to preserve the substances outside of him. (ML 421)

Compare G IV, 515/AG 165; G IV, 567–68/L 583.

9. In "Occasionalism and General Will in Malebranche," *Journal of the History of Philosophy* (forthcoming), Steven Nadler argues that the former more accurately represents Malebranche's position: "that God always acts in accordance with the laws he has established in the realm of nature . . . does not rule out an infinite number of temporalized and individual acts of will on God's part" (pp. 20–21).

10. Compare G III, 519. I discuss this requirement in detail in my essay "Leibniz's Principle of Intelligibility" (*History of Philosophy Quarterly,* forthcoming).

11. This is the objection that Leibniz raises against Locke's notion of "thinking matter":

As for thought, it is certain, as our author more than once acknowledges, that it cannot be an intelligible modification of matter and be comprehensible and explicable in terms of it. That is, a sentient or thinking being is not a mechanical thing like a watch or a mill: one cannot conceive of sizes and shapes and motions combining mechanically to produce something which thinks, and senses too, in a mass where [formerly] there was nothing of the kind—something which would likewise be extinguished by the machine's going out of order. So sense and thought are not something which is natural to matter, and there are only two ways in which they could occur in it: through God's combining it with a substance to which thought is natural, or through his putting thought into it by a miracle. (NE 66–67).

Compare his letter to Lady Masham of 30 June 1704 (G III, 355/AG 290).

It is quite true that, speaking with metaphysical rigor, there is no real influence of one created substance on another, and that all things, with all their reality, are continually produced by the power [*vertu*] of God. But in solving problems it is not sufficient to make use of the general cause and to invoke what is called a *Deus ex machina*. For when one does that without giving any other explanation derived from the order of secondary causes, it is, properly speaking, having recourse to miracle. (G IV, 483/AG 143).

13. See "Remark H" to the article "Rorarius" in Pierre Bayle, *Historical and Critical Dictionary: Selections*, trans. Richard H. Popkin (Indianapolis, Ind.: Hackett, 1991), p. 238.

14. Compare *Traité de la Nature et de la Grace*, I, lix (OC V, 63); and *Dialogues on Metaphysics* VIII, iii (OC XII–XIII, 177–78/D 175).

15. Similar statements appear in the *Theodicy*, §207 (G VI, 240–41/H 257) and §355 (G VI, 326/H 338–39), in his comments on Lamy (G IV, 587–88, 594–95), and in his letters to Basnage de Beauval, c. 1696 (G III, 122), and Conti, 9 April 1716 (GB 277). Leibniz does not deny the possibility of God's extraordinary intervention in the world, but only claims that it is necessary to draw a clear distinction between the ordinary course of nature, which can be understood through the natures of created things, and genuine miracles. Thus, he writes to Lady Masham in 1704 that "the ways of God are of two sorts, the one natural, the other miraculous" (G III, 353).

16. See section III below.

17. Responding to François Lamy's critique of the doctrine of preestablished harmony in his *Connaissance de soi-même* (1699), Leibniz writes that according to occasionalists "a miracle is only an exception to general rules or laws that God has established arbitrarily. Thus once God has made it a general law or rule that the body should always agree with the soul, and vice versa, there would be no miracle about it; and in this sense, a miracle would only differ from another action of God by an external denomination, that is, by its rarity" (G IV, 594). There is no question that in Leibniz's mind occasionalists are committed to the arbitrariness of the laws of nature, insofar as they do not see God as constrained to will contingent events "in conformity with" the external natures of things (cf. G III, 529; G IV, 594–95). Malebranche would obviously contest this charge. Not only, he believes, is God "obliged to act always in a manner worthy of Him, by ways which are simple, general, constant and uniform" (OC V, 49), but all of his actions are subordinated to the highest aim of creation—the Incarnation of the Word in the person of Jesus Christ; cf. *Traité* I, i, and Additions (OC V, 12–13), and Lennon, "Philosophical Commentary," in LO, 824. For more on this issue, see section III.

18. Sleigh remarks that, for Leibniz, "Laws of nature are . . . characterized as generalizations that are true of created substances in virtue of their natures" (*Leibniz and Arnauld*, p. 162). I believe that this account needs to be emended slightly. As I read Leibniz, laws of nature are in the first place expressive not of the individual natures of substances, but of the natures of *types* or *species* of being (e.g., body or soul), only some of which are, strictly speaking, substances. What needs to be emphasized, I think, is the conceptual relation for Leibniz between the idea of a "law of nature" (including the laws that govern corporeal phenomena) and the notion of intelligibility (or explainability in

terms of natures) described above. I take it to be consistent with my position that the causal powers of any given species of being (e.g., material being) supervene on the causal powers of individual substances—the only true sources of activity for Leibniz.

19. This is how Sleigh understands the criticism. He sees Leibniz as objecting to "Malebranche's belief that some physical events have as their sole immediate quasi-cause, a mental event" ("Leibniz on Malebranche on Causality," pp. 167–68; cf. *Leibniz and Arnauld,* pp. 164–68) on the grounds that it is inconsistent with his "great principle of physics"—that "a body never receives a change in motion except by another body in motion that pushes it" (G VI, 541/L 587). On Sleigh's account, Malebranche is guilty of no more than a mistaken belief about the sequences of events that in fact obtain in the world: namely, that there are some physical events for which there are no identifiable physical causes. And this is a belief that Malebranche could easily have given up while preserving his system of occasional causes. I see Leibniz's criticism as going beyond this.

20. I take this point to be implicit in the following version of Leibniz's "elimination argument" (see above, n. 5):

> [H]aving assumed that ordinary things must occur naturally and not by miracle, it seems that one can say that according to this my hypothesis is demonstrated. For the two other hypotheses necessarily make recourse to miracle. . . . And in all one can find no other hypothesis than these three. For either the laws of bodies and of souls are interfered with [*troublées*], or else they are conserved. If these laws are interfered with (what must come about from something outside), it is necessary either that one of these two things interferes with the other, which is the hypothesis of influence common in the Schools, or that it is a third thing which interferes with them, that is, God, in the hypothesis of occasional causes. But finally, if the laws of souls and of bodies are conserved without being interfered with, that is the hypothesis of preestablished harmony, which is consequently the only natural one. (letter to Lady Masham, 30 June 1704 [G III, 355])

21. Malebranche's fullest defense of this position is in *The Search after Truth,* Bk. 6, Pt. 2, Ch. 3, and in the "Fifteenth Elucidation."

22. Likewise, they raise the question of the proper understanding of two different divine attributes: God's power and God's wisdom.

23. He writes to Jaquelot: "I have said to you that it is as far from reasonable to attribute to the soul an immediate physical influence on the body as to attribute to matter the faculty of thinking. My reason is that the one is as inexplicable as the other by the modifications of the thing to which it is attributed" (G VI, 569; cf. 570).

24. The case of bodies raises special problems. Although I cannot argue the point here, on Leibniz's understanding of the body-soul relation any fundamental commitment to the substantiality of bodies is given up; instead, every body is, in the final analysis, an "aggregate" of soul-like monads. (On this, see

my essay "Leibniz's 'Analysis of Multitude and Phenomena into Unities and Reality,' " *Journal of the History of Philosophy* 28 [1990]: 525–52.). Thus, while in many of his published writings Leibniz represents the theory of preestablished harmony as a response to the views of Descartes and Malebranche on the issue of mind-body interaction, this posture is to a degree deceptive. At a deeper level, the preestablished harmony of body and soul is revealed to be a preestablished harmony among the perceptions of a universe of unextended, soul-like substances.

25. Roger Woolhouse has argued that Leibniz's objection that occasionalism introduces a perpetual miracle "turns on his view of substances as active and as containing in their own natures the principle of their changes" ("Leibniz and Occasionalism," in *Metaphysics and Philosophy of Science in the Seventeenth and Eighteenth Centuries,* ed. R. Woolhouse [Dordrecht: D. Reidel, 1988], pp. 166–67). I see his position as largely consistent with my own, although it collapses the distinction between what I regard as two separate argumentative strategies in Leibniz—the one bearing on the nature of substances as persisting principles of activity, the other on the intrinsic intelligibility of nature as a whole. Again, I would stress the point made with respect to Sleigh: Leibniz's arguments concerning miracles and intelligibility are in the first place concerned with the sorts of effects that can be conceived as following from the natures of different *types* of being.

26. In his first reply to Bayle, Leibniz claims that "it is the soul's own God-given nature to represent everything that takes place in its organs by virtue of its own laws" (G IV, 519/L 493). Compare *Theodicy,* §355: "The true means whereby God causes the soul to have sensations of what happens in the body have their origin in the nature of the soul, which represents bodies, and is so made beforehand that the representations which arise from one another within it, by a natural sequence of thoughts, correspond to the changes of bodies" (G VI, 326).

27. In the "New System, Leibniz writes that the "internal perceptions in the soul itself must arise because of its own original constitution, that is, they must arise through the representative nature (capable of expressing external things as they relate to its organs) given to the soul from its creation, which constitutes its individual character" (G IV, 484/AG 143). He further remarks that the "organized mass" of the body contains the "point of view" of the soul, and that "the soul has its seat in the body by an immediate presence" (G IV, 484–85/AG 144). For reasons of space, I omit here any discussion of the special sense Leibniz gives to the terms 'expression' and 'representation'. Such a discussion would obviously be necessary for a complete account of his position.

28. For more on this topic, see my essay "Leibniz's Principle of Intelligibility."

29. "Leibniz's 'Crossing from Occasional Causes to the Preestablished Harmony,' " in *Leibniz: Tradition und Aktualität. Vorträge, V. Internationaler Leibniz-Kongress,* ed. I. Marchlewitz (Hannover: Schlütersche Verlagsanstalt, 1988), pp. 116–23.

30. A forceful statement of Leibniz's concern on this issue appears in the Preface to the *New Essays*:

I acknowledge that we must not deny what we do not understand, but I add that we are entitled to deny (within the natural order at least) whatever is absolutely unintelligible and inexplicable. . . . The distinction between what is natural and explicable and what is miraculous and inexplicable removes all the difficulties. To reject it would be to uphold something worse than occult qualities, and thereby to renounce philosophy and reason, giving refuge to ignorance and laziness by means of an irrational system which maintains not only that there are qualities which we do not understand—of which there are only too many—but further that there are some which could not be comprehended by the greatest intellect if God gave it every possible opportunity, i.e. [qualities] which are either miraculous or without rhyme or reason. And indeed it would be without rhyme or reason for God to perform miracles in the ordinary course of events. So this idle hypothesis would destroy not only our philosophy which seeks reasons but also the divine wisdom which provides them. (NE 65–66)

31. Compare his letter to Lady Masham of 30 June 1704: "[T]he very reason and order of divine wisdom determines that one not have recourse to miracles unless necessary. . . . Thus it seems that my hypothesis is something more than a hypothesis, being not only entirely possible, but also the one which is most in conformity with the wisdom of God and the order of things" (G III, 353–54).

32. Compare *Traité* I, xiv:

God could undoubtedly make a world more perfect than the one we inhabit. He could, for example, make it in such a way that the rain, which serves to render the earth fertile, should fall more regularly on lands that are worked than in the ocean where it is not so necessary. But in order to make this world more perfect, it would have been necessary for him to have changed the simplicity of his ways, and to have multiplied the laws of the communication of motion by which our world subsists; and then there would no longer have been between the action of God and his work that proportion which is necessary in order to determine an infinitely wise being to act, or at least there would not have been the same proportion between the action of God and this world, however perfect, as there is between the laws of nature and the world we inhabit. For our world, as imperfect one may want to imagine it being, is founded on laws of motion so simple and so natural that it is completely worthy of the infinite wisdom of its author." (OC V, 29)

See also *Dialogues* IX, x (OC XII, 213–14/D 213)

33. "Leibnizian Optimism," *Journal of Philosophy* 80 (1983): 765–83, and *Leibniz's Metaphysics: A Historical and Comparative Study* (Princeton: Princeton University Press, 1989), pp. 281–88.

34. A somewhat subtle distinction is involved here. My claim is not that the mode of God's willing (God's "ways") is irrelevant for Leibniz in determining the perfection of a world, but only that it is not a factor that is set against the perfection of the "work," as in Malebranche. According to Leibniz, God's

assessment of a world's degree of perfection requires that he foresee the results of certain free decrees of his will. (In the Arnauld correspondence, Leibniz says that God considers these decrees *sub ratione possibilitatis*; cf. G II, 51–52/ LA 56–58.) These free decrees are responsible for the specific causal order of any world, and thus contribute to determining its intrinsic perfection. The difference between the positions of Leibniz and Malebranche is that for Leibniz the mode of God's willing is relevant to the assessment of the perfection of God's creative act only insofar as it contributes to the intrinsic perfection of the *product* of creation. For Malebranche, by contrast, the mode of God's willing becomes a factor that is in competition with the perfection of the work. The apparent similarity between their two positions allows Leibniz to claim (when it suits him) that he is really just saying the same thing as Malebranche. Reading carefully, however, the distance between the two becomes clear. In the *Theodicy* (§208), for example, Leibniz defends the Malebranchian view that the "ways of God are those most simple and most uniform"; but he immediately goes on to stress that these are also the means that are the "most productive" and that they lead "to a single advantage, which is to produce as much perfection as is possible" (G VI, 241/H 257; cf. ML 392). This is a point that is reiterated in a number of texts suggesting that God's decision in creation is to be seen not as a balancing of two competing sources of perfection—richness of existence (perfection of the "work") versus simplicity of laws (perfection of the "ways")—but that a simplicity of laws is merely the means by which the greatest quantity of intrinsic perfection can be realized (cf. G I, 331/L 211; G VII, 303/L 487). Compare Martial Gueroult, *Malebranche,* 3 vols. (Paris: Aubier, 1959), vol. 2, pp. 194–207, and Geneviève Rodis-Lewis, *Nicolas Malebranche* (Paris: Presses Universitaires de France, 1963), pp. 310–12.

35. "[T]he Incarnation of the Word is the first and principal of the plans of God" (OC XII–XIII, 207/D 205). Compare *Traité* I, i–ii, and *Dialogues* IX, iii–vi. I am grateful to Thomas Lennon for making this point clearer to me; see his "Philosophical Commentary," in LO, p. 284; see also Gueroult, *Malebranche,* vol. 2, ch. 5.

36. "God wants His conduct, as well as His work, to bear the character of His attributes. Not satisfied that the Universe honor Him by its excellence and its beauty, He wants His ways to glorify Him by their simplicity, their fecundity, their universality, their uniformity, by all the characteristics expressing qualities which He glories in possessing" (OC XII–XIII, 214/D 213).

37. "God [is] obliged to act always in a manner worthy of him, by ways simple, general, constant and uniform, in a word, by ways conforming to the idea we have of a general cause whose wisdom has no limits" (OC V, 49).

38. Compare *Traité,* "Premier Éclaircissement," III:

On the basis of these definitions, one sees that far from denying providence I assume on the contrary that it is God who bring about everything in all things; that the nature of pagan philosophers is a chimera; and that properly speaking what is called *nature* is nothing other than the general laws that God has established in order to construct or conserve his work by means of very simple ways, by an action that is always uniform, constant, perfectly worthy of an infinite wisdom and universal cause (OC V, 148).

39. On the first point, see *Causa Dei*, §§25–26: "The antecedent will of God tends toward actualizing all good and repelling all evil, as such, and in proportion to the degree of goodness and evil. . . . The consequent will arises from the concurrence of all antecedent acts of will. When the effects of all antecedent acts of will cannot be carried out together, the maximum effect which can be obtained by wisdom and power will be obtained" (G VI, 442–43/S 119). On the second point, see *Causa Dei*, §30: "*Metaphysical* good or evil, in general, consists in the perfection or imperfection of all creatures, even those not endowed with intelligence" (G VI, 443/S 120). In an appendix to the *Theodicy*, Leibniz defines a "perfection" as "any purely positive or absolute reality" (G VI, 383/H 384).

40. Leibniz maintains that God would only not create if it were impossible to fix on a single best possible world; see *Theodicy*, §8.

41. Leibniz's standard examples of perfections are the attributes of power, knowledge, and will. The nature of any possible substance can be defined by limitations of these primary perfections. See "Monadology," §48, "Principles of Nature and Grace," §9, Preface to the *Theodicy* (G VI, 27/H 51), and, especially, Grua, 126.

42. Compare *Theodicy* §225: "The wisdom of God, not content with embracing all the possibles, penetrates them, compares them, weighs them one against the other, to estimate their degrees of perfection or imperfection. . . . The result of all these comparisons and deliberations is the choice of the best from among all these possible systems, which wisdom makes in order to satisfy goodness completely; and such is precisely the plan of the universe as it is" (G VI, 252/H 267–68). See also "Observations on the Book Concerning 'The Origin of Evil,' Published Recently in London," §21 (G VI, 423/H 428).

43. I am here merely sketching a line of argument that needs to be filled out in greater detail.

44. Compare Wilson, *Leibniz's Metaphysics*, pp. 297–303. Wilson's book emphasizes another strand of Leibniz's thinking that is at odds with orthodox Christianity: his sympathy for a Neoplatonic account of creation as emanation (see pp. 275–81). Arguably, this is a point on which Malebranche's position is also at risk.

45. In a somewhat unlikely place, Hume's *Enquiry Concerning Human Understanding*, we find a compelling statement of this distinctively Leibnizian complaint. According to the occasionalists, Hume writes,

> every thing is full of God. Not content with the principle, that nothing exists but by his will, that nothing possesses any power but by his concession: They rob nature, and all created beings, of every power, in order to render their dependence on the Deity still more sensible and immediate. They consider not, that, by this theory, they diminish, instead of magnifying, the grandeur of those attributes, which they affect so much to celebrate. It argues surely more power in the Deity to delegate a certain de-

gree of power to inferior creatures, than to produce every thing by his own immediate volition. It argues more wisdom to contrive at first the fabric of the world with such perfect foresight, that, of itself, and by its proper operation, it may well serve all the purposes of providence, than if the great Creator were obliged at every moment to adjust its parts, and animate by his breath all the wheels of that stupendous machine. (sec. vii)

12

Leibniz's Theory of Relations

David Wong

I. Introduction

Discussion of Leibniz's theory of relations has focused on the question of whether he thought that propositions about relations between substances are reducible to propositions containing nonrelational predicates only. Russell and Rescher have interpreted his doctrine that relations between substances are ideal mental entities as entailing the reducibility of relational propositions to nonrelational ones. Hintikka and Ishiguro have argued that the doctrine should not be interpreted as yielding such a strong result. I agree with Hintikka and Ishiguro on the question of reducibility. I will argue, however, that there is an important connection between relational and nonrelational propositions in Leibniz's theory which has been overlooked. The connection is not quite one of reducibility, and it has been overlooked because commentators have been preoccupied with the question of reducibility. I will explain how Leibniz's assertion of the connection is consistent with his distinction between possibility and compossibility. I will also explain how his assertion sheds new light on Leibniz's doctrine of expression. I conclude by applying the theory of relations to the relations between simple substances or monads and explaining how the world of monads makes up the world of everyday experience. If my interpretation is correct, Leibniz's theory of relations is the key to understanding some of his most central and notoriously obscure doctrines.

II. The Ideality Doctrine

It is well known that in Leibniz's ontology there are only substances and their modifications. Relations can only be considered as abstract mental entities, if they are considered apart from substances and their modifications:

> I do not believe that you will admit an accident that is in two subjects at the same time. My judgment about relations is that paternity in David is one thing, sonship in Solomon another, but that the relation common to both is a merely mental thing whose basis is the modifications of the individuals. [L, 609]

David's paternity is a relational property. He is the father of someone. His relational property is different from the relation common to him and Solomon.

To explain the difference between a relation and a relational property, Leibniz gives the example of the ratio between two lines *L* and *M*. *L* has the relational property of being greater than *M*, while *M* has the property of being less than *L*. If we conceive of the ratio as a relation rather than a property, we conceive of it as "something abstracted" from *L* and *M*, "without considering which is the antecedent, or which the consequent; which the subject and which the object." This way of conceiving of the ratio is "useful," but we must not forget that a relation is a "mere ideal thing." (LC, 71)

This conception of the relation corresponds to the open sentence '*xRy*' with two free variables *x* and *y*, reading '*x* and *y* have the ratio of greater to lesser'. Because we are using two variables, we are not "considering which is the antecedent, or which the consequent; which the subject, and which the object." The relation is an abstraction formed by us upon consideration of pairs of lines with relational properties that seem to have something in common. Leibniz was worried that we may think the relation exists independently of the pairs of lines.

III. The Ideality Doctrine and Reducibility

The doctrine of the ideality of relations is taken to have implications for the reducibility of relational propositions. Relational propositions contain relational predicates. I characterize a relational predicate as involving essential reference to some thing other than the one to which it is attributed. It may be explicitly relational. Following Rescher, I will say that the form of the explicitly relational predicate is the following:

$(\lambda z)zRa$ = the characteristic of standing in the relation R to the object a.[1]

An implicitly relational predicate does not refer to particular individuals:

$(\exists x)bRx = b$ has the characteristic of standing in the relation R to something.[2]

I maintain that the doctrine of the ideality of relations entails no more than

R1) All relational propositions are logically equivalent to subject-predicate propositions containing relational predicates.

The doctrine that relations are abstractions entails that relational propositions do not have any additional content beyond that which can be expressed by subject-predicate propositions containing relational predicates. Relations do not really exist, so all that can be said about what exists can be said with relational and nonrelational predicates along with subject terms. For instance, propositions about spatial relations between objects are always logically equivalent to propositions about the spatial properties of the objects. The ideality doctrine does not require that relational propositions be reducible to propositions with nonrelational predicates only. Russell and Rescher suggest that the doctrine does require this, but the passages cited above contrast 'ideal' relations to relational properties.[3] Relations are ideal because they cannot be present in two subjects at once. Relational properties belong to one subject only and cannot be called ideal, at least for the reason that relations are. Hintikka and Ishiguro claim that the ideality doctrine entails nothing more than R1, and I must agree.[4]

An examination of Leibniz's actual attempts to reduce relational propositions provides support for their interpretation. Some of his reductions contain nonrelational predicates only. "Peter is similar to Paul" is reducible to "Peter is A now and Paul is A now" (LP, 13). However, Leibniz reduces "Paris loves Helen" to "Paris loves, *and by that very fact (et eo ipso)* Helen is loved" (LP, 14). The reduction contains a non-truth-functional operator, *"eo ipso,"*[5] and it contains implicitly relational terms, 'loves' and 'loved'.

It is possible that Leibniz never meant the above reduction to be viewed as an ultimate reduction, but there is no evidence to suggest that he had another one in mind. Parkinson points to a letter of 1679 in which Leibniz states that the purpose of reduction is to cast all reasonings in a "certain and indubitable form" (A, ii, I, 498).[6] He recognized that some arguments requiring the use of relational propositions could not be explicated in terms of traditional subject-predicate logic.

He presents as an example the "oblique inference": "Jesus Christ is God; therefore the mother of Jesus Christ is the mother of God" (NE, 560). Elsewhere, Leibniz argued that subject-predicate logic needed supplementation, a "rational grammar" which could be used to transform relational arguments into forms which traditional logic could handle (C, 36, 244). Leibniz's main purpose in giving reductions may have been to transform relational arguments into a form whose validity can be commonly agreed upon, and it is not clear that this requires the reduction of relational propositions to ones containing nonrelational predicates only.

IV. The Doctrine of Extrinsic Denomination

So far, the evidence shows that Leibniz held a reducibility doctrine R1 but nothing stronger in the way of a *reducibility doctrine*. I argue that he believed in a connection between relational and nonrelational propositions which is not one of reducibility. My argument begins with his doctrine of extrinsic denomination:

> There is no denomination so extrinsic as not to have an intrinsic one for its foundation. [L, 526–527. See also L, 268.]

Ishiguro points out that Leibniz probably used 'denomination' as the medieval logicians did.[7] Anselm means by 'denomination' the appellation of an object by an expression which refers to a quality the object has. Extrinsic and intrinsic denominations are probably different properties. A passage from *Opuscules et fragments inédits* indicates that the contrast between the properties boils down to a contrast between relational and nonrelational properties:

> the category of relations such as quantity and position do not constitute intrinsic [nonrelational] denominations themselves, and furthermore, need a basis taken from the category of quality, or intrinsic denomination of accidents. [C, 9]

Leibniz never explicitly stated what he meant by saying that nonrelational properties are the 'basis' or 'foundation' of relational properties. The result has been that the doctrine of extrinsic denomination is not taken seriously as an expression of an important connection between relational and nonrelational propositions. Take John Earman's interpretation of the passage, for instance.[8] If the doctrine is interpreted as a claim about what is true in the ordinary world of physical objects, says

Earman, it involves nothing more than Leibniz's belief that all proposi-tions can be translated into subject-predicate form and his containment theory of truth. Leibniz was merely pointing out that the relational predicates of ordinary physical objects are contained in their corre-sponding subject concepts, in such a way that the predicates are deriv-able from the subject concepts.[9]

However, in the passages quoted above, Leibniz is not merely claim-ing that relational predicates are derivable from subject concepts. He is saying relational properties need a foundation in *intrinsic* or *nonre-lational* properties. Furthermore, there are other passages which strongly suggest that Leibniz meant something quite significant when he said there must be a foundation for relational properties in nonrela-tional properties. In the *New Essays*, Locke's spokesman says that a subject may remain unchanged even though its relation to some other substance may change. A father may be unchanged by his son's death, for instance, even though he is no longer a father. Leibniz replies,

> That statement may very well be made in view of things which are per-ceived; although in metaphysical strictness it is true that there is no entire exterior denomination (*denominatio pure extrinseca*) because of the real connection of all things. [NE, 236]

Elsewhere, Leibniz remarks that

> there are no extrinsic denominations, and no one becomes a widower in India by the death of his wife in Europe unless a real change occurs in him. [L, 365]

These passages suggest that a change in the relational properties of a substance must be accompanied by a change in its nonrelational prop-erties.

It does not seem too great a leap to infer that Leibniz believed the relational properties of a substance to be determined by its nonrela-tional properties. Given that a substance has a certain set of nonrela-tional properties (and perhaps certain other premises), it follows that the substance has a certain set of relational properties. Given changes in the nonrelational properties (and perhaps certain other premises), changes in the relational properties follow. This interpretation gives a natural sense to the claim that the relational properties of a substance have a foundation in its nonrelational properties.

To complete this interpretation, it is necessary to specify the sense in which the relational properties of a substance and changes in these properties follow (at least in part) from its nonrelational properties and changes in these properties. There is no direct textual evidence on this matter. A highly plausible interpretation is suggested by Leibniz's distinction between two ways in which a predicate may be deduced from a subject concept.

One of Leibniz's most notorious doctrines is that the nature of a substance is to have a concept so complete that it is sufficient to allow the deduction from it of all the predicates truly attributable to the substance (DM, 12–13). God can clearly apprehend the notion of Alexander and can deduce all that ever happened to him, all the predicates truly attributable to him. A predicate can be deduced in one of two ways. One kind of deduction or "consecution" is absolutely necessary, in which the contrary of what is deduced entails contradiction. The other kind "is only necessary *ex hypothesi,* and so to speak by accident, but in itself is contingent, the contrary implying no contradiction" (DM, 19–20). Examples of predicates that must be deduced in the second way are predicates attributable to Caesar which would inform us why he "resolved rather to cross the Rubicon than to stop at it and why he won rather than lost the day at Pharasalus." To deduce the predicates is to know "that it was reasonable and consequently assured that this would happen, but not that it is necessary in itself nor that the contrary implies contradiction" (DM, 21). In order to perform the demonstration, it is necessary to suppose the "sequence of things that God has freely chosen and which is founded on the first free decree of God, the import of which is always to do what is most perfect, and the decree which God made with regard to human nature, which is that man will always do that which appears to him best." Thus contingent truths about a substance are deducible only on the supposition of God's free decrees and the resulting physical laws. Necessary truths are deducible solely on the basis of the principle of contradiction, without regard to the free decrees of God (DM, 22).

The predicates which are contained in necessary truths about a substance could be said to be more basic to it, and indeed, in correspondence with Arnauld, Leibniz writes of "basic" predicates:

> For all the predicates of Adam depend or do not depend upon other predicates of the same Adam. Setting aside, therefore, those which do depend upon others, one has only to consider together all the basic predicates in order to form the complete concept of Adam adequate to deduce from it everything that is ever to happen to him, as much as is necessary to be able to account for it. [LA, 48]

Perhaps the basic predicates are contained in necessary truths about Adam, while other predicates are contained in contingent truths about him. From the basic predicates, all the others can be deduced according to supposition of the free decrees of God and ancillary physical laws.

In different possible worlds, a set of nonrelational properties could be combined with different sets of relational properties. In the best possible world, a certain set of relational predicates is deducible from a given set of nonrelational ones on the supposition that God chooses to create the best. In a mediocre world, the relational predicates are deducible from nonrelational ones on a different supposition, that God chooses to create the mediocre, for instance. Thus each conception of a possible world contains God's possible decision. God considers his own possible decisions when he surveys the possible worlds and chooses which one to create.

It is important to note that the conception of contingency which Leibniz uses in distinguishing between two kinds of deduction differs from the conception that has become standard for us. Under the standard conception, to say that a relational predicate is contingently true of Adam is to say that in some possible world Adam lacks that predicate. Leibniz denies that an individual could lack a predicate in the actual world but possess it in another:

> For by the individual concept of Adam I mean, to be sure, a perfect representation of a particular Adam who has particular individual conditions and who is thereby distinguished from an infinite number of other possible persons who are very similar but yet different from him (as every ellipse is different from the circle, however much it approximates to it), and to whom God has preferred him, because it has pleased God to choose precisely this particular order of the universe. . . . There is a possible Adam whose posterity is thus, and an infinite number of other Adams whose posterity would be different; is it not true that these possible Adams (if one may so call them) differ among themselves and that God has chosen just one who is precisely our Adam? [LA, 15–16]

Each merely possible Adam stands in relation to the actual one as each ellipse to the circle. Each is a unique individual.

When Leibniz says that a contingent truth is a proposition whose contrary does not entail a contradiction, he is using "does not entail a contradiction" to attribute a proof-theoretical property to the proposition; that is, that its truth is deducible only through infinite analysis:

> In contingent truths, however, though the predicate inheres in the subject, we can never demonstrate this, nor can the proposition ever be reduced to an equation or an identity, but the analysis proceeds to infinity, only God being able to see not the end of the analysis indeed, since there

is no end, but the nexus of terms or the inclusion of the predicate in the subject, since he sees everything which is in the series. [L, 265]

That this world is the best of all possible worlds is deducible only through infinite analysis. One would have to examine the infinite characteristics of this world in order to assign a value to it and then compare it to an infinite number of other worlds in order to establish it as the best (see C, 19). Since any deduction of a relational predicate of Adam must proceed on the supposition that this is the best of all possible worlds, it must be a proof of a contingent truth. For Leibniz, the contingently true is true by virtue of the relations of subject and predicate concepts.[10] That is why he can assert that two possible individuals who do not share the same predicates cannot be the same individual.

Having specified Leibniz's conception of contingency, I am now in a position to state the sense in which the relational properties of a substance can be said to follow from its nonrelational ones. The corresponding relational predicates are deducible from the corresponding nonrelational predicates, and the deduction is of the kind that results in contingent truths. The basic predicates of a substance are its nonrelational ones, or some subset of them. If there is a change in the relational predicates which apply to a substance, then it must be deducible from some change in nonrelational predicates which apply to the substance.

Earman was partly correct in saying that the doctrine of extrinsic denomination involves nothing more than subject–predicate logic and the containment theory of truth. However, he neglected some important features of the containment theory and the way in which Leibniz applied the theory to the question of the deducibility of nonrelational predicates from subject concepts. If I am correct in my interpretation, Leibniz believed in an important connection between relational and nonrelational propositions, but it is not a connection of reducibility:

R2) All relational propositions concerning a substance S are deducible from the free decrees of God and ancillary physical laws together with propositions containing only nonrelational predicates attributable to S, and the deduction is of the kind that results in contingent truths. Propositions describing a change in the relations of S are deducible from the above premises and propositions describing a change in S's nonrelational properties.

The second sentence of R2 covers Leibniz's claim that no one becomes a widower in India by the death of his wife in Europe unless a real change occurs in him. The claim seems far-fetched but is understandable given Leibniz's view that everything which happens to an individual is deducible from his basic, nonrelational predicates and the free decrees of God with ancillary laws. If God chooses the best world, a man becomes a husband because it is best for a man with his intrinsic properties to become a husband. If he becomes a widower, that is best also. Since God has changed the man's status, he must have a reason for the change. The reason is to be found partly in the man's intrinsic properties. There is a change in his internal state which makes the relational change one for the best. Perhaps the man's character has changed so that it is no longer best that he have a wife. In the *Discourse on Metaphysics,* Leibniz says that God can know a priori whether Alexander died a natural death or by poison. Indeed, "we can say that there are at times in the soul of Alexander vestiges of all that has happened to him and the marks of all that will happen to him" (DM, 13).

V. Possibility and Compossibility

A test for any interpretation of Leibniz's theory of relations is whether it permits him to make a distinction he wanted to make: the one between possibility and compossibility. A possible substance is one whose existence does not involve contradiction. Two substances are compossible when they can coexist. Not all possible substances are compossible. A possible world is composed of possible substances which can coexist, and there is more than one possible world. Hintikka expresses the distinction between possibility and compossibility by comparing

a) $M(\exists x)Ax$ & $M(\exists x)Bx$
b) $M((\exists x)Ax$ & $(\exists x)Bx)$

where '*M*' is "it is possible that."[11] a) says that substances of the kind '*A*' are possible and that substances of the kind '*B*' are possible. b) says that substances of both kinds can coexist.

If '*A*' and '*B*' are nonrelational, monadic predicates,

c) $(\exists x)Ax$ & $(\exists x)Bx$

is satisfiable if and only if $(\exists x)Ax$ and $(\exists x)Bx$ are both separately satisfiable. a) and b) are not really distinct. However, if '*A*' and '*B*' are complex, relational predicates, it may happen that $(\exists x)Ax$ and $(\exists x)Bx$ are both satisfiable while c) is not. For instance, "There exists everybody's master" and "There exists nobody's slave" are separately satisfiable but incompatible. Hintikka claims that Leibniz will lose the distinction between possibility and compossibility if he holds that all relational predicates can be reduced to nonrelational ones. Relational predicates must be included as nonreducible parts of subject concepts if Leibniz is to preserve the distinction.

In fact, Hintikka's claim is false if the distinction between possibility and compossibility is interpreted in such a way that it is sufficient that a) not entail b) for some choice of 'A' and 'B'. Suppose all relations are deducible from nonrelational predicates of the relata (such as 'x is the same color as y'). Let 'Ax' be '($\exists y$) ($y \neq x$ & (y) ($y \neq x \rightarrow x$ is the same color as y)' and let 'Bx' be '($\exists y$) ($y \neq x$ & (y) ($y \neq x \rightarrow x$ is not the same color as y))'. Then a) is true and b) is not. On the other hand, suppose the distinction between possibility and compossibility is interpreted in such a way that it is required that it be impossible for two possible individuals in different worlds to coexist in the same world. Since the impossibility of their coexistence cannot be derived from their nonrelational predicates alone, Hintikka has a case for saying that Leibniz loses the distinction between possibility and compossibility if he does not include relational predicates and nonreducible parts of subject concepts.[12]

Under my interpretation, Leibniz could have held the second interpretation of the distinction (which seems a reasonable one to me) and preserved the distinction at the same time. Under my interpretation, he held that the relational predicates which apply to a substance can be deduced from a set of its basic, nonrelational predicates and the free decrees of God, but he did not hold that relational predicates can be eliminated from the concept of the substance. Indeed, we have seen that Leibniz's special conception of contingency is such that he believed predicates which are contingently true of a substance cannot be eliminated from its concept. Human beings are not able to know a priori that a relational predicate belongs to a possible substance, but God can know this when he examines its concept. He will know that two possible substances with conflicting relational predicates do not exist in the same possible world, even though the nonrelational predicates are compatible.

VI. Relations and Expression

A standard puzzle for readers of Leibniz has been the expression doctrine:

Each individual substance is an expression of the entire universe after its own manner, and . . . in its concept all events that occur in it are included with all their circumstances and the whole succession of external things. [LA, 5]

Hintikka has suggested that the expression doctrine means that the concept of an individual substance includes "complex predicates," which seem to be implicitly relational predicates. The complex predicates which apply to a substance implicitly refer to all other substances standing in some relation to it. Because its concept contains these predicates, a substance expresses everything in the possible world containing it.[13]

This could be part of what Leibniz meant by expression, but it cannot be all:

> One thing expresses another . . . when there exists a constant and fixed relationship between what can be said of one and the other . . . this expression occurs everywhere, because every substance is in harmony with every other and undergoes some proportionate change which corresponds to the smallest change occurring in the whole universe, although this change is more or less noticeable to the extent that other bodies or their actions have more or less connexion with ours. [LA, 144. See also GI, 383; C, 15; GVII, 263.]

It is possible to interpret the talk of "constant and fixed relationship" in a way that is consistent with Hintikka's interpretation. However, the talk of change indicates that a fuller interpretation is needed.

A natural interpretation is the following: a substance stands in some relation to every other substance in the same possible world; if it undergoes a change in nonrelational properties, all the other substances will undergo a change in their relational properties (if a thin man becomes fat everyone now has some property of being related to a fat rather than a thin man); by R2, this means that each substance undergoes a change in nonrelational properties.

There is some evidence that this is the reasoning which led Leibniz to postulate the wave effect of expression. In "First Truths," Leibniz affirms his doctrines that there is no purely extrinsic denomination and that each substance expresses the entire universe. Then he says that each created substance exerts action on all others:

> For if a change occurs in one, *some corresponding change results in all others, because their denomination is changed.* This is confirmed by our experience of nature, for we observe that in a vessel full of liquid (the whole universe is such a vessel) a motion made in the middle is propagated to the edges, though it may become more and more insensible as it recedes farther from its origin. [L, 269; italics mine]

The change in denomination occurs because of the change in relational properties and because change in relational properties does not occur without change in nonrelational properties.

VII. Relations between Monads

I have discussed R2 as it applies to all sorts of individuals, including ones like Caesar and Adam. R2 can be used to explain the relations between simple substances or monads.

Leibniz believed each monad was characterized in terms of its perceptions of the entire universe or possible world to which it belongs. I agree with Furth's claim that these perceptions must be interpreted as purely intensional entities. To say that a monad perceives an object is not to presuppose that the object exists.[14] When Des Bosses asserts that God cannot create any one monad without creating the rest because their perceptions must correspond with each other and be perceptions of the same universe, Leibniz replies,

> There would be no deception of rational creatures, however, even if everything outside of them did not correspond exactly to their experiences, or indeed, if nothing did, just as if there were only one mind; because everything would happen just as if all other things existed, and this mind, acting with reason, would not charge itself with any fault. For this is not to err. [L, 611]

Elsewhere, Leibniz says that each monad represents the entire universe but is "confused as regards the variety of particular things in the whole universe, and can be distinct only as regards a small part of things." Monads are "limited and differentiated through the degrees of their distinct perceptions" (M, 250). Thus the internal state of a monad is constituted by its perceptions along with the intensity and clarity of its perceptions.

I suggest that the nonrelational predicates which apply to a monad specify such a state. Relational predicates apply to a monad also, but these predicates do not stand for perceptions only. They stand for relational properties which make it possible for monads to constitute individuals like Adam. Adam was composed of a collection of monads which constituted his organic body. A "dominant" monad unifies the collection, makes it into the body of one individual. A relational proposition about a monad might inform us about what collection of monads it belongs to.

When we apply R2 to monads, we get the claim that all relational propositions about a monad are deducible from the free decrees of God and ancillary laws together with propositions about its perceptions. To understand how such a deduction could be made, we can start with the plausible supposition that a dominant monad unifies a collection of monads into a single body through its perceptions. Perhaps the clearest and most intense of its perceptions are of certain monads; as intentional objects these monads correspond to the collection it unifies into a body. That is, the dominant monad perceives the monads it dominates. The latter are differentiated by *their* perceptions, so the dominant monad perceives monads with certain perceptions. The following passage is some evidence that Leibniz thought of the relations between monads in this way:

> And each outstanding simple substance or monad which forms the center of a compound substance (such as an animal, for example), and is the principle of its uniqueness, is surrounded by a mass composed of an infinity of other monads which constitute the body belonging to this central monad, corresponding to the affections by which it represents, as in a kind of center, the things which are outside it. [L, 637]

Perhaps all monads perceived by the dominant one have similar perceptions in that they perceive approximately the same part of the universe. By perceiving the perceptions of the monads constituting its body, the dominant monad could represent, as "in a kind of center, the things which are outside it."

R2 tells us that the relational proposition that a monad belongs to the body of Adam could be deduced from a proposition about the perceptions of the monad, together with the free decrees of God and ancillary laws. Presumably, God can see through infinite analysis that in the best world a monad with certain perceptions and not others belongs to the body of Adam and is perceived by the dominant monad of Adam.

VIII. Concluding Remarks

If I am right in my interpretation, there is a remarkable and previously unnoticed coherence among Leibniz's doctrine of truth, his theory of relations, his doctrine of expression, and his theory of monads. The key to discovering this coherence is to shift the focus of attention from the question of the reducibility of relations to the question of how relational properties are founded upon nonrelational properties. Once this shift is made, Leibniz's theory of relations assumes a central place

in his philosophy and is the link between the theory of truth and the
metaphysical doctrines.

Abbreviations

The following abbreviations are used for Leibniz's works:

A for *Sämtliche Schriften und Briefe,* Academy edition (Darmstadt and Berlin,
   1923–), cited by series, volume, and page;
C for *Opuscules et fragments inédits,* ed. L. Couturat (Paris, 1903);
DM for *Discourse on Metaphysics,* trans. P. G. Lucas and L. Grint (Manchester,
   1953);
G for *Philosophische Schriften von G. W. Leibniz,* ed. C. I. Gerhardt (Berlin,
   1875–90);
L for *Philosophical Papers and Letters* 2d ed. (Dordrecht, 1969);
LA for *The Leibniz-Arnauld Correspondence,* ed. H. T. Mason (Manchester,
   1967);
LC for *The Leibniz-Clarke Correspondence,* ed. H. G. Alexander (Manchester,
   1956);
LP for *Logical Papers,* ed. G. H. R. Parkinson (New York, 1966);
M for *The Monadology,* trans. Robert Latta (London, 1898);
NE for *New Essays Concerning Human Understanding,* ed. Alfred Langley
   (Chicago, 1916);
T for *Theodicy,* trans. E. M. Huggard (Ontario, 1966).

Notes

   I wish to thank Margaret Wilson, Fred Sommers, and the referee for *The
Philosophical Review* for helpful comments on earlier versions of this essay.
   1. Nicholas Rescher, *The Philosophy of Leibniz* (Englewood Cliffs, 1967),
p. 73.
   2. Jaakko Hintikka treats this sort of predicate as monadic (($\exists x$) . . . Rx to
b). See his "Leibniz on Plenitude, Relations and the 'Reign of Law'," in *Leibniz:
A Collection of Critical Essays,* ed. Harry G. Frankfurt (New York, 1972), p. 162.
Still, '*R*' is originally a two-place predicate, and the truth conditions for a proposition containing its ascription to a subject involve essential reference to some
individual other than the one explicitly named. I prefer to call nonrelational
those predicates which do not have these characteristics.
   3. Rescher, *Philosophy of Leibniz,* pp. 72–75; Bertrand Russell, *A Critical
Exposition of the Philosophy of Leibniz* (London, 1937), pp. 12–14.
   4. Hintikka, "Plentitude," pp. 164–168; Hidé Ishiguro, "Leibniz's Theory of
the Ideality of Relations," in *Leibniz: A Collection of Critical Essays,* ed. Harry
G. Frankfurt (New York, 1972), pp. 198–200; see also Hidé Ishiguro, *Leibniz's
Philosophy of Logic and Language* (New York, 1972), pp. 88–93.

5. As Ishiguro points out, material equivalence does not capture the sense of the operator; there are many propositions which can be related through material equivalence and which cannot be related through the "*eo ipso*" operator, e.g., "Snow is white ≡ 2 + 2 = 4"; Ishiguro, "Leibniz's Theory," p. 208.

6. G. H. R. Parkinson, *Logic and Reality in Leibniz's Metaphysics* (Oxford, 1965), pp. 51–52.

7. Ishiguro, "Leibniz's Theory," p. 193, n.6.

8. John Earman, "Perceptions and Relations in the Monadology," *Studia Leibnitiana,* Band IX (1977), p. 223.

9. Earman believes the doctrine of extrinsic denomination can be interpreted as the claim that there must be a founding of the world of physical objects with their relational properties on the world of monads with nonrelational properties only; I believe there must be some kind of founding, but not the kind Earman has in mind. I also believe that the founding involves relational properties of monads. Of course, I differ from Earman in interpreting the doctrine of extrinsic denomination as saying something significant about the connection between the relational properties of physical objects and the nonrelational properties of those *same* objects. Earman holds nothing like R2, but it should be noted that R2 is compatible with his interpretation of Leibniz.

10. It would therefore seem that possible world semantics must be applied carefully to Leibniz's talk of contingent propositions, if it is to be applied at all. For a discussion of the application of possible world semantics for modal logic to Leibniz, see Fabrizio Mondadori, "Leibniz and the Doctrine of Inter-World Identity," *Studia Leibnitiana,* Band VII (1975), pp. 21–57, and Benson Mates, "Individuals and Modality in the Philosophy of Leibniz," *Studia Leibnitiana,* Band IV (1972), pp. 81–118. For discussions of the difficulties of applying the semantics to Leibniz, see Robert M. Adams, "Leibniz's Theories of Contingency," *Rice University Studies: Essays on the Philosophy of Leibniz,* ed. Mark Kulstad (Houston, 1977), pp. 1–41, and Dennis Fried, "Necessity and Contingency in Leibniz," *The Philosophical Review,* LXXXVII (1978), pp. 575–584. The Adams article contains an enlightening discussion of Leibniz's proof-theoretic conception of contingency.

11. Hintikka, "Plenitude," pp. 159–160.

12. I thank the referee for *The Philosophical Review* for pointing out to me the consequences of the different interpretations of the distinction between possibility and compossibility. The choice of '*A*' and '*B*' described in the example was suggested by the referee.

13. Hintikka, "Plenitude," pp. 168–170.

14. Montgomery Furth, "Monadology," *Leibniz: A Collection of Critical Essays,* ed. Harry G. Frankfurt (New York, 1972), p. 103.

13

Occasionalism and General Will in Malebranche

Steven Nadler

Occasionalism is a much more complex and interesting doctrine than the traditional textbook mythology would have us believe. First, it is clear that occasionalism was not simply an *ad hoc* remedy for a perceived mind–body problem facing Cartesian dualism. Rather, it was a full-bodied philosophical account of the nature of causal relations generally, motivated in part by the desire to demonstrate the true metaphysical foundations of Cartesian physics and the mechanical philosophy.[1] Moreover, occasionalism had to reconcile in a single theory of causation several distinct (and often apparently irreconcilable) sets of concerns, both philosophical and theological. It is this second issue I wish to focus on here, particularly as it pertains to how we understand Malebranche's version of the doctrine.

There has been a great deal of inconsistency and disagreement in the way in which Malebranche's occasionalism has been interpreted by commentators, whether by his critics or partisans, among both his contemporaries and recent scholars. In fact, at least two distinct and apparently incompatible readings of his theory emerge, and we are left having to choose between two different pictures of causation and God's role therein. On one picture, God's activity as cause is constant and ubiquitous, and is required in order to maintain a lawlike correspondence in the states of things. The other picture more closely resembles Leibniz's preestablished harmony, with God originally establishing such a correspondence once and for all by means of a few general volitions. In other words, there is something funny about the way in which Malebranche's occasionalism has been read. In this chapter, I try to get to the bottom of the confusion and point out the proper way to understand his account.

The mechanics of Malebranche's doctrine most easily lends itself to the following reading, which I here call the "traditional" reading. Finite creatures, whether bodies or minds, have no causal efficacy, no power whatsoever to effect real changes in each other. God is the only true causal agent. The apparent causal interactions among finite entities are, in fact, simply ongoing manifestations of the divine activity. God, then, is constantly engaged in the workings of the world, bringing about changes in and among souls and physical objects on the occasion either of contact between bodies or of a volition in a human mind. To be sure, God's activity as cause is not *ad hoc,* but is governed by general laws instituted by God at creation. But unlike Descartes's God, Malebranche's deity does not simply let nature take its course once motion has been imparted to it.[2] Rather, Malebranche's God is personally, directly, and immediately responsible for bringing about effects and causal changes in nature—for example, for altering the direction and velocity of the motion of one billiard ball when it is struck by another.

There is no question that many of Malebranche's contemporaries understood his position to involve a constant activity by God. Leibniz, for example, takes such an ongoing participation by God in the affairs of the world to be one of the important differences between his own theory of preestablished harmony and occasionalism. The system of occasional causes, he insists, demands "a perpetual supervisor . . . a little as if a man were charged with constantly synchronizing two bad clocks which are in themselves incapable of agreeing"; while his own theory suggests "the natural agreement" of substances, such as would exist between two very exact clocks.[3] He accuses Malebranche of introducing "continuous miracles" into the course of nature at every moment, and of having God "intervene" with the laws of bodies and of thought.[4] To Leibniz's mind, there is no mistaking occasionalism for a preestablished harmony.

Now I shall argue that we ought to keep to this traditional reading of Malebranche's occasionalism. In this regard, I am not offering any new or groundbreaking theses. But when we look at the alternative reading of his doctrine, and at the textual basis for it, it becomes clear that there is a certain *prima facie* tension in Malebranche's system—a tension between the occasionalist theory of causation as it is presented in the *Search after Truth* and the *Dialogues on Metaphysics,* on the one hand, and, on the other hand, his account of the nature of divine volition in the *Treatise on Nature and Grace* and elsewhere. Resolving this tension will not mean giving up the traditional reading. But it will require putting that reading in the context of the more properly theological works. The result is a deeper understanding of Malebranche's doctrine. And we will see that what initially appears to be a tension in Malebranche's system is, in fact, simply the result of isolating one dimension of divine volition at the expense of the other.

1.

Arnauld is well-known for being Malebranche's harshest, most rigorous, and perhaps most insightful critic. Thus, it comes as a bit of a surprise to find that Arnauld's understanding of what occasionalism involves, particularly with regard to God's activity as cause, differs from what has come to be the traditional interpretation. In a letter to Leibniz (March 4, 1687), Arnauld insists that Leibniz's position on mind-body "interaction" really is, in essence, no different from what he understands to be the occasionalist position. According to Leibniz's theory of preestablished harmony, my desire to raise my arm is not the real cause of my arm's rising. Rather, the desire occurs in the mind (in consequence of some prior mental state) at the very moment when the body, "by virtue of its own laws," moves itself. This "wonderful but unfailing agreement of things" is the result of God's initial resolution at creation upon the sequences of all things in the universe; it does not come about by God's moment-to-moment causal intervention in the world.[5] For Arnauld,

> this is to say the same thing in other terms that those say who maintain that my will is the occasional cause for the movement of my arm and that God is its real cause; for they do not claim that God does this at the moment by a new act of will each time that I wish to raise my arm, but by a single act of the eternal will by which he has chosen to do everything which he has foreseen that it will be necessary to do, in order that the universe might be such as he has decided it ought to be.[6]

I take Arnauld, in his claim that Leibniz's position is simply an "occasionalism" in different clothes, to be understanding the occasionalist position as one whereby God foresees and then, by a few initial simple and general acts of will, chooses and institutes an ongoing correspondence between the states of things, without having to "intervene" and maintain appearances with a constant activity. God, in his prescience, chooses at creation a world with all its present and future states of affairs, details, and dynamics or correspondences. This choice of a world which unfolds over time takes place once and for all by means of "a single act of the eternal will," to use Arnauld's phrase, by means of a general volition which has the whole universe (in all its present and future states) as its scope. Thus, on Arnauld's reading of occasionalism, God's will or resolve is responsible for the movement of my arm on the occasion of a desire in my soul only in the sense that God, by a simple and general volition, originally willed the series of corresponding events to be such as it is; but *not* in the sense that God wills at time *t* on occasion *o* to move arm *a*.[7]

How is it that Arnauld understands the occasionalist position to resemble, in this regard, Leibniz's preestablished harmony? Since, at the time of his letter to Leibniz, Arnauld's most recent and thorough acquaintance with the doctrine of occasional causes comes by way of Malebranche's *Search after Truth* and *Treatise on Nature and Grace*,[8] we should turn to the relevant texts of both Malebranche and Arnauld for an answer to this question.

Under its most well-known guise, the Arnauld-Malebranche debate is an epistemological debate over the direct and immediate objects of perception. For Arnauld, these are bodies in the world; for Malebranche, they are representative ideas in the divine understanding. This picture of the debate pits Arnauld's direct realism against Malebranche's visionary representative theory.[9] But the polemic over "true and false ideas" is merely a preliminary, a warm-up for the more important debate over theological issues. In Arnauld's eyes, one of the most unacceptable features of Malebranche's system is his understanding of the mode of God's operations in both the realm of nature and the realm of grace.

In his *Treatise on Nature and Grace,* Malebranche undertakes the theodicy problem, the task of explaining how God's omnipotence, benevolence, and perfection can be reconciled with the persistence of evil and imperfections in the natural world and with the apparent unfairness in the distribution of divine grace and everlasting happiness. (Since we are concerned here with Malebranche's occasionalism as a theory of natural causation, I restrict my discussion to God's activity in the realm of nature.) Our conception of God tells us that God is infinitely wise, good, powerful, and perfect. God's knowledge and benevolence are without bounds, and God's will and power are necessarily efficacious (*Treatise* I.12, OC 5:27). Moreover, God wishes to make the most beautiful and perfect world possible, the better to express and honor the qualities and perfections possessed by God himself. Nonetheless, the world which God has, in fact, created certainly appears to us to be quite imperfect in its details and full of disorders of every variety. Monsters and deformed creatures are born; there is sin and misery among human beings; even the rain regularly falls on the sea, where it is not needed, rather than on fertile soil (*Treatise* I.13–14, OC 5:28–30). As Theodore, Malebranche's spokesman in the *Dialogues on Metaphysics,* exclaims, "The Universe then is the most perfect that God can make? But really! So many monsters, so many disorders, the great number of impious men—does all this contribute to the perfection of the universe?" (*Dialogues* IX.9, OC 12:211 = D 211). Aristes, his interlocutor, is led thereby to wonder about either the efficacy of God's will or the benevolence of God's intentions:

> God wishes to make a work that is the most perfect possible. For, the more perfect it is, the more it will honor Him. This appears evident to me. Yet I understand that the work would be more accomplished if it were free of thousands upon thousands of defects which disfigure it. Here is a contradiction that stops me quite short. It seems that God did not accomplish His plan, or that He did not adopt the plan most worthy of His attributes. (*Dialogues* IX.9, OC 12:211 = D 211)

The resolution of this conundrum, as presented in both the *Dialogues* and the *Treatise,* is to be found in the consideration not just of the details of the visible universe, not just of the particular effect wrought by God, but also of the means undertaken to achieve and sustain this product. God, according to Malebranche, when creating looks not only to the final result of the creative act (that is, to the goodness and perfection of the world *per se*). God is honored not just by the *creatatum,* but also by his work or ways. And the activities or means most expressive of God's nature are of maximum simplicity, uniformity, fecundity, and universality (*Treatise* I.13, OC 5:28). God does not accomplish by complex means that which can be accomplished by simple means; and God does not execute with many particular volitions that which can be executed by a few general volitions. This holds true even if it means that the world created by God could be spared some imperfections were God to compromise the simplicity and generality of his operations. That is, the perfection of the world in its details as a product is completely relative to the mode of activity which is most worthy of God. God might have increased the absolute perfection of the world, perhaps by decreasing the number of defects or evils therein. But this would have entailed greater complexity in the divine ways. God might, for example, keep the rain from falling on anything but fertile and inseminated soil. But this would involve departing from the general laws of nature established at creation.

> In a sense, it can be said that God wants all his creatures to be perfect; that he does not want infants to perish in their mother's wombs; that he does not like monsters, and that he has not made the laws of nature in order to engender them; and that if he had been able, by equally simple ways, to create and conserve a more perfect world, he would not have established laws from which so many monsters necessarily result. But it

> would have been unworthy of his wisdom to multiply his volitions in
> order to prevent certain particular disorders. (*Treatise* I.22, OC 5:35)

The world which God has created is the one out of the infinitely many
which best reconciles perfection of design with simplicity and generality of means of production and conservation (*Treatise* I.13, OC 5:28).[10]
By a number of "particular volitions" (*volontés particulières*), God
could correct deformities of birth, keep fruit from rotting on trees,
prevent physical disasters about to occur by the regular course of the
laws of nature (floods, droughts, etc.), and forestall sin and wickedness.
But, Malebranche insists, "we must be careful not to require constant
miracles from God, nor to attribute them to him at every moment"
(*Treatise* I.21, OC 5:34). God, in other words, only acts by "general
volitions" (*volontés générales*) and the most simple ways (*les voies les
plus simples*), and *never* by particular volitions (*Dieu n'agit point par
des volontez particulières*), except in the case of miracles. The solution
to the problem of evil is found in the simplicity and uniformity of God's
conduct, in the generality of the divine will.[11]

From this general outline of Malebranche's account of the nature of
divine volition and activity in the realm of nature, we can begin to get
a sense both of a *prima facie* tension in Malebranche's system, and of
a possible explanation for the kind of reading of Malebranche's occasionalism we find in Arnauld and others. The tension, briefly stated,
appears when this emphasis on the generality, simplicity, and uniformity of God's ways is considered in conjunction with what at least appears to be a demand within the occasionalist theory of causation for
an infinite number of *particular* volitions on God's part. Recall that on
the traditional reading, God's activity as efficient cause of natural effects is constant and omnipresent. It is God who directly and immediately moves the second billiard ball upon impact with the first. And this
would seem to entail a particular volition on God's part—that is, a volition at time *t* to move object *x* on occasion *o*. Before trying to resolve
this tension in favor of the traditional reading, let us return to Arnauld's
alternative reading and see whence it comes.

Arnauld, in the *Réflexions,* undertakes to demonstrate that, *pace*
Malebranche, it is false that God only acts by means of general volitions
and never by particular volitions. Part of his strategy is to show that
Malebranche simply mistakes both the manner of operating which is
most worthy of God and the import of what it means to act by particular volitions. And we find in Arnauld's critique that his (mis)understand-
ing of Malebranche's conception of what it is for God to act by *volontés
générales* informs his interpretation of Malebranche's occasionalism.

Malebranche, according to Arnauld, makes the mistake of identifying 'acting in accordance with general laws' with 'acting by general volitions', where general volitions are understood by Arnauld as volitions whose content is general and nonspecific, and which do not directly regard particulars. God, Arnauld insists, clearly acts in accordance with general laws. Laws are simply the "order" according to which things are done (*les loix sont l'ordre selon lequel les choses se font*), and by nature are general. Thus, if God does things in an orderly way, as he must, then God acts in accordance with general laws (*Réflexions,* 175). But the *means* by which (*ce par quoi*) God actually brings something about according to law (that is, the volition itself) cannot be general. Everything God does, he does in particular, not in general. When God creates a soul, he creates it by a particular action. And since 'to do' and 'to will' are one and the same for God, if God *does* something in particular it is by means of a particular *volition* (*Réflexions,* 175). To be sure, these particular volitions occur in accordance with general law (*Dieu agit par des volontés particulières en conséquence des loix générales*). But this does not imply that the volitions themselves are general in nature or universal in scope. God always desires "every effect in particular positively and directly, although in conformity with a general law" (*Réflexions,* 174–75). Any other mode of action is unworthy of God, who must take a direct and constant interest in every aspect of his creation. Malebranche does not understand this, Arnauld insists, and mistakenly thinks that if God acts "in accordance with general law," then God must thereby act by general volitions.

Another way of putting this point, Arnauld suggests, is to consider the ambiguity in the concept of 'general cause'. An agent can be a general cause in the sense that its concern or activity extends to all things, but by means of taking a particular interest or concern in (and, thus, a particular volition for) each and every particular thing. This is the sense in which it *is* proper to speak of God as a general cause. On the other hand, an agent can be a general cause in the way in which a distant and detached king governs a kingdom solely by means of general decrees (e.g., "There shall be no begging in the streets"), without any concern as to how they relate to or affect individual subjects, or without any interest in the details and quality of execution of the decree; or the way in which a bishop has a general care for the whole of a very large diocese, without necessarily concerning himself for each and every individual in particular (*Réflexions,* 178). In Arnauld's eyes, Malebranche treats God as a general cause in this second sense, a sense which is unworthy of God's goodness, and which conditionalizes God's power by assuming that the scope of God's concern for particulars is limited by the enormous population of his "diocese."[12]

This, then, is the general thrust of Arnauld's attack on Malebranche's

Treatise. In that attack, Arnauld's interpretation of Malebranche's view of divine activity has Malebranche's God acting only by general and universal decrees, callously unconcerned with particular events and objects. Thus, when Malebranche claims that "God acts only by general volitions," Arnauld clearly reads him as *denying* that God acts by means of particular volitions in a lawlike manner.

Now it is only a small and natural step from this reading of divine volition in Malebranche's *Treatise* to the alternative reading of his occasionalism. If the phrase 'God acts only by general volitions' is taken in the sense in which Arnauld understands Malebranche to mean it— whereby God acts only by decrees which are general in scope, and never upon individuals as an efficient cause of particular changes— then it clearly *must* be the case that with respect to natural events God, by a few original and general acts of will, establishes once and for all "everything which he has foreseen that it will be necessary to do, in order that the universe might be such as he has decided it ought to be." Only such a reading would seem to preserve in God's will and activity the kind of simplicity and generality Arnauld thinks Malebranche intends. Nor should we be surprised that Arnauld's reading of the occasionalism in the *Search after Truth* is influenced by his understanding of divine volition in the *Treatise,* since his immediate and primary concern is with the theological implications of Malebranche's doctrine of God's *volontés générales,* and not with the philosophical aspects of his theory of causation.[13] (In fact, Arnauld did not even conceive the project of criticizing Malebranche's *Search after Truth,* which he does in *Des vraies et des fausses idées,* until he became convinced that it was merely a philosophical prolegomena to the doctrine of grace in the *Treatise*).[14]

Interestingly, Arnauld is not alone in reading Malebranche's occasionalism in this way. Several recent commentators have adopted a similar (but not identical) understanding of his doctrine. Charles McCracken, for example, focuses, like Arnauld, on Malebranche's discussion of divine volition, and even compares Malebranche to Leibniz in this regard.

> Malebranche, too, took a richness of effects wrought by the simplest possible means to be the mark of a creator's perfection. Accordingly, he explicitly rejected the view that God performs a separate "act of will" to cause each event that occurs in nature. He denied that when one billiard ball strikes another, God, by a "particular volition," sets the second ball in motion; nor did he think that each time I will to raise my arm, God, by a particular act, causes it to rise. Instead, God rules all things by a few "general volitions."[15]

According to McCracken, these "few general volitions" just are general decrees instituting universal laws of motion, of thought, and of mind–body union. They are sufficient by themselves to determine how bodies will behave, or what state a thing will be in on any particular occasion, once things are set going.[16] No further divine volitions are required; no "particular acts" on God's part are necessary to bring any effects about. God, by a general volition wills a certain law governing impact between moving bodies. That law takes the form of a conditional: if body *a* is moving in a certain way, and it comes into contact with body *b* moving in a certain way, then body *b* will change its motion in such and such a manner. The fulfillment of the antecedent of the conditional is the "occasion" for the operation of the law, hence for the change in *b*'s motion. "[God] need not, in addition, will that this particular moving body, on this particular occasion," take on this particular motion.[17] God's will, on this reading (as on Arnauld's reading), is still the "cause" of effects in the world. Since the law just *is* God's general volition, and since the law is necessary and sufficient to bring about the effect when the requisite "occasion" obtains, then it is ultimately God's volition which is the necessary and sufficient condition for the effect.

Nicholas Jolley takes a similar line. Rejecting Foucher's suggestion that the preestablished harmony is simply occasionalism with all the adjustments made at once (a characterization grounded in the traditional reading), Jolley denies that Malebranche's occasionalism involves a series of discrete divine acts. This picture, he asserts, rests on a "gross misinterpretation" of Malebranche's doctrine. "For Malebranche just as much as for Leibniz, God acts through general laws, not through a series of particular volitions," by which Jolley apparently means that God wills only general laws, not particular events. He even cites Arnauld as his authority here, using as evidence precisely the same passage from the 1687 letter to Leibniz examined above, as well as Arnauld's complaints regarding Malebranche's hypergeneralizing of divine volition.[18]

Desmond Clarke insists that "apart from the chronological connotations of *pre*established harmony," there is no significant difference between occasionalism and Leibniz's doctrine. "In fact, Malebranche's emphasis on the simplicity of the divine agency and his manifest endorsement of Descartes' identification of creation and conservation suggest that God does nothing more than create/conserve both physical phenomena and the laws which determine their interactions. Creation and conservation is an atemporal, unique action on God's part which bears little comparison with the repeated interventions of the assiduous watchmaker."[19] From his reference to Malebranche's emphasis on divine simplicity, it appears that Clarke, in his reading of Malebranche's occasionalism, falls into the same trap as Arnauld, Jolley, and McCracken.[20]

2.

The alternative readings offered by Arnauld *et al.* misrepresent Malebranche's occasionalism, and are based on a misunderstanding of what it means, for Malebranche, to say that God acts only by general volitions. Arnauld, in a sense, simply gets it backwards. Malebranche is not taking 'acting in accordance with general laws' to mean 'acting by general volitions', where the latter are understood as volitions whose content is of a general and nonspecific nature. On the contrary, he is explaining 'acting by general volitions' in terms of action in accordance with general laws. When we understand this, and when we grasp the real contrast in Malebranche between general volitions and particular volitions, the *prima facie* tension between Malebranche's discussion of God's general volitions and the demands of occasionalism as it is traditionally understood disappears, and we are left with a consistent picture of God's activity as cause in the realm of nature. By the same token, there is no longer the temptation towards the alternative readings.

It is clear, in spite of the Arnauldian reading to the contrary, that Malebranche's God *is* directly and immediately responsible for each and every particular effect in nature; that is, that God's activity as efficient cause is constant, ubiquitous, and necessary. At the very moment when one billiard ball strikes another, God wills efficaciously then and there to move the second ball. The second ball's motion is not the *immediate* result of some general volitions by God at creation with regard to the motions of bodies (although, as we shall see, such general volitions *qua* laws of nature do have a *mediate* role to play in this causal story). Rather, it is the immediate result of a discrete volitional act by God on this particular occasion (on the axiomatic assumption that if God moves an object on a particular occasion, God must will or have a volition to move the object on that occasion).

This becomes especially clear if we remember that one of Malebranche's arguments for his occasionalism is based on God's role as sustainer of the universe by means of its continuous creation. At every moment, God must recreate the universe in order to maintain it in existence. Now, this continuous creation of the universe involves a continuous creation of every object therein. Hence, God must constantly will that our billiard ball exist; otherwise, it would cease to exist. Moreover, God must will it to exist in some relative place or another, in some spatial relationship to other bodies. When God recreates the ball in the same relative place from moment to moment, it is at rest. When God conserves it in different successive relative places, it is in motion. This implies that unless there is a volition by God at time t to create body b in a particular relative place, different from its relative place at the previous moment (time $t - 1$), there will be no motion in body b. But this is tantamount to saying that God wills at time t to move body b (as opposed to simply willing at t to preserve b in the same state as it was at $t - 1$).

> Now the moving force of a body in motion is simply the volition of the Creator who conserves it successively in different places. . . . Hence, bodies cannot move one another, and their encounter or impact is only an occasional cause of the distribution of their motion. Since bodies are impenetrable, it is a kind of necessity that God, who I suppose acts at all times [*Dieu, que je suppose agir toujours*] with the same efficacy or quantity of moving force, distributes, as it were, the moving force from the striking body to the body struck.
>
> What is a body in motion? It is a body transported by divine action. . . . [Matter] does not have an active capacity, and it is in fact moved only by the continual action of the Creator [*l'action continuelle du Créateur*]. . . . Their encounter is but an occasional cause which, because of their impenetrability, obliges the Mover or Creator to distribute His action. (*Dialogues* VII.11–12, OC 12:162–64 = D 159–61)[21]

Other passages can easily be found in Malebranche which involve God in constant causal activity in the world. In the *Search,* Malebranche insists that "a natural cause is not a real and true, but only an occasional cause, which determines the Author of nature to act in such and such a manner in such and such a situation" (VI.2.iii, OC 2:373 = LO 448).[22] Elsewhere, he stipulates that in order for God to act as a motive cause, "there has to be in God a positive volition [*il faut donc en Dieu une volonté positive*] to put a ball in motion . . . and it is sufficient for it to be at rest that He stops willing it to be moved; just as in order for God to create a world . . . He must will positively the mode in which it must exist" (*Search* VI.2.ix, OC 2:431 = LO 516–17, translation modified).

While this clearly suggests that Malebranche's God does *not* act only by what Arnauld understood as "general volitions" (viz., volitions which are general in scope), it does *not* mean that Malebranche's God ordinarily acts by what Malebranche understood as "particular volitions." What it *does* mean is that Malebranche's God acts by means of what Arnauld understood as "particular volitions" and what Malebranche understood as "general volitions"—that is, by means of individual volitions in accordance with general laws. At time *t,* on such and such an occasion, God positively wills then and there to move a certain body in such and such a way. In this sense, there is a discrete and temporalized volition with a *particular* content (e.g., "Let this body now move thus") in God. But God's volitions to move bodies or cause events generally are always in accordance with the general laws he has established. God always acts in a lawlike and orderly manner, never arbitrarily and *ad hoc.* When God moves bodies on the occasion of contact with other bodies, God is, by means of such individual acts of will, simply executing or following through the laws instituted at creation.[23] And this is all Malebranche means when he says that God acts only by general volitions.

> When a needle pricks me, God makes me feel pain as a consequence of the general laws regarding the union of the soul and the body, in accordance with which he is constantly acting in us [*il agit en nous sans cesse*]. (*Réponse aux Réflexions,* OC 8:651)

> God acts by general volitions when he acts in consequence of the general laws he has established. For example, I say that God acts in me by general volitions when he makes me feel pain when I am pricked—since, in accordance with the general and efficacious laws regarding the union of the soul with the body which he has established, he makes me suffer pain whenever my body is ill-disposed. Likewise, when one ball strikes another, I say that God moves the second by a general volition, since he moves the second in accordance with the general and efficacious laws regarding the communication of motions. (*Treatise,* First Elucidation, OC 5:147)

One such physical law might stipulate, for example, that whenever a body at rest is struck by another body moving in a particular direction with a given velocity, it will behave in such and such a way. Thus, God does not move the second ball unless it is struck by some other body; and he moves it only in the way it ought to move, as stipulated by the relevant law.

To act by particular volitions, on the other hand, is to act in a capricious and *ad hoc* way, in an unorderly and arbitrary manner, without regard to general laws. "God acts by particular volitions, when the efficacy of his will is not at all determined by some general law to produce some effect. Thus, God acts by particular volitions when he makes me feel the pain of a prick without there occurring in my body . . . any change which determines him to act in me according to some general laws" (*Treatise,* First Elucidation, OC 5:147–48). God *never* acts by particular volitions understood in this way except in the case of miracles, since such a mode of operation in the ordinary course of nature would be unworthy of God's wisdom, simplicity, and goodness. Were God to act in this manner, there would be no difference between natural effects and miraculous events (*Treatise* I.59, OC 5:63).[24]

Now it may seem *prima facie* odd, if not in fact incoherent, to speak as I have of "temporalized" volitions in God. God, after all, is an eternal, hence atemporal being. This would seem to argue, then, for Arnauld's reading and against mine. In fact, the issue would be a problem for either reading of Malebranche's occasionalism, since even on Arnauld's "Leibnizian" interpretation God must act "in time" to create the world with all its implicit future states. Moreover, there is no indication that the "temporal" problem of the causal activity of an eternal God ever occurred to Malebranche (or his critics, as far as I can tell). He explicitly speaks of what God "will do in the course of time" (*Dialogues*, OC 12:59 = D 157). Nonetheless, we can make sense of such language in the following way. Natural events—caused by and thus linked to God's volitions—appear to us to occur in and unfold over time. Hence, from our finite, temporal point of view, we are compelled to regard God's volitions themselves as temporal. Absolutely speaking, however, from God's eternal point of view, this is not the way things are. Each volition is indexed to a particular event (an event which to us appears in time), but is still comprehended by God in the eternal present (or however things appear to God). The reading for which I am arguing does not require a temporal sequence of volitions in God. God's will remains eternal and unchanging; there is not literally a succession of volitions, one following another. All that is required is a one-to-one correspondence between temporal events and divine volitions, such that for each event x (physical or mental) there is an individual volition (with a particular content) in God causing that event to occur when it does ("Let it be the case that x at t"). And the volition that x should occur at t is in God not just at t, but eternally, as befits an atemporal and immutable God. But note, God still wills particular events that occur in time, and not just general laws.

This is precisely how Malebranche states his account in *Dialogues* VIII. Theodore is explaining to Aristes how God's immutability is reconcilable with his causal activity, which involves free volitions. The divine decrees, Theodore insists, are eternal and immutable.

> God made these decrees, or rather He fashions them unceasingly on eternal Wisdom, which is the inviolable rule of his volitions. And, although the effects of these decrees are infinite and produce thousands upon thousands of changes in the universe, the decrees are at times the same.

This is because the efficacy of these immutable decrees is determined to action [*déterminée à l'action*] only by the circumstances of the causes which are called natural and which I believe we ought to call "occasional," for fear of encouraging the dangerous prejudice of a "nature" or efficacy which is distinguished from the will of God and His omnipotence.

After Aristes wonders how there can be even a *possible* change of volition in God, as his freedom would appear to require, Theodore continues:

> You must understand that, in God, there is no succession of thoughts and volitions—that, by an eternal and immutable act, He knows everything and wills everything that He wills. God wills, with a perfect freedom and a total indifference, to create a world. He wills to make decrees and establish simple and general laws in order to govern it in a way that bears the character of His attributes. But, these decrees posited, they cannot be changed—not that they are necessary absolutely but are so *ex hypothesi*. Take note: it is simply that they are posited and that, when God made them, He knew so well what He was doing that they cannot be revoked. For, though some of them He made [only] for a time [*fait . . . pour un tems*], it is not that He changed His mind and will when the time comes; but rather one and the same act of His will refers to differences in time [*se rapporte aux differences des tems*] which are contained in His eternity. (OC 12:175–76 = D 173)

The talk of "an immutable and eternal act" and the claim that "in God, there is no succession of thoughts and volitions" would appear to support the alternative, Arnauldian reading. But Malebranche's point here is simply that for an immutable God, his causally efficacious volitions— although linked to temporal events ("made [only] for a time," "referring to differences in time")—are eternal and unchanging, and abide atemporally in God. As he says, their efficacy is activated (*déterminée à l'action*) by the occurrence in time of the proper occasion.

One final point: it should be clear that the traditional reading of occasionalism I am arguing for does not imply that, as Leibniz charges, God *intervenes* in nature and disrupts or suspends the laws of bodies and thought. For on this reading it is precisely those physical and psychophysical laws that God is carrying out in the ordinary course of nature. There is no "intervention" at all; only a divine maintenance of the lawlike correlation in the states of finite substances.[25]

3.

When Malebranche's discussion of God's acting only by *volontés générales* is read in the way I suggest, the apparent tension between the details of his theodicy and his occasionalism is eased.[26] As he insists in the *Treatise on Nature and Grace,* God only acts by general volitions. But this can easily be reconciled with the demands of his occasionalism, since it simply means that God always acts in accordance with the laws he has established in the realm of nature. It does not rule out an infinite number of temporalized and individual acts of will on God's part. God as universal cause acting only by general volitions is consistent with God as the sole and constant efficient agent of natural change.

Moreover, we see that there is more agreement between Malebranche and Arnauld on the nature of divine volition than Arnauld, at least, was willing to recognize. Given, however, the low point in their personal relations at this stage in their correspondence, and the high degree of rancor involved in the debate, it certainly would take a *volonté particulière* by God to get Arnauld to admit any kind of agreement between himself and Malebranche.[27]

References

Works by Malebranche:

OC = Nicolas Malebranche, *Oeuvres Complètes,* 20 vols., André Robinet, dir. (Paris: J. Vrin, 1959–66), referred to by volume number:page number.

Search = The Search after Truth (De la recherche de la vérité).

Treatise = Treatise on Nature and Grace (Traité de la nature et de la grace).

Dialogues = Dialogues on Metaphysics and Religion (Entretiens sur la métaphysique et sur la religion).

Réponse aux Réflexions = Réponse au livre I des Réflexions philosophiques et theologiques.

LO = English translation of *Search,* Thomas M. Lennon and Paul J. Olscamp, trans. (Columbus: Ohio State University Press, 1980).

D = English translation of *Dialogues,* Willis Doney, trans. (New York: Abaris Books, 1980).

Works by others:

Réflexions = Réflexions philosophiques et théologiques sur le nouveau système de la nature et de la grace, in vol. 39 of *Oeuvres de Messire Antoine Arnauld,* 43 vols. (Paris: Sigismond D'Arnay, 1775).

G = *Die Philosophischen Schriften von Gottfried Wilhelm Leibniz,* 7 vols., C.J. Gerhardt, ed. (Hildesheim: Georg Olms, 1960–62).

M = Leibniz, *Discourse on Metaphysics/Correspondence with Arnauld/Monadology,* George Montgomery, trans. (LaSalle: Open Court, 1980).

Notes

An early version of this paper was read to the Conference on Early Modern Philosophy at the University of Massachusetts, Amherst, May, 1989. I am grateful to the participants in the discussion that followed, and particularly to Robert

C. Sleigh, Jr., who commented on the paper. I also want to thank Donald Ruth-erford and Charles McCracken for reading and commenting on a draft.

1. See Thomas M. Lennon, "Occasionalism and the Cartesian Metaphysic of Motion," *Canadian Journal of Philosophy,* Supplementary Volume 1 (1974): 29–40. See also Steven Nadler, "Occasionalism and the Mind-Body Problem," *Oxford Studies in the History of Philosophy,* forthcoming; and "Doctrines of Explanation in Late Scholasticism and the Mechanical Philosophy," *The Cam-bridge History of Seventeenth-Century Philosophy,* forthcoming.

2. Descartes's God is, of course, also responsible for sustaining the uni-verse in existence and maintaining the total quantity of motion therein once he has imparted motion to it; see *Principles of Philosophy* II.36–43.

3. "Clarification of the difficulties which Mr. Bayle has found in the new system of the union of soul and body," G IV, 520.

4. Letter to Arnauld, July 14, 1686, G II, 57–58 = M 134; see also the draft of this letter, May 1686, G II, 47 = M 119. See also *New System of the Nature and the Communication of Substances,* §§12–13, G IV, 483–84.

5. See Leibniz to Arnauld, November 28–December 8, 1686, G II, 74–75 = M 158–59. God *is* required, however, to sustain all beings in existence by a continuous conservation/creation; see *Discourse on Metaphysics,* §30; *Theod-icy,* §§385–86; and the letter to Arnauld, April 30, 1687, G II, 91–92 = M 183.

6. Arnauld to Leibniz, March 4, 1687, G II, 84 = M 173. Arnauld's response here is in marked contrast with his remarks in an earlier letter, in which he seems clear on the differences between Leibniz's account and occasionalism; see his letter to Leibniz, September 28, 1686, G II, 65 = M 145. Leibniz himself, in a draft of the letter to which Arnauld is responding, explicitly contrasts his preestablished harmony with the "hypothesis of occasional causes," which de-mands "a particular intervention of God"; see Leibniz to Arnauld (draft of letter of November 28–December 6, 1686), G II, 70–71 = M 153. He does so again in his response to Arnauld's identification of the two doctrines; see Leibniz to Arnauld, April 30, 1687, G II, 92–94 = M 185. For a discussion of the differ-ences between occasionalism and preestablished harmony as analyses of natu-ral causation, see Thomas M. Lennon, "Philosophical Commentary," in LO, 826f., 832f.

7. It might be argued that the passage from Arnauld really is in line with the traditional reading of Malebranche's occasionalism (and with Arnauld's earlier remarks—see note 6). Although, as Arnauld says, God originally chooses "by a single act of the eternal will . . . to do everything which he has foreseen that it will be necessary to do," God does not actually perform the selected and re-quired actions until the occasion presents itself. But this implies that God's will, by which he chooses to perform an action, and God's deed (the action itself) are distinct. It also implies that when God fulfills the original volition and actually moves my arm, no "new act of will" is required (not even a will to fulfill the original volition on this occasion). Neither Arnauld nor Malebranche would accept such a bifurcation in God between will and action. Nor does such a reading even seem coherent on its own terms.

8. In 1687, when he is writing Leibniz, Arnauld has just completed his *Ré-*

flexions (1685), in which he attacks Malebranche's *Treatise* and the account therein of divine will and causation.

9. For an examination of this aspect of the debate, see Steven Nadler, *Arnauld and the Cartesian Philosophy of Ideas* (Princeton: Princeton University Press, 1989); and Monte Cook, "Arnauld's Alleged Representationalism," *Journal of the History of Philosophy* 12 (1974): 53–64.

10. For a discussion of this relativizing of the relationship between end (world) and means (laws), and its subsequent influence on Leibniz's theodicy, see Catherine Wilson, "Leibnizian Optimism," *Journal of Philosophy* 80 (1983): 765–83.

11. Patrick Riley examines the concept of general will in Malebranche (as well as its eventual transformation into a political concept in Rousseau) in *The General Will before Rousseau* (Princeton: Princeton University Press, 1986), chapters 1–3. See also André Robinet, *Système et existence dans l'oeuvre de Malebranche* (Paris: J. Vrin, 1965), 76–81, 92–95; and Martial Guéroult, *Malebranche*, 3 vols. (Paris: Aubier, 1959), vol. 2, chapter 6.

12. For Malebranche's response to these particular criticisms, see *Réponse au livre I des Réflexions philosophiques et théologiques* (OC 8:650–56).

13. One reason Arnauld's understanding of the *Treatise* may have the effect I am arguing it has on his reading of Malebranche's occasionalism is that the details of occasionalism as a theory of natural causation as presented in the *Search* are somewhat vaguer than in the presentation of the doctrine in the *Dialogues on Metaphysics* (1688, in which we see the very strong "continuous creation" argument). Arnauld of course has not seen the *Dialogues* by the time of his writings to Leibniz in 1687.

14. The *Search* was published in 1674; Arnauld probably read it soon thereafter (in *Des vraies et des fausses idées* [VFI], he worked from the fourth, 1678, edition—see OC 1:xxvii), and was one of its early praisers. He did not read the *Treatise* (completed in 1679) until 1680. He only then conceived the project of criticizing Malebranche's entire system, epistemology and all, with VFI in 1683 and the *Réflexions* in 1685—see Arnauld to Quesnel, August 12, 1680 (OC 18:181); and Arnauld to De Roucy, for Malebranche, January 4, 1682 (OC 18:223).

15. Charles McCracken, *Malebranche and British Philosophy* (Oxford: Oxford University Press, 1983), 100–101.

16. More accurately, a law is only sufficient to bring about an effect when taken in conjunction with the existence of the state of affairs which fulfills the conditions necessary to instantiate the law (i.e., which "occasions" the operation of the law).

17. McCracken, *Malebranche and British Philosophy*, 101.

18. Nicholas Jolley, *The Light of the Soul: Theories of Ideas in Leibniz, Malebranche, and Descartes* (Oxford: Oxford University Press, 1990), 106–107. Jolley describes Leibniz's characterization of the differences between preestablished harmony and occasionalism as being either a case of "polemical exaggeration" or the result of "a very poor understanding of occasionalism." In fact, as my argument in this paper implies, both Foucher and Leibniz had a very good grasp of the differences between the two doctrines.

19. Desmond Clarke, *Occult Powers and Hypotheses: Cartesian Natural Philosophy under Louis XIV* (Oxford: Clarendon Press, 1989), 121.

20. See also Riley, *The General Will before Rousseau*, 120–21. Donald Rutherford, in defense of this reading, cites the following passage from the *Dialogues:* "From all eternity God has willed, and to all eternity He will continue to will—or, to speak more accurately, God wills unceasingly though without variation, without succession, without necessity—everything He will do in the course of time" (OC 12:159 = D 157; see Rutherford, "Natures, Laws, and Miracles: The Roots of Leibniz's Critique of Occasionalism," in *Causation in Early Modern Philosophy,* ed. S. Nadler [University Park: Pennsylvania State University Press, 1993], 135–58). But note that Malebranche speaks here of God acting "in the course of time." The reference to God willing "without variation [*sans variété*]" can be explained in terms of the constancy and law-likeness of his general volitions, as discussed below; and the phrase "without succession" should be read as descriptive of God's atemporal perspective on his own volitions.

21. See also *Search,* Elucidation XV, OC 3:208–209 = LO 660. A similar argument is found in Louis de la Forge, *Traité de l'esprit de l'homme* (1666), chapter XVI; and in a nonoccasionalist form in Descartes, *Principles of Philosophy,* II.36–39. See Daniel Garber, "How God Causes Motion: Descartes, Divine Sustenance, and Occasionalism," *Journal of Philosophy* 84 (1987): 567–80.

22. "Une cause naturelle n'est donc point une cause réelle et véritable, mais seulement une cause occasionnelle, & qui détermine l'Auteur de la nature à agir de telle & telle manière, en telle & telle rencontre."

23. Along these lines, R. C. Sleigh, Jr. urges a distinction in Malebranche between (a) God *acting by* a particular volition, and (b) a particular volition in God being the real cause of an event, with God still acting in such a case by a general volition. See his *Leibniz and Arnauld: A Commentary on Their Correspondence* (New Haven: Yale University Press, 1990), 156.

24. "[Les miracles] ne seroient point des miracles differens des effets qu'on appelle naturels, s'il étoit vrai que Dieu agît ordinairement par des volontez particulières; puisque les miracles ne sont tels, que parce qu'ils n'arrivent point selon les loix generales." See also *Réponse aux Réflexions,* OC 8:695–96. Here we see Malebranche's defense against Leibniz's charge that, according to Malebranche, all natural effects are miraculous. In these passages, Malebranche asserts that God acts by particular volitions when performing miracles. But elsewhere, he modifies this, and insists that miracles, too, are divine acts performed in accordance with certain laws or an Eternal Order—except that in this case the relevant laws are of a different order from the laws of nature and are unknown to us; see *Dialogues* VIII.3, OC 12:177–78 = D 175.

25. There is, however, another dimension to Leibniz's "intervention" objection to which my argument is *not* an answer. The problem with occasionalism, for Leibniz, is not only with God's perpetual activity in the course of nature, but also with the fact that God, on the occasionalist view, causes a physical event on the occasion of a mental event—and this is to "intervene" in or interrupt the laws of (physical) nature. In this sense, with mental events occasion-

ing physical events, occasionalism is, in Leibniz's eyes, no better than Cartesian interactionism. For a discussion of this, see R. S. Woolhouse, "Leibniz and Occasionalism," in Woolhouse, ed., *Metaphysics and Philosophy of Science in the Seventeenth and Eighteenth Centuries* (The Netherlands: Kluwer, 1988), 172–78.

26. Such a reading of Malebranche's conception of God's *volontés générales* is also offered by Daisie Radner, *Malebranche* (Amsterdam: Van Gorcum, 1978), 30–33.

Bibliography

I. Descartes

Descartes's Works

Oeuvres de Descartes, ed. Ch. Adam and P. Tannery (revised edition). Paris: Vrin/C.N.R.S., 1964–76.

The Philosophical Writings of Descartes, tr. J. Cottingham, R. Stoothoff, and D. Murdoch, 3 volumes. Cambridge: Cambridge University Press, 1985.

Descartes: His Moral Philosophy and Psychology, tr. with an introduction and conceptual index by J. J. Blom. New York: New York University Press, 1978.

Descartes: Philosophical Letters, tr. and ed. A. Kenny. Minneapolis: University of Minnesota Press, 1981.

The Passions of the Soul, tr. and annotated by S. Voss. Indianapolis: Hackett, 1989.

Secondary Sources

Beyssade, J.-M. *La Philosophie première de Descartes*. Paris: Flammarion, 1979.

Burnyeat, M. (ed.). *The Skeptical Tradition*. Berkeley and Los Angeles: University of California Press, 1983.

Cottingham, J. *The Cambridge Companion to Descartes*. Cambridge: Cambridge University Press, 1992.

———. *Descartes*. Oxford: Blackwell, 1986.

Curley, E. *Descartes against the Skeptics*. Oxford: Blackwell, 1978.

Doney, W. (ed.). *Descartes: A Collection of Critical Essays*. New York: Doubleday, 1967.

Frankfurt, H. G. *Demons, Dreamers, and Madmen*. Indianapolis, Ind.: Bobbs-Merrill, 1970.

Gaukroger, S. (ed.). *Cartesian Logic*. Oxford: Oxford University Press (Clarendon), 1989.

———. *Descartes: Philosophy, Mathematics and Physics*. Sussex: Harvester, 1980.

Gilson, E. *La Doctrine cartésienne de la liberté et le théologie*. Paris: Alcan, 1913.

———. *Etudes sur le rôle de la pensée médiévale dans la formation su système cartésien*, 4ᵗʰ ed. Paris: Vrin, 1975.

———. *Index Scolastico-Cartésien*. Paris: Alcan, 1913.

Gouhier, H. *Cartésianisme et augustinisme au XVIIe siècle*. Paris: Vrin, 1978.

———. *La Pensée métaphysique de Descartes*. Paris: Vrin, 1962.

———. *La Pensée religieuse de Descartes*. Paris: Vrin, 1924.

———. *Les Premières Pensées de Descartes*. Paris: Vrin, 1958.

Grene, M. *Descartes*. Minneapolis: University of Minnesota Press, 1985.

Gueroult, M. *Descartes selon l'ordre des raisons*. Paris: Montaigne, 1953. English translation by R. Ariew, *Descartes' Philosophy Interpreted According to the Order of Reasons*. Minneapolis: University of Minnesota Press, 1984.

Hooker, M. (ed.). *Descartes: Critical and Interpretive Essays*. Baltimore: Johns Hopkins University Press, 1978.

Kenny, A. *Descartes: A Study of His Philosophy*. New York: Random House, 1968.

Lennon, T. *The Battle of Gods and Giants: The Legacies of Descartes and Gassendi: 1655–1715*. Princeton: Princeton University Press, 1993.

Marion, J.-L. *Questions Cartésiennes*. Paris: Presses Universitaires de France, 1991.

———. *Sur la théologie blanche de Descartes*. Paris: Presses Universitaires de France, 1981; 2ⁿᵈ edn. 1991.

———. *Sur le prisme métaphysique de Descartes*. Paris: Presses Universitaires de France, 1986.

———. *Sur l'ontologie grise de Descartes*. Paris: Vrin, 1975; 2ⁿᵈ edn. 1981.

Markie, P. *Descartes's Gambit*. Ithaca: Cornell University Press, 1986.

Menn, S. *Descartes and Augustine*. Cambridge: Cambridge University Press, 1998.

Rodis-Lewis, G. *Descartes*. Paris: Libraire Généale Française, 1984.

———. *Idées et vérités eternelles chez Descartes et ses successeurs*. Paris: Vrin, 1985.

———. *L'antropologie cartésienne*. Paris: Presses Universitaires de France, 1991.

———. *L'oeuvre de Descartes*. Paris: Vrin, 1971.

Rorty, A. O. (ed.). *Essays on Descartes' Meditations*. Berkeley and Los Angeles: University of California Press, 1986.

Rozemond, M. *Descartes's Dualism*. Cambridge: Harvard University Press, 1998.

Voss, S. (ed.). *René Descartes: Metaphysics and the Classification of the Sciences in 1637*. Proceedings of the conference at San Jose State University, Calif., 1988.

Williams, B. *Descartes: The Project of Pure Enquiry*. Harmondsworth: Penguin Books, 1978.

Wilson, M. D. *Descartes*. London: Routledge and Kegan Paul, 1978.

II. Spinoza

Spinoza's Works

Spinoza Opera, ed. C. Gebhardt, 4 volumes. Heidelberg: Carl Winter, 1925.
The Collected Works of Spinoza, volume 1, ed. and tr. E. M. Curley. Princeton: Princeton University Press, 1985.
A Spinoza Reader, ed. E. M. Curley. Princeton: Princeton University Press, 1994.

Secondary Sources

Bennett, J. *A Study of Spinoza's Ethics.* Indianapolis: Hackett Publishing Company, 1984.
Curley, E. *Behind the Geometrical Method: A Reading of Spinoza's Ethics.* Princeton, Princeton University Press, 1988.
————. *Spinoza's Metaphysics: An Essay in Interpretation.* Cambridge, Mass.: Harvard University Press, 1969.
Curley, E., and P.-F. Moreau (eds.). *Spinoza: Issues and Directions, Brill's Studies in Intellectual History*, vol. 14. Leiden: Brill, 1990.
Delahunty, R. J. *Spinoza.* London: Routledge and Kegan Paul, 1985.
Della Rocca, M. *Representation and the Mind-Body Problem in Spinoza.* Oxford: Oxford University Press, 1996.
Donagan, A. *Spinoza.* Hertfordshire: Harvester Wheatsheaf, 1988.
Garrett, D. *The Cambridge Companion to Spinoza.* Cambridge: Cambridge University Press, 1996.
Grene, M. (ed.). *Spinoza: a Collection of Critical Essays.* Modern Studies in Philosophy. Garden City: Doubleday/Anchor Press, 1973.
Grene, M., and D. Nails (eds.). *Spinoza and the Sciences.* Boston Studies in the Philosophy of Science, vol. 91. Dordrecht: Reidel, 1986.
Gueroult, M. *Spinoza.* Vol. I: *Dieu (Ethique I)*; Vol. 2: *L'âme (Ethique 2)* 2 Vols. Paris: Aubier, 1968–74.
Hampshire, S. *Spinoza.* New York: Penguin, 1951.
Parkinson, G. H. R. *Spinoza's Theory of Knowledge.* Oxford: Clarendon Press, 1954.
Yovel, Y. *Spinoza on Knowledge and the Human Mind: Papers Presented at the Second Jerusalem Conference (Ethica II).* Leiden: Brill, 1994.
————. *Spinoza and Other Heretics.* Vol. I: *The Marrano of Reason*; Vol. 2: *The Adventures of Immanence.* Princeton: Princeton University Press, 1989.

III. Leibniz

Leibniz's Works

G. W. Leibniz. *Die philosophischen Schriften*, ed. C. I. Gerhard, 7 vols. Hildesheim: Olms, 1965.

G. W. Leibniz. *Philosophical Essays*, tr. R. Ariew and D. Garber. Indianapolis, Hackett, 1989.

G. W. Leibniz. *Philosophical Papers and Letters*, tr. and ed. L. E. Loemker, second edition. Dordrecht and Boston: D. Reidel Publishing Company, 1969.

New Essays on Human Understanding, tr. and ed. J. Bennett and P. Remnant. Cambridge: Cambridge University Press, 1981.

Nouvelles lettres et opuscules inedits de Leibniz. Foucher de Careil, A. Paris, 1857.

Opuscules et Fragments inédits de Leibniz, ed. L. Couturat. Paris, 1903.

Secondary Sources

Adams, R. *Leibniz: Determinist, Theist, Idealist.* Oxford: Oxford University Press, 1994.

Couturat, L. *La Logique de Leibniz, d'après des documents inédits.* Paris: Alcan, 1901; reprinted Hildesheim: Olms, 1961.

Frankfurt, H. G. (ed.). *Leibniz: A Collection of Critical Essays.* New York: Doubleday Anchor, 1972.

Gueroult, M. *Leibniz: Dynamique et Métaphysique.* Paris: Aubier-Montaigne, 1967.

Hooker, M. (ed.). *Leibniz: Critical and Interpretive Essays.* Minneapolis: University of Minnesota Press, 1982.

Ishiguro, H. *Leibniz's Philosophy of Logic and Language.* London: Duckworth, 1972.

Jolley, N. *The Cambridge Companion to Leibniz.* Cambridge: Cambridge University Press, 1995.

———. *Leibniz and Locke.* Oxford: Oxford University Press, 1984.

Kulstad, M. *Leibniz on Apperception, Consciousness, and Reflection.* Munich: Philosophia Verlag, 1991.

Mates, B. *The Philosophy of Leibniz: Metaphysics and Language.* Oxford: Oxford University Press, 1986.

McRae, R. *Leibniz: Perception, Apperception, and Thought.* Toronto: University of Toronto Press, 1976.

Mercer, C. *Leibniz's Metaphysics: Its Origins and Development.* Cambridge: Cambridge University Press, forthcoming.

Parkinson, G. H. R. *Leibniz on Human Freedom, Studia Leibnitiana, Sonderheft 2.* Wiesbaden: Franz Steiner, 1970.

———. *Logic and Reality in Leibniz's Metaphysics.* Oxford: Oxford University Press, 1965.

Rescher, N. *The Philosophy of Leibniz.* Englewood Cliffs: Prentice-Hall, 1967.

Russell, B. *A Critical Exposition of the Philosophy of Leibniz.* London, 1900.

Sleigh, R. *Leibniz and Arnauld.* New Haven: Yale University Press, 1990.

Wilson, C. *Leibniz's Metaphysics: A Comparative and Historical Study.* Princeton: Princeton University Press, 1989.

Woolhouse, R. S., ed. *Leibniz: Metaphysics and Philosophy of Science.* Oxford: Oxford University Press, 1981.

IV. Malebranche

Malebranche's Works

Malebranche, N. *Dialogues on Metaphysics*, tr. W. Doney. New York: Abaris Books, 1980.

———. *Dialogues on Metaphysics and Religion*, tr. M. Ginsberg. New York: Macmillan, 1923.

———. *Oeuvres complètes de Malebranche*, 20 vols., ed. A. Robinet. Paris: J. Vrin, 1959–66.

———. *The Search After Truth*, tr. T. M. Lennon and P. J. Olscamp. Columbus: Ohio State University Press, 1980.

Secondary Sources

Alquié, F. *Le cartésianisme de Malebranche*. Paris: J. Vrin, 1974.

Gouhier, H. *La philosophie de Malebranche et son expérience religieuse*, 2nd edition. Paris: J. Vrin, 1948.

———. *La vocation de Malebranche*. Paris: J. Vrin, 1926.

Gueroult, M. *Etendue et psychologie chez Malebranche*, Publications de la faculté des lettres de l'Université de Strasbourg, no. 91. Paris: Les belles lettres, 1939.

———. *Malebranche*, Vol. 1, *La Vision en Dieu*. Paris: Aubier, 1955.

———. *Malebranche*, Vol. 2, *Les cinq abîmes de la providence: l'Ordre et l'occasionalisme*. Paris: Aubier, 1959.

———. *Malebranche*, Vol. 3, *Les cinq abîmes de la providence; la Nature et la Grâce*. Paris: Aubier, 1959.

Luce, A. A. *Berkeley and Malebranche*. Oxford: Oxford University Press, 1934.

McCracken, C. *Malebranche and British Philosophy*. Oxford: Clarendon Press, 1983.

Nadler, S. *Malebranche and Ideas*. Oxford: Oxford University Press, 1992.

Radner, D. *Malebranche: A Study of a Cartesian System*. Assen: Van Gorcum, 1978.

Robinet, A. *Système et existence dans l'oeuvre de Malebranche*. Paris: J. Vrin, 1965.

Rodis-Lewis, G. *Nicholas Malebranche*. Paris: Presses Universitaires de France, 1963.

Schmaltz, T. *Malebranche's Theory of the Soul*. Oxford: Oxford University Press, 1996.

V. General Studies of Rationalist Themes

Ayres, M., and Garber, D. (eds.). *Cambridge History of Seventeenth Century Philosophy*. Cambridge University Press, 1998.

Cottingham, J. *The Rationalists*. Oxford: Oxford University Press, 1988.

Gueroult, M. *Études sur Descartes, Spinoza, Malebranche et Leibniz*, Vol. 1970. Hildesheim: Georg Olms, 1970.

Jolley, N. *The Light of the Soul: Theories of Idea in Leibniz, Malebranche, and Descartes.* Oxford: Oxford University Press, 1990.

Loeb, L. *From Descartes to Hume: Continental Metaphysics and the Development of Modern Philosophy.* Ithaca: Cornell University Press, 1981.

Woolhouse, R. S. *Descartes, Spinoza, and Leibniz: The Concept of Substance in Seventeenth Century Metaphysics.* London: Routledge and Kegan Paul, 1993.

Authors

Robert Adams is professor of philosophy at Yale University. He is the author of *Leibniz: Determinist, Theist, Idealist* (Oxford, 1994), of *The Virtue of Faith and Other Essays in Philosophical Theology* (Oxford, 1987), and of many articles on Leibniz, Kant, and in philosophy of religion, metaphysics, and ethics.

Janet Broughton is professor of philosophy, University of California, Berkeley, and is the author of a number of articles on philosophers in the modern period.

John Carriero is professor of philosophy at the University of California, Los Angeles. He is the author of a number of articles on Descartes, Spinoza, and Leibniz.

Michael Della Rocca is professor of philosophy at Yale University. He is the author of *Representation and the Mind-Body Problem in Spinoza* (Oxford, 1996) and of several articles on Spinoza.

Daniel Garber is professor of philosophy, University of Chicago. He is the author of *Descartes' Mathematical Physics* (Chicago, 1988), and of numerous articles on Descartes, Leibniz, and in philosophy of science.

Don Garrett is professor of philosophy, University of North Carolina, Chapel Hill. He is the author of *Cognition and Commitment in Hume's Philosophy* (Oxford, 1996), and of a number of articles on Spinoza and Hume.

Paul Hoffman is professor of philosophy, University of California, Riverside. He is the author of several articles on Descartes, Spinoza, and Leibniz, and in metaphysics.

Christia Mercer is professor of philosophy at Columbia University, and the author of *Leibniz's Metaphysics: Its Origins and Development* (Cambridge, forthcoming).

Steven Nadler is professor of philosophy at the University of Wisconsin. He is the author of *Arnauld and the Cartesian Philosophy of Ideas* (Princeton, 1989), and of *Malebranche and Ideas* (Oxford, 1992), and of a number of articles on Descartes, Arnauld, and Malebranche.

Derk Pereboom is professor of philosophy at the University of Vermont. He is the author of articles in history of modern philosophy and in philosophy of mind.

Marleen Rozemond is professor of philosophy at Kansas State University. She is the author of *Descartes's Dualism* (Harvard, 1998) and of several articles on Descartes.

Donald Rutherford is professor of philosophy at Emory University, and the author of *Leibniz and the Rational Order of Nature* (Cambridge, 1995) and of a number of articles on Leibniz.

Margaret Wilson was professor of philosophy at Princeton University for many years. She is the author of *Descartes* (Routledge, 1978), and author of many articles on Descartes, Spinoza, Locke, Leibniz, Berkeley, and Kant.

David Wong is professor of philosophy at Brandeis University. He is the author of *Moral Relativity* (University of California, 1984), and of articles in ethics and in Chinese philosophy.